Y0-DEW-521

INDIANA ELECTION RETURNS

1816-1851

INDIANA HISTORICAL COLLECTIONS

VOLUME XL

INDIANA ELECTION RETURNS
1816-1851

Compiled by

Dorothy Riker and Gayle Thornbrough

INDIANA HISTORICAL BUREAU

1960

CONTENTS

Page

Editorial Note vii

Introduction ix

Presidential and Vice-Presidential Electors 1

Congress

Representatives 71

Senators 127

Governor and Lieutenant Governor

Governor 137

Lieutenant Governor 159

General Assembly 181

Constitution

Referendums on Calling a Constitutional Convention 367

Delegates to the Constitutional Convention of 1850-1851 378

Ratification of the Constitution of 1851 and the Negro Exclusion Clause 388

Appendix

Acts Forming and Organizing Counties 393

Governors, 1816-1851 395

Congress: Apportionment of Representatives 396

General Assembly: Apportionment of Members 399

Index 409

EDITORIAL NOTE

In publishing the present volume of Election Returns, the Historical Bureau is carrying out one of its principal functions—that of making valuable source materials available to students of state and local history. Interest in such a volume was aroused at the time the editors first used some of these records in preparing for publication the volume of *Executive Proceedings, 1816-1836 (Indiana Historical Collections,* Vol. 29). The frequency of inquiries received regarding election returns is indicative of the need for such a volume. In some respects it may be considered as a companion volume to the *Executive Proceedings,* inasmuch as the latter deals primarily with the commissioning of local officials, while the present volume covers the elections of presidential electors, governors and lieutenant governors, members of the General Assembly, Congressmen, United States senators, and delegates to the Constitutional Convention of 1850-51.

The original election certificates or returns were sent by the county clerks to the Secretary of State and were retained in that office until the completion of the State Library and Historical Building in 1934, when they were transferred to the Archives Division of the State Library. They have been separated from the other archival material and arranged by years and months.

The returns for the early years are incomplete. In cases where no official return was found, but the votes were reported in the newspapers, those figures have been inserted in brackets. Before 1843 the clerks were not required to forward to the Secretary of State certificates for the election of members of the General Assembly. For this reason it has been possible to obtain only a limited number of the returns prior to that date. From 1816 to 1830 only the names of the persons elected to the Assemblies are given; from 1830 through 1843 all available returns are given.

In reporting the election of delegates to the Constitutional Convention of 1850-51, the county clerks in many instances gave only the names of the persons elected. The official returns have been supplemented by newspaper sources wherever possible.

The political affiliation of the candidates for the various offices has been added from newspaper sources, and should not be considered as official. The newspaper editors were not always in accord. In most cases it has been possible to check only the Indianapolis papers for this information.

United States senators were elected by joint ballot of the two houses of the General Assembly. The results are published in the House and Senate Journals. Since the Journals for this early period are available in only a few libraries, the results of these elections have been included in the present volume.

Referendums were held on a variety of questions during the period under consideration. The most important were those regarding the calling of a convention to revise the Constitution. This question was voted on five times. The results of these referendums and the one on the adoption of the Constitution of 1851 are presented in Part V of this volume.

The spelling of the names of the candidates is that given on the election returns and in the House and Senate Journals unless there was good reason to believe that this was wrong. An asterisk before a candidate's name indicates that he was elected.

Our sincere thanks are due the staffs of the Archives and Indiana divisions of the State Library for their help in the preparation of the volume. Letters were mailed to individuals in most of the counties of the state soliciting help in finding election returns in their respective courthouses or in newspaper files available in local libraries and museums. Many of these persons spent hours in searching without the reward of finding anything. Our sincere thanks are due to them as well as to those few who met with success.

INTRODUCTION

The summer of 1816 was an important one for the people of Indiana. The plans for rising from the rank of a territory to that of a state were advanced one step by the passage of the Indiana Enabling Act by Congress on April 19. This provided for the election of delegates who were to meet on June 10 to prepare a constitution for the new state. The document which they framed in nineteen days was not submitted to the voters for ratification. It set up the framework for the government of the new state, leaving to subsequent General Assemblies the filling in of the details.

Under the Constitution the executive power was to be vested in a governor who was to be chosen by the qualified electors every three years. A lieutenant governor was to be chosen at the same time and for the same term. He was to serve as president of the Senate, and, in case of impeachment of the governor, his removal from office, death, resignation, or absence from the state, the lieutenant governor was to exercise all the powers and authority of the governor. In the event the lieutenant governor assumed the duties of the governorship, the Senate was then to elect a president *pro tem.* from its own members who would be next in line for the governorship.[1]

The legislative authority of the state was to be vested in a General Assembly, consisting of a Senate and House of Representatives, both to be elected by the people. Representatives were to be chosen annually; senators were to serve three years, one third of them being elected each year.

The number and apportionment of representatives and senators were to be fixed by the General Assembly every five years following an enumeration of white male inhabitants over the age of twenty-one years. The membership of the lower house was not to be less than twenty-five nor more than one hundred; the number of senators was not to be less than one third the number of representatives nor more than one half. Section 9 of Article XII provided for the first apportion-

---

1 It was by virtue of this provision that James Brown Ray became acting governor in February, 1825, although the circumstances were not exactly those set out in the Constitution. In this case the lieutenant governor had resigned the year before upon his election to Congress. Then when the governor was elected United States senator, Ray, the president *pro tem.* of the Senate, was sworn in as acting governor.

ment of members of the Assembly among the counties of the state; there were to be twenty-nine representatives and ten senators.

The qualifications for members of the General Assembly were set out in Sections 4 and 7 of Article III. A representative was to be twenty-one years of age or over, a citizen of the United States, and a resident for one year of the state and of the county or district from which he was chosen; a senator was to be twenty-five years of age or over, a citizen of the United States, a resident of the state for two years, and of the county or district one year. In case of a vacancy in either house, the governor was to issue a writ calling a special election to fill the vacancy.

Section 25 of the same Article provided that the General Assembly should meet the first Monday in November of 1816; thereafter it was to meet annually on the first Monday in December unless otherwise directed. The Assemblies of 1824 and 1850 failed to meet on time. In the first instance, the opening was postponed until January 10, 1825, pending removal of the state offices from the first state capital at Corydon to Indianapolis and the completion of the new courthouse where the Assembly was to meet. In 1850 the opening was postponed until December 30 because the Constitutional Convention was meeting in the legislative hall. In 1820 the Assembly met a week earlier than the time stipulated in the Constitution, and in 1821 it met two weeks earlier.

The judicial power of the state was to be vested in a Supreme Court, circuit courts, and such other inferior courts as the General Assembly might establish from time to time. The judges of the Supreme Court were to be appointed by the governor with the advice and consent of the Senate, while the president judges of the circuit courts, as well as the secretary of state, state auditor, and state treasurer were to be elected by joint ballot of the two branches of the General Assembly. The appointment and election of these officials are not treated in the present volume. United States senators were to be elected by joint ballot of the two houses of the General Assembly according to a provision in the Federal constitution. The result of these elections is presented in Part II.

Article VI of the Constitution dealt with elections and qualifications of voters. Any free white male, twenty-one years of age or over, who was a citizen of the United States and a resident of the state for one year, was entitled to vote in the county in which he resided. All elections were to be by ballot. This represented a change from the *viva voce* method which had been in use, and those in favor of the latter method were able to insert a proviso in the Constitution to the effect that after five years the General Assembly could change the method of voting if it so desired; if no change was made at that time the method of voting by ballot was to remain unaltered.[2]

On the last day of the convention, writs for the first election to be held under the new Constitution were issued to the county sheriffs by the convention president, Jonathan Jennings. The election was to be held August 5 to choose a governor, lieutenant governor, representative in Congress, members of the General Assembly, sheriffs, and coroners. The Enabling Act had stipulated that Indiana was to have one representative in Congress until after the Census of 1820 was taken.

The time between the close of the convention and the 1816 election was so short (only five weeks) that there must have been quite a flurry of excitement over the state as prospective candidates made known their intentions. Printing presses were available at Vincennes, Lexington, Corydon, and Vevay, and possibly at such other towns as Salem, Brookville, and Lawrenceburg. The campaign literature shows that the candidates of this period did not boldly announce their plans to run. Rather, their statements indicate a modest diffidence, real or assumed. The following are typical: "without my previty or consent, my name has been introduced"; "partly from the friendly solicitations of some of my friends and partly from a wish that you should have an opportunity of making a choice, is the reasons which have induced me to offer"; "I am induced to offer myself as a candidate . . . by urgent considerations that are nearly allied with your best interest"; "having been requested by some respectable characters of this county to offer myself

---

[2] The year before the question was to come up for consideration, the General Assembly passed an act authorizing the voters to express their preference on the method of voting at the election to be held in August, 1821. According to a committe report to the House of Representatives at the 1821-22 session, the secretary of state received returns on the referendum from only fifteen of the thirty-nine counties. The method of voting was warmly debated in both houses of the Assembly. A bill passed the lower house changing to *viva voce* voting, but the Senate took no action on it and thus no change was made. Charles Kettleborough (ed.), *Constitution Making in Indiana. Volume I, 1780-1851 (Indiana Historical Collections,* Vol. I, Indianapolis, 1916) xxvii-xxxii. Only the votes in Harrison and Parke counties on this matter were found on the returns in the Archives Division. The Vincennes *Western Sun* of August 11 reported the vote in Knox County and the Charlestown *Indiana Intelligencer* of August 15 gave the vote in Clark and Jefferson counties. The results in the above five counties were as follows: for *viva voce,* Clark 512; Harrison 764; Jefferson 704; Knox 250; Parke 43; total 2273; for use of ballot, Clark 386; Harrison 141; Jefferson 296; Knox 387; Parke 126; total 1336.

as a candidate." Fourth of July gatherings no doubt offered opportunities for prospective candidates to make themselves known. The pages of the only Indiana newspaper of the period that has survived indicate that spirited contests were waged in some parts of the territory. The fact that 9,145 votes were cast for governor out of a possible 12,112 shown in the enumeration taken a year earlier indicates the widespread interest in the election.

After the votes were counted and the results announced there was a lull in public activity until the meeting of the General Assembly on November 4. Jonathan Jennings and Christopher Harrison were sworn in as governor and lieutenant governor, respectively, on the seventh, and the following day, Waller Taylor and James Noble were elected to the United States Senate by the Assembly. The two senators and William Hendricks, the elected representative, appeared at the opening of Congress on December 2. Hendricks was seated on the opening day, and the senators on December 12, the day after Indiana was formally admitted into the Union as the nineteenth state.

No provision had been made in the Enabling Act or in the Constitution whereby the Indiana electorate could participate in the presidential election of 1816. The Assembly therefore chose three presidential electors on November 16, who met shortly thereafter and cast their votes for James Monroe for president and Daniel Tompkins for vice-president. When the two houses of Congress met the following February to count the electoral votes, the question was raised whether or not Indiana's votes should be counted since they had been cast previous to her admission into the Union. After Representative Hendricks made a forceful presentation of the case for his state, the decision was made to include Indiana's three votes.[3]

The transition having been made from territorial status to statehood, the first General Assembly took up the task of passing the legislation necessary to fill in the framework of government set up by the Constitution. The territorial election law of January 5, 1814, was replaced by a new one setting out the procedure for holding elections.[4]

The county commissioners were to appoint an inspector of elections in each township, who, in turn, was to appoint two qualified voters to serve with him as judges of each election; the judges, in turn, were to appoint two clerks. Poll books and blank returns were to be pro-

---

[3] *Annals of Congress,* 14 Congress, 2 session, 943-50.

[4] *Laws of Indiana,* 1816-17, pp. 85-92.

vided by the county commissioners and forwarded by the sheriff to the inspector at least ten days before the time of the election. Voting places were to be opened between the hours of nine and eleven in the morning of election day and remain open until four o'clock in the afternoon or until closed by the inspectors.

The inspectors were to proclaim in a loud voice the opening of the polls in their respective townships. The name of each person wishing to vote was to be called out by the inspector and if no objection was raised as to his qualifications, he was to be given a "ticket" (apparently a blank sheet of paper in the early years) on which to write the names of the candidates for whom he wished to vote together with the offices for which they were running.[5] Having prepared his "ticket," the voter, in the presence of the judges, put it into a box prepared for the purpose, whereupon the name of the voter was again repeated by one of the judges in the presence of the clerks, each of whom was to keep a separate list of the voters, numbering every name taken down.

After the polls were closed, the judges were to open the box and canvass the votes, the inspector opening each "ticket" and reading in a loud voice the name or names entered thereon and the office each was to fill. He was then to hand it to one of the judges who was to repeat the information, and then hand it to the other judge, who was to "string it on a thread of twine" prepared for that purpose.

As the inspector opened and read the "tickets," each clerk was to mark the votes each candidate received. When all the "tickets" had been read and the votes counted, the judges were to make out a certificate stating the number of votes each candidate received, the number to be written in words at full length. The certificate together with one of the lists of voters and one of the tally papers was then to be given to one of the judges to be delivered to the county clerk at the courthouse the following Wednesday. On that day, between the hours of twelve and four o'clock, the clerk of the circuit court, in the presence of all the judges of elections in attendance from the different townships, was to compare the different certificates and declare duly elected the persons having the highest number of votes for the different offices. In case of a tie, the clerk and judges were to make a choice by lot. Those elected to the General Assembly were to receive certificates of their election from the clerk.

---

5 After political organizations came into existence, the "tickets" were usually printed by the parties with the names of their candidates and the offices for which they were running.

A certificate showing the number of votes each candidate for governor and lieutenant governor received was to be made out by the county clerk in a fair hand, in words at full length, and transmitted to the Speaker of the House of Representatives. When the General Assembly next met, the certificates were to be opened and the votes tabulated in the presence of the two houses. Certificates showing the votes received by the candidates for Congress and for county sheriffs and coroners were to be forwarded to the Secretary of State. That officer was then to lay them before the Governor who in turn was to issue certificates or commissions to those elected. As mentioned in the Editorial Note, no return was required to be made of the votes received by candidates for the General Assembly until after 1843.[6] These certificates, now in the Archives Division of the State Library, are the documents from which most of the election returns given in this volume have been taken.

When two or more counties were joined together to compose a senatorial or representative district, the clerks of each county, on the Wednesday following each election, were to make out a return of the votes received by each candidate and deliver the same to the sheriff of his particular county; the sheriffs of the various counties were then to meet on the Saturday following the election at the courthouse of the oldest county in the district, where they were to compare the several returns and jointly give the person having the highest number of votes a certificate of his election; in case of a tie, it was to be decided by lot who should serve.

As compensation for their services, the inspector, judges, and clerks were to receive credit for one day's work on the public roads for every day employed in holding elections. It was almost twenty years before any further provision was made for paying these officials. Then they were allowed $1.00 per day if they were not eligible for exemption from road work. In townships where more than three hundred votes were taken, they were to be allowed additional compensation.[7]

In addition to the general elections which were held each year, township elections were held frequently to choose justices of the peace. During the early years of statehood, there was only one voting place in each township. Considering the distances to be traveled and the lack of roads and adequate transportation, the proportion of voters who turned out shows the deep interest early Hoosiers displayed in their

---

6 *Revised Laws of Indiana,* 1843, p. 133.

7 *Laws of Indiana,* 1835-36 (general), p. 60.

government.[8] An act of 1834 gave the boards doing county business the privilege of opening an additional polling place at the county seat or in any township where the number of voters exceeded one hundred. This was repealed in 1850 to allow additional polling places wherever they were deemed necessary.[9]

The possibility of fraud was not overlooked by the early lawmakers. Any person convicted of attempting to vote more than once or to hand in two or more "tickets" folded together was to be fined not exceeding $50 and rendered incapable of voting or holding any office in the state for two years. Any person convicted of using threats, force, or violence to awe any voter so as to restrain him in his freedom of choice, or offer any fee or reward in meat, drink, or otherwise, in order to persuade any voter to vote contrary to his mind, should be fined not exceeding $500 and rendered incapable of holding office for two years. This last provision must not have been enforced very rigidly if the accounts of "treating" on election days are true. Still another provision of the law was aimed at election officials; any official found guilty of refusing or neglecting to perform the duties enjoined upon him, or having taken up his duties was found guilty of fraud and corruption in performing them, was to be fined not exceeding $500.[10]

The election certificates in the Archives Division of the State Library reveal that township returns were sometimes late in being transmitted to the county seat or that often some irregularity occurred which left the clerk in doubt whether or not to include the vote. He would usually give the details to the Secretary of State and leave to that official the decision as to whether the vote should be counted. In most instances such irregularities or delinquency did not affect the outcome, but in one instance in which the election of a Congressman was at stake, the Governor ruled that the returns from one township which had been received by the county clerk on time but were unaccompanied by the tally papers should be counted.[11] One common reason for discarding votes was the failure on the part of the person voting to give the name of the candidate correctly. Such votes were often reported separately by the clerks.

---

[8] Indiana compared favorably with other states in this respect. See Logan Esarey, "Pioneer Politics," in *Indiana Magazine of History,* 13(1917):100.

[9] *Laws of Indiana,* 1833-34, p. 78; 1849-50 (general), p. 71.

[10] *Ibid.,* 1816-17, pp. 85-92, secs. 6, 17, 19.

[11] See *post,* 109n.

The total votes for governor and lieutenant governor which may be obtained by tabulating the election returns available often differ and sometimes are larger than those recorded in the Journals of the General Assembly. Although the returns were dated before the opening of the Assembly, evidently some were not available to the Speaker of the House at the time the votes were countd. The returns as given in the newspapers often differ from both the official returns and those recorded in the Journals. For example, in 1831, when Noah Noble was elected governor, the returns from only 43 of the 64 counties were included in the count made by the General Assembly, yet the returns from 61 counties were found in the Archives Division, and the other three were available in the newspapers of that year.

Organized political parties played little or no part in the first state elections, for practically all the voters gave their allegiance to the Jeffersonian Republican party. The geographic factionalism that had existed in territorial days between the settlers around Vincennes and those on the eastern border had all but disappeared, though a faint echo of this might have been detected in the contest for governor in 1816 between Jonathan Jennings and Thomas Posey, who were residents of Clark and Knox counties respectively.

Prior to the development of political parties, candidates announced their intentions to run for office by inserting a notice in the local newspaper, if there was one, or by circulating printed handbills. The original handbills were usually followed by others as the campaign progressed. As noted above, in the early days of statehood it was considered bad taste for a candidate to announce himself for office; instead, he was supposed to come out in response to the demands of his friends. James Brown Ray broke this precedent in 1825 when he announced his intention of running for governor.

It was almost impossible for candidates to cover the entire state or even a Congressional district in their campaigning. Log rollings, muster rallies, and other public gatherings offered opportunities for candidates to slip in unobtrusively and show themselves to be friendly. Stump speaking came into fashion in the 1820's. From 1840 to 1860 the barbecue was an important part of political meetings. It was also the fashion for candidates to hold joint debates on the issues of the day.

In the newspaper files that have been preserved one can read long articles, many signed by fictitious names, praising candidates or making personal attacks on them. The latter often appeared a day or so before the election when there was no time left to refute the charges made. Candidates had to meet these newspaper attacks as well as all kinds of oral rumors and false reports spread by the opposition.

Sixteen of the forty-two members of the Constitutional Convention were elected to the first legislature; some accepted other state jobs. Jennings, who had been president of the Convention, became the state's first governor. James Noble, another member of the Convention, was elected to the United States Senate in 1816 and continued to serve until his death in 1831. William Hendricks, the state's first representative in Congress, had been secretary of the Convention. These three, it was claimed, by virtue of their influence and positions, ruled the state in the early years. By the middle 1820's complaints were being made that an office-holding aristocracy had developed. This became one of the issues as political parties began to emerge. Other issues were internal improvements, reduction of the price of public land, and banking policies. The first real political contest in the state came in the presidential election of 1824.

In response to the agitation of the people for a greater voice in the election of the president and vice-president, an act was passed by the General Assembly in January, 1824, providing for the selection of presidential electors (equal to the number of senators and representatives in Congress) by the voters on the second Monday of November in that year and the first Monday in November every fourth year thereafter.[12] The election was to be conducted in the same manner as the state elections in August, except that marshals were to be appointed from the election districts in which the state was divided to carry the certificates made out by county clerks to the secretary of state on the fourth Monday in November. The secretary was to compare the certificates and make out an abstract of the votes received by the electors in the various counties, after which the governor was to certify the ones elected. The electors were then to meet on the day directed by Congress to perform the duties enjoined on them by the Federal constitution.

The presidential candidates in 1824 were Henry Clay, John Quincy Adams, Andrew Jackson, and William Crawford. The necessity of reaching an agreement among the followers of each of these on a slate of electors brought into existence the first political machinery in the state.

The businessmen and well-to-do farmers usually favored Clay on account of his position on the tariff and internal improvements. Adams stood well with the lawyers and other professional men. The Clay and

---

[12] The time of the presidential election was changed to the Tuesday after the first Monday beginning in November, 1848, in compliance with a Federal statute. *Laws of Indiana,* 1847-48 (general), 29.

Adams men were the office holders in Indiana and had little trouble in getting together to choose their electoral tickets. Those who favored Jackson were mostly farmers and young men who had little means of contact except in the militia musters. The result was that three Jackson electoral tickets appeared. To solve this dilemma, the editor of the *Western Sun,* in the issue of July 31, suggested the holding of county conventions to choose delegates to a state convention to meet at Salem the first Monday in September. Eleven counties were represented in this convention. In addition to choosing the five electors, a state committee of three was appointed to manage the campaign for Jackson in Indiana; county committees, usually consisting of three men, were to look after the local campaigns, and a vigilance committee in each township was to look after the individual voters. Crawford was not popular in Indiana and had no electoral ticket.

The Jackson electors carried the state by a margin of 2,123 votes over the Clay electors, and 4,351 over those of Adams. Nationally, Jackson received a plurality of the electoral votes but not the majority necessary to elect. The choice of a president therefore devolved upon the House of Representatives. In the balloting in the House, Indiana's vote was cast for Jackson but Adams was elected. Clay was accused of throwing his strength to Adams in exchange for his appointment as secretary of state. Resentment over the "corrupt bargain" spurred the Jackson men to vigorous efforts four years later. Their state and county organizations were continued with the result that by the time of the next presidential election they had captured most of the township and county offices and had a small but quite vocal group in the General Assembly. In addition, they had the backing of a number of newspaper editors.

At the Jackson state convention in January, 1828, a larger number of counties were represented than at the first attempt four years earlier. At this time the party organization was further perfected, one new innovation being to request the township assessors to note the political preference of each voter at the time they assessed the property. Poll books were then to be made up from the assessors' records and turned over to the vigilance committees. Presumably the opposition party would have had access to this information also, since the assessor was a public officer. The Adams and Clay men comprised the Administration party, and though nearly all the experienced politicians of the state were affiliated with it, their state and county organization was not as closely knit as that of the Jacksonians.

During the 1820's the state elections were still determined largely by the personal popularity of the candidates. Governor Jennings and

Representative Hendricks switched position in 1822, with Lieutenant Governor Ratliff Boon serving out Jennings' term as governor. When Hendricks was elected to the United States Senate in February, 1825, James Brown Ray, president *pro tem.* of the Senate, filled out Hendricks' term as governor, the lieutenant governor having previously resigned. Ray was then elected to the office for two terms on an independent ticket. He was the last governor to be chosen without the backing of a political party.

In his first campaign, Ray defeated Isaac Blackford, an Adams elector in the presidential election of 1824, by a majority of 1,687. Ray, himself, had favored Clay in that election. In 1828, he had two opponents, Israel T. Canby, a Jackson man, and Harbin H. Moore, who was brought forward by the Administration forces. Ray sought the support of both parties by making promises to both and ended up in losing friends on both sides.[13] He had the advantage, however, of being better known than either of the other candidates and was able to draw sufficient strength from both parties to win the election by a majority of 2,880 over Canby, and 4,233 over Moore.

The Enabling Act had provided that Indiana should be entitled to one representative in Congress until after the Census was taken in 1820. Provision for the election in August, 1816, of a representative in the second session of the Fourteenth Congress was included in the writ issued by the president of the Constitutional Convention. As noted above, William Hendricks was elected. The first General Assembly then passed an act calling for the election of a Congressman for the Fifteenth Congress in August, 1817, and the election of one for the Sixteenth Congress in August, 1818. After that the representative or representatives were to be elected biennially. Hendricks was a candidate for re-election in 1817, 1818, and 1820, defeating his opponents Thomas Posey and Reuben W. Nelson by decisive majorities.

Following the tabulation of the 1820 Census, Indiana was allowed three representatives. The number was increased to seven in 1833, and to ten in 1843. To avoid having the Congressional elections fall in the same years as the presidential campaigns, an act was passed in 1829 moving the 1830 election up to 1831, and providing for holding succeeding elections every two years thereafter. This meant that in the odd-numbered years, Indiana had no elected representatives from March 4 until after the August election. In the event the President

---

[13] *Messages and Papers relating to the Administration of James Brown Ray, Governor of Indiana, 1825-1831 (Indiana Historical Collections,* Vol. 34, Indianapolis, 1954), 13-14.

should call a special session (as happened in 1841), the Governor was to call a special election for representatives. As in the elections for the governor, lieutenant governor, and the General Assembly, political parties played little or no part in the Congressional elections in the 1820's nor in the elections for United States senators by the Assembly.

With the backing of a good political organization, the Jacksonian presidential electors were again able to win in the state in 1828, and this time they succeeded in electing their candidate nationally. As soon as Jackson became President, proscription was inaugurated for Federal office holders in Indiana. Dismissals began with the postmasters and continued down the line of Federal appointees until practically all had been replaced with staunch Jacksonians.

Apparently national politics were not decisive in the elections for the General Assembly in 1828, nor in the organization of the two houses. Isaac Howk, an Adams man, was elected speaker of the House over Samuel Judah, a Jacksonian. In the Congressional elections of that year, Ratliff Boon, Jonathan Jennings, and John Test won. Boon was for Jackson and Test for Adams; Jennings was elected over a Jackson man on the basis of his personal popularity.

Members of the General Assembly were the only state officials elected in 1829. Again, the national issues did not enter into the campaign. When the Assembly met, Ross Smiley, a Jacksonian, was elected speaker. At the following session of the Assembly (1830-31), Hendricks was re-elected to the United States Senate, defeating Boon 44 to 26, with 12 votes distributed between John Law and Charles Dewey, both of whom had been Administration men. The following year, 1831-32, it became necessary to elect a Senator to fill out the term of James Noble who had died in February, 1831. John Tipton, a Jackson man, was elected but not on a party vote.

In August of 1831, Noah Noble, described as anti-Jackson and anti-Ray, won the governorship over James G. Read, a Jacksonian, and Milton Stapp, running as an independent. In the Congressional elections of that year, three Jackson men (Boon, John Carr, and Jonathan McCarty) were elected.

The presidential election of 1832 saw Jackson and Clay pitted against each other, with the former again winning the electoral vote of Indiana. By this time the parties were called Democratic and National Republicans. A third national party, the anti-Masons, nominated William Wirt for president. This party had only a small following in Indiana. David G. Mitchell, of Corydon, a brother-in-law of Jennings, was one of its leaders. The anti-Masonic electoral ticket received a total of 27 votes from six counties.[14]

The local elections of 1832 were overshadowed by the national campaign. Both parties claimed a majority in the General Assembly. The election of a United States senator was again before that body, it being the end of the term for which James Noble had been elected. John Tipton, who had filled out Noble's term, was again a candidate. He had lost some of his Jackson support due to his failure to support the President in some of his policies. This time it took two days and nineteen ballots before he could be re-elected. As was the case the year before, Tipton's election was due to the faithfulness of the personal following he had built up during his years as Indian agent at Fort Wayne and Logansport.[15]

The sharpest struggle of the Assembly at this session came over the effort to create a state bank. Although Indiana had not had a branch of the United States Bank, the branches at Louisville and Cincinnati had met, at least partially, the needs of Indiana's citizens. Now with the veto of the Bank's charter by President Jackson, the necessity for a new national bank or a state bank was urgent. Several proposals were considered by the Assembly, but none could be agreed upon.[16] Members of both parties were disappointed at this failure to relieve the situation, and the bank question became an issue in the election of Assembly members the following August. Public opinion was strongly in favor of a state bank and when the next legislature met a bill was passed creating one.

The first Congressional election under the new apportionment act was held in August, 1833. The Democrats were successful in six of the districts, while the National Republicans won only one seat (the Second District) and that by a narrow margin of two votes.

---

[14] Charles McCarthy in an article on Anti-Masons in the American Historical Association *Report,* 1902, Vol. 1: 556, says eleven Indiana counties participated in the election, giving the Albany (N.Y.) *Argus,* November 21, 1832, as a reference. Returns from only six counties were found in the Archives Division. The Indianapolis *Indiana Journal* did not report the Anti-Masonic vote.

[15] Tipton was anxiously awaiting the result in Washington while the voting was going on in Indianapolis. Letters from his friends tell something of the efforts made to elect him. See the *John Tipton Papers* (3 vols. *Indiana Historical Collections,* Vols. 24-26, Indianapolis, 1942), 2:722 ff.

[16] See *Messages and Papers relating to the Administration of Noah Noble, Governor of Indiana, 1831-1837 (Indiana Historical Collections,* Vol. 38, Indianapolis, 1958), 31-34, 210n-11n.

In the campaign for governor the following year (1834), Noble and Read were again the candidates, the latter being nominated by the Democratic state party convention, thus establishing a new precedent. Noble was the candidate of the Whig party, which was just getting started and represented a coalition of the National Republicans, anti-Jackson Democrats, and Anti-Masons. Having conducted a rather extensive speaking campaign in 1831, Noble and Read both agreed to stay home and not campaign outside of certain districts in 1834. However, as the time of the election drew near, both candidates became uneasy about the other's activities and ended up in making a number of speeches over the state. The General Assembly of 1834-45 would probably have been anti-Jacksonian if there had been any occasion for a political division.

In the Congressional election of 1835, all six Democrats were re-elected and a seventh one replaced the Whig in the Second District. With William Henry Harrison as their standard bearer, the Whig presidential electoral ticket was victorious in the state in 1836, though the Democrats won in the nation. The Whigs also had a majority in the Assembly. Hendricks' second term as United States senator was due to expire the following March, and he was a candidate for re-election. Governor Noble was the first choice of the Whigs with Oliver H. Smith as an alternate. When the Democrats found they could not elect Hendricks, they threw their support to Smith, thus preventing Noble's election. Nine ballots were taken.[17]

The most important legislation of the session of 1835-36 was the mammoth internal improvement bill, providing for a network of roads, canals, and railroads covering the entire state. The popularity of this measure contributed to Whig success in 1837 when the party won six of the seats in Congress, the governorship, and a majority of the seats in the General Assembly. The Democrats were so completely dejected after their defeat in 1836 that they did not bring out a candidate for governor. David Wallace, the lieutenant governor, won an easy victory over a Whig rival, John Dumont.

In 1838 the only state elections were those for the General Assembly. The result left the Whigs with a substantial majority in the two houses. The most bitterly contested senatorial election of the period before 1850 occurred at this session, with thirty-six ballots being taken before any one candidate could muster sufficient strength to obtain a majority. Thomas H. Blake and Noah Noble, both Whigs, were

---

[17] *Messages and Papers of Noah Noble,* 500-2n; Oliver H. Smith, *Early Indiana Trials and Sketches* (Cincinnati, 1858), 141-43.

the principal candidates. Albert S. White, another Whig, was brought forward as a compromise on the thirty-second ballot; he gained support rapidly and received the required seventy-five votes on the thirty-sixth ballot.[18]

The Panic of 1837 brought hard times to the state. The internal improvement program entered upon so enthusiastically had to be halted for lack of funds. The Whigs were blamed for the bankrupt condition of the state, and the Democrats took advantage of the situation to make a comeback. Five Democrats and two Whigs were elected to Congress in 1839. The Democrats also gained control of the General Assembly.

The 1840 presidential campaign was the greatest political demonstration of the period before 1850. Harrison and Van Buren were again the opposing candidates. The Liberty party nominated James G. Birney. The highlight of the campaign in Indiana was the gathering at the Tippecanoe Battleground on May 29 which drew an estimated thirty thousand Whigs from all parts of the state. Tilghman A. Howard, Democratic congressman from the Seventh District, resigned his seat to make the race for governor against Samuel Bigger, a Whig. The popularity of Harrison swept the Whigs to victory in the state and local elections as well as in the presidential contest.

The Whigs were still riding the crest a year later and succeeded in recapturing four of the seats in Congress, leaving only one for the Democrats. Two years later, with the state in a bankrupt condition, the Whigs were overthrown, with the Democrats winning the governorship and eight of the ten Congressional seats to which the state now became entitled under the 1840 Census. The Democrats continued in power in Indiana, electing the governors in 1846 and 1849, the presidential electors in 1844 and 1848, and continuing to elect a majority of the Congressmen. This continued success was due in part to a departure from the old issues and a new emphasis which party leaders placed on human rights, individual liberties, and private initiative. Such talented orators as Robert Dale Owen, Edward A. Hannegan, Joseph A. Wright, and John W. Davis were eloquent advocates of this new trend. Schools for the Deaf and Dumb and for the Blind were opened, and the first steps were taken to provide hospital care for the mentally ill. Such old issues as the tariff continued to be debated in the state during election campaigns as well as in the halls of Congress, and the need for internal improvements remained a vital issue. Indianans were disappointed with the lack of Southern

[18] *John Tipton Papers,* 771, 776-79; *post,* 132-33.

support in obtaining Federal appropriations for these improvements, and when President Polk vetoed the Rivers and Harbors bill in 1846, the Democrats lost some of their support in the state. Hoosier politicians tended to avoid the slavery issue as long as possible.

The Liberty party, an anti-slavery group, picked up strength slowly, winning two thousand votes in the 1844 presidential campaign as against thirty votes four years earlier. Its principal support came from the Quaker communities. Stephen C. Stevens, their gubernatorial candidate in 1846, won 2301 votes as against 1683 that Elizur Deming received in 1843. From this same area in 1848 came the Free Soil strength and most of its party leadership. Led nationally by Martin Van Buren, the Indiana group was able to cut into the Whig strength, thus helping the Democrats win in the state. James H. Cravens, their candidate for governor the following year, received 3076 votes.

Article VIII of the Constitution of 1816 provided that every twelfth year thereafter the voters should have the opportunity to express their opinion regarding the calling of a convention to revise or amend the Constitution. If a majority of the voters were in favor of a revision, the governor was to inform the General Assembly, which should then provide for calling a convention. From the wording of the article it was not clear whether the question of revision had to be submitted to the voters at least once every twelve years but could be submitted sooner and oftener, or whether the question could be voted on only once in every twelve-year period. Proponents of the first theory were in the majority in the General Assembly of 1822-23 when a bill was passed authorizing the first referendum to be held the following August. The second and third referendums were held in 1828 and 1840 in accordance with the twelve-year intervals; the fourth in 1846 and the fifth in 1849 were provided for by special legislation. The first three referendums showed decided majorities against calling a convention. The report on the fourth referendum, as received by the General Assembly, was 32,721 in favor and 27,485 votes against calling a convention.[19] Less than half the voters had expressed an opinion.

As soon as the result became known, discussion began as to whether the referendum was legal and how binding it was on the Assembly. Provision for the referendum had been made by a General Assembly that was predominantly Democratic, while the one that assembled in December, 1846, had a slight Whig majority. Bills providing for the

---

19 As tabulated from the returns in the Archives Division, the vote was 34,192 in favor and 30,394 against calling a convention, the total being slightly more than half the votes cast for governor. See *post,* 373-75.

election of delegates to a convention were introduced in both houses; neither measure passed although considerable time was spent in discussion.

Two years later the General Assembly provided for a fifth referendum. The vote this time was much larger and the result showed a decided majority in favor of revising the Constitution. The Assembly of 1849-50, with the Democrats in control of both houses, made the necessary provisions for calling a convention. With a few exceptions, the delegates were apportioned in the same manner as the members of the General Assembly, there being fifty delegates from the senatorial districts and one hundred from the representative districts. Of the fifty senatorial delegates, thirty-three were Democrats and seventeen were Whigs; of the one hundred representative delegates, sixty-two were Democrats and thirty-eight were Whigs.

The convention met October 7, 1850, and adjourned February 10, 1851. The Constitution which the delegates framed was submitted to the electors for their approval or disapproval at the August election, 1851, and at the same time the electors were to vote separately on Article XIII, prohibiting Negroes or Mulattoes from coming into or settling in the state. If a majority of those voting were in favor of this article it was to become a part of the Constitution; otherwise, it should be void and form no part of it. The result was favorable both as to the ratification of the Constitution and the inclusion of Article XIII. The new Constitution went into effect on November 1, 1851. Senators whose terms had not expired and the senators and representatives elected in August, 1851, were to continue in office until the first general election under the new document which was to be held the second Tuesday in October, 1852.

PRESIDENTIAL AND VICE-PRESIDENTIAL ELECTORS

PRESIDENTIAL AND VICE-PRESIDENTIAL ELECTORS

1816

In accordance with a joint resolution of the Indiana General Assembly, the House and Senate met in joint session on November 13, 1816, and chose Joseph Bartholomew, of Clark County, Thomas H. Blake, of Knox County, and Jesse L. Holman, of Dearborn County, as presidential electors. The Governor was to notify them of their election and set the time and place when they should meet to cast their vote for president and vice-president. The returns from the various states were opened and counted before the two houses of Congress on February 12, 1817. Indiana's three electors cast their votes for James Monroe as president and Daniel D. Tompkins as vice-president.[1]

1820

Two joint resolutions were passed at the beginning of the 1820-21 session of the Indiana General Assembly; the first of these provided for the selection of three presidential electors by joint ballot of the House and Senate on November 30, 1820, and the second resolution provided that the electors should meet in the office of the secretary of state to cast their ballots. Daniel J. Caswell, of Franklin County, John H. Thompson, of Clark County, and Nathaniel Ewing, of Knox County, were chosen as presidential electors. They met December 6 and cast their votes for James Monroe as president and Daniel D. Tompkins as vice-president. Robert Buntin was selected to carry the votes to Washington where they were opened and counted along with the votes of other states before the two houses of Congress on February 14, 1821.[1]

[1] Indiana *House Journal,* 1820-21, pp. 38-39; *Laws of Indiana,* 1820-21, p. 251; U. S. *Senate Journal,* 14 Congress, 2 session, 229.

---

[1] *Indiana House Journal,* 1820-21, pp. 38-39; *Laws of Indiana,* 1820-21, pp. 131-32; Vincennes *Centinel & Public Advertiser,* December 23 and 30, 1820; U. S. *Senate Journal,* 16 Congress, 2 session, 191.

Election November 8, 1824[1]

County	Electors for Andrew Jackson and John C. Calhoun				
	Jonathan McCarty	John Carr	David Robb	Elias McNamee	Samuel Milroy
Allen	11	11	11	11	11
Bartholomew	96	96	96	96	96
Clark	589	587	588	588	589
Crawford	34	34	34	34	34
Daviess	114	114	114	114	114
Dearborn	668	668	668	668	668
Decatur	55	55	55	55	55
Dubois	32	32	32	32	32
Fayette	355	354	355	354	354
Floyd	216	216	216	216	216
Franklin	471	471	471	471	471
Gibson	133	133	133	133	133
Greene	28	28	28	28	28
Hamilton	4	4	4	4	4
Harrison	185	185	185	185	182[2]
Hendricks	6	6	6	6	6
Henry	42	42	42	42	42
Jackson	176	176	175	176	176
Jefferson	298	298	298	298	298
Jennings	131	131	131	131	131
Johnson	28	28	28	28	28
Knox	171	171	171	171	171
Lawrence	228	228	223[3]	228	228
Madison	6	6	6	6	6
Marion	99	99	99	99	99
Martin	44	44	44	44	44
Monroe	149	149	149	149	149
Montgomery	40	40	22	22	22
Morgan	71	71	71	71	71
Orange	213	213	213	213	213
Owen	33	34	30[4]	34	34
Parke	45	45	45	45	45
Perry	5	5	5	5	5
Pike	62	62	62	62	62
Posey	173	173	173	173	173
Putnam	27	27	27	26	27

County	Electors for Andrew Jackson and John C. Calhoun				
	Jonathan McCarty	John Carr	David Robb	Elias McNamee	Samuel Milroy
Randolph	62	62	62	62	62
Ripley	119	119	119	119	119
Rush	118	119	119	119	119
Scott	123	123	123	123	123
Shelby	144	144	144	144	144
Spencer	10	10	10	10	10
Sullivan	104	104	104	104	104
Switzerland	161	161	161	161	161
Union	254	254	254	254	254
Vanderburgh	32	32	32	32	32
Vermillion	2	2	2	2	2
Vigo	54	54	54	54	54
Warrick	54	54	54	54	54
Washington	668	669	669	669	667
Wayne	501	500	501	501	501
	7444	7443	7418	7427	7423

County	Electors for Henry Clay and Nathan Sanford				
	Moses Tabbs	Marston G. Clark	James Rariden	Walter Wilson	William W. Wick
Allen	44	44	44	44	44
Bartholomew	99	99	99	99	99
Clark	156	156	156	156	156
Crawford	45	45	45	45	45
Daviess	92	92	92	92	92
Dearborn	116	116	122	116	116
Decatur	72	72	72	72	72
Dubois	18	18	18	18	18
Fayette	277	277	277	277	277
Floyd	50	50	50	50	50
Franklin	244	244	244	244	244
Gibson	169	169	169	169	169
Greene	10	10	10	10	10
Hamilton	31	31	31	31	31
Harrison	128	129	129	129	129
Hendricks	30	30	30	30	30
Henry	96	96	96	96	96
Jackson	23	23	23	23	23
Jefferson	371	371	371	371	371
Jennings	76	76	76	76	76
Johnson	38	38	38	38	38
Knox	280	280	280	280	280
Lawrence	44	44	44	44	44
Madison	54	54	54	54	54
Marion	213	213	213	213	213
Martin	30	30	30	30	30
Monroe	71	71	71	71	71
Montgomery	57	57	57	57	57
Morgan	83	83	83	82	83
Orange	145	145	145	145	145
Owen	77	77	77	77	77
Parke	111	111	111	111	111
Perry	12	12	12	12	12
Pike	73	73	73	73	73
Posey	228	228	228	228	228
Putnam	31	31	31	31	31
Randolph	7	7	7	7	7

County	Electors for Henry Clay and Nathan Sanford				
	Moses Tabbs	Marston G. Clark	James Rariden	Walter Wilson	William W. Wick
Ripley	102	102	102	102	102
Rush	108	108	108	108	108
Scott	83	84	83	84	84
Shelby	104	99	104	99	104
Spencer	33	33	33	33	33
Sullivan	175	175	175	175	175
Switzerland	108	108	108	108	108
Union	135	135	135	135	135
Vanderburgh	56	56	56	56	56
Vermillion	79	79	79	79	79
Vigo	227	227	225	227	227
Warrick	44	44	44	45	43
Washington	55	55	55	55	55
Wayne	306	306	306	304	306
	5316	5313	5321	5311	5317

County	Electors for John Quincy Adams and John C. Calhoun				
	James Scott	Jesse L. Holman	Isaac Blackford	Christopher Harrison	David H. Maxwell
Allen	14	14	14	14	14
Bartholomew	20	20	20	20	20
Clark	233	231	233	233	233
Crawford	43	43	43	43	43
Daviess	19	19	19	19	19
Dearborn	365	367	367	367	367
Decatur	17	17	17	17	17
Dubois	9	9	9	9	9
Fayette	92	92	92	92	92
Floyd	118	118	118	118	118
Franklin	219	219	219	219	219
Gibson	15	15	15	15	15
Greene	12	12	12	12	12
Hamilton	10	10	10	10	10
Harrison	132	132	132	132	132
Hendricks	1	1	1	1	1
Henry	22	22	22	22	22
Jackson	57	57	57	57	57
Jefferson	61	61	61	61	61
Jennings	91	91	91	91	91
Johnson	14	14	14	14	14
Knox	34	34	34	34	34
Lawrence	8	28	28	28	28
Madison	4	4	4	4	4
Marion	16	16	16	16	16
Martin	38	38	38	38	38
Monroe	51	51	51	51	51
Montgomery	17	17	17	17	17
Morgan	10	10	10	10	10
Orange	61	61	61	61	61
Owen	12	12	2	11	12
Parke	7	7	7	7	7
Perry	9	9	9	9	9
Pike	3	3	3	3	3
Posey	13	13	13	13	13
Putnam	25	25	25	25	25
Randolph	72	72	72	72	72

County	Electors for John Quincy Adams and John C. Calhoun				
	James Scott	Jesse L. Holman	Isaac Blackford	Christopher Harrison	David H. Maxwell
Ripley	33	33	33	33	33
Rush	15	15	15	15	15
Scott	26	26	26	26	26
Shelby	9	9	9	9	9
Spencer	5	5	5	5	5
Sullivan	21	21	21	21	21
Switzerland	28	28	28	28	28
Union	85	85	85	85	85
Vanderburgh	33	33	33	33	33
Vermillion	4	4	4	4	4
Vigo	44	44	44	44	44
Warrick	11	11	11	11	11
Washington	272	272	272	271	272
Wayne	541	541	541	541	541
	3071	3091	3083	3092	3093

1 The votes are compiled from the official election returns in the Archives Division of the State Library.

2 In Harrison County three voters who intended to vote for Samuel Milroy gave the name as John Milroy.

3 In Lawrence County five votes intended for Robb were given to David Gibson. The name had first appeared as Gibson in the newspapers but was later corrected. Robb was from Gibson County.

4 In Owen County David Gibson received three votes and David Paten, one vote.

Election November 3, 1828[1]

County	Electors for Andrew Jackson and John C. Calhoun				
	Benjamin V. Beckes	Ratliff Boon	Jesse B. Durham	William Lowe	Ross Smiley
Allen	64	64	64	64	64
Bartholomew	445	445	445	445	445
Clark	953	953	953	953	953
Clay	83	83	83	83	83
Crawford	230	230	230	230	230
Daviess	291	291	291	291	291
Dearborn	1066	1066	1066	1066	1066
Decatur	346	346	346	346	346
Delaware	91	91	91	91	91
Dubois	180	180	180	180	180
Fayette	650	650	650	650	650
Floyd	590	590	590	590	590
Fountain	468	468	468	468	468
Franklin	693	693	693	693	693
Gibson	380	380	380	380	380
Greene	320	320	320	320	320
Hamilton[2]	55	55	53	55	55
Hancock	65	65	65	65	65
Harrison	[705]	[705]	[705]	[705]	[705]
Hendricks	204	204	204	204	204
Henry	284	284	284	283	284
Jackson	405	405	405	405	405
Jefferson	627	627	627	627	627
Jennings	204	204	204	204	204
Johnson	298	298	298	298	298
Knox	420	420	417	420	420
Lawrence	823	823	823	823	823
Madison	58	58	58	58	58
Marion[3]	379	379	379	379	379
Martin[4]	191	191	191	191	191
Monroe	570	570	570	570	570
Montgomery	359	359	359	359	359
Morgan	235	235	235	235	235
Orange	631	631	631	631	631
Owen	187	187	187	187	187
Parke	480	480	469	469	469

County	Electors for Andrew Jackson and John C. Calhoun				
	Benjamin V. Beckes	Ratliff Boon	Jesse B. Durham	William Lowe	Ross Smiley
Perry[5]	134	109	133	71	134
Pike	149	149	149	149	149
Posey	646	646	646	646	646
Putnam	632	632	632	632	632
Randolph	123	123	123	123	123
Ripley	307	322	307	307	307
Rush	649	649	649	649	649
Scott	283	283	283	283	283
Shelby	458	458	458	458	458
Spencer	173	173	173	173	173
Sullivan	432	432	432	432	432
Switzerland[6]	439	439	439	439	439
Tippecanoe	210	210	210	210	210
Union	547	547	547	547	547
Vanderburgh	108	108	108	108	108
Vermillion	282	282	277	276	277
Vigo	186	185	162	162	161
Warren[7]	63	53	63	62	63
Warrick	318	314	318	318	318
Washington	1083	1083	1083	1083	1083
Wayne	888	885	888	887	888
	22,140	22,122	22,114	22,033	22,099

County	Electors for John Quincy Adams and Richard Rush				
	Joseph Orr	John Watts	Amaziah Morgan	Joseph Bartholomew	Isaac Montgomery
Allen	74	74	74	74	74
Bartholomew	235	235	235	235	235
Clark	615	615	615	615	615
Clay	25	25	25	25	25
Crawford	206	206	206	206	206
Daviess	210	210	210	210	210
Dearborn	986	986	986	986	986
Decatur	292	292	292	292	292
Delaware	63	63	63	63	63
Dubois	49	49	49	49	49
Fayette	516	516	516	516	516
Floyd	374	374	374	374	374
Fountain	224	224	224	224	224
Franklin	656	656	656	656	656
Gibson	239	239	239	239	239
Greene	161	161	161	161	161
Hamilton	156	156	156	156	156
Hancock	67	67	67	67	67
Harrison	[457]	[457]	[457]	[457]	[457]
Hendricks	164	164	164	164	164
Henry	328	328	325	328	328
Jackson	182	182	182	182	182
Jefferson	709	709	709	709	709
Jennings	290	290	290	290	290
Johnson	199	199	199	199	199
Knox	405	405	405	405	405
Lawrence	213	213	213	213	213
Madison	72	72	71	72	72
Marion[3]	582	582	582	582	582
Martin[4]	68	68	68	68	68
Monroe	223	223	223	223	223
Montgomery	243	243	243	243	243
Morgan	232	232	232	232	232
Orange	285	285	285	285	285
Owen	201	201	201	201	201
Parke	328	328	339	339	339

County	Electors for John Quincy Adams and Richard Rush				
	Joseph Orr	John Watts	Amaziah Morgan	Joseph Bartholomew	Isaac Montgomery
Perry	180	180	180	180	180
Pike	140	140	140	140	140
Posey	278	278	278	278	278
Putnam	309	309	309	309	309
Randolph	250	250	250	250	250
Ripley	325	325	325	325	325
Rush	345	345	345	345	345
Scott	147	147	147	147	147
Shelby	310	310	310	310	310
Spencer	74	74	74	74	80
Sullivan	168	168	168	168	168
Switzerland[6]	335	335	335	335	335
Tippecanoe	184	182	184	184	184
Union	518	518	518	518	518
Vanderburgh	134	134	134	134	134
Vermillion	283	282	287	287	287
Vigo	520	520	544	544	544
Warren[7]	77	61	61	77	77
Warrick	73	73	73	73	73
Washington	612	612	612	612	612
Wayne	1343	1343	1343	1343	1342
	16,934	16,915	16,956	16,973	16,978

[1] The votes are compiled from the official election returns with the exception of those for Harrison County which are from the Indianapolis *Indiana Journal* (semiweekly), December 3, 1828.

[2] Hamilton County gave two votes to Israel T. Canby as a Jackson elector.

[3] In Marion County the votes from Franklin Township were received too late to be included. They were: for Adams electors, nine; for Jackson electors, seven.

[4] The Martin County clerk reported that the returns from one township were not properly reported; if set aside, it would take 22 votes from the Jackson electors and none from the Adams electors.

[5] In Perry County in addition to the five Jackson electors listed, David Robb received 25 votes and Jacob Lowe, 63.

[6] The returns from Cotton Township, Switzerland County, were not included because of an irregularity. The vote was: for Adams electors, 66; for Jackson electors, 53.

[7] In Warren County in addition to the electors listed, Joseph Watts received 16 votes as an Adams elector and David Robb, ten votes as a Jackson elector.

Election November 5, 1832[1]

County	Electors for Andrew Jackson and Martin Van Buren								
	George Boon	James Blake	Arthur Patterson	Nathan B. Palmer	Marks Crume	Thomas Givens	Alexander S. Burnett	Walter Armstrong	John Ketcham
Allen	126	126	126	126	126	126	126	126	126
Bartholomew	489	489	489	489	489	489	489	489	489
Boone	216	216	216	216	216	216	216	216	216
Carroll	258	258	258	258	258	258	258	258	258
Cass	162	162	162	162	162	162	162	162	162
Clark	1058	1058	1058	1058	1058	1058	1058	1058	1058
Clay	230	230	230	230	230	230	230	230	230
Clinton	252	252	252	252	252	252	252	252	252
Crawford	222	222	222	222	222	222	222	222	222
Daviess	363	363	363	363	363	363	363	363	363
Dearborn	1198	1198	1198	1198	1198	1198	1198	1194	1198
Decatur	405	405	405	405	405	405	405	405	405
Delaware	197	197	197	197	197	197	197	197	197
Dubois	191	191	191	191	191	191	191	191	191
Elkhart	129	129	129	129	129	no vote	129	129	129
Fayette	762	762	762	762	762	761	762	761	762
Floyd	625	625	625	625	625	625	625	625	625
Fountain	920	920	920	920	920	920	920	920	920
Franklin	738	738	738	738	738	738	738	738	738
Gibson	446	446	446	446	446	446	446	446	446
Grant	34	34	34	34	34	34	34	34	34

Greene	471	471	471	471	471	471	471	471	471
Hamilton	166	166	166	166	166	166	166	166	166
Hancock	310	310	310	310	310	310	310	310	310
Harrison	603	603	603	603	603	603	603	603	603
Hendricks	483	483	483	483	483	483	483	483	483
Henry	583	583	583	583	583	583	583	583	583
Jackson	533	533	533	533	533	533	533	529	533
Jefferson	730	729	729	730	730	729	730	729	729
Jennings	317	317	317	317	317	317	317	317	317
Johnson	653	653	653	653	653	653	653	653	653
Knox	482	481	481	481	481	481	481	481	481
LaGrange	44	44	44	44	44	44	44	44	44
LaPorte	46	46	46	46	46	46	46	46	46
Lawrence	877	877	877	877	877	877	877	877	877
Madison	285	287	269	268	269	271	270	268	271
Marion	771	771	771	771	771	771	771	771	771
Martin	202	202	202	202	202	202	202	202	202
Monroe	811	811	811	811	811	811	811	811	811
Montgomery	796	796	796	796	796	796	796	796	796
Morgan	522	522	522	522	522	522	522	522	522
Orange	615	615	615	615	615	615	615	615	615
Owen	322	322	322	322	322	322	322	322	322
Parke	882	882	882	882	882	882	882	882	882
Perry[2]	86	86	86	86	86	86	86	86	86
Pike	186	186	186	186	186	186	186	186	186
Posey	623	623	623	623	623	623	623	623	623

County	Electors for Andrew Jackson and Martin Van Buren								
	George Boon	James Blake	Arthur Patterson	Nathan B. Palmer	Marks Crume	Thomas Givens	Alexander S. Burnett	Walter Armstrong	John Ketcham
Putnam	950	950	950	950	950	950	950	950	950
Randolph[3]	175	175	175	175	175	175	175	175	175
Ripley	393	393	393	393	393	393	393	393	393
Rush	927	927	927	926	927	927	927	927	928
St. Joseph	121	121	121	121	121	121	121	121	121
Scott	342	342	342	342	342	342	342	342	342
Shelby	733	733	733	733	733	733	733	733	733
Spencer	139	139	139	139	139	139	139	139	139
Sullivan	647	648	648	648	648	648	648	648	648
Switzerland	520	520	520	514	520	520	519	520	520
Tippecanoe[4]	618	618	618	618	618	618	618	617	618
Union	568	568	568	568	568	568	568	568	568
Vanderburgh	102	102	102	102	102	102	102	102	102
Vermillion	545	545	545	545	545	545	545	545	541
Vigo	425	425	425	425	425	425	425	425	425
Warren	265	266	264	266	266	266	262	264	266
Warrick	354	354	354	354	354	354	354	354	354
Washington	1088	1088	1088	1088	1088	1088	1088	1088	1088
Wayne	1072	1072	1072	1072	1072	1072	1072	1070	1072
	31,404	31,406	31,387	31,387	31,389	31,260	31,386	31,377	31,387

County	Electors for Henry Clay and John Sergeant								
	Jacob Kuykendall	John Hawkins	Dennis Pennington	Samuel Henderson	Walter Wilson	Stephen Ludlow	Abel Lomax	Sylvanus Everts	John I. Neely
Allen	98	98	98	98	98	98	98	98	98
Bartholomew	372	372	372	372	372	372	372	372	372
Boone	125	125	125	125	125	125	125	125	125
Carroll	173	173	173	173	173	173	173	173	173
Cass	153	153	153	153	153	153	153	153	153
Clark	502	502	502	502	502	502	502	502	502
Clay	36	36	36	36	36	36	36	36	36
Clinton	176	176	176	176	176	176	176	176	176
Crawford	166	166	166	166	166	166	166	166	166
Daviess	315	315	315	315	315	315	315	315	315
Dearborn	1196	1196	1196	1196	1196	1197	1196	1196	1196
Decatur	539	539	539	538	539	539	539	539	539
Delaware	112	112	112	112	112	112	112	112	112
Dubois	82	82	82	82	82	82	82	82	82
Elkhart	60	60	60	60	60	60	60	60	60
Fayette	762	762	762	762	762	762	762	762	762
Floyd	436	436	436	436	436	436	436	436	436
Fountain	559	559	559	559	559	559	559	559	559
Franklin	790	790	790	790	790	790	790	790	790
Gibson	414	414	414	414	414	414	414	414	414

County	Electors for Henry Clay and John Sergeant								
	Jacob Kuykendall	John Hawkins	Dennis Pennington	Samuel Henderson	Walter Wilson	Stephen Ludlow	Abel Lomax	Sylvanus Everts	John I. Neely
Grant	33	33	33	33	33	33	33	33	33
Greene	180	180	180	180	180	180	180	180	180
Hamilton	251	251	251	251	251	251	251	251	251
Hancock	179	179	179	179	179	179	179	179	179
Harrison	426	426	425	426	426	426	426	426	426
Hendricks	374	374	374	374	374	374	374	374	374
Henry	769	769	769	769	769	769	769	769	769
Jackson	321	321	321	321	321	321	321	321	321
Jefferson	700	700	700	699	700	700	700	700	699
Jennings	355	355	355	355	355	355	355	355	355
Johnson	270	270	270	270	270	270	270	270	270
Knox	561	561	561	561	561	561	561	560	561
LaGrange	37	37	37	37	37	37	37	37	37
LaPorte	59	59	59	59	59	59	59	59	59
Lawrence	368	368	368	368	368	368	368	368	368
Madison	217	217	217	217	217	217	217	217	217
Marion	817	817	817	817	817	817	817	817	817
Martin	91	91	91	91	91	91	91	91	91
Monroe	235	235	235	235	235	235	235	235	235
Montgomery	639	639	639	639	639	639	639	639	639

Morgan	417	417	417	417	417	417	417	417	417
Orange	365	365	365	365	365	365	365	365	365
Owen	279	279	279	279	279	279	279	279	279
Parke	540	540	540	540	540	540	540	540	540
Perry[2]	187	187	187	187	187	187	187	187	187
Pike	174	174	174	174	174	174	174	174	174
Posey	303	303	303	303	303	303	303	303	303
Putnam	493	493	493	493	493	493	493	493	493
Randolph[3]	254	254	254	254	254	254	254	254	254
Ripley	444	444	444	444	444	444	444	444	444
Rush	796	796	796	796	796	796	796	796	796
St. Joseph	123	123	123	123	123	123	123	123	123
Scott	171	171	171	171	171	171	171	171	171
Shelby	485	485	485	485	485	485	485	485	485
Spencer	84	84	84	84	84	84	84	84	84
Sullivan	160	160	160	160	160	160	160	160	160
Switzerland	535	535	535	535	535	535	535	535	535
Tippecanoe[4]	523	523	523	523	523	523	523	523	523
Union	643	643	643	643	643	643	643	643	643
Vanderburgh	170	170	170	170	170	170	170	170	170
Vermillion	430	430	430	430	430	430	430	430	430
Vigo	637	637	637	637	637	637	637	637	637
Warren	301	301	301	301	301	301	301	301	301
Warrick	121	121	121	121	121	121	121	121	121

County	Electors for Henry Clay and John Sergeant								
	Jacob Kuykendall	John Hawkins	Dennis Pennington	Samuel Henderson	Walter Wilson	Stephen Ludlow	Abel Lomax	Sylvanus Everts	John I. Neely
Washington	623	623	623	623	623	623	623	623	623
Wayne	2031	2031	2031	2031	2031	2031	2031	2031	2031
	25,237	25,237	25,236	25,233	25,237	25,238	25,237	25,236	25,237

[1] The votes have been compiled from the official election returns. In addition to the two main parties, a third group, the Anti-Masons, also nominated the following electors: Aaron Davis, David Jewett (or Jerrett, or Spencett), Daniel (or David) Bardon, Andrew House (or Housh), John Morgan, David G. Mitchell, Cyrus Douglass, Hugh Morse, and Aaron Farmer. They received the following votes: from Bartholomew, five; from Dearborn, three; from Decatur, one; from Franklin, five; from Jennings, six; from Johnson, seven.

[2] The Perry County clerk certified that returns from the townships of Union, Anderson, and Clark were not included. The vote in these townships was: for Jackson, 84; and for Clay, 38.

[3] The returns from Washington and Ward townships, Randolph County, were not included because they were not properly made out. The vote was: for Clay, 99 votes; for Jackson, 17 votes.

[4] The Tippecanoe County clerk reported that in addition to the votes recorded, the Jackson electors received 147 votes that were not properly returned, and that the Clay electors received 99 votes each, with the exception of Walter Wilson who received 98.

Election November 7, 1836[1]

County	Electors for William Henry Harrison and Francis Granger (W)								
	John G. Clendenin	Hiram Decker	Milton Stapp	Enoch McCarty	Achilles Williams	Austin W. Morris	Albert S. White	Marston G. Clark	Abraham P. Andrew
Adams	68	68	68	68	68	68	68	68	68
Allen	353	353	353	353	353	353	353	353	354
Bartholomew	608	608	608	608	608	608	608	608	608
Boone	464	464	464	464	464	464	464	464	464
Carroll	375	375	375	375	375	375	375	375	375
Cass	513	513	513	513	513	513	513	513	513
Clark	893	893	893	893	893	893	893	893	893
Clay	153	153	153	153	153	153	153	153	153
Clinton	331	331	331	331	331	331	331	331	331
Crawford	196	196	196	196	196	196	196	196	196
Daviess	438	438	438	438	438	438	438	438	438
Dearborn	1203	1203	1203	1201	1203	1203	1203	1203	1203
Decatur	950	950	950	950	950	950	950	950	950
Delaware	369	369	369	369	369	369	369	369	369
Dubois	165	165	165	165	165	165	165	165	165
Elkhart[2]	354	354	354	354	354	354	354	354	354
Fayette	965	965	965	965	965	965	965	965	964
Floyd	[574]	[574]	[574]	[574]	[574]	[574]	[574]	[574]	[574]
Fountain	697	697	697	697	697	697	697	697	697

County	Electors for William Henry Harrison and Francis Granger (W)								
	John G. Clendenin	Hiram Decker	Milton Stapp	Enoch McCarty	Achilles Williams	Austin W. Morris	Albert S. White	Marston G. Clark	Abraham P. Andrew
Franklin	963	963	963	963	963	963	963	963	963
Fulton	55	55	55	55	55	55	55	55	55
Gibson	496	496	496	496	496	496	496	496	496
Grant	238	238	238	238	238	238	238	238	238
Greene	366	366	366	366	366	366	366	366	366
Hamilton	569	569	569	569	569	569	569	569	569
Hancock	366	366	366	366	366	366	366	366	366
Harrison	747	747	747	747	747	747	747	747	747
Hendricks	731	731	731	731	731	731	731	731	731
Henry	1304	1304	1304	1304	1304	1304	1304	1304	1304
Huntington	52	52	52	52	52	51	52	52	52
Jackson	439	439	439	439	439	439	439	439	439
Jefferson	1172	1172	1172	1172	1172	1172	1172	1172	1172
Jennings	626	626	626	626	626	626	626	626	626
Johnson	438	438	438	438	438	438	438	438	438
Knox	736	736	736	736	736	736	736	736	736
Kosciusko	160	160	160	160	160	160	160	160	160
LaGrange	138	138	138	138	138	138	138	138	138
LaPorte	490	490	490	490	490	490	490	490	489
Lawrence	670	670	670	670	670	670	670	670	670

Madison	487	487	487	487	487	487	487	487	487
Marion	1409	1409	1409	1409	1409	1409	1409	1409	1409
Marshall	94	94	94	94	94	94	94	94	94
Martin	142	139	139	139	139	139	139	142	139
Miami	133	133	133	133	133	129	133	133	133
Monroe	424	424	424	424	424	424	424	424	424
Montgomery	1066	1066	1066	1066	1066	1066	1066	1066	1066
Morgan	666	666	666	666	666	666	666	666	666
Noble	46	46	46	46	46	46	46	46	46
Orange	483	483	483	483	483	483	483	483	483
Owen	427	427	427	427	427	427	427	427	427
Parke	828	828	828	828	828	828	828	828	828
Perry[3]	392	392	392	392	392	392	392	392	392
Pike	226	226	226	226	226	326	226	226	226
Porter	87	87	87	87	87	87	87	87	87
Posey	330	330	330	330	330	330	330	330	330
Putnam	1067	1067	1067	1067	1067	1067	1067	1067	1067
Randolph	633	633	633	633	633	633	633	633	633
Ripley	663	663	663	663	663	663	663	663	663
Rush	1167	1167	1167	1167	1167	1166	1167	1167	1167
St. Joseph	480	480	480	480	480	480	480	480	480
Scott	294	294	294	294	294	294	294	294	294
Shelby	688	688	688	688	688	688	688	688	688
Spencer	171	171	171	171	171	171	171	171	171

County	Electors for William Henry Harison and Francis Granger (W)								
	John G. Clendenin	Hiram Decker	Milton Stapp	Enoch McCarty	Achilles Williams	Austin W. Morris	Albert S. White	Marston G. Clark	Abraham P. Andrew
Sullivan[4]	203	203	203	203	203	203	203	203	203
Switzerland	630	630	630	630	630	630	630	630	630
Tippecanoe	1244	1244	1244	1244	1244	1244	1244	1244	1244
Union[5]	700	700	700	700	700	700	700	700	700
Vanderburgh	269	269	269	269	269	269	269	269	269
Vermillion	574	574	574	574	574	573	574	573	574
Vigo	963	963	963	963	963	963	963	963	963
Wabash	122	122	122	122	122	122	122	122	122
Warren	541	541	541	541	541	541	540	541	541
Warrick	157	157	157	157	157	157	157	157	157
Washington	656	656	656	656	656	656	656	656	656
Wayne	2285	2282	2285	2284	2283	2285	2284	2285	2283
White	109	109	109	109	109	109	109	109	109
	41,281	41,275	41,278	41,275	41,276	41,271	41,276	41,280	41,276

County	Electors for Martin Van Buren and Richard M. Johnson (D)								
	John Myers	William Rockhill	Thomas C. Stewart	George W. Moore	Jesse Jackson	Marinus Willett	Elisha Long	Jonathan Williams	William White
Adams	28	28	28	28	28	28	28	28	28
Allen	266	266	266	266	266	266	266	266	266
Bartholomew	412	412	412	412	412	412	412	412	412
Boone	421	421	421	421	421	421	421	421	421
Carroll	565	565	565	565	565	565	565	565	565
Cass	286	286	286	286	286	286	286	286	286
Clark	978	978	978	978	978	978	978	978	978
Clay	251	251	251	251	251	251	251	251	251
Clinton	427	427	427	427	427	427	427	427	427
Crawford	166	166	166	166	166	166	166	166	166
Daviess	253	253	253	253	253	253	253	253	253
Dearborn	1282	1282	1282	1282	1278	1282	1278	1278	1282
Decatur	513	513	513	513	513	513	513	513	513
Delaware	307	307	307	307	307	307	307	307	307
Dubois	127	127	127	127	127	127	127	127	127
Elkhart[2]	305	305	305	305	305	305	305	305	305
Fayette	545	545	545	545	545	545	545	545	545
Floyd	[999]	[999]	[999]	[999]	[999]	[999]	[999]	[999]	[999]
Fountain	948	948	948	948	948	948	948	948	948
Franklin	875	875	875	875	875	875	875	875	875
Fulton	39	39	39	39	39	39	39	39	39

County	Electors for Martin Van Buren and Richard M. Johnson (D)								
	John Myers	William Rockhill	Thomas C. Stewart	George W. Moore	Jesse Jackson	Marinus Willett	Elisha Long	Jonathan Williams	William White
Gibson	425	425	425	425	425	425	425	425	425
Grant	130	130	130	130	130	130	130	130	130
Greene	330	330	330	330	330	328	328	329	330
Hamilton	262	262	262	262	262	262	262	262	262
Hancock	293	293	293	293	293	293	293	293	293
Harrison	456	456	456	456	456	456	456	456	456
Hendricks	390	390	390	390	390	390	390	390	390
Henry	712	712	712	712	712	712	709	712	712
Huntington	67	67	67	67	67	67	67	67	67
Jackson	307	307	307	307	307	307	307	307	307
Jefferson	679	678	678	678	678	678	678	678	678
Jennings	292	292	292	292	292	292	292	292	292
Johnson	559	559	559	559	559	559	559	559	559
Knox	437	437	437	437	437	437	437	437	437
Kosciusko	149	149	149	149	149	149	149	149	149
LaGrange	150	150	150	150	150	150	150	150	150
LaPorte	452	452	452	452	452	452	452	452	452
Lawrence	815	815	815	815	815	815	815	815	815
Madison	367	367	367	367	367	367	367	367	367
Marion	1043	1043	1043	1043	1043	1043	1043	1043	1043
Marshall	42	42	42	42	42	42	42	42	42

Martin	197	197	197	197	197	197	197	197	197
Miami[6]	80	80	80	80	80	80	79	80	79
Monroe	604	604	604	604	604	604	604	604	604
Montgomery	752	752	752	752	752	752	752	752	752
Morgan	543	543	543	543	543	543	543	543	543
Noble	80	80	80	80	80	80	80	80	80
Orange	564	564	564	564	564	564	564	564	564
Owen	286	286	286	286	286	286	286	286	286
Parke	534	534	534	534	534	534	534	534	534
Perry[3]	114	114	114	114	114	114	114	114	114
Pike	218	218	218	218	218	218	218	218	218
Porter	69	69	69	69	69	69	69	69	69
Posey	751	751	751	751	751	751	751	751	751
Putnam	694	694	694	694	694	694	694	694	694
Randolph	234	234	234	234	234	234	234	234	234
Ripley	453	453	453	453	453	453	453	453	453
Rush	749	747	749	749	749	747	749	748	748
St. Joseph	255	255	255	255	255	255	255	255	255
Scott	267	267	267	267	267	267	267	267	267
Shelby	675	675	675	675	675	675	675	675	675
Spencer	179	179	179	179	179	179	179	179	179
Sullivan	558	558	558	558	558	558	558	558	558
Switzerland	519	519	519	519	519	519	519	519	519
Tippecanoe	1041	1041	1041	1041	1041	1041	1041	1041	1041
Union[5]	568	568	568	568	568	568	568	568	568

County	Electors for Martin Van Buren and Richard M. Johnson (D)								
	John Myers	Rockhill William	Thomas C. Stewart	George W. Moore	Jesse Jackson	Marinus Willett	Elisha Long	Jonathan Williams	William White
Vanderburgh	130	130	130	130	130	130	130	130	130
Vermillion	433	433	433	433	433	433	433	433	433
Vigo	287	287	287	287	287	287	287	287	287
Wabash	47	47	47	47	47	47	47	47	47
Warren	329	329	329	329	329	329	329	329	329
Warrick	380	380	380	380	380	380	380	380	380
Washington	947	947	947	947	947	947	947	947	947
Wayne	985	985	985	985	985	985	983	985	985
White	106	106	106	106	106	106	106	106	106
	32,978	32,975	32,977	32,977	32,977	32,973	32,967	32,971	32,975

[1] Compiled from the original election returns in the Archives Division with the exception of the vote of Floyd County which is from the Indianapolis *Indiana Democrat,* December 13, 1836.

[2] The returns from Middlebury Township, Elkhart County, were not included in the totals because the certificate did not set forth the names of the electors. The vote was: for Van Buren electors, 38; for Harrison electors, 17.

[3] The votes from Clark Township, Perry County, were received too late to be included. They were: for Van Buren electors, 15; for Harrison electors, 14.

[4] The Sullivan County clerk reported that 203 votes were cast for Harrison electors while the same men as electors for vice-president received only 126 votes.

[5] The election returns from Union Township, Union County, were rejected because they were not transmitted in proper form. They were: for Van Buren electors, 45; for Harrison electors, 27.

[6] The Miami County clerk reported that eight ballots carrying only the names of Van Buren and Johnson were not counted.

Election November 2, 1840[1]

County	Electors for William Henry Harrison and John Tyler (W)								
	Jonathan McCarty	Joseph G. Marshall	John W. Payne	Richard W. Thompson	Joseph L. White	James H. Cravens	Caleb B. Smith	William Herod	Samuel C. Sample
Adams	193	193	193	193	193	193	193	193	193
Allen	640	640	640	640	640	640	640	639	637
Bartholomew	982	982	982	982	982	982	982	982	982
Benton	26	26	26	26	26	26	26	26	26
Blackford	77	77	77	77	77	77	77	77	69
Boone	700	700	700	700	700	700	700	700	700
Brown	54	54	54	54	54	54	54	54	54
Carroll	699	699	699	699	699	699	699	699	699
Cass	649	649	649	649	649	649	649	649	649
Clark	1132	1132	1132	1132	1132	1132	1132	1132	1132
Clay	398	398	398	398	398	398	398	398	398
Clinton	582	582	582	582	582	582	582	582	582
Crawford	435	435	435	435	435	435	435	435	435
Daviess	738	738	738	738	738	738	738	738	738
Dearborn	1771	1771	1771	1771	1771	1771	1771	1771	1771
Decatur	1298	1298	1298	1298	1298	1298	1298	1298	1298
DeKalb	177	177	147	177	177	177	177	177	177
Delaware	918	920	920	920	920	920	920	920	920
Dubois	264	264	264	264	264	264	264	264	264
Elkhart	640	640	640	640	640	640	640	640	640
Fayette	1085	1090	1090	1090	1089	1090	1090	1090	1090

County	Electors for William Henry Harrison and John Tyler (W)								
	Jonathan McCarty	Joseph G. Marshall	John W. Payne	Richard W. Thompson	Joseph L. White	James H. Cravens	Caleb B. Smith	William Herod	Samuel C. Sample
Floyd	869	869	869	869	869	869	869	869	869
Fountain	938	938	938	938	938	938	938	938	938
Franklin	1187	1188	1188	1188	1188	1188	1188	1188	1188
Fulton	241	241	241	241	241	241	241	241	241
Gibson	788	788	788	788	788	788	788	788	788
Grant	470	470	470	470	470	470	470	470	470
Greene	704	704	704	704	704	704	704	704	704
Hamilton	972	972	972	972	972	972	972	972	972
Hancock	721	721	721	721	721	721	721	721	721
Harrison	1285	1285	1285	1285	1285	1285	1285	1285	1285
Hendricks	1189	1189	1189	1189	1190	1190	1189	1190	1190
Henry	1651	1652	1652	1652	1652	1652	1652	1652	1652
Huntington	142	142	143	143	143	143	143	143	143
Jackson	680	680	679	680	680	680	680	680	680
Jasper	73	73	73	73	73	73	73	73	73
Jay	283	282	283	282	283	283	283	283	283
Jefferson	1674	1673	1674	1674	1672	1674	1674	1674	1674
Jennings	908	908	908	908	908	908	908	908	908
Johnson	631	631	631	631	631	631	631	631	631
Knox	1077	1077	1077	1077	1077	1077	1077	1077	1077
Kosciusko	496	496	496	496	496	496	496	496	496
LaGrange	390	391	391	391	391	391	391	391	391

Lake	115	115	115	115	115	115	115	115	115
LaPorte	1068	1068	1069	1069	1069	1068	1069	1069	1069
Lawrence	989	989	989	989	989	989	989	989	989
Madison	910	911	911	911	911	911	911	911	911
Marion	1636	1636	1636	1636	1636	1636	1636	1636	1636
Marshall	154	154	154	154	154	154	154	154	154
Martin	311	311	311	311	311	311	311	311	311
Miami	312	312	312	312	312	312	312	312	312
Monroe	719	719	719	719	719	719	719	719	719
Montgomery	1413	1413	1413	1413	1413	1413	1413	1413	1413
Morgan	1012	1012	1012	1012	1012	1012	1012	1012	1012
Noble	241	241	241	241	241	241	241	241	241
Orange	707	707	708	708	708	708	708	708	708
Owen	709	709	709	709	709	709	709	709	709
Parke	1360	1360	1360	1360	1360	1360	1360	1360	1360
Perry	560	560	560	560	560	560	560	560	560
Pike	474	474	474	474	474	474	474	474	474
Porter	220	220	220	220	220	220	220	220	220
Posey	706	706	706	706	706	706	706	706	706
Pulaski	51	51	51	51	51	51	51	51	51
Putnam	1571	1571	1571	1571	1571	1571	1571	1571	1571
Randolph	1068	1068	1068	1068	1068	1068	1068	1068	1068
Ripley	1000	1000	1000	1000	1000	1000	1000	1000	1000
Rush	1526	1525	1526	1525	1526	1526	1526	1526	1526
St. Joseph	809	809	809	809	809	809	809	809	809
Scott	399	399	399	399	399	399	399	399	399

County	Electors for William Henry Harrison and John Tyler (W)								
	McCarty Jonathan	Joseph G. Marshall	John W. Payne	Richard W. Thompson	Joseph L. White	James H. Cravens	Caleb B. Smith	William Herod	Samuel C. Sample
Shelby	1016	1016	1016	1016	1016	1016	1016	1016	1016
Spencer	589	589	589	589	589	589	589	589	589
Steuben	238	238	238	238	238	238	238	238	238
Sullivan	417	417	417	417	417	417	417	417	417
Switzerland	1023	1023	1023	1023	1023	1023	1023	1023	1023
Tippecanoe	1508	1508	1508	1508	1508	1508	1508	1508	1508
Union	760	760	760	760	760	760	760	760	760
Vanderburgh	628	628	628	628	628	628	628	628	628
Vermillion	847	847	847	847	847	847	847	847	847
Vigo	1511	1511	1511	1511	1511	1511	1511	1511	1511
Wabash	307	307	307	307	307	307	307	307	307
Warren	737	737	737	737	737	737	737	737	737
Warrick	355	355	355	355	355	355	355	355	355
Washington	1131	1131	1138	1138	1138	1138	1138	1138	1138
Wayne	2865	2869	2869	2869	2869	2869	2868	2869	2869
Wells	131	131	131	131	131	131	131	131	131
White	206	206	206	206	206	206	206	206	206
Whitley	144	144	144	144	144	144	144	133	133
	63,216	63,225	63,237	63,235	63,235	63,237	63,237	63,227	63,217

County	Electors for Martin Van Buren and Richard M. Johnson (D)								
	William Hendricks	Tilghman A. Howard	Robert D. Owen	Henry Secrest	Thomas J. Henley	John L. Robinson	Andrew Kennedy	William J. Peaslee	John M. Lemon
Adams	153	94	153	94	153	153	153	152	152
Allen	394[2]	399	399	399	399	399	399	399	399
Bartholomew	703	703	703	703	703	703	703	703	703
Benton	42	42	42	42	42	42	42	42	42
Blackford	147	145	147	146	148	148	148	148	148
Boone	686	686	686	686	686	686	686	686	686
Brown	270	270	270	270	270	270	270	270	270
Carroll	765	765	765	765	765	765	764	764	764
Cass	372	372	372	372	372	372	372	372	372
Clark	1278	1278	1278	1278	1277	1277	1278	1278	1278
Clay	487	487	487	487	487	487	487	487	487
Clinton	698	698	698	698	698	697	697	698	698
Crawford	281	281	281	281	281	281	281	281	281
Daviess	509	509	509	509	509	509	509	509	509
Dearborn	1583	1583	1583	1583	1583	1583	1583	1583	1583
Decatur	759	759	759	759	759	759	759	759	759
DeKalb	169	119	168	167	168	168	167	168	168
Delaware	531	526	532	532	531	532	531	532	532
Dubois	239	239	239	239	239	239	239	239	239
Elkhart	596	595	596	595	596	596	596	596	596
Fayette	728	728	728	728	728	728	728	728	728
Floyd	796	796	796	796	796	796	796	796	796

County	Electors for Martin Van Buren and Richard M. Johnson (D)								
	William Hendricks	Tilghman A. Howard	Robert D. Owen	Henry Secrest	Thomas J. Henley	John L. Robinson	Andrew Kennedy	William J. Peaslee	John M. Lemon
Fountain	1166	1166	1166	1166	1166	1166	1166	1166	1166
Franklin	1115	1115	1115	1115	1115	1115	1115	1115	1115
Fulton	107	108	108	108	108	108	108	108	108
Gibson	594	568	594	594	594	594	594	594	594
Grant	364	364	364	364	364	364	364	364	364
Greene	634	634	634	634	634	634	634	634	634
Hamilton	688	688	688	688	688	688	688	688	688
Hancock	537	537	537	537	537	537	537	537	537
Harrison	861	861	861	861	861	861	861	861	861
Hendricks	651	652	651	651	651	651	651	652	651
Henry	839	839	839	839	839	839	839	839	839
Huntington	177	177	177	177	177	177	177	177	177
Jackson	737	737	737	737	737	737	737	737	737
Jasper	95	95	95	95	95	95	95	95	95
Jay	267	204	267	205	266	264	264	265	217
Jefferson	1026	1025	1026	1026	1026	1026	1026	1026	1026
Jennings	503	503	503	499	503	503	503	503	503
Johnson	948	948	948	948	948	948	948	948	948
Knox	658	658	658	658	658	658	658	658	657
Kosciusko	329	329	329	329	329	329	329	329	329
LaGrange	225	224	224	224	224	224	224	224	224
Lake	125	125	125	125	125	125	125	125	125

LaPorte	640	640	639	639	639	639	640	639	639
Lawrence	898	898	898	898	898	898	898	898	898
Madison	625	625	625	625	625	625	625	625	625
Marion	1279	1279	1279	1279	1279	1279	1279	1279	1279
Marshall	194	194	194	194	194	194	194	194	194
Martin	366	366	366	366	366	366	366	366	366
Miami	244	244	244	244	244	244	244	244	244
Monroe	943	943	943	943	943	943	943	943	943
Montgomery	1222	1222	1222	1222	1222	1222	1222	1222	1222
Morgan	815	815	815	815	815	815	815	815	815
Noble[3]	228	217	225	228	227	227	227	224	228
Orange	879	844	879	879	879	879	879	879	879
Owen	604	604	604	604	604	604	604	604	604
Parke	948	948	948	948	948	948	948	948	947
Perry	221	221	220	221	221	221	221	221	221
Pike	318	318	318	318	318	318	318	318	318
Porter	194	186	194	194	194	194	194	194	194
Posey	965	950	965	965	965	965	965	965	965
Pulaski	60	60	60	60	60	60	60	60	60
Putnam	1049	1049	1049	1049	1049	1049	1049	1049	1049
Randolph	553	496	553	482	553	553	553	553	553
Ripley	623	623	623	623	623	623	623	623	623
Rush	1170	1170	1170	1170	1170	1170	1170	1170	1170
St. Joseph	440	440	440	440	440	440	440	440	440
Scott	361	361	361	361	361	361	361	361	361
Shelby	1070	1070	1070	1070	1070	1070	1070	1070	1070

County	Electors for Martin Van Buren and Richard M. Johnson (D)								
	William Hendricks	Tilghman A. Howard	Robert D. Owen	Henry Secrest	Thomas J. Henley	John L. Robinson	Andrew Kennedy	William J. Peaslet	John M. Lemon
Spencer	324	324	324	324	324	324	324	324	324
Steuben	176	176	176	176	176	176	176	176	176
Sullivan	1014	1014	1014	1014	1014	1014	1014	1014	1014
Switzerland	735	735	735	735	735	735	735	735	735
Tippecanoe	1200	1200	1200	1200	1200	1200	1200	1200	1200
Union	614	614	614	614	614	614	614	614	614
Vanderburgh	370	370	370	370	370	370	370	370	370
Vermillion	663	663	663	663	663	663	663	663	663
Vigo	583	583	583	583	583	583	583	583	583
Wabash	198	197	197	198	195	198	198	185	198
Warren	347	347	347	347	347	347	347	347	347
Warrick	662	662	662	662	662	661	661	662	662
Washington	1381	1381	1381	1381	1381	1381	1381	1381	1381
Wayne	1258	1256	1258	1256	1257	1258	1258	1258	1258
Wells	140	138	140	140	140	140	140	140	140
White	144	139	144	144	144	144	144	144	144
Whitley	141	126	141	141	141	139	141	141	141
	51,691	51,339	51,690	51,494	51,688	51,687	51,688	51,676	51,642

County	Electors for James G. Birney and Thomas Earle (Liberty)								
	Thomas Johns	Thomas Hicklin	William Smith	Cyrus Hamilton	Daniel Worth	James Clayton	Samuel Stephenson	Lesmon Basye	Thomas Maxwell
Dearborn	3	3	3	3	3	3	3	3	3
Jefferson	3	3	3	3	3	3	3	3	3
Jennings	8	8	8	8	8	8	8	8	8
Morgan	16	16	16	16	16	16	16	16	16

[1] Compiled from the official election returns in the Archives Division. In addition to the votes cast for the electors of the Whig, Democrat, and Liberty parties, the following persons received votes without the backing of any party: J. M. Simmons 51 votes in Jay County; George Boon 59 votes in Adams County, 62 in Jay, four in Jennings, 70 in Randolph, and two in Wayne; George W. Ewing received 59 votes in Adams County, 49 in DeKalb, five in Delaware, 26 in Gibson, 62 in Jay, 11 in Noble, 35 in Orange, eight in Porter, 15 in Posey, 57 in Randolph, two in Wayne, two in Wells, five in White, and 15 in Whitley, making a total of 351 votes.

[2] In Allen County five other votes intended for William Hendricks were not counted because the name was given as William J. Hendricks.

[3] In Noble five other votes probably intended for Robert Dale Owen were not counted because the name was given as Robert Dale.

Election November 4, 1844[1]

County	Electors for James K. Polk and George M. Dallas (D)											
	Graham N. Fitch	James G. Read	William A. Bowles	Elijah Newland	John M. Johnston	Samuel E. Perkins	William W. Wick	Paris C. Dunning	Austin M. Puett	Henry W. Ellsworth	Charles W. Cathcart	John Gilbert
Adams	296	296	296	296	296	296	296	296	296	296	296	296
Allen	849	849	849	849	849	849	849	849	849	849	849	847
Bartholomew	1068	1068	1068	1068	1068	1068	1068	1068	1068	1068	1068	1068
Benton	59	60	60	60	60	60	60	60	60	59	60	59
Blackford	205	205	205	205	205	205	205	205	205	205	205	205
Boone	871	871	871	871	871	871	871	871	871	871	871	871
Brown	432	432	432	432	432	432	432	432	432	432	432	432
Carroll	965	965	965	965	965	965	965	965	965	962	965	965
Cass	671	671	671	671	671	671	671	671	671	671	671	670
Clark	1417	1417	1417	1417	1417	1417	1417	1417	1417	1417	1417	1417
Clay	662	662	662	662	662	662	662	662	662	662	662	662
Clinton[2]	944	944	944	944	944	944	944	944	944	944	944	943
Crawford[3]	395	397	397	397	397	397	397	397	397	397	397	394
Daviess	764	764	764	764	764	764	764	764	764	764	764	764
Dearborn	1971	1971	1971	1971	1971	1971	1971	1971	1971	1971	1971	1971
Decatur	1091	1091	1091	1091	1091	1091	1091	1091	1091	1091	1091	1091

DeKalb	327	327	327	327	327	327	327	327	327	326	327	327
Delaware	732	732	732	732	732	732	732	732	732	732	732	732
Dubois	501	501	501	501	501	501	501	501	501	501	501	501
Elkhart	963	964	964	964	964	964	964	964	964	964	963	964
Fayette	908	908	908	908	908	908	908	908	908	907	907	906
Floyd	981	981	981	981	981	981	981	981	981	980	979	979
Fountain	1387	1387	1387	1387	1387	1387	1387	1387	1387	1387	1387	1387
Franklin	1583	1583	1583	1583	1584	1583	1583	1583	1583	1583	1583	1583
Fulton	308	308	308	308	308	308	308	308	308	308	308	308
Gibson	810	810	810	810	810	810	810	810	810	810	810	810
Grant	423	423	423	422	423	423	423	423	423	423	423	423
Greene	909	909	909	909	909	909	909	909	909	909	909	909
Hamilton	766	766	766	766	766	766	766	766	766	766	766	766
Hancock	736	736	736	736	736	736	736	736	736	736	736	736
Harrison	1144	1144	1144	1144	1144	1144	1144	1144	1144	1144	1144	1144
Hendricks	844	844	844	844	844	844	844	844	844	844	844	844
Henry	1005	1005	1005	1005	1005	1005	1005	1005	1004	1004	1005	1005
[Howard] Richardville	133	133	133	133	133	133	133	133	133	133	133	133
Huntington	317	317	316	316	316	316	316	316	316	316	316	316
Jackson[4]	1048	1048	1048	1048	1048	1048	1048	1048	1048	1048	1048	1045
Jasper	175	175	175	175	175	175	175	175	175	175	175	175
Jay	352	352	352	352	352	352	352	352	352	352	352	352
Jefferson	1427	1427	1427	1427	1427	1427	1427	1427	1427	1427	1427	1427
Jennings	669	669	669	669	669	669	669	669	669	669	669	669

County	Electors for James K. Polk and George M. Dallas (D)											
	Graham N. Fitch	James G. Read	William A. Bowles	Elijah Newland	John M. Johnston	Samuel E. Perkins	William W. Wick	Paris C. Dunning	Austin M. Puett	Henry W. Ellsworth	Charles W. Cathcart	John Gilbert
Johnson	1150	1150	1150	1150	1150	1150	1149	1150	1150	1150	1150	1150
Knox	821	821	821	821	821	821	821	821	821	821	821	821
Kosciusko	553	553	553	553	553	553	553	553	553	553	553	553
LaGrange	457	457	457	457	457	457	457	457	457	457	457	457
Lake	206	206	206	206	206	206	206	206	206	206	205	206
LaPorte	831	831	831	831	831	831	831	831	831	831	831	831
Lawrence	1085	1085	1085	1085	1085	1085	1085	1085	1085	1085	1085	1085
Madison	854	854	854	854	854	854	854	854	854	854	854	854
Marion	1634	1634	1634	1634	1634	1634	1633	1634	1634	1634	1634	1634
Marshall	256	256	256	256	256	256	256	256	256	256	256	256
Martin	516	516	516	516	516	516	516	517	516	516	516	516
Miami	517	517	517	517	517	517	517	517	517	517	517	517
Monroe	1118	1118	1118	1118	1118	1118	1118	1118	1118	1118	1118	1118
Montgomery	1521	1521	1521	1521	1521	1521	1521	1521	1521	1521	1521	1521
Morgan	1078	1078	1078	1078	1078	1078	1078	1078	1078	1078	1078	1078
Noble	438	438	438	438	438	438	438	438	438	438	438	438
Ohio	168	168	168	168	168	168	168	168	168	168	168	168

Orange	1036	1036	1032	1036	1036	1036	1036	1036	1036	1036	1036	1036
Owen	888	888	888	888	888	888	888	888	888	888	888	888
Parke	1329	1329	1329	1329	1329	1329	1329	1329	1329	1329	1329	1329
Perry	334	334	335	334	334	334	334	334	334	334	334	334
Pike	491	491	491	491	491	491	491	491	491	491	491	491
Porter	305	305	305	305	305	305	305	305	305	305	305	305
Posey	1154	1154	1154	1154	1154	1154	1154	1154	1154	1154	1154	1154
Pulaski	124	124	124	124	124	124	124	124	124	124	124	124
Putnam	1367	1367	1367	1367	1367	1367	1367	1367	1367	1367	1367	1367
Randolph	809	809	809	809	809	809	809	809	809	809	809	809
Ripley	908	908	908	908	908	908	908	908	908	908	908	908
Rush	1362	1362	1362	1362	1362	1362	1362	1362	1362	1362	1362	1362
St. Joseph	683	683	683	683	683	683	683	683	683	683	683	683
Scott	441	441	441	441	441	441	441	441	441	441	441	441
Shelby	1342	1342	1342	1342	1342	1342	1342	1342	1342	1342	1342	1342
Spencer	496	496	496	496	496	496	496	496	496	496	496	496
Steuben	303	303	303	303	303	303	303	303	303	303	303	303
Sullivan	1221	1221	1221	1221	1221	1221	1221	1221	1221	1221	1221	1221
Switzerland	1006	1006	1006	1006	1006	1006	1006	1006	1006	1006	1006	992
Tippecanoe	1551	1551	1551	1551	1551	1551	1552	1551	1551	1550	1551	1551
Tipton	119	119	119	119	119	119	119	119	119	119	119	119
Union	672	672	672	672	672	672	672	672	672	672	672	672
Vanderburgh	556	556	556	556	556	556	556	556	556	556	556	556
Vermillion	762	762	762	762	762	762	762	762	762	762	762	762

County	Electors for James K. Polk and George M. Dallas (D)											
	Graham N. Fitch	James G. Read	William A. Bowles	Elijah Newland	John M. Johnston	Samuel E. Perkins	William W. Wick	Paris C. Dunning	Austin M. Puett	Henry W. Ellsworth	Charles W. Cathcart	John Gilbert
Vigo	856	856	856	856	856	856	856	856	856	856	856	856
Wabash	575	575	575	575	575	575	575	575	574	574	573	575
Warren	470	470	470	470	470	470	470	470	470	470	470	470
Warrick	850	850	850	850	850	850	850	850	850	849	848	849
Washington	1660	1660	1660	1659	1660	1660	1660	1660	1660	1660	1660	1660
Wayne	1437	1436	1436	1436	1437	1437	1437	1436	1436	1436	1436	1436
Wells	306	306	306	306	306	306	306	306	306	306	306	306
White	218	218	218	218	218	218	218	218	218	218	218	218
Whitley	237	237	237	237	237	237	237	237	237	237	237	237
	70,179	70,182	70,178	70,179	70,183	70,182	70,181	70,182	70,179	70,170	70,172	70,151

County	Henry S. Lane	Joseph G. Marshall	John A. Brackenridge	James Collins, Jr.	John A. Matson	Samuel W. Parker	Hugh O'Neal	George G. Dunn	Richard W. Thompson	Albert L. Holmes	Horace P. Biddle	Lewis G. Thompson
	Electors for Henry Clay and Theodore Frelinghuysen (W)											
Adams	198	198	198	198	198	198	198	198	198	198	198	198
Allen	861	861	861	861	861	861	861	861	861	861	861	862
Bartholomew	1035	1035	1035	1035	1035	1035	1035	1035	1035	1035	1035	1035
Benton	40	40	40	40	40	40	40	40	40	40	40	40
Blackford	81	81	81	81	81	81	81	81	81	81	81	81
Boone	816	816	816	816	816	816	816	816	816	816	816	816
Brown	59	59	59	59	59	59	59	59	59	59	59	59
Carroll	712	712	712	712	712	711	711	712	712	711	712	712
Cass	768	768	768	767	768	768	768	768	768	768	768	768
Clark	1132	1132	1132	1132	1132	1132	1132	1132	1132	1132	1132	1132
Clay	429	429	429	429	429	429	429	429	429	429	429	429
Clinton	645	645	645	645	645	645	645	645	645	645	645	645
Crawford	462	462	462	461	462	462	462	462	462	462	462	462
Daviess	807	807	807	807	807	807	807	807	807	807	807	807
Dearborn	1616	1616	1615	1616	1616	1616	1616	1616	1616	1616	1616	1616
Decatur	1275	1275	1275	1275	1275	1275	1275	1275	1275	1275	1275	1275
DeKalb	269	269	269	269	269	269	269	269	269	269	269	269

County	Henry S. Lane	Joseph G. Marshall	John A. Brackenridge	James Collins, Jr.	John A. Matson	Samuel W. Parker	Hugh O'Neal	George G. Dunn	Richard W. Thompson	Albert L. Holmes	Horace P. Biddle	Lewis G. Thompson
Delaware	940	940	940	940	940	940	940	940	940	940	940	940
Dubois	229	229	229	229	229	229	229	229	229	229	229	229
Elkhart	758	759	758	758	758	758	756	756	756	758	758	758
Fayette	1051	1051	1051	1050	1051	1049	1051	1051	1051	1051	1051	1051
Floyd	956	956	956	955	956	956	956	956	956	956	956	956
Fountain	947	947	947	947	947	947	947	947	947	947	947	946
Franklin	1325	1324	1325	1325	1325	1325	1325	1325	1325	1325	1325	1325
Fulton	344	344	344	344	344	344	344	344	344	344	344	344
Gibson	796	796	796	796	796	796	796	796	796	796	796	796
Grant	353	353	353	353	353	353	353	353	353	353	353	353
Greene	762	762	762	762	762	762	762	762	762	762	762	762
Hamilton	859	859	859	859	859	859	859	859	859	859	859	859
Hancock	719	719	719	719	719	719	719	719	719	719	719	719
Harrison	1252	1252	1252	1252	1252	1252	1252	1252	1252	1252	1252	1252
Hendricks	1262	1262	1262	1262	1262	1262	1262	1262	1262	1262	1262	1262
Henry	1458	1458	1458	1458	1458	1458	1458	1458	1458	1458	1458	1458
[Howard] Richardville	129	129	129	129	129	129	129	129	129	129	129	129

Huntington	277	277	277	277	277	277	277	277	277	277	277	277
Jackson	662	662	662	662	662	662	662	662	662	662	662	662
Jasper	128	128	128	128	128	128	128	128	128	128	128	128
Jay	331	331	331	331	331	331	331	331	331	331	331	331
Jefferson	1835	1831	1835	1832	1835	1835	1835	1835	1835	1835	1835	1835
Jennings	872	872	872	872	872	872	872	872	872	872	872	872
Johnson	659	659	659	659	659	659	659	659	659	659	659	659
Knox	1079	1079	1079	1079	1079	1079	1079	1079	1079	1078	1078	1078
Kosciusko	623	623	623	623	623	623	623	623	623	623	623	623
LaGrange	590	590	590	590	590	590	590	590	590	590	590	590
Lake	114	114	114	114	114	114	114	114	114	114	114	114
LaPorte	1009	1009	1009	1009	1009	1009	1009	1009	1009	1009	1009	1009
Lawrence	1019	1019	1019	1019	1019	1019	1019	1018	1019	1019	1019	1019
Madison	813	813	813	813	813	813	813	813	813	813	813	813
Marion	1715	1715	1715	1714	1715	1715	1714	1715	1715	1715	1715	1715
Marshall	199	199	199	199	199	199	199	199	199	199	199	199
Martin	277	277	276	276	276	276	276	276	276	276	276	276
Miami	569	569	569	569	569	569	569	569	569	569	569	569
Monroe	721	721	721	719	721	721	721	721	721	721	721	721
Montgomery	1449	1450	1450	1450	1450	1450	1450	1450	1450	1450	1450	1450
Morgan	1023	1023	1023	1023	1023	1023	1023	1023	1023	1023	1023	1023
Noble	390	390	390	390	390	390	390	390	390	390	390	390
Ohio	193	193	193	193	193	193	193	193	193	193	193	193
Orange	707	707	707	707	707	707	707	707	707	707	707	707

County	Henry S. Lane	Joseph G. Marshall	John A. Brackenridge	James Collins, Jr.	John A. Matson	Samuel W. Parker	Hugh O'Neal	George G. Dunn	Richard W. Thompson	Albert L. Holmes	Horace P. Biddle	Lewis G. Thompson
	Electors for Henry Clay and Theodore Frelinghuysen (W)											
Owen	754	754	754	754	754	754	754	754	754	754	754	754
Parke	1377	1377	1377	1377	1377	1377	1377	1377	1377	1377	1377	1377
Perry	564	564	564	564	564	564	564	564	564	564	564	564
Pike	459	459	459	459	459	459	459	459	459	459	459	459
Porter	311	311	311	311	311	311	311	311	311	311	311	311
Posey	673	673	673	673	673	673	673	673	673	673	673	673
Pulaski	123	123	123	123	123	123	123	123	123	123	123	123
Putnam	1540	1540	1540	1540	1540	1540	1540	1540	1540	1540	1540	1540
Randolph	818	818	818	818	818	818	818	818	818	818	818	818
Ripley	1060	1060	1060	1060	1060	1060	1060	1060	1060	1060	1060	1060
Rush	1580	1580	1580	1580	1580	1580	1580	1580	1580	1580	1580	1580
St. Joseph	863	863	863	863	863	863	863	863	863	863	863	863
Scott	481	481	481	481	481	481	481	481	481	481	481	481
Shelby	1107	1107	1107	1107	1107	1107	1107	1107	1107	1107	1107	1107
Spencer	586	586	586	586	586	586	586	586	586	586	586	586
Steuben	328	328	328	328	328	328	328	328	328	328	328	328
Sullivan	464	464	464	464	464	464	464	464	464	464	464	464

Switzerland	961	960	961	961	961	961	961	961	961	961	961	961
Tippecanoe	1548	1550	1550	1550	1550	1550	1550	1550	1550	1548	1545	1545
Tipton	100	100	100	100	100	100	100	100	100	100	100	100
Union	682	682	682	681	682	682	682	682	682	682	682	682
Vanderburgh	675	675	675	675	675	675	675	675	675	675	675	675
Vermillion	787	787	787	787	787	787	787	787	787	787	787	787
Vigo	1515	1515	1515	1515	1515	1515	1515	1515	1515	1515	1515	1515
Wabash	601	601	601	601	601	601	601	601	601	601	600	601
Warren	778	779	779	779	779	779	779	779	779	779	779	779
Warrick	394	394	394	391	394	394	394	394	394	394	394	394
Washington	1149	1148	1149	1149	1149	1149	1149	1149	1149	1149	1149	1149
Wayne	2322	2321	2321	2322	2321	2322	2321	2321	2321	2321	2321	2322
Wells	185	185	185	185	185	185	185	185	185	185	185	185
White	258	258	259	259	257	259	259	259	259	259	259	259
Whitley	222	222	222	222	222	222	222	221	221	222	222	222
	67,864	67,861	87,866	67,854	61,865	67,865	67,863	67,863	67,864	67,863	67,860	67,749

County	Elizur Deming	Stephen S. Harding	Matthew R. Hull	Stephen C. Stevens	Roger Ide	Ziba Casterline	Eli J. Sumner	William Benbow	John K. Lovejoy	John J. Deming	Benjamin S. Noble	Daniel Worth	E. Davis
Adams	......	......	......	......	......	......	......	......	......	......	......	......	......
Allen	......	......	......	......	......	......	......	......	......	......	......	......	......
Bartholomew[5]	13	13	13	13	13	13	13	......	13	......	13	13	......
Benton	1	1	1	1	1	1	1	1	1	1	1	1	......
Blackford[6]	......	......	3	3	3	3	3	3	3	......	3	3	......
Boone	8	8	8	8	8	8	8	8	8	......	8	8	......
Brown	......	......	......	......	......	......	......	......	......	......	......	......	......
Carroll	8	8	8	8	8	8	8	8	8	8	8	8	......
Cass[7]	18	18	18	18	18	18	18	18	18	1	18	18	......
Clark	......	......	......	......	......	......	......	......	......	......	......	......	......
Clay	......	......	......	......	......	......	......	......	......	......	......	......	......
Clinton	12	12	12	12	12	12	12	12	12	6	12	12	......
Crawford	......	......	......	......	......	......	......	......	......	......	......	......	......
Daviess	......	......	......	......	......	......	......	......	......	......	......	......	......
Dearborn	50	50	50	51	51	50	50	50	50	51	50	50	......
Decatur	68	68	68	68	68	68	68	68	68	68	68	68	......
DeKalb[8]	6	6	6	6	6	6	6	6	6	......	6	6	......
Delaware	3	3	3	3	3	3	3	3	3	......	3	3	1

Dubois	......	......	......	......	......	......	......	......	......	......	......	......	......
Elkhart	1	1	1	1	1	1	1	1	1	1	1	1	......
Fayette	17	17	17	17	17	17	17	17	17	17	17	17	......
Floyd	......	......	......	......	......	......	......	......	......	......	......	......	......
Fountain	......	......	......	......	......	......	......	......	......	......	......	......	......
Franklin	8	8	8	8	8	8	8	8	8	7	8	8	......
Fulton	6	6	6	6	6	6	6	6	6	6	6	6	......
Gibson[9]	8	8	8	8	8	8	8	8	8	......	8	8	......
Grant	197	197	196	197	197	197	197	196	197	......	197	197	5
Greene	......	......	......	......	......	......	......	......	......	......	......	......	......
Hamilton	139	139	139	139	139	139	139	139	139	139	139	139	......
Hancock	2	2	2	2	2	2	2	2	2	2	2	2	......
Harrison	......	......	......	......	......	......	......	....	......	......	......	......	......
Hendricks	26	26	26	26	26	26	26	26	26	26	26	26	......
Henry	188	188	188	188	188	188	188	188	188	......	188	188	150
[Howard] Richardville	14	14	14	14	14	14	14	14	14	......	14	14	6
Huntington	8	8	8	8	3	8	8	8	3	......	8	8	3
Jackson[10]	1	1	1	1	1	1	1	......	1	......	1	......	......
Jasper	8	8	8	8	8	8	8	8	8	8	8	8	......
Jay	42	42	42	42	42	42	42	42	42	......	42	42	38
Jefferson	50	50	50	50	50	50	50	50	50	......	50	50	38
Jennings	14	14	14	14	14	14	14	14	14	8	14	14	6
Johnson	15	15	15	15	15	15	15	15	15	......	15	15	......
Knox	1	1	1	1	1	1	1	1	1	......	1	1	......

County	Electors for James G. Birney and Thomas Morris (Liberty)												
	Elizur Deming	Stephen S. Harding	Matthew R. Hull	Stephen C. Stevens	Roger Ide	Ziba Casterline	Eli J. Sumner	William Benbow	John K. Lovejoy	John J. Deming	Benjamin S. Noble	Daniel Worth	E. Davis
Kosciusko	5	5	5	5	5	5	5	5	5	5	5	5	......
LaGrange	30	30	38	38	38	38	38	38	38	38	38	38	......
Lake	5	6	5	4	5	5	5	5	5	5	5	5	......
LaPorte	53	53	53	53	53	53	53	53	53	53	53	53	......
Lawrence	3	3	3	3	3	3	3	3	3	3	3	3	......
Madison	20	20	21	20	20	20	20	20	20	......	20	20	10
Marion	25	25	25	25	25	25	25	25	25	4	25	25	......
Marshall	54	54	54	54	54	54	54	54	54	54	54	54	......
Martin	......	......	......	......	......	......	......	......	......	......	......	......	......
Miami	......	......	......	......	......	......	......	......	......	......	......	......	......
Monroe	12	12	12	12	12	12	12	12	12	1	12	12	......
Montgomery	8	8	8	8	8	8	8	8	8	8	8	8	......
Morgan	24	24	24	24	24	24	24	24	24	......	24	24	13
Noble	......	......	......	......	......	......	......	......	......	......	......	......	......
Ohio	......	......	......	......	......	......	......	......	......	......	......	......	......
Orange	3	3	3	3	3	3	3	3	3	2	3	3	......
Owen	1	1	1	1	1	1	1	1	1	1	1	1	......
Parke	12	12	12	12	12	12	12	12	12	12	12	12	......

Perry	......	......	......	......	......	......	......	......	......	......	......	......	......
Pike	......	......	......	......	......	......	......	......	......	......	......	......	......
Porter	14	14	14	14	14	14	14	14	14	11	14	14	......
Posey	......	......	......	......	......	......	......	......	......	......	......	......	......
Pulaski	1	1	1	1	1	1	1	1	1	1	1	1	......
Putnam	9	9	9	9	9	9	9	9	9	5	9	9	......
Randolph	206	206	206	206	206	206	206	204	205	......	206	206	190
Ripley	89	89	89	89	89	89	89	89	89	81	89	89	......
Rush	42	42	42	42	42	42	42	42	42	1	42	42	......
St. Joseph	33	33	33	33	33	33	33	33	33	33	33	33	......
Scott[11]	1	1	1	1	1	1	1	1	1	......	1	1	......
Shelby	7	7	7	7	7	7	7	7	7	......	7	7	......
Spencer	......	......	......	......	......	......	......	......	......	......	......	......	......
Starke	......	......	......	......	......	......	......	......	......	......	......	......	......
Steuben	42	42	42	42	42	42	42	42	42	42	42	42	......
Sullivan	1	1	1	1	1	1	1	1	1	......	1	1	......
Switzerland	8	8	8	8	8	8	8	7	6	8	8	2	......
Tippecanoe	38	37	37	37	37	37	37	37	37	31	37	37	......
Tipton	......	......	......	......	......	......	......	......	......	......	......	......	......
Union	60	60	60	60	60	60	60	60	60	......	60	60	......
Vanderburgh	1	1	1	1	1	1	1	1	1	......	1	1	......
Vermillion	......	......	......	......	......	......	......	......	......	......	......	......	......
Vigo	......	......	......	......	......	......	......	......	......	......	......	......	......
Wabash	19	19	19	19	19	19	19	19	19	......	19	19	......
Warren	10	10	10	10	10	10	10	10	10	10	10	10	......

County	Electors for James G. Birney and Thomas Morris (Liberty)												
	Elizur Deming	Stephen S. Harding	Matthew R. Hull	Stephen C. Stevens	Roger Ide	Ziba Casterline	Eli J. Sumner	William Benbow	John K. Lovejoy	John J. Deming	Benjamin S. Noble	Daniel Worth	E. Davis
Warrick	......	......	......	......	......	......	......	......	......	......	......	......	......
Washington	5	5	5	5	5	5	5	5	5	5	5	5	......
Wayne	318	318	319	318	318	319	318	319	318	318	318	319	......
Wells	3	3	3	3	3	3	3	3	3	......	3	3	3
White	......	......	......	......	......	......	......	......	......	......	......	......	......
Whitley	2	2	2	2	2	2	2	2	2	2	2	2	......
	2096	2096	2107	2106	2102	2107	2106	2089	1780	1078	2106	2100	731

1 Compiled from the official returns in the Archives Division.

2 In Clinton County Lucian P. Ferry received one vote.

3 In Crawford County Tilghman A. Howard received two votes and Lucian P. Ferry, two.

4 In Jackson County Ferry received two votes.

5 In Bartholomew County John Boggs received one vote.

6 In Blackford County Thomas Beckford received one vote.

7 In Cass County Lewis Falley received one vote.

8 In DeKalb County Thomas Gail received six votes.

9 In Gibson County William Paul received eight votes.

10 In Jackson County William Berford received one vote.

11 In Scott County William Hughes received one vote.

Election November 7, 1848[1]

County	Electors for Lewis Cass and William O. Butler (D)											
	Robert D. Owen	E. M. Chamberlain	Nathaniel Albertson	Cyrus L. Dunham	William McCarty	Charles H. Test	James Ritchey	George W. Carr	James M. Hanna	Daniel Mace	Graham N. Fitch	Andrew J. Harlan
Adams	398	398	398	398	398	398	398	398	398	398	398	398
Allen	1059	1059	1059	1059	1059	1059	1059	1059	1059	1059	1059	1058
Bartholomew	1167	1167	1167	1167	1167	1167	1167	1167	1167	1167	1167	1167
Benton	78	78	78	78	78	78	78	78	78	78	78	78
Blackford	231	231	231	231	231	231	231	231	231	231	231	231
Boone	916	916	916	916	916	916	916	916	916	916	916	916
Brown	503	503	503	503	503	503	503	503	503	503	503	503
Carroll	1008	1008	1008	1008	1008	1008	1008	1008	1008	1008	1008	1008
Cass	829	829	829	829	829	829	829	829	829	829	829	829
Clark	1510	1510	1510	1510	1510	1509	1509	1510	1510	1510	1510	1509
Clay	734	734	734	734	734	734	734	734	734	734	734	734
Clinton	964	964	964	964	964	964	964	964	964	964	964	964
Crawford	397	397	397	397	397	397	397	397	397	397	397	397
Daviess	701	701	708	708	708	708	702	702	708	708	708	708
Dearborn	1801	1799	1801	1801	1801	1801	1801	1801	1801	1801	1801	1800

Electors for Lewis Cass and William O. Butler (D)

County	Robert D. Owen	E. M. Chamberlain	Nathaniel Albertson	Cyrus L. Dunham	William McCarty	Charles H. Test	James Ritchey	George W. Carr	James M. Hanna	Daniel Mace	Graham N. Fitch	Andrew J. Harlan
Decatur	1096	1096	1096	1096	1096	1096	1096	1096	1096	1096	1096	1096
DeKalb	577	577	577	577	577	577	577	577	577	577	577	577
Delaware	694	694	694	694	694	694	694	694	694	694	694	694
Dubois	579	579	579	579	579	579	579	579	579	579	579	579
Elkhart	1050	1049	1050	1050	1050	1050	1050	1050	1050	1050	1050	1050
Fayette	765	765	765	765	765	764	765	765	765	765	764	764
Floyd	1154	1154	1154	1154	1154	1154	1154	1154	1154	1154	1154	1154
Fountain	1304	1304	1304	1304	1304	1304	1304	1304	1304	1304	1304	1304
Franklin	1694	1694	1694	1694	1692	1694	1694	1694	1695	1694	1694	1694
Fulton	404	404	404	404	404	404	404	404	402	404	404	404
Gibson	802	802	802	802	802	802	802	802	802	802	802	802
Grant	623	623	623	623	623	623	623	623	621	623	623	623
Greene	921	921	921	921	921	921	921	921	921	921	921	921
Hamilton	805	806	805	805	805	805	805	805	805	805	805	805
Hancock	806	806	806	806	806	806	806	806	806	806	806	806
Harrison	1046	1047	1047	1047	1047	1047	1047	1047	1047	1047	1047	1047
Hendricks	775	775	775	775	775	775	775	775	775	775	775	775

Henry	1005	1005	1005	1005	1005	1005	1005	1005	1005	1005	1005	1005
Howard	355	355	355	355	355	355	355	355	355	355	355	355
Huntington	463	463	463	463	463	463	463	463	463	463	463	463
Jackson	1071	1071	1071	1071	1071	1071	1071	1071	1071	1071	1071	1071
Jasper	190	190	190	190	190	190	190	190	190	190	190	190
Jay	392	392	392	392	392	392	392	392	392	392	392	392
Jefferson	1609	1609	1609	1609	1609	1609	1609	1609	1609	1609	1609	1609
Jennings	784	784	784	784	784	784	784	784	784	784	784	784
Johnson	1114	1114	1114	1114	1114	1114	1114	1114	1114	1114	1114	1114
Knox	741	741	741	741	741	741	741	741	741	741	741	741
Kosciusko	676	676	676	676	676	676	676	676	676	676	676	676
LaGrange	636	636	636	636	636	636	636	636	636	636	636	636
Lake	208	208	208	208	208	208	208	208	208	208	208	208
LaPorte	876	877	877	877	877	877	877	877	877	877	877	877
Lawrence	1030	1031	1031	1031	1031	1031	1031	1030	1031	1031	1031	1031
Madison	993	993	993	993	993	993	993	993	993	993	993	993
Marion	1789	1789	1789	1789	1789	1789	1789	1789	1789	1789	1789	1789
Marshall	428	428	428	428	428	428	428	428	428	428	428	428
Martin	497	497	497	497	497	497	497	497	497	497	497	497
Miami	770	770	770	770	770	770	770	770	0[2]	770	770	770
Monroe	1084	1084	1084	1084	1084	1084	1084	1084	1084	1084	1084	1084
Montgomery	1547	1547	1547	1547	1547	1547	1547	1547	1547	1547	1547	1547
Morgan	1029	1029	1029	1029	1029	1029	1029	1029	1029	1029	1029	1029
Noble	613	613	613	613	613	613	613	613	613	613	613	613

County	Robert D. Owen	E. M. Chamberlain	Nathaniel Albertson	Cyrus L. Dunham	William McCarty	Charles H. Test	James Ritchey	George W. Carr	James M. Hanna	Daniel Mace	Graham N. Fitch	Andrew J. Harlan
	Electors for Lewis Cass and William O. Butler (D)											
Ohio	459	459	459	459	459	459	459	459	459	459	459	459
Orange	959	961	961	961	961	961	961	961	961	961	961	961
Owen	953	953	953	953	953	953	953	953	953	953	953	953
Parke	1318	1318	1318	1318	1318	1318	1318	1318	1318	1319	1319	1319
Perry	335	335	335	335	335	335	335	335	335	335	335	335
Pike	510	510	510	510	510	510	510	510	510	510	510	510
Porter	401	401	401	401	401	401	401	401	401	401	401	400
Pcsey	1226	1226	1226	1226	1226	1226	1226	1226	1226	1226	1226	1226
Pulaski	224	224	224	224	224	224	224	224	224	224	224	224
Putnam	1300	1300	1300	1300	1300	1300	1300	1300	1300	1300	1300	1300
Randolph	787	788	789	789	789	789	789	789	789	789	789	789
Ripley	988	988	988	988	988	988	988	988	987	988	988	988
Rush	1392	1392	1392	1392	1392	1392	1392	1392	1392	1392	1392	1391
St. Joseph	667	667	667	667	667	667	667	667	667	667	667	667
Scott	477	477	477	477	477	477	477	477	477	477	477	477
Shelby	1414	1414	1414	1414	1414	1414	1414	1414	1414	1414	1414	1414
Spencer	469	471	471	471	471	471	471	471	471	471	471	471

Steuben	352	352	352	352	352	352	352	352	352	351	352	352
Sullivan	1141	1141	1142	1142	1142	1142	1142	1142	1142	1142	1142	1142
Switzerland	1106	1106	1106	1106	1106	1106	1106	1106	1106	1106	1106	1106
Tippecanoe	1523	1523	1523	1523	1523	1523	1523	1523	1523	1522	1523	1523
Tipton	235	235	235	235	235	235	235	235	235	235	235	235
Union	637	637	637	637	637	635	637	637	637	637	637	637
Vanderburgh	667	667	667	667	667	667	667	667	667	667	667	667
Vermillion	763	763	763	763	763	763	763	763	763	763	763	763
Vigo	852	851	851	851	851	852	852	852	852	852	851	850
Wabash	739	739	739	739	739	739	739	739	739	739	739	739
Warren	460	460	460	460	460	460	460	460	460	460	460	460
Warrick	861	862	862	862	862	862	862	862	862	862	862	862
Washington	1643	1643	1643	1643	1642	1642	1642	1642	1642	1642	1642	1642
Wayne	1432	1432	1432	1432	1432	1429	1432	1432	1432	1432	1432	1432
Wells	416	416	416	416	416	416	416	416	416	416	416	417
White	305	305	305	305	305	305	305	305	305	305	305	305
Whitley	373	373	373	373	373	373	373	373	373	373	373	373
Total	74,675	74,680	74,692	74,692	74,691	74,685	74,691	74,685	73,912	74,691	74,691	74,686

County	Joseph G. Marshall	Godlove S. Orth	James E. Blythe[3]	John S. Davis	Milton Gregg	David P. Holloway	Lovel H. Rousseau	Edward W. McGaughey	James F. Suit	Daniel D. Pratt	David Kilgore	Thomas D. Walpole
Adams	261	261	261	261	261	261	261	261	261	261	261	261
Allen	991	991	991	991	991	991	991	991	991	991	991	991
Bartholomew	1011	1011	1011	1011	1011	1011	1011	1011	1011	1011	1011	1011
Benton	60	60	60	60	60	60	60	60	60	60	60	60
Blackford	61	61	61	61	61	61	61	61	61	61	61	61
Boone	773	773	773	773	773	773	773	773	773	773	773	773
Brown	70	70	70	70	70	70	70	70	70	70	70	70
Carroll	822	821	822	822	822	822	822	822	822	822	821	822
Cass	881	881	881	881	881	881	881	881	881	881	881	881
Clark	1200	1200	1200	1200	1200	1200	1200	1200	1200	1200	1200	1200
Clay	500	500	500	500	500	500	500	499	500	500	500	500
Clinton	726	726	726	726	726	726	726	726	725	726	726	726
Crawford	520	520	520	520	520	520	520	520	520	520	520	520
Daviess	735	735	735	735	735	735	735	735	735	735	735	735
Dearborn	1378	1378	1378	1378	1378	1378	1378	1378	1378	1377	1377	1378
Decatur	1245	1245	1245	1245	1245	1245	1245	1245	1245	1245	1245	1245
DeKalb	347	347	347	347	347	347	347	347	347	347	347	347

Delaware	822	821	821	821	821	821	821	821	821	821	822	822
Dubois	258	258	258	258	258	258	258	258	258	258	258	258
Elkhart	756	756	756	756	756	756	756	756	756	756	756	756
Fayette	1040	1040	1040	1040	1040	1040	1040	1040	1040	1040	1039	1040
Floyd	1018	1018	1018	1017	1018	1018	1018	1018	1018	1018	1017	1018
Fountain	840	840	840	840	840	840	840	840	840	840	840	840
Franklin	1411	1411	1411	1411	1411	1411	1411	1411	1411	1410	1411	1411
Fulton	423	423	423	423	423	423	423	423	423	423	423	423
Gibson	860	860	860	860	860	860	860	860	860	860	860	860
Grant	325	325	325	325	325	325	325	325	325	325	325	325
Greene	918	916	918	918	918	918	918	918	918	918	918	918
Hamilton	809	809	809	809	809	809	809	809	809	809	808	809
Hancock	665	665	665	665	665	665	665	665	665	665	665	665
Harrison	1277	1277	1277	1277	1277	1277	1277	1277	1277	1277	1277	1277
Hendricks	1158	1158	1158	1158	1158	1158	1158	1158	1158	1158	1158	1158
Henry	1215	1215	1215	1215	1215	1215	1215	1215	1215	1214	1214	1215
Howard	275	275	275	275	275	275	275	275	275	275	274	275
Huntington	457	457	457	457	457	457	457	457	457	457	457	457
Jackson	632	632	632	632	632	632	632	632	632	632	632	632
Jasper	86	86	68	86	86	86	86	86	86	86	86	86
Jay	276	276	276	276	276	276	276	276	276	276	276	276
Jefferson	2075	2075	2075	2075	2075	2075	2075	2075	2075	2075	2075	2075
Jennings	926	926	926	926	926	926	926	926	926	926	926	926
Johnson	676	676	676	676	676	676	676	676	676	676	676	676

County	Joseph G. Marshall	Godlove S. Orth	James E. Blythe[3]	John S. Davis	Milton Gregg	David P. Holloway	Lovel H. Rousseau	Edward W. McGaughey	James F. Suit	Daniel D. Pratt	David Kilgore	Thomas D. Walpole
	Electors for Zachary Taylor and Millard Fillmore (W)											
Knox	1044	1044	1044	1044	1044	1044	1044	1044	1044	1044	1044	1044
Kosciusko	797	797	797	797	797	797	797	797	797	797	797	797
LaGrange	629	629	629	629	629	629	629	629	629	629	629	629
Lake	138	138	117	138	138	138	138	138	138	138	138	138
LaPorte	1027	1027	1027	1027	1027	1027	1027	1027	1027	1027	1026	1027
Lawrence	1070	1070	1070	1070	1070	1070	1070	1070	1070	1070	1070	1070
Madison	824	824	824	824	824	824	824	824	824	824	824	824
Marion	1877	1877	1877	1877	1877	1877	1877	1877	1877	1877	1877	1877
Marshall	305	305	305	305	305	305	305	305	305	305	305	305
Martin	325	325	341	342	342	342	342	342	342	342	342	342
Miami	731	731	731	731	731	731	731	731	731	731	730	731
Monroe	780	780	780	780	780	780	780	780	780	780	780	780
Montgomery	1501	1501	1501	1501	1501	1501	1501	1501	1501	1501	1501	1509
Morgan	986	986	986	986	986	986	986	986	986	985	985	986
Noble	497	497	497	497	497	497	497	497	497	497	497	497
Ohio	439	439	413	439	439	439	439	439	439	439	439	439
Orange	760	760	760	760	760	760	760	760	760	760	758	760

Owen	882	882	882	882	882	882	882	882	882	882	882	882
Parke	1398	1398	1398	1398	1398	1398	1398	1398	1398	1398	1398	1398
Perry	599	599	599	599	599	599	599	599	599	599	599	599
Pike	519	519	519	519	519	519	519	519	519	519	519	519
Porter	343	343	343	343	343	343	343	343	343	343	343	343
Posey	763	763	763	763	763	763	763	763	763	763	763	763
Pulaski	135	135	127	135	135	135	135	135	135	135	135	135
Putnam	1647	1647	1647	1647	1647	1647	1647	1647	1647	1647	1647	1647
Randolph	631	631	631	631	631	631	631	631	631	631	631	631
Ripley	1114	1114	1114	1114	1114	1114	1114	1114	1114	1114	1114	1114
Rush	1442	1442	1442	1442	1442	1442	1442	1442	1442	1442	1442	1442
St. Joseph	817	817	817	817	817	817	817	817	817	817	817	817
Scott	486	486	486	486	486	486	486	486	486	486	486	487
Shelby	1122	1122	1122	1122	1122	1122	1122	1122	1122	1122	1121	1122
Spencer	681	681	681	681	681	681	681	681	681	681	681	681
Steuben	315	315	315	315	315	315	315	315	315	315	315	315
Sullivan	465	465	465	465	465	465	465	465	465	465	465	465
Swizerland	1093	1093	1093	1093	1093	1093	1092	1092	1092	1092	1091	1093
Tippecanoe	1269	1269	1269	1269	1269	1269	1269	1269	1269	1269	1269	1269
Tipton	183	183	183	183	183	183	183	183	183	183	183	183
Union	526	526	526	526	526	526	526	526	526	526	526	526
Vanderburgh	734	734	735	734	734	734	734	734	734	732	733	734
Vermillion	830	830	830	830	830	830	830	830	830	830	830	830
Vigo	1585	1583	1585	1585	1585	1585	1584	1585	1584	1584	1584	1585

Electors for Zachary Taylor and Millard Fillmore (W)

County	Joseph G. Marshall	Godlove S. Orth	James E. Blythe[3]	John S. Davis	Milton Gregg	David P. Holloway	Lovel H. Rousseau	Edward W. McGaughey	James F. Suit	Daniel D. Pratt	David Kilgore	Thomas D. Walpole
Wabash	847	847	847	847	847	847	847	847	847	847	847	847
Warren	708	708	708	708	708	708	708	708	708	708	708	708
Warrick	457	457	457	457	457	457	457	457	457	457	457	457
Washington	1126	1126	1126	1126	1126	1126	1126	1125	1125	1125	1125	1126
Wayne	2085	2085	2085	2085	2085	2085	2085	2085	2085	2085	2085	2085
Wells	252	252	252	252	252	252	252	252	252	252	252	252
White	268	268	268	268	268	268	268	268	268	268	268	268
Whitley	318	318	318	318	318	318	318	318	318	318	318	318
Total	70,149	70,145	70,135	70,164	70,165	70,165	70,163	70,163	70,162	70,157	70,151	70,175

County	Henry L. Ellsworth	John H. Bradley	Nathaniel Little	John R. Cravens	James H. Cravens	George W. Julian	Ovid Butler	Milton Short	Albert G. Coffin	Samuel A. Huff	Joseph L. Jernegan	Daniel Worth[4]
	Electors for Martin Van Buren and Charles Francis Adams (Free Soil)											
Adams	1	1	1	1	1	1	1	1	1	1	1	1
Allen	13	13	13	13	13	13	13	13	13	13	13	13
Bartholomew	28	28	28	28	28	28	28	28	28	28	28	3
Benton	3	3	3	3	2	3	3	3	3	3	3	2
Blackford	28	28	27	28	27	27	28	28	27	27	28	28
Boone	66	66	66	66	66	66	66	66	66	66	66	66
Brown	......	......	......	......	......	......	......	......	......	......	......	......
Carroll	76	76	76	76	76	76	76	76	76	76	76	76
Cass	55	55	55	55	55	55	55	55	55	55	55	55
Clark	28	28	28	28	28	28	28	28	28	28	28	......
Clay	5	5	5	5	5	5	5	5	5	5	5	5
Clinton	87	87	87	87	86	87	87	87	87	87	87	84
Crawford	......	......	......	......	......	......	......	......	......	......	......	......
Daviess	2	2	2	2	2	2	2	2	2	2	2	0
Dearborn	176	176	176	176	176	176	176	176	176	176	176	......
Decatur	143	143	143	143	142	143	143	143	143	143	143	143
DeKalb	45	45	45	45	45	45	45	45	45	45	45	30
Delaware[5]	58	58	58	58	58	58	58	58	58	52	58	58
Dubois	1	1	1	1	1	1	1	1	1	1	1	......

County	Electors for Martin Van Buren and Charles Francis Adams (Free Soil)											
	Henry L. Ellsworth	John H. Bradley	Nathaniel Little	John R. Cravens	James H. Cravens	George W. Julian	Ovid Butler	Milton Short	Albert G. Coffin	Samuel A. Huff	Joseph L. Jernegan	Daniel Worth[4]
Elkhart[6]	141	141	142	142	142	142	142	142	142	142	142	142
Fayette	86	86	86	86	86	86	86	86	86	86	86	73
Floyd	17	17	17	17	17	17	17	17	17	17	17	9
Fountain	138	138	138	138	138	138	138	138	138	138	138	137
Franklin	51	51	51	51	51	51	51	51	51	51	51	37
Fulton	39	39	39	39	39	39	39	39	39	39	39	39
Gibson	15	15	15	15	15	15	15	15	15	15	15	15
Grant	359	359	359	359	359	359	359	359	359	359	359	359
Greene	6	6	6	6	6	6	6	6	6	6	6	6
Hamilton	314	315	316	317	317	317	317	317	317	317	317	316
Hancock	40	40	40	40	40	40	40	40	40	40	40	40
Harrison	1	1	1	1	1	1	1	1	1	1	1	0
Hendricks	173	173	173	173	173	173	173	173	173	173	173	173
Henry	455	455	455	455	455	455	455	455	455	455	455	455
Howard	152	152	152	152	152	152	152	152	152	152	152	152
Huntington	46	46	46	46	46	46	46	46	46	46	46	46
Jackson	7	7	7	7	7	7	7	7	7	7	7	1
Jasper	128	128	128	128	128	128	128	128	128	128	128	128
Jay	142	142	142	142	142	142	142	142	142	142	142	142

Jefferson	167	167	167	167	167	167	167	167	167	167	167	167
Jennings	96	96	96	96	96	96	96	96	96	96	96	0
Johnson	46	46	46	46	46	46	46	46	46	46	46	46
Knox	0	0	0	0	0	0	0	0	0	0	0	0
Kosciusko	64	64	64	64	64	64	64	64	64	64	64	39
LaGrange	114	114	114	114	114	114	114	114	114	114	114	......
Lake	139	139	139	139	139	139	139	139	139	139	139	127
LaPorte	226	226	226	226	226	226	226	226	226	226	227	226
Lawrence	18	18	18	18	18	18	16	18	18	18	18	16
Madison	55	55	55	55	55	55	55	55	55	55	55	55
Marion	109	107	109	109	110	109	110	109	109	110	109	106
Marshall	91	91	91	91	91	91	91	91	91	91	91	91
Martin[7]	7	7	7	3	7	7	7	7	7	7	7	1
Miami	70	70	68	70	69	70	70	70	70	70	70	70
Monroe	59	59	59	59	59	59	59	59	59	59	59	59
Montgomery	109	109	109	109	109	109	109	109	109	109	109	109
Morgan	121	121	121	121	121	121	121	121	121	121	121	121
Noble	53	53	53	53	53	53	53	53	53	53	53	7
Ohio	6	6	6	6	6	6	6	6	6	6	6	3
Orange	6	6	6	6	6	6	6	6	6	6	3[8]	......
Owen	13	13	13	13	13	13	13	13	13	13	13	3
Parke	56	56	53	57	57	57	57	57	57	56	56	28
Perry	8	8	8	8	8	8	8	8	8	8	8	8
Pike	1	1	1	1	1	1	1	1	1	1	1	......
Porter	73	73	77	77	75	77	77	77	77	77	77	43
Posey	19	19	19	19	19	19	19	19	19	19	19	......

County	Henry L. Ellsworth	John H. Bradley	Nathaniel Little	John R. Cravens	James H. Cravens	George W. Julian	Ovid Butler	Milton Short	Albert G. Coffin	Samuel A. Huff	Joseph L. Jernegan	Daniel Worth[4]
	Electors for Martin Van Buren and Charles Francis Adams (Free Soil)											
Pulaski	1	1	1	1	1	1	1	1	1	1	1	1
Putnam	29	29	29	29	29	29	29	29	29	29	29	29
Randolph	523	523	523	523	523	523	523	523	523	523	523	523
Ripley[9]	173	173	173	173	173	173	173	173	169	173	173	......
Rush	87	87	87	87	87	87	87	87	87	87	87	84
St. Joseph	332	332	332	332	332	332	332	332	332	332	332	332
Scott	16	16	16	13	16	16	16	16	16	16	16	......
Shelby	18	18	18	18	18	18	18	18	18	18	18	12
Spencer	......	......	......	......	......	......	......	......	......	......	......	......
Steuben	194	194	194	194	194	194	194	194	194	194	194	194
Sullivan	2	2	3	2	3	3	3	3	3	3	3	1
Switzerland	44	44	44	44	44	44	44	44	44	44	44	44
Tippecanoe	405	405	405	405	405	405	405	405	405	405	405	405
Tipton	3	3	3	3	3	3	3	3	3	3	3	3
Union	208	208	208	208	208	208	208	208	208	208	208	208
Vanderburgh	22	22	22	22	22	22	22	22	22	22	22	22
Vermillion[10]	9	9	9	9	9	9	9	9	9	9	9	9
Vigo	10	10	10	10	10	10	10	10	10	10	10	10
Wabash	140	140	140	140	140	140	140	140	140	140	140	140

Warren	68	67	68	68	68	68	68	68	68	67	68	68
Warrick	21	21	21	21	21	21	21	21	21	21	21	21
Washington	22	22	22	22	22	22	22	22	22	22	22	22
Wayne	839	839	839	839	839	839	839	839	838	839	839	835
Wells	18	18	18	18	18	18	18	18	18	18	18	18
White	34	34	34	34	34	34	34	34	34	34	34	34
Whitley	21	21	21	21	21	21	21	21	21	21	21	21
Total	8090	8088	8092	8095	8097	8099	8099	8100	8098	8098	8097	7195

1 Compiled from the official election returns in the Archives Division.

2 In place of Hanna, Miami County gave Henry Secrest 770 votes.

3 John Pitcher was a candidate for elector in opposition to Blythe and received the following votes: in Jasper County, 20; Lake, 21; Martin, one; Ohio, 26; Pulaski, eight.

4 Lewis Beecher and Joseph Morrow were opposing candidates of Worth and received a share of the votes that Worth might otherwise have obtained. Beecher's support came from the following counties: Bartholomew, 28 votes; Clark, 11; Clinton, 3; Dearborn, 43; Franklin, 3; Jennings, 96; Kosciusko, 19; Lake, 12; Martin, 3; Miami, 1; Ohio, 3; Parke, 11; Pike, 1; Posey, 19; Putnam, 3; Ripley, 173; Rush, 3; Scott, 13; Shelby, 1; Sullivan, 3; total, 449. Joseph Morrow received votes in the following counties: Clark, 17; Daviess, 2; Dearborn, 134; DeKalb, 15; Dubois, 1; Floyd, 8; Franklin, 11; Green, 4; Harrison, 1; Jackson, 7; Kosciusko, 6; LaGrange, 114; Martin, 3; Noble, 46; Orange, 6; Owen, 10; Parke, 16; Porter, 13; Putnam, 1; Scott, 3; Shelby, 1; total, 419.

5 Delaware County gave six votes to Samuel A. Taffee.

6 In addition to the votes recorded here, Elkhart County gave fourteen votes to each of the following: Joseph H. Leeper, W. H. Marvin (?), D. W. Gray, H. H. Beardsley, William Proctor, N. F. Brodrick, E. Beach, A. Bassett, J. Frush, J. Primley, E. Beardsley, and M. A. Brodrick.

7 In Martin County, there were two ballots for James R. Cravens, two for John H. Cravens, and one for John Cravens.

8 On three other Orange County ballots intended for Jernegan, the name was spelled Hernegan.

9 In addition to the votes recorded here, Ripley gave three votes to each of the following: Stephen S. Harding, Richard Workman, James L. Yater, Squire H. Knapp, Jesse L. Holman, George Walker, Thomas Smith, John M. Patrick, Roger Ide, Isaiah W. Robinson, Samuel Ball, and Jonas Walker. Benjamin Dwight Sheldon, received one vote; Henry Secrest, one, and A. C. Cooper, four.

10 In addition to the votes recorded here, Vermillion gave one vote to each of the following: William B. Ogdon, John Bufferm, Henry B. Evans, Levi F. Torrey, Thomas Hogue, Samuel H. Davis, A. Hose, Jonathan Blanchard, and George B. Arnold.

CONGRESS

REPRESENTATIVE IN THE FOURTEENTH CONGRESS

Election August 5, 1816[1]

County	*William Hendricks	Allan D. Thom	George R. C. Sullivan
Clark			
Dearborn			
Franklin			
Gibson			
Harrison			
Jackson	[93]	[41]	
Jefferson			
Knox	[170]	[543]	
Orange	[191]	[96]	
Perry			
Posey			
Switzerland			
Warrick			
Washington	[499]	[85]	
Wayne			

1 The official election returns have not been found. The vote in Jackson, Knox, Orange, and Washington counties is from the Vincennes *Western Sun,* August 17 and 24, 1816.

REPRESENTATIVE IN THE FIFTEENTH CONGRESS

Election August 4, 1817[1]

County	*William Hendricks	Thomas Posey
Clark	467	368
Daviess	[135]	[165]
Dearborn	365	208
Franklin	1019	48
Gibson	116	181
Harrison	457	430
Jackson	192	30
Jefferson	453	280

	*William Hendricks	Thomas Posey
Jennings and Ripley	[80]	[18]
Knox	35	346
Orange[2]	458	203
Perry	56	152
Pike	71	71
Posey	121	453
Sullivan[3]	102	127
Switzerland	222	126
Warrick	0	195
Washington	[383]	[242]
Wayne	961	135
Total	5693	3778

1 Compiled from the official election returns with the exception of the votes in Daviess, Jennings and Ripley, and Washington counties which are from the Vincennes *Western Sun,* August 16, 23, and 30, 1817.

2 The return for Leatherwood Township, Orange County, was received too late to be included. The vote was: Hendricks, 24; Posey, 7.

3 The return for Dixon Township, Sullivan County, was received too late to be included. The vote was: Posey, 28; Hendricks, 26.

REPRESENTATIVE IN THE SIXTEENTH CONGRESS

Election August 3, 1818[1]

County	Candidates	
	*William Hendricks	Reuben W. Nelson
Clark	1122	40
Dearborn	903	27
Dubois	68	0
Franklin	1389	5
Gibson	163	18
Harrison	664	398
Jackson	285	13
Jefferson	741	26
Jennings	121	1
Knox[2]	179	343
Lawrence	151	1
Monroe	132	20
Orange	492	1
Perry	180	26
Pike	79	46

Posey	284	26
Ripley	72	0
Switzerland	394	6
Vanderburgh	75	6
Vigo	169	2
Warrick	6	92
Washington	878	20
Wayne	1408	1
Total	9955	1118

1 Compiled from the official election returns in the Archives Division. No returns were found for Daviess and Sullivan counties.

2 Knox County also gave one vote to Waller Taylor and one to R. W. Noble.

REPRESENTATIVE IN THE SEVENTEENTH CONGRESS

Election, August 7, 1820[1]

County	Candidates	
	*William Hendricks	Reuben W. Nelson
Clark	907	267
Crawford	211	26
Daviess	375	8
Dearborn	1177	19
Dubois	74	1
Fayette	757	5
Floyd	248	72
Franklin	1364	16
Gibson	461	3
Harrison	820	339
Jackson	382	74
Jefferson	985	55
Jennings	222	6
Knox	[302]	[477]
Lawrence	524	5
Martin	137	1
Monroe	[320]	[0]
Orange	719	7
Owen	88	0
Perry	251	5
Pike	188	0

	*William Hendricks	Reuben W. Nelson
Posey	559	2
Randolph	165	0
Ripley	224	0
Scott	[228]	[8]
Spencer	185	0
Sullivan	417	95
Switzerland	604	3[2]
Vanderburgh	174	5
Vigo	495	30
Warrick	115	0
Washington	[868]	[94]
Wayne	1785	0
Total	16,331	1623

1 Compiled from the official election returns in the Archives Division with the exception of the votes from Knox, Monroe, Scott, and Washington counties which are from the Corydon *Indiana Gazette,* August 31 and September 17, 1820.

2 The name was given as Newton W. Nelson by two of these voters in Switzerland County.

REPRESENTATIVE IN THE SEVENTEENTH CONGRESS

Special Election August 5, 1822[1]

County	Candidates[2]	
	*Jonathan Jennings	Davis Floyd
Bartholomew		
Clark	800	267
Crawford	185	82
Daviess	268	171
Dearborn	1006	570
Decatur	104	38
Dubois	121	31
Fayette	558	149
Floyd		
Franklin	789	350
Gibson	57	344
Greene	75	70
Harrison	724	382
Henry	34	65

Jackson	460	111
Jefferson	392	739
Jennings	351	23
Knox	158	454
Lawrence	384	42
Marion	282	15
Martin	177	13
Monroe	296	117
Morgan	125	16
Orange	422	95
Owen	61	68
Parke	225	0
Perry	160	46
Pike[3]	148	29
Posey	307	133
Putnam	81	19
Randolph[4]	107	0
Ripley	335	35
Rush		
Scott	204	167
Shelby	192	28
Spencer	180	49
Sullivan	[288]	[74]
Switzerland	566	108
Union	286	161
Vanderburgh	117	120
Vigo	412	6
Warrick	[226]	[26]
Washington	824	288
Wayne	[724]	[425]
Total	13,211	5926

1 Compiled from the official election returns in the Archives Division with the exception of the votes in Sullivan, Warrick, and Wayne counties which are from the Vincennes *Western Sun,* August 17 and 31, 1822. No returns were found for Bartholomew, Floyd, and Rush counties. This election was held to fill the vacancy caused by the resignation of William Hendricks whose term as representative would not expire until March 3, 1823.

2 In addition to the two candidates listed, James Scott received five votes in Clark County, eight in Marion, and three in Morgan.

3 The return from Adams Township, Pike County, was received too late to be included. The vote was: Jennings, 8; Floyd, 14.

4 Randolph County gave one vote to Henry P. Thornton.

REPRESENTATIVES IN THE EIGHTEENTH CONGRESS

Election August 5, 1822[1]

First District	Candidates	
County	*William Prince	Charles Dewey
Daviess	264	181
Dubois	99	62
Gibson	447	18
Greene	124	133
Knox	484	149
Lawrence	321	134
Martin	60	131
Monroe	239	216
Morgan	3	120
Orange	80	572
Owen	92	34
Parke	9	225
Perry	117	90
Pike[2]	154	40
Posey	587	145
Putnam	5	91
Spencer	223	59
Sullivan	[341]	[82]
Vanderburgh	[192]	[102]
Vigo	50	463
Warrick	[246]	[20]
Total	4137	3067

Second District	Candidates	
County	*Jonathan Jennings	James Scott
Bartholomew		
Clark[3]	763	328
Crawford	203	58
Floyd		
Harrison	779	239
Jackson	320	295
Jefferson	352	785
Jennings	296	70

Marion	175	133
Scott	246	137
Shelby	171	48
Washington	666	505
Total	3971	2598

Third District	Candidates		
County	*John Test	Samuel C. Vance	Ezra Ferris
Dearborn	272	789	572
Decatur	85	43	47
Fayette	600	63	59
Franklin	744	342	125
Henry	70	12	20
Randolph	77	23	33
Ripley	97	256	60
Rush			
Switzerland	331	285	64
Union	365	151	48
Wayne	[537]	[274]	[397]
Total	3178	2238	1425

[1] Compiled from the official election returns in the Archives Division with the exception of the votes of Sullivan, Vanderburgh, and Warrick counties which are from the Vincennes *Western Sun,* August 10 and 17, 1822, and Wayne County which is from the Richmond *Weekly Intelligencer,* August 7, 1822. No returns were found for Bartholomew, Floyd, and Rush counties. The state had been divided into three Congressional districts by act of January 3, 1822. *Laws of Indiana,* 1821-22, pp. 43-45.

[2] The return from Adams Township, Pike County, was not received in time to be included. The vote was: Prince, 19; Dewey, 5.

[3] Clark County also gave eleven votes to David H. Maxwell.

REPRESENTATIVES IN THE NINETEENTH CONGRESS

Election August 2, 1824[1]

First District	Candidates		
County	*Ratliff Boon	Jacob Call	Thomas H. Blake
Daviess	233	272	117
Dubois	178	51	8

County	*Ratliff Boon	Jacob Call	Thomas H. Blake
Gibson	327	202	14
Greene[2]	62	69	247
Hendricks	15	0	95
Knox	37	615	95
Lawrence	168	392	223
Martin	26	164	68
Monroe	256	81	288
Montgomery	0	79	19
Morgan	88	20	95
Orange	355	285	208
Owen	55	32	234
Parke	43	138	103
Perry	343	33	0
Pike	209	68	1
Posey	643	105	17
Putnam	20	38	208
Spencer	388	3	1
Sullivan	160	109	262
Vanderburgh	294	52	2
Vermillion	85	103	49
Vigo	21	300	306
Warrick	275	11	1
Total	4281	3222	2661

Second District	Candidates	
County	*Jonathan Jennings	Jeremiah Sullivan
Bartholomew	204	132
Clark	795	498
Crawford	335	63
Floyd	357	178
Hamilton	32	74
Harrison	1162	168
Jackson	206	275
Jefferson	221	1021
Jennings	166	233
Johnson	51	68
Madison	[21]	[29]
Marion	172	256

Scott	104	321
Shelby	59	68
Washington	795	735
Total	4680	4119

Third District	Candidates		
County	*John Test	James Brown Ray	Daniel J. Caswell
Allen	72	2	6
Dearborn	670	118	614
Decatur	46	307	17
Fayette	403	329	54
Franklin	614	579	73
Henry	112	129	1
Randolph			
Ripley			
Rush	241	89	56
Switzerland	238	197	186
Union	413	163	62
Wayne	625	558	319
Total	3434	2471	1388

1 Compiled from the official election returns in the Archives Division with the exception of the votes of Madison County which are from the Indianapolis *Gazette,* August 10, 1824. The sheriff of Madison County was prevented from making his return at the proper time because of high water. No returns were found for Randolph and Ripley counties.

2 Greene County also gave eight votes to William Call.

REPRESENTATIVE IN THE EIGHTEENTH CONGRESS

Special Election November 8, 1824[1]

First District	Candidates[2]	
County	*Jacob Call	Thomas H. Blake
Daviess	123	84
Dubois	45	11
Gibson	151	150
Greene	34	16
Hendricks		
Knox	306	167

County	*Jacob Call	Thomas H. Blake
Lawrence	210	120
Martin	48	57
Monroe	138	117
Montgomery	52	51
Morgan	44	76
Orange	248	137
Owen	23	94
Parke	62	100
Perry	6	17
Pike	73	60
Posey	192	213
Putnam	7	77
Spencer	20	25
Sullivan	117	177
Vanderburgh	44	59
Vermillion	31	52
Vigo	110	202
Warrick	71	25
Total	2155	2087

[1] Compiled from the official election returns in the Archives Division. This election was held to fill the vacancy caused by the death of William Prince on September 4, 1824. No return was found for Hendricks County. In the August election of this same year Hendricks County had given Blake 95 votes and Call none. The Indianapolis *Western Censor,* December 7, 1824, reported that Call was elected by a majority of about twenty votes, which would have meant that Blake's majority in Hendricks County was about forty-eight.

[2] In addition to the two candidates listed, Ratliff Boon received twenty-nine votes in Morgan County, three each in Lawrence and Montgomery, and one in Owen County, making a total of thirty-six votes.

REPRESENTATIVES IN THE TWENTIETH CONGRESS

Election August 7, 1826[1]

First District	Candidates		
County	*Thomas H. Blake	Ratliff Boon	Lawrence S. Shuler
Clay	100	4	1
Daviess	329	227	38
Dubois	2	228	6
Fountain	225	18	62
Gibson	61	260	135

Greene	413	78	9
Hendricks	154	19	0
Knox	201	153	454
Lawrence	347	485	133
Martin	99	129	25
Monroe	317	137	209
Montgomery	247	1	2
Morgan	154	160	14
Orange	288	655	21
Owen	297	3	29
Parke	312	116	84
Perry	1	398	4
Pike	32	245	29
Posey	38	655	123
Putnam	[496]	[19]	[2]
Spencer	2	326	3
Sullivan	344	208	16
Tippecanoe	124	3	8
Vanderburgh	27	256	29
Vermillion	112	102	119
Vigo	484	38	150
Warrick	17	279	18
Total	5223	5202	1723

Second District	Candidate
County	*Jonathan Jennings
Bartholomew	424
Clark	1272
Crawford	
Floyd	503
Hamilton	187
Harrison	1108
Jackson	224
Jefferson[2]	1410
Jennings	473
Johnson	230
Madison	75
Marion[3]	558
Scott	

County	*Jonathan Jennings
Shelby	404
Washington	1045
Total	7913

Third District	Candidates	
County	*Oliver H. Smith	John Test
Allen	10	101
Dearborn	1290	734
Decatur	397	168
Fayette	884	187
Franklin	402	710
Henry	240	144
Randolph	182	103
Ripley	150	449
Rush	611	166
Switzerland	455	421
Union	438	446
Wayne	956	1317
Total	6015	4946

1 Compiled from the official election returns with the exception of the votes of Putnam County which are from the Vincennes *Western Sun,* August 26, 1826. No returns were found for Crawford and Scott counties in the second district.

2 Jefferson County also gave 12 votes to John H. Scott and one to Jeremiah Sullivan.

3 Marion County also gave twenty votes to Jacob Colip, seven to George L. Kinnard, two to Jeremiah Sullivan, and one to Thomas Chinn.

REPRESENTATIVES IN THE TWENTY-FIRST CONGRESS

Election August 4, 1828[1]

First District	Candidates	
County	*Ratliff Boon	Thomas H. Blake
Carroll	26	28
Clay	28	84
Daviess	201	401
Dubois	211	52
Fountain	215	302

Gibson	271	381
Greene	196	349
Hendricks	105	135
Knox	[418]	[433]
Lawrence	809	237
Martin	212	86
Monroe	471	332
Montgomery	234	219
Morgan	[213]	[344]
Orange	653	298
Owen	115	295
Parke	333	344
Perry	162	276
Pike	113	169
Posey	601	289
Putnam	287	473
Spencer	311	79
Sullivan	370	227
Tippecanoe	54	212
Vanderburgh	145	169
Vermillion	173	296
Warren	29	89
Warrick	316	72
Total	7272	6671

Second District	Candidates	
County	*Jonathan Jennings	John H. Thompson
Bartholomew	451	161
Eel Twp. attached to Carroll	60	0
Clark	1147	262
Crawford	323	157
Floyd	576	143
Hamilton	180	39
Hancock	61	37
Harrison	981	338
Jackson		
Jefferson	875	570
Jennings	404	107
Johnson[2]	200	171
Madison	143	35

County	*Jonathan Jennings	John H. Thompson
Marion	629	246
Scott		
Shelby	577	75
Washington	1052	444
Total	7659	2785

Third District	Candidates	
County	*John Test	Jonathan McCarty
Allen	122	10
Dearborn	1129	966
Decatur	373	326
Delaware	60	59
Fayette	504	687
Franklin	825	496
Henry	322	250
Randolph	223	121
Ripley	447	196
Rush	419	644
Switzerland	489	452
Union	556	441
Wayne	1398	785
Total	6867	5433

1 Compiled from the official election returns in the Archives Division with the exception of the votes of Knox and Morgan counties which are from the Indianapolis *Indiana Journal,* September 25, 1828. No returns have been found for Jackson and Scott counties in the second district.

2 Johnson County also gave three votes to Henry S. Handy.

REPRESENTATIVES IN THE TWENTY-SECOND CONGRESS

Election August 1, 1831[1]

First District	Candidates	
County	*Ratliff Boon	John Law
Carroll	151	166
Clay	159	105
Clinton[2]	36	163
Daviess	286	539

Dubois	261	50
Fountain	561	686
Gibson	424	403
Greene	441	204
Hendricks	332	281
Knox	[368]	[584]
Lawrence	482	620
Martin	143	177
Monroe	757	355
Montgomery	471	500
Morgan	440	324
Orange	592	358
Owen	351	284
Parke	729	567
Perry	218	244
Pike	228	204
Posey[3]	618	399
Putnam	704	612
Spencer	258	123
Sullivan	544	273
Tippecanoe	518	549
Vanderburgh	142	276
Vermillion	412	515
Vigo	190	816
Warren	99	330
Warrick	365	142
Total	11,280	10,849

Second District	Candidates					
County	*John Carr	William W. Wick	Jonathan Jennings	John H. Thompson	James B. Ray	Isaac Howk
Bartholomew	234	502	24	7	129	4
Boone	4	75	4	10	52	0
Cass	9	185	18	0	2	0
Clark	972	85	193	208	11	135
Crawford	196	2	149	74	61	24
Elkhart	4	32	129	0	12	0

County	*John Carr	William W. Wick	Jonathan Jennings	John H. Thompson	James B. Ray	Isaac Howk
Floyd	281	99	250	200	70	36
Hamilton	8	144	2	34	95	12
Hancock	95	116	2	2	44	0
Harrison	270	14	509	372	18	62
Jackson	477	86	75	63	21	0
Jefferson	507	920	44	114	8	14
Jennings	238	372	14	38	15	19
Johnson	205	354	24	10	98	6
Madison	110	232	2	9	87	2
Marion	143	463	33	9	609	5
Shelby	268	491	39	3	142	4
St. Joseph[4]	0	30	65	0	27	0
Scott	214	151	8	86	6	3
Washington	[619]	[252]	[96]	[247]	[225]	[127]
Total	4854	4605	1680	1486	732	453

Third District	Candidates		
County	*Jonathan McCarty	Oliver H. Smith	John Test
Allen	99	97	5
Dearborn	994	467	476
Decatur	421	117	441
Delaware	160	121	31
Fayette	770	588	68
Franklin	421	379	395
Grant	46	51	10
Henry	425	639	36
Randolph	172	314	7
Ripley	306	179	375
Rush	699	363	314
Switzerland	372	225	400
Union	455	341	270
Wayne	898	1416	279
Total	6238	5297	3107

1 Compiled from the official election returns in the Archives Division with the exception of the votes of Knox and Washington counties which are from

the Indianapolis *Indiana Journal,* August 20, 1831. The Indiana General Assembly, by an act of January 19, 1829, had advanced the time of holding the next Congressional election from 1830 to 1831. *Laws of Indiana,* 1828-29, pp. 28-29. Some changes were made in the Congressional districts at this session to take care of the many new counties that had been formed since 1822.

2 The return from Michigan Township, Clinton County, was not included in the count because it was not made as required by law. The vote was: Law, 19; Boon, none.

3 The returns from Robb and Lynn townships of Posey County were rejected because of irregularities.

4 St. Joseph County also gave Robert Hanna two votes.

REPRESENTATIVES IN THE TWENTY-THIRD CONGRESS

Election August 5, 1833[1]

First District	Candidates					
County	*Ratliff Boon	Dennis Pennington	Robert M. Evans	James R. E. Goodlet	Seth M. Levenworth	David G. Mitchell
Crawford	203	35	18	19	263	17
Dubois	227	31	13	47	13	2
Gibson	394	258	206	48	4	1
Harrison	423	537	47	63	135	192
Orange	518	22	138	15	99	46
Perry	218	21	59	246	48	13
Pike	311	106	20	13	23	1
Posey	807	58	223	162	7	0
Spencer	306	9	8	115	13	16
Vanderburgh	164	7	254	18	2	0
Warrick	402	36	83	42	4	0
Total	3973	1120	1069	788	611	288

Second District	Candidates					
County	*John Ewing	John W. Davis	John Law	George Boon	William C. Linton	Hugh L. Livingston
Clay	31	51	87	180	55	9
Daviess	244	82	363	41	......	22

	Ewing	Davis	Law	Boon	Linton	Livingston
Greene	67	235	43	151	40	212
Knox	622	93	302	112	3	2
Lawrence	36	278	140	78	94	651
Martin	135	164	41	18	1	21
Owen	179	249	162	80	10	38
Putnam	520	396	309	114	239	63
Sullivan	31	358	123	457	37	1
Vigo	56	13	98	228	704	3
Total	1921	1919	1668	1459	1183	1022

Third District	Candidates	
County	*John Carr	Harbin H. Moore
Clark	1035	430
Floyd	397	628
Jackson	619	386
Jefferson	794	761
Jennings	358	394
Scott	419	169
Washington	908	489
Total	4530	3257

Fourth District	Candidates		
County	*Amos Lane	John Test	Enoch McCarty
Dearborn	1341	795	62
Decatur	479	583	43
Franklin	663	606	204
Ripley	421	357	71
Rush	825	669	189
Switzerland	533	445	107
Total	4262	3455	676

Fifth District	Candidates	
County	*Jonathan McCarty	Oliver H. Smith
Allen	199	75
Delaware	323	114

Fayette	845	711
Grant	160	76
Henry	659	696
LaGrange	90	33
Randolph	275	433
Union	578	504
Wayne	1461	1626
Total	4590	4268

Sixth District	Candidates		
County	*George L. Kinnard	William W. Wick	James B. Ray
Bartholomew	482	628	0
Boone	229	136	2
Cass	25	378	0
Hamilton	214	235	0
Hancock	214	223	0
Hendricks	462	492	0
Johnson	587	338	4
Madison	234	362	0
Marion	917	719	2
Monroe	813	366	0
Morgan	605	456	1
Shelby	630	485	7
Total	5412	4818	16

Seventh District	Candidates			
County	*Edward A. Hannegan	Albert S. White	Harrison R. Thomas	Joseph M. Hayes
Carroll	320	146	0	0
Clinton	135	74	0	0
Elkhart	146	113	0	0
Fountain	1009	456	10	0
LaPorte	41	103	0	5
Montgomery	629	805	0	0
Parke	815	743	9	0
St. Joseph	71	166	0	8

County	*Edward A. Hannegan	Albert S. White	Harrison R. Thomas	Joseph M. Hayes
Tippecanoe	647	644	0	0
Vermillion	687	451	1	0
Warren	294	355	0	0
Total	4794	4056	20	13

[1] Compiled from the official election returns in the Archives Division. The state was redistricted on the basis of the 1830 Census by an act of January 8, 1833. The number of districts was increased from three to seven. *Laws of Indiana,* 1832-33, pp. 3-4.

REPRESENTATIVES IN THE TWENTY-FOURTH CONGRESS

Election August 3, 1835[1]

First District	Candidates	
County	*Ratliff Boon (D)	John G. Clendenin (W)
Crawford	210	344
Dubois	103	193
Gibson	435	416
Harrison	407	859
Orange	362	822
Perry	231	303
Pike	254	206
Posey	1002	248
Spencer	345	121
Vanderburgh	242	193
Warrick	437	110
Total	4028	3815

Second District	Candidates	
County	*John W. Davis (D)	John Ewing (W)
Clay	362	137
Daviess	387	421
Greene	409	366
Knox	406	742
Lawrence	858	552
Martin	226	174

Owen	510	342
Putnam	1233	783
Sullivan	689	208
Vigo	419	715
Total	5499	4440

Third District	Candidates	
County	*John Carr (D)	Charles Dewey (W)
Clark	1087	670
Floyd	493	678
Jackson	675	291
Jefferson	857	1148
Jennings	384	376
Scott	311	236
Washington	1241	555
Total	5048	3954

Fourth District	Candidates	
County	*Amos Lane (D)	George H. Dunn (W)
Dearborn	1384	1161
Decatur	607	665
Franklin	710	699
Ripley	497	466
Rush[2]	1108	1008
Switzerland	463	688
Total	4769	4687

Fifth District	Candidates		
County	*Jonathan McCarty (D)	James Rariden (W)	John Finley
Allen	250	94	61
Delaware	378	197	33
Fayette	813	395	88
Grant	132	50	54
Henry	753	464	442

County	*Jonathan McCarty (D)	James Rariden (W)	John Finley
Huntington	46	11	76
LaGrange	118	113	1
Randolph	408	163	228
Union	523	283	280
Wabash	106	16	99
Wayne	1297	898	991
Total	4824	2684	2353

Sixth District	Candidates	
County	*George L. Kinnard (D)	Jacob B. Lowe
Bartholomew	639	529
Boone	306	175
Cass	486	137
Hamilton	300	210
Hancock	339	273
Hendricks	678	404
Johnson	[786]	[310]
Madison	505	221
Marion	1247	553
Miami	188	45
Monroe	393	765
Morgan	595	558
Shelby	1021	478
Total	7483	4658

Seventh District	Candidates	
County	*Edward A. Hannegan (D)	James Gregory (W)
Carroll	449	120
Clinton	359	108
Elkhart	301	205
Fountain	1037	326
LaPorte	612	163
Montgomery	857	587

Parke	912	646
St. Joseph	420	73
Tippecanoe	853	549
Vermillion	774	259
Warren	277	442
White	59	37
Total	6910	3515

[1] Compiled from the official election returns in the Archives Division with the exception of the votes of Johnson County which are from the Indianapolis *Indiana Journal,* August 21, 1835.

[2] Rush County also gave three votes to James B. Cobb.

REPRESENTATIVE IN THE TWENTY-FOURTH CONGRESS

Special Election January 2, 1837[1]

Sixth District	Candidates	
County	*William Herod (W)	William W. Wick
Bartholomew	526	98
Boone	236	232
Cass	127	149
Hamilton	277	179
Hancock	127	244
Hendricks	548	245
Johnson	322	334
Madison	197	223
Marion	509	460
Miami	62	38
Monroe	150	412
Morgan	365	380
Shelby	257	499
Total	3703	3493

[1] Compiled from the official election returns in the Archives Division. The election was held to fill the vacancy caused by the death of George L. Kinnard on November 26, 1836.

REPRESENTATIVES IN THE TWENTY-FIFTH CONGRESS

Election August 7, 1837[1]

First District	Candidates	
County	*Ratliff Boon (D)	John Pitcher (W)
Crawford	235	287
Dubois	184	170
Gibson	471	639
Harrison	466	984
Orange	751	427
Perry	324	319
Pike	284	286
Posey	762	468
Spencer	364	259
Vanderburgh	222	372
Warrick	471	256
Total	4534	4467

Second District	Candidates	
County	*John Ewing (W)	John Law (D)
Clay	339	271
Daviess	587	403
Greene	506	315
Knox[2]	847	432
Lawrence	683	694
Martin	250	184
Owen	511	449
Putnam	1088	817
Sullivan	249	703
Vigo	760	619
Total	5820	4887

Third District	Candidates	
County	*William Graham (W)	John S. Simonson (D)
Clark	729	1218
Floyd	681	593

Jackson	709	402
Jefferson	1462	698
Jennings	727	161
Scott	385	250
Washington	1024	1068
Total	5717	4390

Fourth District	Candidates	
County	*George H. Dunn (W)	Amos Lane (D)
Dearborn	1323	1605
Decatur	995	620
Franklin	962	911
Ripley	664	478
Rush	1279	896
Switzerland	868	547
Total	6091	5057

Fifth District	Candidates	
County	*James Rariden (W)	Jonathan McCarty (W)
Adams	31	39
Allen	186	340
Delaware	511	397
Fayette	630	766
Fulton[3]	46	55
Grant	205	123
Henry	1084	707
Huntington	82	40
Jay	50	66
LaGrange	182	174
Noble	64	77
Randolph	576	419
Steuben[4]	51	24
Union	649	386
Wabash	109	86

County	Rariden (W)	McCarty (W)
Wayne	2130	1099
Wells	13	47
Total	6599	4845

Sixth District	Candidates	
County	*William Herod (W)	James B. Ray (D)
Bartholomew	1075	97
Boone	554	315
Brown	116	131
Cass	598	311
Hamilton	637	250
Hancock	494	396
Hendricks	1058	372
Johnson	692	564
Madison	867	253
Marion	1014	1397
Miami	226	42
Monroe	831	438
Morgan	649	618
Shelby	824	704
Total	9635	5888

Seventh District	Candidates	
County	*Albert S. White (W)	Nathan Jackson
Carroll	534	467
Clinton	412	259[5]
Elkhart	322[6]	289
Fountain	1003	510
Kosciusko	265	90
Lake	81	53
LaPorte	701	223
Marshall	147	35
Montgomery	1623	353
Parke	1459	279
Porter	145	75

St. Joseph	899	138
Tippecanoe	1461	559
Vermillion	1027	219
Warren	681	176
White	177	64
Total	10,937	3789

1 Compiled from the official election returns in the Archives Division.

2 Knox County gave Edwin M. Jones one vote.

3 Fulton County gave James Brown Ray two votes.

4 Fifteen voters in Steuben County who intended to vote for James Rariden gave the name as Samuel Rariden; seven others gave his name as John Rariden. John Knott also received one vote in the county.

5 Twenty voters in Clinton County who intended to vote for Nathan Jackson gave the name as John Jackson.

6 Two other voters who intended to vote for Albert S. White gave the name as Albert A. White.

REPRESENTATIVES IN THE TWENTY-SIXTH CONGRESS

Election August 5, 1839[1]

First District	Candidates	
County	*George H. Proffit (W)	Robert Dale Owen (D)
Crawford	381	320
Dubois	228	262
Gibson	687	495
Harrison	1032	936
Orange	632	828
Perry	492	219
Pike	528	227
Posey	716	748
Spencer	433	355
Vanderburgh	614	204
Warrick	265	635
Total	6008	5229

Second District	Candidates	
County	*John W. Davis (D)	John Ewing (W)
Clay	590	268

County	Davis (D)	Ewing (D)
Daviess	585	578
Greene	618	526
Knox	646	808
Lawrence	1003	852
Martin	395	250
Owen	705	449
Putnam	1341	1106
Sullivan	935	244
Vigo	698	1136
Total	7516	6217

Third District	Candidates	
County	*John Carr (D)	William Graham (W)
Clark	1392	838
Floyd	930	687
Jackson	759	525
Jefferson	1330	1289
Jennings	566	561
Scott	413	335
Washington	1608	886
Total	6998	5121

Fourth District	Candidates	
County	*Thomas Smith (D)	George H. Dunn (W)
Dearborn	1829	1165
Decatur	934	855
Franklin	1016	869
Ripley	683	753
Rush	1173	1170
Switzerland	906	730
Total	6541	5542

Fifth District	Candidates		
County	*James Rariden (W)	William Thompson (D)	Jonathan McCarty (W)
Adams	93	55	32
Allen[2]	413	272	49
Blackford	21	60	34
DeKalb	100	56	4
Delaware	351	356	463
Fayette	576	593	575
Fulton	93	75	45
Grant	308	241	98
Henry	815	629	571
Huntington	56	101	10
Jay	140	163	24
LaGrange	238	246	29
Noble	121	282	9
Randolph	512	394	445
Steuben	113	71	1
Union	389	521	349
Wabash	159	126	28
Wayne	1638	982	1155
Wells	46	64	32
Whitley	53	40	6
Total	6235	5327	3959

Sixth District	Candidates	
County	*William W. Wick (D)	William Herod (W)
Bartholomew	553	878
Boone	546	588
Brown	275	58
Cass	452	429
Hamilton	744	533
Hancock	562	426
Hendricks	601	1029
Johnson	936	514
Madison	744	724
Marion	1192	915

County	Wick (D)	Herod (W)
Miami	235	212
Monroe	816	716
Morgan	784	775
Shelby	1065	697
Total	9505	8494

Seventh District	Candidates	
County	*Tilghman A. Howard (D)	Thomas J. Evans (W)
Carroll	751	469
Clinton	651	381
Elkhart[3]	557	410
Fountain	1048	758
Jasper	111	45
Kosciusko	312	219
Lake	75	64
LaPorte	563	683
Marshall	163	117
Montgomery	1066	1100
Parke	[1254]	[741]
Porter	210	123
Pulaski	32	22
St. Joseph	475	584
Tippecanoe	1270	1121
Vermillion	825	433
Warren	363	601
White	148	135
Total	9874	8006

1 Compiled from the official election returns in the Archives Division with the exception of the votes of Parke County which are from the Indianapolis *Indiana Journal,* August 23, 1839.

2 The returns from one township in Allen County were received too late to be included. They gave Rariden 22; Thompson 6; McCarty 2.

3 Returns in Elkhart County that were received too late to be included would have given Howard an additional 55 votes and Evans an additional 30 votes.

REPRESENTATIVE IN THE TWENTY-SIXTH CONGRESS

Special Election August 3, 1840[1]

Seventh District	Candidates	
County	*Henry S. Lane (W)	Edward A. Hannegan (D)
Benton	31	36
Carroll	678	798
Clinton	543	741
Elkhart	614	667
Fountain	953	1209
Jasper	62	82
Kosciusko	396	349
Lake	108	133
LaPorte	1015	760
Marshall	160	159
Montgomery	1425	1241
Parke	1349	1020
Porter	223	216
Pulaski	59	58
St. Joseph	810	464
Tippecanoe	1517	1269
Vermillion	854	642
Warren	733	380
White	196	152
Total	11,726	10,376

[1] To fill the vacancy caused by resignation of Tilghman A. Howard. Election Returns, August 1840, Archives Division.

REPRESENTATIVES IN THE TWENTY-SEVENTH CONGRESS

Election May 3, 1841[1]

First District	Candidates	
County	*George H. Proffit (W)	James Lockhart (D)
Crawford	319	227
Dubois	190	202

County	Proffit (W)	Lockhart (D)
Gibson	612	329
Harrison	1082	725
Orange	644	640
Perry	407	102
Pike	337	234
Posey	541	635
Spencer	408	179
Vanderburgh	511	238
Warrick	260	435
Total	5311	3946

Second District	Candidates	
County	*Richard W. Thompson (W)	John W. Davis (D)
Clay	259	387
Daviess	574	426
Greene	523	510
Knox	759	477
Lawrence	755	769
Martin	256	306
Owen[2]	537	545
Putnam	1212	959
Sullivan	294	864
Vigo	1125	425
Total	6294	5668

Third District	Candidates	
County	*Joseph L. White (W)	John Carr (D)
Clark	996	1141
Floyd	706	643
Jackson	476	663
Jefferson	1385	923
Jennings	719	388
Scott	361	315
Washington	953	1177
Total	5596	5250

Fourth District	Candidates	
County	*James H. Cravens (W)	Thomas Smith (D)
Dearborn[3]	1254	1368
Decatur	1012	664
Franklin	909	902
Ripley[4]	847	579
Rush	1252	919
Switzerland	782	594
Total	6056	5026

Fifth District		Candidates[5]	
County	*Andrew Kennedy (D)	Jonathan McCarty (W)	Caleb B. Smith (W)
Adams	101	84	26
Allen	275	251	144
Blackford	98	54	0
DeKalb	29	67	5
Delaware	401	605	21
Fayette	656	288	575
Fulton	27	38	76
Grant	303	139	82
Henry	597	713	527
Huntington	143	79	1
Jay	193	189	13
LaGrange	180	27	173
Noble	174	60	81
Randolph	500	326	347
Steuben	102	41	85
Union	541	113	459
Wabash	167	168	75
Wayne	1050	935	1351
Wells	78	94	0
Whitley	49	16	7
Total	5664	4287	4048

Sixth District	Candidates	
County	*David Wallace (W)	Nathan B. Palmer (D)
Bartholomew	748	521
Boone	505	436
Brown	20	149
Cass	392	286
Hamilton	637	439
Hancock	568	384
Hendricks	860	532
Johnson	449	692
Madison	517	301
Marion	1324	976
Miami	213	159
Monroe	506	654
Morgan	705	634
Shelby	762	846
Total	8206	7009

Seventh District	Candidates	
County	*Henry S. Lane (W)	John Bryce (D)
Carroll	562	505
Clinton[6]	361	411
Elkhart	552	532
Fountain	766	784
Jasper	47	51
Kosciusko	308	204
Lake	65	76
LaPorte	779	469
Marshall	129	100
Montgomery[7]	1228	761
Parke	973	530
Porter	156	104
Pulaski	37	21
St. Joseph	682	302
Tippecanoe	1308	851
Vermillion	694	386

Warren	653	191
White	177	114
Total	9477	6392

[1] Compiled from the official election returns in the Archives Division. The election was held in May rather than in August in order that Indiana might be represented in the special session of Congress called to meet on May 31, 1841.

[2] In the second district, the returns from Harrison Township, Owen County, were received too late to be included. They were: for Thompson, 29; for Davis, two.

[3] In the fourth district, Dearborn County gave six votes to John Hansell, four to Adrian V. Eggert, five to Herman Wright, and one to Milton Gregg.

[4] Ripley County gave 28 votes to Herman Wright.

[5] In the fifth district, DeKalb County had two votes for John A. Spencer, and one for Charles H. Test. Delaware County had four for Test; two for James Rariden, and five for Jacob Crowsaw. Fulton County had one vote for Ebenezer Ward. Grant County had six for Test, 43 for Daniel Worth, and eight for Rariden. Henry County gave Daniel Worth 43 votes. In Huntington County, Test received four votes. In LaGrange County, Rariden received three votes. In Randolph County, Worth received two votes, Rariden, one. In Union County, Worth received thirteen, Test, four. In Wabash County, Test received three votes, Rariden, one. In Wayne County, Worth received 51 votes. In Wells County, twelve returns intended for Jonathan McCarty were credited to John McCarty. In Whitley County, Test received eight votes.

[6] In the seventh district, the clerk of Clinton County reported that the returns had not been received from two townships because of high water. He estimated that Bryce would have had a small majority in those townships.

[7] Montgomery County gave one vote to Isaac C. Reed.

REPRESENTATIVES IN THE TWENTY-EIGHTH CONGRESS

Election August 7, 1843[1]

First District	Candidates	
County	*Robert Dale Owen (D)	John W. Payne (W)
Crawford	393	416
Dubois	356	232
Gibson	652	760
Harrison	1005	1083
Orange	933	642
Perry	283	452
Pike	417	394
Posey	917	711
Spencer[2]	409	520

County	Owen (D)	Payne (W)
Vanderburgh	521	531
Warrick	773	341
Total	6659	6082

Second District	Candidates	
County	*Thomas J. Henley (D)	Joseph L. White (W)
Clark	1349	973
Floyd	914	883
Jackson	875	548
Jefferson	1350	1479
Jennings	605	808
Scott	445	415
Washington	1482	964
Total	7020	6070

Third District	Candidates	
County	*Thomas Smith (D)	John A. Matson (W)
Dearborn	1817	1464
Decatur	1009	1176
Franklin	1273	1057
Ripley	743	879
Rush	1177	1316
Switzerland	1002	874
Total	7021	6766

Fourth District	Candidates			
County	*Caleb B. Smith (W)	Charles H. Test	Hiram P. Bennett	Wilson Thompson
Fayette	842	774	23	0
Henry	1052	914	206	0
Union	545	498	62	52
Wayne	1658	1256	458	0
Total	4097	3442	749	52

Fifth District	Candidates	
County	*William J. Brown (D)	David Wallace (W)
Bartholomew	911	893
Brown	423	43
Hamilton	775	840
Hancock	747	619
Johnson	1054	616
Madison	803	762
Marion	1485	1627
Shelby	1201	914
Total	7399	6314

Sixth District	Candidates	
County	*John W. Davis (D)	George G. Dunn (W)
Daviess	603	756
Greene	711	705
Knox[3]	661	907
Lawrence	894	926
Martin	361	280
Monroe	947	722
Morgan	993	824
Owen	811	653
Sullivan	1125	414
Total	7106	6187

Seventh District	Candidates	
County	*Joseph A. Wright (D)	Edward W. McGaughey (W)
Clay[4]	547(78)	302(12)
Hendricks[5]	796	978
Parke	1124	1220
Putnam	1388	1215

County	Wright (D)	McGaughey (W)
Vermillion	688	590
Vigo	820	1121
Total	5363	5426
	78	12
	5441	5438

Eighth District	Candidates	
County	*John Pettit (D)	James R. M. Bryant (W)
Boone	752	709
Carroll	814	607
Clinton	760	547
Fountain	1220	790
Montgomery	1219	1287
Tippecanoe[6]	1296	1299
Warren	342	746
Total	6403	5985

Ninth District	Candidates		
County	*Samuel C. Sample (W)	Ebenezer M. Chamberlain (D)	Jacob Bigelow
Benton	24	28	0
Cass	667	546	3
Elkhart	690	811	3
Fulton	273	213	1
Jasper	125	181	0
Kosciusko	496	446	0
Lake	112	185	4
LaPorte	841	696	53
Marshall	167	235	29
Miami	483	450	0
Porter	232	248	10
Pulaski	98	95	0
St. Joseph	792	591	24
Wabash	491	480	0
White	202	174	0
Total	5693	5379	127

Tenth District	Candidates	
County	*Andrew Kennedy (D)	Lewis G. Thompson (W)
Adams	235	227
Allen	646	739
Blackford	214	67
DeKalb	291	216
Delaware	726	758
Grant	470	483
Huntington	281	200
Jay	368	347
LaGrange	392	436
Noble	339	280
Randolph[7]	761	787
Steuben	221	266
Wells	248	170
Whitley	166	122
Total	5358	5098

1 Compiled from the official election returns in the Archives Division.

2 The returns from Carter Township, Spencer County, were not included because they were not accompanied by a list of the voters. The vote was: for Payne, 45; for Owen, 20. Spencer County Election Return, August 1843, Archives.

3 The returns of Decker Township, Knox County, were not included because they were not received within the legal time. The vote was: for Davis, 61; for Dunn, 18.

4 The returns from Perry Township, Clay County, were not included in the original report made by the county clerk. After it was discovered that the acceptance or rejection of the vote in this township would change the final result, a full explanation was made to Governor Bigger, after which he ruled that the returns should be included. The vote was: for Wright, 78; for McGaughey, 12. The person bringing the return to the county seat had arrived within the legal time, but had neglected to bring the tally papers. See letter with Clay County Election Returns, August 1843, Archives Division.

5 Hendricks County gave three votes to James T. Moffatt.

6 Tippecanoe County gave two votes each to Othniel L. Clark and Samuel Milroy and one to James W. Wilson.

7 Randolph County gave sixteen votes to Levi Stout.

REPRESENTATIVES IN THE TWENTY-NINTH CONGRESS

Election August 4, 1845[1]

First District	Candidates	
County	*Robert Dale Owen (D)	George P. R. Wilson (W)
Crawford	417	500
Dubois	496	219
Gibson	703	656
Harrison	1088	1228
Orange	[967]	[636]
Perry	301	517
Pike	459	400
Posey	992	651
Spencer	530	615
Vanderburgh	577	615
Warrick	806	294
Total	7336	6331

Second District	Candidates	
County	*Thomas J. Henley (D)	Roger Martin (W)
Clark	1306	1041
Floyd	973	847
Jackson	883	533
Jefferson	1414	1646
Jennings	688	791
Scott	450	467
Washington	1505	1051
Total	7219	6376

Third District	Candidates		
County	*Thomas Smith (D)	Joseph C. Eggleston (W)	Angus C. McCoy
Dearborn	1590	1138	34
Decatur	945	981	75
Franklin	1267	973	10

Ohio	405	397	0
Ripley[2]	906	909	68
Rush	1210	1341	32
Switzerland	923	967	0
Total	7246	6706	219

Fourth District		Candidates	
County	*Caleb B. Smith (W)	John Finley (D)	Matthew R. Hull (Liberty)
Fayette	976	625	19
Henry	1332	842	140
Union	661	594	61
Wayne	1894	1140	333
Total	4863	3201	553

Fifth District		Candidates	
County	*William W. Wick (D)	James P. Foley (W)	Asa Bales
Bartholomew	1025	893	0
Brown	374	75	0
Hamilton	638	650	179
Hancock	712	608	3
Johnson	1048	535	23
Madison	797	742	20
Marion	1498	1404	51
Shelby	1252	890	2
Tipton	115	86	0
Total	7459	5883	276

Sixth District	Candidates	
County	*John W. Davis (D)	Eli P. Farmer (W)
Daviess	759	680
Greene	921	676
Knox	731	971

County	Davis (D)	Farmer (W)
Lawrence	1018	932
Martin	477	185
Monroe	1125	311
Morgan[3]	1065	807
Owen[4]	955	264
Sullivan	1132	627
Total	8183	5253

Seventh District — Candidates

County	*Edward W. McGaughey (W)	Joseph A. Wright (D)
Clay	398	704
Hendricks	1072	895
Parke	1286	1347
Putnam	1477	1455
Vermillion	729	720
Vigo	1230	902
Total	6192	6023

Eighth District — Candidates

County	*John Pettit (D)	Albert L. Holmes (W)	Elizur Deming
Boone	758	735	0
Carroll	651	646	0
Clinton	588	363	8
Fountain	1090	734	1
[Howard] Richardville	146	171	0
Montgomery	1275	1209	2[5]
Tippecanoe[6]	1360	1169	75
Warren	392	744	5
Total	6260	5771	91

Ninth District — Candidates

County	*Charles W. Cathcart (D)	Samuel C. Sample (W)	John J. Deming
Benton	67	41	0
Cass	640	672	0

Elkhart	826	574	31
Fulton	246	282	6
Jasper	185	142	0
Kosciusko	577	622	20
Lake	197	115	1
LaPorte	[873]	[834]	[41]
Marshall	245	195	49
Miami	558	558	0
Porter	308	277	28
Pulaski	127	137	0
St. Joseph	589	747	74
Wabash	574	535	22
White	219	228	1
Total	6141	5959	273

Tenth District		Candidates	
County	*Andrew Kennedy (D)	Lewis G. Thompson (W)	Daniel Worth
Adams	278	185	0
Allen	755	843	1
Blackford	202	74	0
DeKalb	316	237	13
Delaware	747	799	0
Grant	450	444	97
Huntington	320	273	0
Jay	301	307	0
LaGrange	472	546	48
Noble	438	377	4
Randolph	706	724	171
Steuben	289	309	22
Wells	307	171	1
Whitley	256	193	0
Total	5837	5482	357

1 Compiled from the official election returns with the exception of the votes of Orange and LaPorte counties which are from the Indianapolis *Indiana State Journal* (weekly), August 27, 1845.

2 In Ripley County, J. H. Cravens received two votes, Ebenezer Ridlin one.

3 Morgan County gave one vote each to John Eccles and A. B. Conduit.

4 Owen County gave one vote to George G. Dunn.

5 T. Deming received one vote probably intended for Elizur Deming.

6 In Tippecanoe County, Robert Heath and Sandford C. Cox each received one vote.

REPRESENTATIVES IN THE THIRTIETH CONGRESS

Election August 2, 1847[1]

First District	Candidates	
County	*Elisha Embree (W)	Robert Dale Owen (D)
Crawford	595	383
Dubois	273	562
Gibson	842	725
Harrison	1297	1044
Orange	708	899
Perry	596	249
Pike	486	464
Posey	879	886
Spencer	641	478
Vanderburgh	676	538
Warrick	453	826
Total	7446	7054

Second District	Candidates	
County	*Thomas J. Henley (D)	John S. Davis (W)
Clark	1328	1119
Floyd	1033	1073
Jackson	780	595
Jefferson	1377	1773
Jennings	686	951
Scott	451	502
Washington	1515	1117
Total	7170	7130

Third District	Candidates		
County	*John L. Robinson (D)	Pleasant A. Hackleman (W)	Stephen S. Harding
Dearborn	1660	1245	0
Decatur	1080	1166	14
Franklin[2]	1474	1172	0

Ohio	483	372	1
Ripley[3]	917	978	0
Rush	1293	1512	18
Switzerland	1001	977	0
Total	7908	7422	33

Fourth District	Candidates	
County	*Caleb B. Smith (W)	Charles H. Test
Fayette	936	835
Henry	1266	798
Union	714	666
Wayne	2072	1241
Total	4988	3540

Fifth District	Candidates		
County	*William W. Wick (D)	Nicholas McCarty (W)	Levi R. Bowman
Bartholomew	947	899	0
Brown	454	73	0
Hamilton	626	831	140
Hancock	652	687	5
Johnson	1085	682	0
Madison	728	816	8
Marion	1402	1695	8
Shelby	1064	1027	0
Tipton	129	89	2
Total	7087	6799	163

Sixth District	Candidates	
County	*George G. Dunn (W)	David M. Dobson (D)
Daviess	878	635
Greene	856	889
Knox	982	642
Lawrence[4]	936	984

County	Dunn (W)	Dobson (D)
Martin	424	453
Monroe	757	1009
Morgan	1134	938
Owen	847	788
Sullivan	551	1015
Total	7365	7353

Seventh District	Candidates	
County	*Richard W. Thompson (W)	Joseph A. Wright (D)
Clay	389	737
Hendricks[5]	1209	884
Parke	1301	1408
Putnam	1530	1508
Vermillion	713	760
Vigo	1260	927
Total	6402	6224

Eighth District	Candidates		
County	*John Pettit (D)	David Brier (W)	Samuel W. Richey
Boone	816	728	22
Carroll	790	800	0
Clinton	726	540	16
Fountain[6]	1075	909	22
Howard[7]	236	198	0
Montgomery[8]	1380	1303	18
Tippecanoe[9]	1398	1351	48
Warren	368	642	12
Total	6789	6471	138

Ninth District	Candidates		
County	*Charles W. Cathcart (D)	Daniel D. Pratt (W)	Robert Stewart
Benton	67	41	0
Cass	731	811	0

Elkhart[10]	807	509	39
Fulton	348	417	2
Jasper	230	163	0
Kosciusko	611	751	2
Lake	287	128	0
LaPorte	997	913	43
Marshall	375	263	42
Miami	785	737	0
Porter	384	311	17
Pulaski	173	122	0
St. Joseph	592	759	40
Wabash	797	809	0
White	290	261	0
Total	7474	6995	185

Tenth District	Candidates	
County	*William Rockhill (D)	William G. Ewing (W)
Adams	309	251
Allen	866	878
Blackford	263	68
DeKalb	[404]	[341]
Delaware	639	862
Grant	491	414
Huntington	390	375
Jay[11]	307	334
LaGrange	630	723
Noble	536	490
Randolph[12]	722	801
Steuben[13]	433	368
Wells	323	241
Whitley	304	295
Total	6617	6451

1 Compiled from the official election returns with the exception of the vote for DeKalb County which is from the Indianapolis *Indiana Journal* (weekly), August 30, 1847.

2 Franklin County gave one vote to James Conwell.

3 Ripley County gave one vote to James N. Waggoner.

[4] The vote of Bono Township was not included because the inspector failed to return one of the poll books as required by law. The vote was: Dobson, 101, and Dunn, 90.

[5] Hendricks County gave two votes to William Benbow.

[6] The returns from Wabash Township, Fountain County, received too late to be included in the tabulation, gave Pettit, 142; Brier, 40.

[7] Howard County gave one vote to ——— Bowman.

[8] Montgomery County gave one vote each to Samuel C. Willson and Henry S. Lane. One voter wrote Brier's name as Drier.

[9] Tippecanoe County gave one vote to Stephen S. Harding and one vote to Samuel W. Davis.

[10] The vote of Middlebury Township, Elkhart County, was not received in time to be included. It was: for Pratt, 68; for Stewart, 2; for Cathcart, 81.

[11] James Marquis received one vote in Jay County.

[12] James Marquis received 59 votes in Randolph County.

[13] Daniel Worth received 6 votes in Steuben County.

REPRESENTATIVES IN THE THIRTY-FIRST CONGRESS

Election August 6, 1849[1]

First District — Candidates

County	*Nathaniel Albertson (D)	Elisha Embree (W)
Crawford	467	600
Dubois	597	230
Gibson	907	900
Harrison	1047	1220
Orange	1041	804
Perry	371	619
Pike	568	512
Posey	1268	877
Spencer	491	655
Vanderburgh	599	668
Warrick	915	513
Total	8271	7598

Second District — Candidates

County	*Cyrus L. Dunham (D)	William McKee Dunn (W)
Clark[2]	1338	1047
Floyd[3]	1195	1052
Jackson	1091	556
Jefferson	1371	2130

Jennings	728	970
Scott	508	528
Washington	1592	1055
Total	7823	7338

Third District	Candidates	
County	*John L. Robinson (D)	Joseph Robinson (W)
Dearborn	1582	1115
Decatur	1241	1147
Franklin	1299	1209
Ohio	459	414
Ripley	897	928
Rush	1469	1534
Switzerland	1173	1001
Total	8120	7348

Fourth District	Candidates	
County	*George W. Julian (FS)	Samuel W. Parker (W)
Fayette	892	938
Henry	[1373]	[1441]
Union	738	506
Wayne[4]	1734	1698
Total	4737	4583

Fifth District	Candidates	
County	*William J. Brown (D)	William Herod (W)
Bartholomew	1075	997
Brown	513	118
Hamilton	834	894
Hancock	805	666
Johnson	1181	681
Madison	997	882
Marion	1776	1920

County	Brown (D)	Herod (W)
Shelby	1356	934
Tipton	225	173
Total	8762	7265

Sixth District	Candidates	
County	*Willis A. Gorman (D)	John S. Watts (W)
Daviess	799	762
Greene	1070	885
Knox	664	925
Lawrence	997	998
Martin	523	373
Monroe	1047	775
Morgan	1234	1142
Owen[5]	897	853
Sullivan	1235	483
Total	8466	7196

Seventh District	Candidates	
County	*Edward W. McGaughey (W)	Grafton F. Cookerly
Clay	410	739
Hendricks	1084	697
Parke	1435	855
Putnam	1663	1109
Vermillion	800	714
Vigo	1390	795
Total	6782	4909

Eighth District	Candidates	
County	*Joseph E. McDonald (D)	Henry S. Lane (W)
Boone	910	808
Carroll	861	719
Clinton	951	764

Fountain	1167	876
Howard	397	493
Montgomery	1525	1410
Tippecanoe	1171	1328
Warren	450	700
Total	7432	7098

Ninth District	Candidates	
County	*Graham N. Fitch (D)	Williamson Wright (W)
Benton	88	75
Cass	911	957
Elkhart	1269	883
Fulton	458	442
Jasper	235	219
Kosciusko	707	890
Lake	270	184
LaPorte	957	1127
Marshall	459	340
Miami	852	786
Porter	429	376
Pulaski	246	155
St. Joseph[6]	816	924
Wabash[7]	790	886
White	313	275
Total	8800	8519

Tenth District	Candidates	
County	*Andrew J. Harlan (D)	David Kilgore (W)
Adams	445	332
Allen	964	709
Blackford	308	103
DeKalb	565	302
Delaware	484	1105
Grant	751	584
Huntington	360	346
Jay	346	304

County	Harlan (D)	Kilgore (W)
LaGrange	574	645
Noble	656	529
Randolph	752	797
Steuben	424	444
Wells	393	269
Whitley	344	308
Total	7366	6777

[1] Compiled from the official election returns in the Archives Division with the exception of the Henry County vote which is from the Indianapolis *Indiana Journal* (weekly), September 3, 1849.

[2] Clark County gave one vote to John Wright.

[3] Floyd County gave three votes to Stephen C. Stevens and one to Levi McDougle.

[4] Wayne County gave thirteen votes to Oliver P. Morton.

[5] Owen County gave one vote to William Madden.

[6] St. Joseph County gave two votes to John U. Pettit, and four to Joseph L. Jernegan.

[7] Wabash County gave one vote to Michael Black.

REPRESENTATIVES IN THE THIRTY-SECOND CONGRESS

Election August 4, 1851[1]

First District	Candidates	
County	*James Lockhart (D)	Lemuel DeBruler (W)
Crawford	505	511
Dubois	490	432
Gibson	905	939
Harrison	1000	1209
Orange	943	667
Perry[2]	481	653
Pike	606	583
Posey	1172	784
Spencer[3]	486	801
Vanderburgh	703	697
Warrick	882	579
Total	8173	7855

Second District	Candidates	
County	*Cyrus L. Dunham (D)	Roger Martin (W)
Clark	1373	1013
Floyd	1098	1052
Jackson	1168	518
Jefferson	1408	2061
Jennings	916	940
Scott	545	502
Washington	1589	1039
Total	8097	7125

Third District	Candidates	
County	*John L. Robinson (D)	Johnson Watts (W)
Dearborn	1888	1444
Decatur	1088	1363
Franklin	1494	1296
Ohio	414	374
Ripley[4]	890	1185
Rush	1365	1455
Switzerland	1103	1056
Total	8242	8173

Fourth District	Candidates	
County	*Samuel W. Parker (W)	George W. Julian (FS)
Fayette	972	681
Henry	1439	1433
Union	580	610
Wayne	2111	1816
Total	5102	4540

Fifth District	Candidates	
County	*Thomas A. Hendricks (D)	William P. Rush (W)
Bartholomew	1218	945
Brown	676	56
Hamilton	754	753
Hancock	817	640
Johnson	959	426
Madison	1111	783
Marion	1615	1364
Shelby	1494	432
Tipton	418	144
Total	9062	5543

Sixth District	Candidates	
County	*Willis A. Gorman (D)	Eli P. Farmer (W)
Daviess	1038	455
Greene	1228	582
Knox	954	674
Lawrence	813	847
Martin	700	282
Monroe	1091	510
Morgan	1175	717
Owen[5]	1108	418
Sullivan	1367	208
Total	9474	4693

Seventh District	Candidates	
County	*John G. Davis (D)	Edward W. McGaughey (W)
Clay	882	338
Hendricks	948	993
Parke	1132	1121
Putnam	1355	1435

Vermillion	769	744
Vigo[6]	990	1183
Total	6076	5814

Eighth District	Candidates	
County	*Daniel Mace (D)	David Brier (W)
Boone	873	819
Carroll	953	712
Clinton[7]	833	667
Fountain	1173	1086
Howard[8]	410	478
Montgomery	1443	1453
Tippecanoe[9]	1430	1325
Warren	437	754
Total	7552	7294

Ninth District	Candidates	
County	*Graham N. Fitch (D)	Schuyler Colfax (W)
Benton	97	95
Cass	975	841
Elkhart	846	694
Fulton	535	470
Jasper	375	345
Kosciusko	779	900
Lake[10]	362	250
LaPorte	1066	1073
Marshall	491	388
Miami	964	863
Porter	510	435
Pulaski[11]	273	163
St. Joseph	788	1118
Starke	80	26

County	*Graham N. Fitch (D)	Schuyler Colfax (W)
Wabash	819	1070
White	396	387
Total	9356	9118

Tenth District	Candidates	
County	*Samuel Brenton (W, FS)	James W. Borden (D)
Adams	306	455
Allen	1112	1100
Blackford	138	345
DeKalb	485	474
Delaware	941	718
Grant	839	702
Huntington	651	660
Jay	528	478
LaGrange	695	604
Noble	663	610
Randolph	1127	887
Steuben	454	501
Wells	370	518
Whitley	467	431
Total	8776	8483

1 From the official election returns, Archives Division.

2 Perry County gave two votes to Charles H. Mason.

3 Spencer County gave one vote to Andrew L. Robinson.

4 Ripley County gave one vote each to J. P. Millikan and Silas Grimsley.

5 Owen County gave one vote each to George G. Dunn, George W. Carr, and David McDonald.

6 Vigo County gave one vote each to R. W. Thompson, John P. Usher, Ezra Reed, and John Smith.

7 Clinton County gave one vote to Dr. Oiler.

8 Howard County gave 21 votes to Samuel Huff (Hoff).

9 Tippecanoe County gave two votes to Samuel A. Huff (Hoff) and eight votes to Elizur Deming.

10 Lake County gave one vote to Robert Stewart.

11 Pulaski County gave one vote to Samuel Decker.

ELECTION OF UNITED STATES SENATORS BY GENERAL ASSEMBLY

[The majority of those voting constituted an election.]

November 8, 1816[1]

*James Noble	26[2]
*Waller Taylor	20[3]
James Scott	16
Jesse L. Holman	3
Ezra Ferris	2
Davis Floyd	2
Walter Wilson	2
Elias M'Namee	1

December 16, 1818[4]

*Waller Taylor	21
James Scott	15
Isaac Blackford	2

December 6, 1820[5]

*James Noble	20
Jesse L. Holman	13
Davis Floyd	4

January 12, 1825[6]

	Ballots			
	1st	2d	3d	4th
*William Hendricks	25	29	31	32
Isaac Blackford	26	30	30	30
Jonathan Jennings	10	2	—	—
Scattering	1	1	1	—

December 12, 1826[7]

	Ballots			
	1st	2d	3d	4th
*James Noble	32	35	38	40
Isaac Blackford	24	24	26	28
Jonathan Jennings	22	20	15	10

December 18, 1830[8]

	Ballots			
	1st	2d	3d	4th
*William Hendricks	31	34	40	44
Ratliff Boon	26	28	24	26
John Law	12	11	13	9
Charles Dewey	9	7	3	3
Scattering	4	2	2	—

December 8 and 9, 1831[9]

	Ballots						
	1st	2d	3d	4th	5th	6th	7th
*John Tipton	1	4	10	12	19	33	55
Samuel Judah	36	39	36	34	31	20	3
Jesse L. Holman	23	25	32	39	41	42	36
Thomas H. Blake	23	22	19	16	12	9	5
James Rariden	16	14	8	4	1	—	—
Jonathan Jennings	3	—	—	—	1	—	—
Scattering or blank	3	1	—	—	—	1	6

December 8 and 10, 1832[10]

Ballots

	1st	2nd	3rd	4th	5th	6th	7th	8th	9th	10th	11th	12th	13th	14th	15th	16th	17th	18th	19th
*John Tipton	32	35	38	39	42	44	46	40	37	37	35	40	33	32	29	34	42	49	54
Oliver H. Smith	21	25	27	26	28	32	32	29	24	21	15	17	....	....	....	....	....	....	2
Ratliff Boon	24	21	21	19	13	8	5	6	4	2	....	....	....	1	....	....	2	2	1
Jonathan McCarty	13	10	7	8	8	6	2	....	1	6	6	4	18	18	16	14	12	11	16
Robert Hanna	1	1	2	1	1	1	....	....	1	....	....	....	1	....	....	....	1	4	4
James G. Read	1	4	5	5	10	10	13	10	10	5	1	....	....	....	....	....	....	....	....
Isaac Blackford	7	7	3	2	1	2	2	3	5	3	3	1	1	....	....	....	....	....	....
John [James] Rariden	1	....	....	....	....	....	....	....	....	....	....	....	....	....	....	....	....	....	....
Walter Wilson	1	....	....	....	....	....	....	....	....	....	....	....	....	....	....	....	....	....	....
Thomas H. Blake	....	1	....	1	....	....	....	2	1	2	1	....	....	....	....	....	....	....	1
Charles Dewey	....	....	1	1	....	....	....	....	....	....	5	5	11	16	23	24	28	20	9
Noah Noble	....	....	....	....	....	1	3	3	3	....	1	1	....	....	1	....	....	....	....
John Ewing	....	....	....	....	....	....	....	1	....	....	....	....	....	1	....	....	....	....	....
David Robb	....	....	....	....	....	....	....	1	....	1	....	....	....	....	....	....	....	....	....
Arthur Patterson	....	....	....	....	....	....	....	10	16	22	24	24	21	25	25	21	14	9	11
William W. Wick	....	....	....	....	....	....	....	....	1	2	2	2	....	....	....	1	....	1	....
John Law	....	....	....	....	....	....	....	....	1	....	....	....	1	3	2	3	1	2	1
Tilghman A. Howard	....	....	....	....	....	....	....	....	1	3	4	1	....	2	5	1	....	....	....
Harbin H. Moore	....	....	....	....	....	....	....	....	....	2	3	6	1	....	....	....	....	....	....
Bethuel F. Morris	....	....	....	....	....	....	....	....	....	1	2	....	....	....	....	....	....	....	....
James Scott	....	....	....	....	....	....	....	....	....	....	1	1	6	2	....	....	....	....	....
David Wallace	....	....	....	....	....	....	....	....	....	....	....	1	....	....	....	....	....	....	....

December 8 and 10, 1832 (Continued)

Ballots

	1st	2nd	3rd	4th	5th	6th	7th	8th	9th	10th	11th	12th	13th	14th	15th	16th	17th	18th	19th
John Test	....	....	....	....	....	....	....	....	....	....	....	....	1	1	....	1	....	....	....
James B. Ray	....	....	....	....	....	....	....	....	....	....	....	....	2	....	....	....	....	....	....
——— Marshall	....	....	....	....	....	....	....	....	....	....	....	....	1	....	....	....	....	....	....
Israel T. Canby	....	....	....	....	....	....	....	....	....	....	....	....	....	1	....	....	....	1	....
William C. Linton	....	....	....	....	....	....	....	....	....	....	....	....	....	....	1	1	1	1	2
Abel C. Pepper	....	....	....	....	....	....	....	....	....	....	....	....	....	....	2	1	....	....	....
H. C. Hammond	....	....	....	....	....	....	....	....	....	....	....	....	....	....	....	1	....	....	....
George Boon	....	....	....	....	....	....	....	....	....	....	....	....	....	....	....	....	1	....	....
John W. Davis	....	....	....	....	....	....	....	....	....	....	....	....	....	....	....	....	....	....	1
Blank or scattering	4	1	2	3	2	1	1	....	....	....	2	2	4	....	....	1	1	3	1

December 8, 1836[11]

Ballots

	1st	2d	3rd	4th	5th	6th	7th	8th	9th
*Oliver H. Smith	35	41	35	34	38	44	57	73	79
Noah Noble	50	49	55	60	65	58	59	64	63
William Hendricks	31	41	47	50	40	37	25	6	1
Ratliff Boon	22	12	....	....	....	....	....	....	....
Tilghman A. Howard	1	....	....	....	....	....	....	....	....
Scattering	7	3	9	3	3	6	5	3	3

December 7, 8, 11, 1838[12]

Ballots

	1st	2nd	3rd	4th	5th	6th	7th	8th	9th	10th	11th	12th	13th	14th	15th	16th	17th	18th
*Albert S. White	....	....	....	....	....	....	....	....	....	....	....	....	....	....	....	....	....	....
Thomas H. Blake	27	29	28	29	29	28	30	29	34	41	52	57	57	51	42	38	43	57
Ratliff Boon	22	21	19	19	19	19	17	18	12	....	....	....	....	....	....	....	....	....
Milton Stapp	33	34	34	35	35	32	31	23	....	....	....	....	....	....	....	....	....	....
Tilghman A. Howard	22	25	27	27	26	28	31	30	32	38	36	32	33	34	41	45	44	34
Charles Dewey	28	28	28	27	27	26	26	14	14	12	4	3	4	8	14	15	11	5
John Dumont	11	9	7	7	7	7	6	4	9	4	....	....	....	....	....	....	....	....
Noah Noble	1	1	2	1	2	4	3	26	44	50	53	53	51	52	48	47	47	45
William W. Wick	1	....	....	....	....	....	....	....	....	....	....	....	....	....	....	....	....	....
William Hendricks	....	....	....	....	....	....	....	....	....	....	....	....	....	....	....	....	....	3
Samuel Judah	....	....	....	....	....	....	....	....	....	....	....	....	....	....	....	....	....	....
Richard W. Thompson	....	....	....	....	....	....	....	....	....	....	....	....	....	....	....	....	....	....
Dr. David G. Mitchell	....	....	....	....	....	....	....	....	....	....	....	....	....	....	....	....	....	....
J. H. Thompson	....	....	....	....	....	....	....	....	....	....	....	....	....	....	....	....	....	....
John Tipton	....	....	....	....	....	....	....	....	....	....	....	....	....	....	....	....	....	....
———— Dunn	....	....	....	....	....	....	....	....	....	....	....	....	....	....	....	....	....	....
Samuel Hall	....	....	....	....	....	....	....	....	....	....	....	....	....	....	....	....	....	....
———— Kilgore	....	....	....	....	....	....	....	....	....	....	....	....	....	....	....	....	....	....
John Bryce	....	....	....	....	....	....	....	....	....	....	....	....	....	....	....	....	....	....
Seth M. Leavenworth	....	....	....	....	....	....	....	....	....	....	....	....	....	....	....	....	....	....
N. Biddle	....	....	....	....	....	....	....	....	....	....	....	....	....	....	....	....	....	....

December 7, 8, 11, 1838 (continued)

	19th	20th	21st	22d	23d	24th	25th	26th	27th	28th	29th	30th	31st	32d	33d	34th	35th	36th
Albert S. White	....	....	....	....	....	....	....	....	....	....	....	....	....	2	19	28	52	75
Thomas H. Blake	68	34	33	40	46	52	59	54	59	60	59	60	64	66	60	59	49	37
Ratliff Boon	....	38	3	3	4	3	4	3	3	3	3	3	3	5	2	3	3	1
Milton Stapp	....	....	....	....	....	....	....	....	....	....	....	5	2	3	10	22	10	....
Tilghman A. Howard	29	6	40	29	21	22	15	21	17	15	15	8	9	16	15	10	12	16
Charles Dewey	2	15	11	8	10	8	7	8	3	3	5	4	3	2	6	10	4	1
John Dumont	....	....	....	1	....	1	1	....	....	....	....	....	....	....	....	....	....	....
Noah Noble	44	52	58	60	61	59	59	58	62	63	60	63	61	48	23	6	3	11
William W. Wick	....	....	....	....	....	....	....	....	....	....	....	....	....	....	1	....	1	....
William Hendricks	2	....	....	....	....	....	....	....	....	....	....	....	....	....	....	....	2	....
Samuel Judah	....	....	....	3	1	....	....	....	....	....	....	....	....	....	....	....	....	....
Richard W. Thompson	....	....	....	1	....	....	....	....	....	....	....	....	....	....	....	....	....	....
Dr. David G. Mitchell	....	....	....	....	1	....	....	....	....	....	....	....	....	....	....	....	....	....
J. H. Thompson	....	....	....	....	....	....	....	....	1	....	....	....	....	....	1	....	....	....
John Tipton	....	....	....	....	....	....	....	....	....	1	....	....	....	....	....	1	2	1
——— Dunn	....	....	....	....	....	....	....	....	....	....	....	....	....	....	2	....	....	....
Samuel Hall	....	....	....	....	....	....	....	....	....	....	....	....	....	....	1	1	1	....
——— Kilgore	....	....	....	....	....	....	....	....	....	....	....	....	....	....	2	....	1	....
John Bryce	....	....	....	....	....	....	....	....	....	....	....	....	....	....	1	1	....	....
Seth M. Leavenworth	....	....	....	....	....	....	....	....	....	....	....	....	....	....	....	1	....	....
N. Biddle	....	....	....	....	....	....	....	....	....	....	....	....	....	....	....	....	1	....

January 24, 1843[13]

Ballots

	1st	2d	3rd	4th	5th	6th
*Edward A. Hannegan	3	1	3	2	2	76
Oliver H. Smith	72	75	73	73	70	69
Tilghman A. Howard	74	74	73	73	73	1
Joseph G. Marshall	1	....	....	....	....	4
William Hendricks	....	....	1	1	....	....
Jonathan McCarty	....	....	....	1	5	....

December 6, 1845[14]

*Jesse D. Bright	80
Joseph G. Marshall	66
Blank	2

December 14, 1848[15]

*James Whitcomb	75
Edward A. Hannegan	15
Caleb B. Smith	53
John Law	2
Joseph G. Marshall	1
Blank	3

1 Indiana *House Journal,* 1816-17, pp. 16, 17-18.

2 Term to expire March 3, 1821, as determined by lot.

3 Term to expire March 3, 1819, as determined by lot.

4 *House Journal,* 1818-19, p. 58.

5 *Ibid.,* 1820-21, pp. 76-77.

6 *Ibid.,* 1825, pp. 32-33.

7 *Ibid.,* 1826-27, pp. 92-93.

8 *Ibid.,* 1830-31, pp. 137-38.

9 *Ibid.,* 1831-32, pp. 41-42, 44. This election was held to fill the vacancy caused by Noble's death on February 26, 1831. Robert Hanna was appointed to serve until a successor was elected to complete his term which expired March 3, 1833.

10 *Ibid.,* 1832-33, pp. 48-50, 62-63, 65-67.

11 *Ibid.,* 1836-37, pp. 36-38.

12 *Ibid.,* 1838-39, pp. 47-54, 57-61, 62-65, 76-84, 88-97.

13 *Ibid.,* 1842-43, pp. 490-95.

14 *Ibid.,* 1845-46, p. 59.

15 *Ibid.,* 1848-49, p. 87.

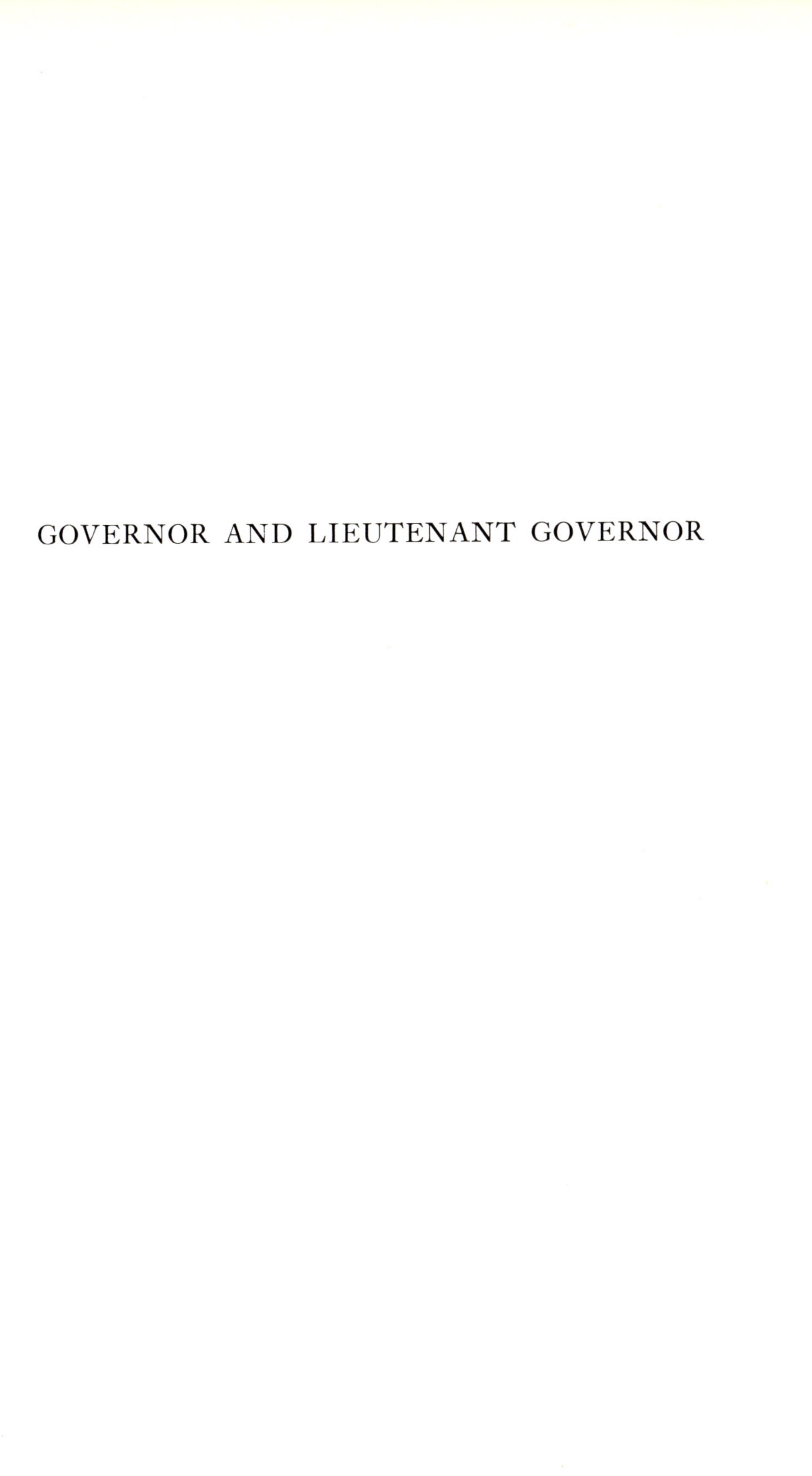

GOVERNOR AND LIEUTENANT GOVERNOR

GOVERNOR

Election August 5, 1816

The official election returns have not been found. The Vincennes *Western Sun* in its issues of August 17 and 24, 1816, gave the vote in four of the state's fifteen counties.

County	Candidates	
	*Jonathan Jennings	Thomas Posey
Jackson	124	22
Knox	174	571
Orange	66	447
Washington	257	359

The total vote for each of the candidates, as given on the returns sent to the Speaker of the House of Representatives and counted in the presence of the two houses of the General Assembly, was: Jennings, 5211; Posey, 3934. *House Journal,* 1816-17, p. 3.

Election August 2, 1819[1]

County	Candidates	
	*Jonathan Jennings	Christopher Harrison
Clark	618	311
Dearborn	1015	161
Fayette	631	20
Floyd	311	6
Franklin	1087	30
Gibson	85	350
Harrison	847	38
Jefferson	447	260
Jennings	189	6
Knox	144	379
Orange	401	170
Pike	99	37
Posey	410	93
Randolph and Wayne	1101	307
Ripley	159	2
Spencer	169	7

	*Jonathan Jennings	Christopher Harrison
Switzerland	516	6
Vigo	349	27
Warrick	125	59
Washington	335	631
Total	9038	2900

[1] The official election returns have not been found. Except for Pike County, the returns given here are from the Corydon *Indiana Gazette,* August 7 to October 23, 1819. They also appeared in the Vincennes *Indiana Centinel,* September 27 to November 6. The Pike County vote is from the *History of Pike and Dubois Counties Indiana* (Goodspeed Bros. & Co., 1885), 291. Returns from the following counties were not given: Crawford, Daviess, Dubois, Jackson, Lawrence, Monroe, Owen, Perry, Sullivan, and Vanderburgh. The total number of votes received by each candidate, as counted on the returns sent to the Speaker of the House, were: Jennings, 9168; Harrison, 2007; Samuel Carr, 80; Peter Allen, one. *House Journal,* 1819-20, p. 26.

August 5, 1822

William Hendricks was unopposed as candidate for governor. He received 18,340 votes. *House Journal,* 1822-23, p. 23.

Election August 1, 1825[1]

County	Candidate	
	*James Brown Ray	Isaac Blackford
Allen	41	55
Bartholomew	238	265
Clark	541	634
Crawford	44	457
Daviess	297	306
Dearborn	886	663
Decatur	278	113
Fayette	690	290
Floyd	305	290
Franklin	824	478
Gibson	55	297
Greene	80	241
Hamilton	79	36
Harrison	490	629
Henry	303	63
Jackson	135	296
Jefferson	299	1040

Jennings	31	432
Johnson	103	64
Knox	230	444
Lawrence	374	386
Madison	91	41
Marion	288	206
Martin	167	65
Monroe	404	158
Montgomery	113	42
Morgan	110	137
Orange	205	608
Owen	91	242
Parke	268	85
Perry	106	171
Pike	43	154
Posey	40	644
Ripley	445	103
Rush	386	120
Scott	maj. of 20	
Shelby	203	122
Spencer	337	73
Sullivan	maj. of 462	
Switzerland	687	133
Union	600	150
Vanderburgh	218	62
Vigo	271	240
Warrick	275	20
Washington	994	515
Wayne	1187	595
Total	13,852	12,165

[1] The official election returns have not been found except for Dearborn County. The other returns given here are from the Vincennes *Western Sun,* with the exception of those for Pike and Union counties. The former are from the *History of Pike and Dubois Counties* (1885), 292, and the latter from the Lawrenceburg *Indiana Polladium,* August 19, 1825. The majorities given for Scott and Sullivan counties are from the Indianapolis *Gazette,* August 16, 1825. No returns have been found for Clay, Dubois, Hendricks, Putnam, Randolph, and Vermillion counties. The total vote for each candidate, as given on the returns sent to the Speaker of the House, were: Ray, 13,040; Blackford, 10,218. *House Journal,* 1825, p. 23. Governor Ray in his first message to the General Assembly stated that returns had not been received from eleven counties. *Messages and Papers of Governor James Brown Ray,* 98-99n.

Election August 4, 1828[1]

County	Candidates		
	*James Brown Ray	Harbin H. Moore	Israel T. Canby
Allen	43	78	14
Bartholomew	233	214	178
Carroll	8	37	77
Clark	335	355	716
Clay	47	35	29
Crawford	170	276	38
Daviess	337	130	123
Dearborn	846	588	674
Decatur	446	127	127
Delaware	45	41	34
Dubois	161	18	84
Fayette	613	227	342
Floyd	156	151	409
Fountain	114	141	258
Franklin	512	573	237
Gibson	19	215	357
Greene	188	171	188
Hamilton	147	74	11
Hancock	83	21	2
Harrison	350	768	203
Hendricks	103	64	0
Henry	470	63	37
Jackson	33	256	335
Jefferson	628	360	506
Jennings	394	74	41
Johnson	258	87	69
Knox	390	158	326
Lawrence	196	95	755
Madison	126	50	6
Marion	600	259	56
Martin	111	92	103
Monroe	168	98	536
Montgomery	142	78	235
Morgan	327	137	92
Orange	41	335	570
Owen	204	145	60
Parke	218	172	278

Perry	279	128	36
Pike	110	97	73
Posey	64	208	524
Putnam	279	273	192
Randolph	93	131	116
Ripley	371	204	75
Rush	500	331	241
Scott	249	114	58
Shelby	170	250	256
Spencer	236	61	60
Sullivan	105	182	314
Switzerland	316	219	393
Tippecanoe[2]	105	87	70
Union	343	369	281
Vanderburgh	43	156	99
Vermillion	177	193	106
Vigo	225	358	76
Warren	64	34	20
Warrick	50	76	217
Washington	531	496	504
Wayne	1559	168	434
Total	15,131	10,898	12,251

[1] Compiled from the official election returns in the Archives Division, Indiana State Library.

[2] The returns from Randolph Township, Tippecanoe County, were not included because they were not properly prepared.

Election August 1, 1831[1]

County	Candidates[2]		
	*Noah Noble	James G. Read	Milton Stapp
Allen	193	9	6
Bartholomew	407	211	311
Boone	58	100	16
Carroll	171	142	4
Cass	191	29	0
Clark	439	931	218
Clay	56	114	89
Clinton	150	38	9
Crawford	312	180	38

	*Noah Noble	James G. Read	Milton Stapp
Daviess	298	503	22
Dearborn	675	1000	268
Decatur	681	241	66
Deleware	92	71	142
Dubois	35	241	43
Elkhart	159	21	2
Fayette	637	690	107
Floyd	347	466	125
Fountain	578	622	56
Franklin	820	306	77
Gibson	399	425	7
Grant	102	7	0
Greene	194	432	28
Hamilton	232	33	35
Hancock	149	112	13
Harrison	762	192	268
Hendricks	[26]	[311]	[55]
Henry	803	275	17
Jackson	316	404	9
Jefferson	130	529	982
Jennings	200	218	280
Johnson	276	213	213
Knox	[399]	[420]	[130]
Lawrence	661	416	104
Madison	357	84	6
Marion	624	422	228
Martin	69	158	89
Monroe	260	769	32
Montgomery	280	391	309
Morgan	437	335	16
Orange	339	588	23
Owen	257	348	28
Parke	675	508	103
Perry	213	148	87
Pike	172	260	2
Posey	370	645	15
Putnam	629	498	198
Randolph	208	139	138
Ripley	514	215	141
Rush	800	396	174

St. Joseph	111	0	12
Scott	176	241	58
Shelby	534	374	52
Spencer	144	218	6
Sullivan	146	594	53
Switzerland	410	350	233
Tippecanoe	540	498	34
Union	460	372	242
Vanderburgh	167	224	30
Vermillion	528	340	56
Vigo	797	123	41
Warren	303	99	24
Warrick	150	325	24
Washington	[704]	[804]	[50]
Wayne	1196	634	740
	23,518	21,002	6,984

1 Compiled from the official election returns in the Archives Division, Indiana State Library. The returns for Hendricks, Knox, and Washington counties were missing; these have been supplied from the returns in the Vincennes *Western Sun,* September 24, 1831.

2 In addition to the candidates listed, James Scott received eight votes in Greene County, four in Lawrence, five in Montgomery, three in Orange, four in Putnam, thirty-two in Sullivan, and five in Warren. Marion County gave one vote to Robert Hanna, Jr.

Election August 4, 1834[1]

County	Candidates	
	*Noah Noble (W)	James G. Read (D)
Allen	246	112
Bartholomew	657	631
Boone	244	227
Carroll	272	344
Cass	449	53
Clark	672	941
Clay	60	333
Clinton	310	178
Crawford	300	198
Daviess	338	402
Dearborn	1293	1039
Decatur	869	326

	*Noah Noble (W)	James G. Read (D)
Delaware	297	163
Dubois	82	249
Elkhart[2]	172	119
Fayette	945	574
Floyd	588	297
Fountain	655	820
Franklin	1061	384
Gibson	502	494
Grant	111	40
Greene	342	448
Hamilton	366	171
Hancock	295	260
Harrison	665	725
Hendricks	552	411
Henry	984	382
Huntington	257	30
Jackson	383	577
Jefferson	1021	689
Jennings	435	321
Johnson	511	440
Knox[3]	700	435
LaGrange	97	54
LaPorte	328	150
Lawrence	618	533
Madison[4]	532	132
Marion	1020	776
Martin	105	299
Miami	70	20
Monroe	548	673
Montgomery	859	466
Morgan	712	488
Orange	383	692
Owen	306	386
Parke	687	654
Perry	325	78
Pike	182	280
Posey	415	722
Putnam	854	748
Randolph	432	138

Ripley	741	239
Rush	1219	704
St. Joseph	348	98
Scott	304	291
Shelby	872	492
Spencer	240	163
Sullivan	242	603
Switzerland	793	297
Tippecanoe	904	597
Union	709	559
Vanderburgh	243	206
Vermillion	563	455
Vigo	939	293
Warren	443	206
Warrick	173	273
Washington	658	1053
Wayne	2225	578
White	50	28
Total	36,773	27,257

[1] Compiled from the official election returns in the Archives Division, Indiana State Library.

[2] In making the returns for Elkhart County, the county clerk listed separately the votes from one township which were received a day late. If these were accepted they would add to the totals listed here 24 votes for Noble, 39 for Read.

[3] Knox County gave one vote to Christopher Harrison.

[4] Twenty-four other votes from Madison County were intended for James G. Read, but the voters had written the name as James B. and James C. Read.

Election August 7, 1837[1]

County	Candidates	
	*David Wallace (W)	John Dumont (W)
Adams[2]	70	0
Allen	548	7
Bartholomew	945	198
Boone	283	558
Brown	32	170
Carroll	367	648
Cass	560	378
Clark	179	1774
Clay	605	20

	*David Wallace (W)	John Dumont (W)
Clinton	287	400
Crawford	16	502
Daviess	799	168
Dearborn	1002	1906
Decatur	608	1011
Delaware	896	22
Dubois	160	172
Elkhart	[718]	[4]
Fayette	[1201]	[278]
Floyd	1280	42
Fountain	1293	228
Franklin	1201	671
Fulton	51	56
Gibson	372	710
Grant	[324]	[30]
Greene	542	292
Hamilton	771	111
Hancock	510	396
Harrison	143	1344
Hendricks	805	602
Henry	1688	230
Huntington	63	63
Jackson	120	1008
Jay	115	5
Jefferson	1289	906
Jennings	677	232
Johnson	876	372
Knox	537	738
Kosciusko	264	78
LaGrange	215	150
Lake	80	52
LaPorte	739	202
Lawrence	559	782
Madison	1121	30
Marion	1473	922
Marshall	129	51
Martin	306	116
Miami	234	36
Monroe	494	777

Montgomery	1759	179
Morgan	737	450
Noble	157	1
Orange	600	486
Owen	337	632
Parke	453	1268
Perry	60	576
Pike	286	267
Porter	157	64
Posey	59	1158
Putnam	1349	528
Randolph	672	382
Ripley	292	839
Rush	1122	1020
St. Joseph[3]	973	61
Scott	[96]	[552]
Shelby	315	1211
Spencer	40	544
Steuben[4]	31	57
Sullivan	98	855
Switzerland	185	1200
Tippecanoe	1199	850
Union	564	500
Vanderburgh	383	200
Vermillion	460	793
Vigo	1112	280
Wabash	136	60
Warren	592	272
Warrick	408	315
Washington	1291	725
Wayne	2414	1028
Wells	61	0
White	122	114
Total	46,067	36,915

[1] Compiled from the official election returns in the Archives Division. Returns from Elkhart, Fayette, Grant, and Scott were missing and have been supplied from the returns in the Indianapolis *Indiana Journal,* August 26 and October 7, 1837.

[2] Two votes were cast in Adams County for Jeremiah Roe.

[3] St. Joseph County gave three votes to Gamaliel Taylor and one to Abel C. Pepper.

[4] Steuben County gave one vote to Jeremiah Tillotson.

Election August 3, 1840[1]

County	Candidates	
	*Samuel Bigger (W)	Tilghman A. Howard (D)
Adams	144	135
Allen	558	471
Bartholomew	983	683
Benton	25	42
Blackford	68	148
Boone	[709]	[720]
Brown	49	279
Carroll	672	805
Cass	593	407
Clark	[1038]	[1243]
Clay	376	521
Clinton	538	750
Crawford	429	357
Daviess	740	564
Dearborn	1813	1676
Decatur	[1268]	[790]
DeKalb[2]	96	122
Delaware	818	512
Dubois	[230]	[281]
Elkhart	610	673
Fayette	1103	765
Floyd	[885]	[819]
Fountain	951	1222
Franklin	1188	1089
Fulton	211	135
Gibson	746	697
Grant	442	347
Greene	667	678
Hamilton	903	685
Hancock	660	574
Harrison	1241	938
Hendricks	1178	716

Henry	1579	844
Huntington	117	159
Jackson	597	791
Jasper	60	84
Jay	250	225
Jefferson	1692	1096
Jennings	799	479
Johnson	610	962
Knox	1024	679
Kosciusko	393	358
LaGrange	407	290
Lake	106	136
LaPorte	1004	778
Lawrence	957	961
Madison	927	474
Marion	1663	1360
Marshall	154	167
Martin	315	378
Miami	297	272
Monroe	739	936
Montgomery	1414	1257
Morgan	1033	921
Noble	213	272
Orange	678	947
Owen	715	660
Parke	1313	1061
Perry	483	232
Pike	472	354
Porter	220	219
Posey	585	1009
Pulaski	[59]	[58]
Putnam	1571	1285
Randolph	1028	514
Ripley	918	569
Rush	1591	1225
St. Joseph	807	470
Scott	406	377
Shelby	964	1123
Spencer	516	394
Steuben	256	196
Sullivan	339	1011

	*Samuel Bigger (W)	Tilghman A. Howard (D)
Switzerland	1044	864
Tippecanoe	1503	1289
Union	[782]	[641]
Vanderburgh	570	384
Vermillion	840	655
Vigo	1408	647
Wabash	278	210
Warren	727	389
Warrick	279	703
Washington	1040	1433
Wayne	2897	1272
Wells	84	112
White	191	159
Whitley	86	89
Total	62,932	54,274

[1] Compiled from the official election returns in the Archives Division. Those from Boone, Clark, Decatur, Dubois, Floyd, Pulaski and Union counties were missing. These have been supplied from the returns in the Indianapolis *Indiana Journal* (semiweekly), August 27, 1840.

[2] The returns from Concord Township, DeKalb County, were received too late to be included. They were: Bigger, 38; Howard, 23.

Election August 7, 1843[1]

County	Candidates		
	*James Whitcomb (D)	Samuel Bigger (W)	Elizur Deming (Liberty)
Adams	236	227	......
Allen	674	720	......
Bartholomew	905	899	9
Benton	27	26	......
Blackford	212	70	......
Boone	764	716	2
Brown	414	50	......
Carroll	825	616	6
Cass	550	668	9
Clark	1310	1031	......
Clay[2]	587	373	......
Clinton	793	522	11

Crawford	381	408	......
Daviess	[592]	[769]	......
Dearborn	1769	1503	25
Decatur	945	1174	63
DeKalb[3]	290	212	4
Delaware	693	808	......
Dubois	363	224	......
Elkhart	843	668	4
Fayette	789	923	4
Floyd	911	900	......
Fountain	1231	799	2
Franklin	1290	1055	7
Fulton	215	272	......
Gibson	707	710	......
Grant	475	336	160
Greene	744	672	......
Hamilton	761	815	130
Hancock	690	685	......
Harrison	976	1091	......
Hendricks	777	1038	3
Henry	902	1110	191
Huntington	279	206	1
Jackson	870	565	......
Jasper	179	123	2
Jay	353	355	......
Jefferson	1289	1576	17
Jennings	543	854	4
Johnson	1066	628	8
Knox[4]	628	934	......
Kosciusko	451	493	......
LaGrange	383	436	12
Lake	193	102	4
LaPorte	699	839	54
Lawrence	908	905	......
Madison	774	790	......
Marion	1523	1583	20
Marshall	229	169	32
Martin	348	287	2
Miami	451	481	......
Monroe	956	696	13
Montgomery	1275	1315	1

	James Whitcomb (D)	Samuel Bigger (W)	Elizur Deming (Liberty)
Morgan	1003	808	10
Noble	340	277	......
Orange	925	642	......
Owen	818	641	1
Parke	1088	1295	......
Perry	264	468	......
Pike	421	390	......
Porter	249	233	7
Posey	933	709	......
Pulaski	95	99	......
Putnam	1362	1320	4
Randolph	701	768	183
Ripley	637	925	62
Rush	1147	1350	24
St. Joseph	606	776	27
Scott	429	432	......
Shelby	1159	960	......
Spencer[5]	380	522	......
Steuben	219	230	40
Sullivan	1144	413	......
Switzerland	974	906	2
Tippecanoe	1361	1266	39
Union	588	560	59
Vanderburgh	488	556	1
Vermillion	692	607	......
Vigo	762	1274	......
Wabash[6]	477	495	5
Warren	382	715	1
Warrick	781	330	......
Washington	1471	1005	......
Wayne	1282	1807	418
Wells	239	173	......
White	173	203	......
Whitley	156	139	......
Total	60,784	58,721	1683

[1] Compiled from the official election returns in the Archives Division. The return from Daviess County was missing and has been supplied from the Indianapolis *Indiana State Journal* (weekly), August 22, 1843.

[2] The returns from Perry Township, Clay County, were first rejected but later included by order of the Governor. See above, 109n. The vote was: for Whitcomb, 73; for Bigger, 17.

[3] William Culbertson received one vote for governor in DeKalb County.

[4] The returns from Decker Township, Knox County, were received too late to be included. They were: for Bigger, 22; for Whitcomb, 56.

[5] The returns from Carter Township, Spencer County, were rejected because the list of voters did not accompany the return. The vote was: for Bigger, 49; for Whitcomb, 17.

[6] Wabash County gave one vote to William Steele.

Election August 3, 1846[1]

County	Candidates		
	*James Whitcomb (D)	Joseph G. Marshall (W)	Stephen C. Stevens (Liberty)
Adams	282	192	......
Allen	793	716	2
Bartholomew	959	840	7
Benton	70	43	......
Blackford	269	78	......
Boone	761	681	28
Brown	407	60	......
Carroll	858	703	......
Cass	676	790	......
Clark	1113	954	......
Clay	597	347	......
Clinton	757	589	15
Crawford	411	410	......
Daviess	716	651	......
Dearborn	1615	1232	23
Decatur	897	1009	68
DeKalb	366	219	5[2]
Delaware	542	734	23
Dubois	496	177	......
Elkhart	882	656	11
Fayette	752	1017	22
Floyd	929	921	......
Fountain	1100	776	36
Franklin[3]	1381	1109	2
Fulton	267	273	1
Gibson	726	682	7
Grant	499	341	206
Greene	804	677	......

	*James Whitcomb (D)	Joseph G. Marshall (W)	Stephen C. Stevens (Liberty)
Hamilton	673	735	168
Hancock	651	624	10
Harrison	971	1108	......
Hendricks	698	1082	53
Henry	814	1180	228
[Howard] Richardville	213	190	27
Huntington	323	270	2
Jackson	802	530	......
Jasper	179	132	9
Jay[4]	359	285	29
Jefferson	1187	1646	25
Jennings	629	747	30
Johnson[5]	973	634	7
Knox	666	862	......
Kosciusko	524	708	4
LaGrange	504	549	50
Lake	184	132	3
LaPorte	867	943	66
Lawrence	1017	927	......
Madison	743	612	24
Marion	1509	1587	43
Marshall	353	253	43
Martin	484	235	3
Miami	582	523	......
Monroe	1002	703	18
Montgomery	1396	1390	14
Morgan	1013	972	29
Noble	506	457	4
Ohio	390	426	8
Orange	956	654	......
Owen	866	742	......
Parke	1249	1215	17
Perry	307	450	......
Pike	508	372	......
Porter	304	294	21
Posey	1104	434	......
Pulaski	159	134	......
Putnam	1327	1420	4
Randolph	751	842	147

Ripley	726	913	76
Rush	1208	1370	37
St. Joseph	702	755	76
Scott	411	474	......
Shelby	1075	948	......
Spencer	490	513	......
Steuben	375	286	30
Sullivan	1108	358	......
Switzerland	870	889	46
Tippecanoe	1454	1425	72
Tipton	137	95	......
Union	599	626	68
Vanderburgh	510	524	......
Vermillion	703	666	......
Vigo	837	1272	......
Wabash	634	670	22
Warren	391	607	6
Warrick	823	314	......
Washington	1334	1039	......
Wayne	1251	1921	310
Wells	269	123	5
White	270	243	7
Whitley	259	231	4
Total	64,104	60,138	2301

1 Compiled from the official election returns in the Archives Division.

2 Another ballot intended for Stevens was discarded because the name was written Stearns.

3 Franklin County gave two votes to John Burk.

4 Jay County gave seventeen votes to Joseph S. Harding.

5 Johnson County gave one vote to J. C. Stephenson and one to David Wallace.

Election August 6, 1849[1]

County	Candidates		
	*Joseph A. Wright (D)	John A. Matson (W)	James H. Cravens (FS)
Adams	455	325	......
Allen	967	725	3
Bartholomew	1121	942	10
Benton	88	75	1

	*Joseph A. Wright (D)	John A. Matson (W)	James H. Cravens (FS)
Blackford	321	91	3
Boone	914	791	25
Brown	545	88	......
Carroll	868	679	28
Cass	923	921	39
Clark	1357	1032	3
Clay	838	399	......
Clinton	974	723	24
Crawford	497	551	......
Daviess	826	678	......
Dearborn	1564	1145	8
Decatur	1170	1286	49
DeKalb	568	298	9
Delaware	754	797	31
Dubois	604	191	4
Elkhart	1266	881	......
Fayette	889	1002	32
Floyd	[1194]	[1056]	[4]
Fountain	1218	784	65
Franklin	1289	1217	11
Fulton	462	437	......
Gibson	930	875	1
Grant	716	631	15
Greene	1142	819	......
Hamilton	833	810	215
Hancock	800	644	29
Harrison	1059	1209	2
Hendricks	774	1006	58
Henry	[1287]	[1437]	[115]
Howard[2]	425	340	......
Huntington	367	351	2
Jackson	1109	542	......
Jasper	232	205	16
Jay	376	273	36
Jefferson	1499	1958	44
Jennings	739	875	73
Johnson	1248	643	4
Knox	675	928	......
Kosciusko	700	864	29

LaGrange	578	622	17
Lake	269	185	......
LaPorte	959	1102	21
Lawrence	1076	935	7
Madison	1018	821	24
Marion	1917	1848	28
Marshall	450	329	22
Martin	575	295	......
Miami	855	771	28
Monroe	1136	723	20
Montgomery	1541	1473	43
Morgan	1262	1109	27
Noble	667	515	8
Ohio	458	414	......
Orange	1053	758	2
Owen	988	798	3
Parke	1322	1298	8
Perry	381	547	......
Pike	591	476	......
Porter	418	352	37
Posey	1341	727	......
Pulaski	248	155	......
Putnam	1558	1509	8
Randolph	753	528	318
Ripley	791	963	122
Rush	1464	1545	63
St. Joseph	767	908	123
Scott	509	525	5
Shelby	1397	916	71
Spencer	534	591	......
Steuben	427	335	112
Sullivan	1279	455	......
Switzerland	1184	988	4
Tippecanoe	1204	1234	129
Tipton[3]	227	170	2
Union	650	520	124
Vanderburgh	660	597	......
Vermillion	792	740	4
Vigo	970	1334	......
Wabash	773	883	40
Warren	439	662	50

	*Joseph A. Wright (D)	John A. Matson (W)	James H. Cravens (FS)
Warrick	952	463	4
Washington	1646	1018	6
Wayne	1282	1741	561
Wells	403	244	21
White	303	265	26
Whitley	346	307	......
Total	76,996	67,218	3076

[1] Compiled from the official election returns in the Archives Division. The returns for Floyd and Henry counties were missing and have been supplied from the Indianapolis *Indiana Journal* (weekly), September 3, 1849.

[2] Howard County gave three votes to Ephraim Trabu (or Trabue).

[3] In Tipton County, James A. Matson received two votes that were no doubt intended for John A. Matson.

LIEUTENANT GOVERNOR

Election August 5, 1816

The official returns for this election have not been found. The Vincennes *Western Sun* in its issues of August 17 and 24, 1816, gave the vote in four of the state's fifteen counties.

County	Candidates					
	*Christopher Harrison	John Vawter	Abel Findley	John Johnson	Davis Floyd	Amos Lane
Jackson	138					
Knox	654	50				
Orange	417	59				
Washington	577	38				

The total vote for each of the candidates, as given on the returns sent to the Speaker of the House of Representatives and counted in the presence of the two houses of the General Assembly, were: Harrison, 6570; Vawter, 847; Findley, 18; Johnson, 14; Floyd, 13; and Lane, 12. *House Journal,* 1816-17, p. 3.

Election August 2, 1819[1]

County	Candidates	
	*Ratliff Boon	John DePauw
Clark	842	156
Dearborn	902	231
Fayette	129	478
Floyd	224	83
Franklin	777	313
Gibson	260	115
Harrison	693	146
Jefferson	320	390
Jennings	6	165
Knox	316	165
Orange	405	169
Posey	418	16
Randolph and Wayne	858	608
Ripley	10	147

	*Ratliff Boon	John DePauw
Spencer	59	7
Switzerland	461	59
Vigo	142	173
Warrick	59	7
Washington	516	454
Total	7397	3882

[1] Copied from the returns in the Corydon *Indiana Gazette,* August 7 to October 23, 1819. They also appeared in the Vincennes *Indiana Centinel* between August 14 and November 6. The returns from Crawford, Daviess, Dubois, Jackson, Lawrence, Monroe, Owen, Perry, Pike, Sullivan, and Vanderburgh are not given. The number of votes received by each candidate, as counted on the returns sent to the Speaker of the House, were: Boon, 7150; DePauw, 3422; James McKnight, five; Dennis Pennington, two; Christopher Harrison, two; and Abraham Markle, two. *House Journal,* 1819-20, p. 26.

Election August 5, 1822[1]

County	Candidates			
	*Ratliff Boon	William Polke	Erasmus Powell	David H. Maxwell
Clark	564	201	47	159
Dearborn	378	408	803	22
Dubois	136	24	2	1
Fayette and Union	339	228	613	50
Franklin	685	45	406	35
Gibson	259	201	......	3
Harrison	410	549	90	9
Jackson	234	12	3	287
Jefferson	230	23	41	837
Jennings	18	41	......	215
Knox	73	519	8	22
Lawrence	419	37	......	18
Marion	88	11	150	61
Martin	177	14	......	......
Monroe	146	36	32	237
Orange	487	43	1	44
Perry	91	108	......	......
Posey	354	151	11	......
Ripley	25	69	306	35
Spencer	170	81	21	1
Vanderburgh	158	138	......	1

Warrick	258	8	1	1
Washington	377	411	216	244
Wayne	538	111	417	27
Total	6614	3469	3168	2309

[1] Copied from the returns in the Vincennes *Western Sun,* August 24, 1822. They are incomplete, the following counties being missing: Crawford, Daviess, Decatur, Greene, Henry, Morgan, Owen, Parke, Pike, Putnam, Randolph, Rush, Scott, Shelby, Sullivan, Switzerland, and Vigo. The total vote on the returns sent to the Speaker of the House and counted in the presence of the House and Senate was: Boon, 7809; Polke, 4044; Powell, 3603; Maxwell, 2366. *House Journal,* 1822-23, pp. 16-17, 23.

Election August 1, 1825[1]

County	Candidates			
	*John H. Thompson	Samuel Milroy	Dennis Pennington	General Washington Johnston	Elisha Harrison

County	*John H. Thompson	Samuel Milroy	Dennis Pennington	General Washington Johnston	Elisha Harrison
Clark	875	197	......	......	......
Dearborn[2]	421	913	14	38	79
Decatur	69	......	283	......	......
Floyd	157	219	92	9	123
Gibson	17	201	25	79	32
Greene	276	50	......	......	......
Hamilton	6	106	......	......	......
Harrison	282	261	505	9	60
Jefferson	1134	13	......	......	......
Jennings	445	12	......	......	......
Knox	60	82	10	474	29
Lawrence	407	279	......	......	......
Madison	47	76	......	......	......
Marion	247	234	......	......	......
Monroe	191	359	......	......	......
Morgan	204	32	......	......	......
Orange	68	18	2	......	106
Owen	254	51	......	......	......
Switzerland	473	351	......	......	......
Vigo	......	371	......	......	......
Washington	783	645	......	......	......
Total	6416	4470	931	609	429

[1] The official election returns have not been found except for Dearborn County. The other returns are from the Vincennes *Western Sun* and Lawrence-

burg *Indiana Palladium* for August, 1825. The latter gave the vote only for the two main candidates. No returns have been found for Allen, Bartholomew, Clay, Crawford, Daviess, Dubois, Fayette, Franklin, Hendricks, Henry, Jackson, Johnson, Martin, Montgomery, Parke, Perry, Pike, Posey, Putnam, Randolph, Ripley, Rush, Scott, Shelby, Spencer, Sullivan, Union, Vanderburgh, Vermillion, Warrick and Wayne counties. The total vote for each candidate, as given on the returns sent to the Speaker of the House were: Thompson, 10,781; Milroy, 7496; Pennington, 1496; Johnston, 851; Harrison, 1434; and Scattering, 84. *House Journal,* 1825-26, p. 23.

[2] Dearborn County also gave 31 votes to Joseph Warner.

Election August 4, 1828[1]

County	Candidates	
	*Milton Stapp	Abel C. Pepper
Allen	93	40
Bartholomew	313	278
Carroll	35	86
Clark	593	739
Clay	79	33
Crawford	356	71
Daviess	360	202
Dearborn	275	1810
Decatur	177	506
Delaware	51	43
Dubois	36	137
Fayette	718	432
Floyd	181	504
Fountain	217	288
Franklin	850	438
Gibson	153	289
Greene	237	243
Hamilton[2]	216	5
Hancock	84	15
Harrison	455	392
Hendricks	140	94
Henry	453	68
Jackson	34	520
Jefferson	1143	337
Jennings	478	20
Johnson	273	47
Knox	454	402
Lawrence	141	741

Madison	177	......
Marion	737	159
Martin	183	85
Monroe	262	532
Montgomery	227	218
Morgan	452	95
Orange	183	627
Owen	200	176
Parke	453	208
Perry	119	22
Pike	79	79
Posey	203	451
Putnam	452	223
Randolph	191	113
Ripley	146	473
Rush	462	576
Scott	228	175
Shelby	159	493
Spencer	85	73
Sullivan	201	383
Switzerland[3]	232	691
Tippecanoe	155	103
Union	633	309
Vanderburgh	174	110
Vermillion	276	193
Vigo	561	86
Warren	87	26
Warrick	70	241
Washington	170	1187
Wayne	1743	375
Total	17,895	17,262

[1] Compiled from the official election returns in the Archives Division, Indiana State Library.

[2] Hamilton County gave one vote to William Stapp.

[3] Switzerland County gave Samuel Milroy ten votes.

Election August 1, 1831[1]

County	Candidates[2]		
	*David Wallace	Ross Smiley	James Gregory
Allen	205	2	......
Bartholomew	180	340	310
Boone	91	27	29
Carroll	167	147	......
Cass	217	1	......
Clark	511	849	97
Clay	129	97	12
Clinton	148	46	3
Crawford	343	56	100
Daviess	629	167	10
Dearborn	764	1033	102
Decatur	253	211	510
Delaware	125	143	23
Dubois	97	93	14
Elkhart	167	10	......
Fayette	442	753	219
Floyd	402	403	53
Fountain	900	302	44
Franklin	926	245	20
Gibson	275	365	5
Grant	76	1	......
Greene	145	112	58
Hamilton	241	31	16
Hancock	78	171	21
Harrison	795	86	215
Hendricks	[139]	[282]	[169]
Henry	110	295	570
Jackson	132	444	112
Jefferson	838	590	160
Jennings	329	136	200
Johnson	166	508	10
Knox	[499]	[350]	[68]
Lawrence	278	336	484
Madison	183	195	31
Marion	531	169	135
Martin	195	52	66

Monroe	356	730	6
Montgomery	534	416	18
Morgan	254	337	108
Orange	333	298	145
Owen	407	166	22
Parke	988	227	30
Perry	236	......	11
Pike	265	38	......
Posey	266	486	2
Putnam	898	343	20
Randolph	244	151	63
Ripley	418	235	190
Rush	467	690	208
St. Joseph	106	6	6
Scott	262	181	......
Shelby	45	373	531
Spencer	116	131	......
Sullivan	300	442	......
Switzerland	246	424	256
Tippecanoe	608	457	......
Union	286	512	255
Vanderburgh	274	78	10
Vermillion	702	185	11
Vigo	857	22	2
Warren	256	38	105
Warrick	176	190	1
Washington	[547]	[623]	[163]
Wayne	648	675	1134
Total	22,801	17,502	7163

[1] Compiled from the official election returns in the Archives Division, Indiana State Library. The returns for Hendricks, Knox, and Washington counties were missing; these have been supplied from the returns in the Vincennes *Western Sun,* September 24, 1831.

[2] In addition to the candidates listed, Amos Lane received 157 votes: one in Elkhart, 121 in Greene, two in Madison, one in Orange, four in Parke, seventeen in Posey, and eleven in Spencer County; Alexander S. Burnett received 73 votes: thirteen in Dearborn, two in Decatur, twenty in Lawrence, one in Morgan, eighteen in Orange, three in Parke, three in Perry, eight in Spencer, four in Vigo, and one in Warren County. Marion County gave one vote to James Brown Ray and Switzerland gave eight to Copeland P. J. Arion.

Election August 4, 1834[1]

County	Candidates	
	*David Wallace (W)	David V. Culley (D)
Allen	244	112
Bartholomew	626	613
Boone	261	187
Carroll	290	312
Cass	459	37
Clark	755	767
Clay	162	167
Clinton	318	166
Crawford	373	14
Daviess	476	233
Dearborn	1012	1292
Decatur	861	330
Delaware	341	49
Dubois	120	118
Elkhart[2]	150	136
Fayette	960	547
Floyd	717	78
Fountain	1226	205
Franklin	162	356
Gibson	441	342
Grant	135	8
Greene	296	402
Hamilton	366	168
Hancock	357	180
Harrison	916	125
Hendricks	571	277
Henry	978	303
Huntington	261	25
Jackson	390	486
Jefferson	1179	495
Jennings	476	242
Johnson	443	250
Knox	839	238
LaGrange	88	62
LaPorte[3]	242	145
Lawrence	608	406

Madison	425	45
Marion	1038	769
Martin	189	196
Miami	88	4
Monroe	541	664
Montgomery	1065	216
Morgan	687	362
Orange	365	485
Owen	306	346
Parke	897	315
Perry	350	29
Pike	129	150
Posey	428	601
Putnam	940	480
Randolph	436	88
Ripley	750	227
Rush	1250	595
St. Joseph	341	83
Scott	377	192
Shelby	694	628
Spencer	155	86
Sullivan	333	448
Switzerland	771	295
Tippecanoe	917	570
Union	699	550
Vanderburgh	198	113
Vermillion	786	213
Vigo	1027	174
Warren	495	150
Warrick	142	224
Washington	971	532
Wayne	2079	638
White[4]	50	23
Total	38,018	20,364

[1] Compiled from the official election returns in the Archives Division.

[2] In making the returns from Elkhart County, the votes from one township which were received a day late were listed separately. If these were accepted they would add to the totals listed here: 24 for Wallace and 39 for Culley.

[3] Five other LaPorte County votes were no doubt intended for David Wallace but the voters had given the name as William Wallace and A. Wallace.

[4] White County also gave five votes to Ross Smiley.

Election August 7, 1837[1]

County	Candidates[2]	
	*David Hillis (W)	Alexander S. Burnett (D)
Adams	68	......
Allen	524	1
Bartholomew	977	61
Boone	569	22
Brown	88	47
Carroll	360	642
Cass	863	21
Clark	412	1449
Clay	577	25
Clinton	338	334
Crawford	270	137
Daviess	268	625
Dearborn	1435	1424
Decatur	1379	174
Delaware	926	......
Dubois	146	70
Elkhart	[705]	......
Fayette	[1034]	[411]
Floyd	502	667
Fountain	1163	185
Franklin	1145	370
Fulton	102	7
Gibson	406	545
Grant	[324]	[7]
Greene	397	118
Hamilton	830	27
Hancock	595	253
Harrison	517	584
Hendricks	1190	49
Henry	1487	130
Huntington	123	......
Jackson	194	755
Jay	110	......
Jefferson	1632	450
Jennings	686	210
Johnson	849	245

Knox	776	424
Kosciusko	284	45
LaGrange	281	......
Lake	88	12
LaPorte	703	104
Lawrence	359	792
Madison	1122	......
Marion	1788	444
Marshall	142	......
Martin	168	217
Miami	270	......
Monroe	781	403
Montgomery	1901	29
Morgan	752	247
Noble	131	......
Orange	260	792
Owen	570	179
Parke	574	637
Perry	402	139
Pike	186	56
Porter	181	25
Posey	76	166[3]
Putnam	885	444
Randolph	806	33
Ripley	714	318
Rush	1152	706
St. Joseph	1027	......
Scott	[99]	[455]
Shelby	50	104
Spencer	294	219
Steuben	43	......
Sullivan	239	646
Switzerland	520	800
Tippecanoe	1198	836
Union	640	277
Vanderburgh	344	214
Vermillion	742	444
Vigo	889	399
Wabash	186	5
Warren	773	6
Warrick	327	194

	*David Hillis (W)	Alexander S. Burnett (D)
Washington	575	1487
Wayne	2831	486
Wells	27	......
White	188	......
Total	49,535	22,829

1 Compiled from the official election returns in the Archives Division. Those from Elkhart, Fayette, Grant, and Scott counties were missing and have been supplied from the returns in the Indianapolis *Indiana Journal,* August 26 and October 7, 1837.

2 In addition to the candidates listed, Abel C. Pepper received 174 votes: one from Hamilton County, two from Henry, 58 from LaGrange, 49 from LaPorte, 27 from Noble, 27 from Steuben, three from Union, and seven from Warren. Gamaliel Taylor received 129 votes: 85 from Henry County, 44 from Union. Jefferson County gave 47 votes to Erastus Colt; St. Joseph gave six to Samuel Williams; Steuben County one to Hiram Parker, and Warren County 31 to Rufus Haymond.

3 Judging from the vote cast in Posey County for the gubernatorial candidates (59 for Wallace and 1158 for Dumont), the vote for Burnett should have been larger. No correction was found for this figure which was given in the original return.

Election August 3, 1840[1]

County	Candidates	
	*Samuel Hall (W)	Benjamin S. Tuley (D)
Adams	149	133
Allen	555	474
Bartholomew	977	684
Benton	25	42
Blackford	69	145
Boone	[704]	[721]
Brown	50	279
Carroll	670	807
Cass	594	402
Clark	[1037]	[1234]
Clay	378	511
Clinton	540	741
Crawford	432	351
Daviess	738	557
Dearborn	1808	1678

Decatur	[1269]	[788]
DeKalb[2]	96	122
Delaware	801	521
Dubois	[235]	[265]
Elkhart	610	671
Fayette	1102	759
Floyd	[882]	[813]
Fountain	951	1213
Franklin	1188	1087
Fulton	216	131
Gibson	744	668
Grant	441	348
Greene	666	674
Hamilton	895	684
Hancock	657	566
Harrison	1244	930
Hendricks	1179	705
Henry	1573	840
Huntington	114	158
Jackson	599	771
Jasper	60	84
Jay	251	223
Jefferson	1686	1091
Jennings	797	476
Johnson	609	953
Knox	1027	666
Kosciusko	397	349
LaGrange	406	291
Lake	107	135
LaPorte	1009	770
Lawrence	958	960
Madison	879	481
Marion	1671	1344
Marshall	156	164
Martin	318	368
Miami	296	271
Monroe	757	912
Montgomery	1421	1246
Morgan	1031	914
Noble	213	269
Orange	690	917

	*Samuel Hall (W)	Benjamin S. Tuley (D)
Owen	716	653
Parke	1322	1042
Perry	476	213
Pike	477	345
Porter	222	217
Posey	595	973
Pulaski	[60]	[57]
Putnam	1561	1256
Randolph	1018	511
Ripley	913	569
Rush	1570	1222
St. Joseph	812	465
Scott	406	372
Shelby	973	1115
Spencer	521	367
Steuben	256	196
Sullivan	331	999
Switzerland	1047	859
Tippecanoe	1512	1279
Union	[783]	[636]
Vanderburgh	572	373
Vermillion	844	649
Vigo	1399	626
Wabash	279	209
Warren	736	385
Warrick	280	691
Washington	1031	1420
Wayne	2875	1274
Wells	84	110
White	190	159
Whitley	86	88
Total	62,874	53,687

[1] Compiled from the official election returns in the Archives Division. The returns from Boone, Clark, Decatur, Dubois, Floyd, Pulaski, and Union counties have not been found; the vote from those counties has been supplied from the Indianapolis *Indiana Journal* (semiweekly), August 27, 1840.

[2] The returns from Concord Township, DeKalb County, were received too late to be included. They were: for Hall, 38; for Tuley, 23.

Election August 7, 1843[1]

County	Candidates		
	*Jesse D. Bright (D)	John H. Bradley (W)	Stephen S. Harding (Liberty)
Adams	240	223	......
Allen	679	705	......
Bartholomew	908	873	8
Benton	27	24	......
Blackford	213	68	......
Boone	752	704	......
Brown	424	39	......
Carroll	834	605	5
Cass	551	668	2
Clark	1329	994	......
Clay[2]	586	331	......
Clinton	789	522	11
Crawford	393	370	......
Daviess	[589]	[670]	......
Dearborn	1775	1464	25
Decatur	941	1146	70
DeKalb	293	210	4
Delaware	688	799	......
Dubois	355	207	......
Elkhart	840	669	4
Fayette	786	926	4
Floyd	911	892	......
Fountain	1264	765	......
Franklin	1285	1059	5
Fulton	218	260	......
Gibson	680	675	......
Grant	472	336	163
Greene	728	617	......
Hamilton	766	798	132
Hancock	747	612	......
Harrison	978	1042	......
Hendricks	775	1012	3
Henry	899	1095	194
Huntington	282	201	......
Jackson	864	552	......
Jasper	179	124	......

	*Jesse D. Bright (D)	John H. Bradley (W)	Stephen S. Harding (Liberty)
Jay	352	357	......
Jefferson	1373	1467	11
Jennings	565	820	4
Johnson	1063	615	8
Knox[3]	618	909	......
Kosciusko	453	491	......
LaGrange	385	434	13
Lake	193	103	2
LaPorte	716	792	54
Lawrence	865	853	......
Madison	782	761	......
Marion	1536	1568	19
Marshall	232	157	31
Martin	329	269	2
Miami	460	473	......
Monroe	967	684	13
Montgomery	1275	1307	......
Morgan	995	808	10
Noble	346	273	......
Orange	919	620	......
Owen	809	621	1
Parke	1094	1279	......
Perry	269	399	......
Pike	393	388	......
Porter	254	223	9
Posey	927	676	......
Pulaski	96	97	......
Putnam	1363	1291	......
Randolph	706	748	182
Ripley	675	847	82
Rush	1140	1333	24
St. Joseph	606	768	28
Scott	433	424	......
Shelby	1181	929	......
Spencer[4]	383	468	......
Steuben	219	229	40
Sullivan	1131	403	......
Switzerland	1015	853	2
Tippecanoe	1352	1282	21

Union	586	555	61
Vanderburgh	487	529	1
Vermillion	692	601	......
Vigo	758	1211	......
Wabash	477	492	5
Warren	379	715	1
Warrick	766	320	......
Washington	1476	975	......
Wayne	1276	1790	423
Wells	239	170	......
White	174	202	......
Whitley	162	127	......
Total	60,982	56,963	1677

[1] Compiled from the official election returns in the Archives Division. No return was found for Daviess County; the vote cast there has been supplied from the returns in the Indianapolis *Indiana State Journal* (weekly), August 22, 1843.

[2] The returns from Perry Township, Clay County, were first rejected but later included by order of the Governor. See above, 109n. The vote was: for Bright, 77; for Bradley, 12.

[3] The returns from Decker Township, Knox County, were received too late to be included. They were: for Bright, 54; for Bradley, 23.

[4] The returns from Carter Township, Spencer County, were rejected because the list of voters did not accompany the return. The vote was: for Bradley, 43; for Bright, 17.

Election August 3, 1846[1]

County	Candidates		
	*Paris C. Dunning (D)	Alexander C. Stevenson (W)	Stephen S. Harding (Liberty)
Adams	277	199	......
Allen	778	723	2
Bartholomew	958	840	5
Benton	70	40	......
Blackford	265	82	......
Boone	748	683	28
Brown	403	55	......
Carroll	855	701	......
Cass	690	774	......
Clark	1100	952	......
Clay	549	367	......

	*Paris C. Dunning (D)	Alexander C. Stevenson (W)	Stephen S. Harding (Liberty)
Clinton	751	594	15
Crawford	404	401	......
Daviess	709	627	......
Dearborn	1603	1221	22
Decatur	862	991	74
DeKalb	366	213[2]	6
Delaware	510	743	22
Dubois	516	168	......
Elkhart	879	639	14
Fayette	765	1005	20
Floyd	926	931	......
Fountain	1093	769	35
Franklin[3]	1406	1089	2
Fulton	266	274	1
Gibson	708	646	......
Grant	492	342	206
Greene	797	660	......
Hamilton	677	720	172
Hancock	643	617	10
Harrison	960	1098	......
Hendricks	686	1082	53
Henry	802	1175	234
[Howard] Richardville	215	188	27
Huntington	327	266	2
Jackson	809	493	......
Jasper[4]	172	130	11
Jay	355	288	12
Jefferson	1153	1659	23
Jennings	596	751	27
Johnson	949	628	8
Knox	654	865	......
Kosciusko	521	709	3
LaGrange	504	549	50
Lake	186	132	3
LaPorte	861	943	66
Lawrence	1002	913	......
Madison	714	610	25

Marion	1519	1588	42
Marshall	362	252	43
Martin	468	223	3
Miami	583	517	......
Monroe	914	696	18
Montgomery	1384	1400	15
Morgan	1001	966	29
Noble	505	461	4
Ohio	402	409	4
Orange	955	646	......
Owen	829	732	......
Parke	1236	1219	12
Perry	271	370	......
Pike	502	372	......
Porter	298	298	25
Posey	959	438	......
Pulaski	157	134	......
Putnam	1252	1452	4
Randolph	734	835	145
Ripley	704	914	72
Rush[5]	1209	1365	36
St. Joseph	704	742	79
Scott	413	470	......
Shelby	1085	924	......
Spencer	467	511	......
Steuben	377	286	30
Sullivan	1083	355	......
Switzerland	872	815	66
Tippecanoe	1455	1431	70
Tipton	136	94	......
Union	613	626	71
Vanderburgh	483	521	......
Vermillion	657	700	......
Vigo	720	1325	......
Wabash	634	669	23
Warren	386	607	5
Warrick	750	302	......
Washington	1323	1035	......
Wayne	1237	1917	317
Wells	264	128	5

	*Paris C. Dunning (D)	Alexander C. Stevenson (W)	Stephen S. Harding (Liberty)
White	271	245	5
Whitley	259	231	4
Total	62,965	59,766	2305

1 Compiled from the official election returns in the Archives Division.

2 Three additional votes in DeKalb County were not counted because the name was written as Alexander C. Stephens.

3 Franklin County gave one vote to Jesse D. Bright.

4 Jasper County gave six votes to Godlove S. Orth.

5 In Rush County Stephen S. Hall received one vote. This was probably intended for Stephen S. Harding.

Election August 6, 1849[1]

County	Candidates		
	*James H. Lane (D)	Thomas S. Stanfield (W)	John W. Wright (FS)
Adams	457	318	......
Allen	969	721	3
Bartholomew	1150	921	2
Benton	88	75	1
Blackford	317	93	1
Boone	927	776	24
Brown	546	86	......
Carroll	870	677	31
Cass	919	918	43
Clark	1374	1005	1
Clay	827	385	......
Clinton	957	742	24
Crawford	496	548	......
Daviess	847	663	......
Dearborn	1566	1090	4
Decatur	1205	1248	23
DeKalb	563	301	4
Delaware	729	775	65
Dubois	605	188	3
Elkhart	1247	903	......
Fayette	884	1001	31
Floyd	[1196]	[1057]	[1]

Fountain	1227	772	66
Franklin	1301	1183	4
Fulton	463	435	......
Gibson	933	843	......
Grant	718	615	12
Greene	1153	791	......
Hamilton	830	812	211
Hancock	840	588	30
Harrison	1056	1215	......
Hendricks	762	1005	51
Henry	[1218]	[1442]	[155]
Howard[2]	421	344	......
Huntington	365	349	2
Jackson	1173	439	......
Jasper	231	205	17
Jay	372	295	13
Jefferson	1522	1938	25
Jennings	752	856	52
Johnson	1247	638	1
Knox	673	923	......
Kosciusko	702	872	29
LaGrange	577	623	18
Lake	269	187	......
LaPorte	954	1105	16
Lawrence	1147	849	17
Madison	1032	797	24
Marion	1902	1859	30
Marshall	449	328	19
Martin	580	282	......
Miami	856	770	26
Monroe	1136	720	18
Montgomery	1537	1475	26
Morgan	1263	1102	27
Noble	656	525	3
Ohio	463	410	......
Orange	1054	754	2
Owen	998	789	1
Parke[3]	1277	1345	1
Perry	374	545	......
Pike	583	479	......
Porter	416	359	37

	*James H. Lane (D)	Thomas S. Stanfield (W)	John W. Wright (FS)
Posey	1374	673	......
Pulaski	255	155	......
Putnam	1487	1515	7
Randolph	746	534	315
Ripley	823	925	114
Rush	1469	1534	53
St. Joseph[4]	695	1015	68
Scott	514	522	......
Shelby	1460	835	5
Spencer	527	570	......
Steuben	420	350	99
Sullivan	1297	422	......
Switzerland	1228	949	3
Tippecanoe	1195	1241	126
Tipton	229	170	2
Union	645	523	122
Vanderburgh	652	569	......
Vermillion	784	741	2
Vigo	983	1232	......
Wabash[5]	790	874	39
Warren	437	670	50
Warrick	938	437	......
Washington	1647	1012	3
Wayne[6]	1148	1741	568
Wells	388	254	17
White	304	261	29
Whitley	346	307	......
Total	77,002	66,385	2816

1 Compiled from the official election returns in the Archives Division. The returns for Henry and Floyd counties have been supplied from the Indianapolis *Indiana Journal* (weekly), September 3, 1849.

2 Howard County gave three votes to Jesse Thatcher.

3 Joseph W. Wright received six votes in Parke County; these may have been intended for John W. Wright.

4 St. Joseph County gave one vote to William Feezler.

5 H. S. Lane received one vote in Wabash County; this was probably intended for James H. Lane.

6 John H. Lane received 117 votes in Wayne County; these were no doubt intended for James H. Lane.

GENERAL ASSEMBLY

ANNUAL ELECTIONS FOR THE GENERAL ASSEMBLY[1]

August 5, 1816

Representatives Elected

First Session, November 4, 1816—January 3, 1817

District	
Clark County	Thomas Carr, Benjamin Ferguson, John K. Graham
Dearborn	Amos Lane, Erasmus Powell
Franklin	James Brownlee, David Mount, James Noble[2]
Gibson	Edmund Hogan[3], John Johnson
Harrison	John Boone, Davis Floyd, Jacob Zenor
Jackson	William Graham
Jefferson	Samuel Alexander, Williamson Dunn
Knox	Isaac Blackford, Henry I. Mills, Walter Wilson
Orange	Jonathan Lindley
Perry	Samuel Connor
Posey	Dan Lynn
Switzerland	John Dumont
Warrick	Ratliff Boon
Washington	Alexander Little, Samuel Milroy
Wayne	Joseph Holman, Ephraim Overman, John Scott

District	Senators Elected[4]
Clark	James Beggs
Dearborn	Ezra Ferris
Franklin	John Conner
Gibson	William Prince
Harrison	Dennis Pennington
Jackson, Orange and Washington	John De Pauw
Jefferson and Switzerland	John Paul
Knox	William Polke
Perry, Posey and Warrick	Daniel Grass
Wayne	Patrick Beard

[1] In the absence of election returns for members of the General Assembly during the first years of statehood, the names of the representatives and senators elected prior to 1830 are given below as they appear in the House and

Senate Journals together with the district they represented. The returns from 1830 through 1851 are from the Secretary of State files in the Archives Division unless otherwise indicated. Prior to 1844 they are very scattered; after that date they are fairly complete. Where no return was available, the names of those elected have been taken from the House and Senate Journals. Beginning in 1836 the political affiliation of the members of the General Assembly has been added as it appeared in the issues of the Indianapolis *Indiana Journal,* the *Indiana State Journal,* and the *Indiana State Sentinel* following the election. Where the returns were taken from local newspapers, the political affiliation is that given with the return.

[2] Noble was elected United States Senator by the General Assembly on November 8, 1816, and resigned his seat in the House the next day. George L. Murdock was elected to succeed Noble and took his seat on December 2. *House Journal,* 1816-17, pp. 16, 18, 48-49.

[3] Hogan died on or before December 21 while the Assembly was in session. Apparently no one was elected to serve the remainder of his term. *Ibid.,* 87.

[4] The Constitution provided that senators should be chosen for a three-year term. In order that their terms might be staggered, the members of the first Senate were classified by casting lots. Those who fell in the first class, to serve one year, were Beggs, Prince, De Pauw, and Beard; in the second class, to serve two years, were Pennington, Polke, and Grass; in the third class, to serve three years, were Ferris, Conner, and Paul. *Senate Journal,* 1816-17, p. 6.

August 4, 1817

Representatives Elected

Second Session, December 1, 1817—January 29, 1818

District	
Clark	Charles Beggs, Thomas Carr, Benjamin Ferguson
Dearborn	Amos Lane, Moses Wiley[1]
Franklin	John Brison (Bryson), James Snowden, Stephen C. Stevens
Gibson	James Campbell, Richard Daniel
Harrison	William D. Littell, James B. Slaughter, Jacob Zenor
Jackson	William Graham
Jefferson	Williamson Dunn, Nathaniel Hunt
Knox	Isaac Blackford,[2] John McClure, George R. C. Sullivan
Orange	Samuel Chambers
Perry	Samuel Connor
Posey	Dan Lynn
Switzerland	Ralph Cotton
Warrick	Ratliff Boon
Washington	Alexander Little, Samuel Milroy
Wayne	Robert Hill, Joseph Holman, John Scott

District	Senators Elected
Clark	James Beggs
Gibson and Pike	Isaac Montgomery
Jackson, Orange, Washington	John De Pauw
Wayne	Patrick Beard

1 Wiley resigned before the beginning of the session. Erasmus Powell was elected in his place and took his seat on December 29, 1817. *House Journal*, 1817-18, pp. 5, 98.

2 Blackford resigned following his appointment to the Indiana Supreme Court on September 10. Robert Buntin, Jr., was elected in November to take his place. *Executive Proceedings of Indiana, 1816-1836*, 42, 43.

August 3, 1818

Representatives Elected

Third Session, December 7, 1818—January 2, 1819

District	
Clark	Joseph Bartholomew, Charles Beggs, John H. Thompson
Dearborn	Erasmus Powell, John Watts[1]
Franklin	Allen Crisler, James Goudie, Jonathan McCarty
Gibson	Richard Daniel,[2] John Johnson
Harrison	Harbin H. Moore, James B. Slaughter, William P. Thomasson
Jackson	William Graham
Jefferson	Williamson Dunn, Nathaniel Hunt
Knox and Sullivan	Robert Buntin, Jr., George R. C. Sullivan, Joseph Warner[3]
Orange	Samuel Chambers
Perry	Samuel Connor
Posey	[no record of a representative]
Switzerland	Ralph Cotton
Warrick	Elisha Harrison
Washington	Jonathan Lyon, Samuel Milroy
Wayne	Zachariah Ferguson, Lewis Johnson, John Sutherland

District	Senators Elected
Crawford and Harrison	Dennis Pennington
Knox, Sullivan, Vigo	William Polke
Perry, Posey, Spencer, Vanderburgh, Warrick	Ratliff Boon

1 Watts resigned as a member of the House on January 5, 1819, three days after the close of the 1818-19 session. He was subsequently appointed president judge of the Third Judicial Circuit. *Executive Proceedings, 1816-1836*, 92.

[2] Daniel resigned December 30, 1818, and three days later was appointed president judge of the Fourth Judicial Circuit. *Ibid.*, 91; *House Journal*, 1818-19, p. 151.

[3] General Washington Johnston contested Warner's election. The House decided in favor of Warner on December 10. *House Journal*, 1818-19, pp. 24-25, 26-27.

August 2, 1819

Representatives Elected

Fourth Session, December 6, 1819—January 22, 1820

District	
Clark	Andrew P. Hay, John F. Ross, John H. Thompson
Dearborn	Samuel Jelley, Isaac Morgan
Franklin	Allen Crisler, Enoch D. John, Conrad Sailor
Gibson	Robert M. Evans, John W. Maddox
Harrison	John N. Dunbar, William P. Thomasson, Jacob Zenor
Jackson	William Graham
Jefferson	Williamson Dunn, Jeremiah Sullivan
Knox, Daviess, Owen, Sullivan, Vigo	Thomas H. Blake, Joseph Warner, Peter Allen
Orange	Samuel Chambers
Perry	John Ewing
Posey	Dan Lynn
Switzerland	Samuel Merrill
Warrick	Daniel Grass
Washington	Samuel Lindley, Samuel Milroy
Wayne	Robert Hill, Joseph Holman, John Sutherland

District	Senators Elected
Dearborn	John Gray
Fayette and Franklin	William C. Drew
Jefferson, Jennings, Ripley, Switzerland	William Cotton
Jackson, Lawrence, Monroe, Orange, Washington	Alexander Little[1]
Perry, Posey, Spencer, Vanderburgh, Warrick	Elisha Harrison[2]

[1] Little was elected to fill out the term of John De Pauw, who resigned on May 24 to run for lieutenant governor. Recommendations, Appointments, Resignations file, Archives Division.

[2] Harrison was elected to fill out the term of Ratliff Boon, who resigned on May 27 to run for lieutenant governor. *Ibid.*

August 7, 1820

Representatives Elected

Fifth Session, November 27, 1820—January 9, 1821

District	
Clark	Joseph Gibson, Andrew P. Hay, John F. Ross
Dearborn	Ezra Ferris, Erasmus Powell
Gibson	David Robb
Franklin	James Goudie, Joseph Hanna, Enoch D. John
Harrison	Henry Green, John Tipton, Jacob Zenor
Jackson	William Graham
Jefferson	Thomas Crawford, Jeremiah Sullivan
Knox	John McDonald, Robert Sturgus, George R. C. Sullivan
Orange	Samuel Chambers
Perry	Samuel Connor[1]
Posey	Charles I. Battell
Switzerland	Samuel Merrill
Warrick	Daniel Grass
Washington	Marston G. Clark, Samuel Milroy
Wayne	Joseph Holman, Thomas Swain, Simon Yandes

District	Senators Elected
Clark and parts of Scott and Floyd	Joseph Bartholomew
Crawford, Harrison, part of Floyd	James B. Slaughter[2]
Dubois, Gibson, Perry, Posey	Richard Daniel
Jackson, Lawrence, Monroe, Orange, Washington	James Gregory
Wayne	Patrick Beard

[1] John Ewing contested Connor's election and a new election was ordered after Connor had been seated. Ewing won in the second election and was seated December 28. *House Journal,* 1820-21, pp. 4, 30, 37, 190.

[2] Slaughter was elected to fill out the unexpired term of Dennis Pennington who had resigned February 2, 1820. *Executive Proceedings, 1816-1836,* 128n.

August 6, 1821

Representatives Elected[1]

Sixth Session, November 19, 1821—January 3, 1822

District	
Bartholomew	John Lindsey
Clark	John Miller, John H. Thompson
Crawford	Henry Green

Daviess and Martin	James G. Read
Dearborn	Ezra Ferris, Amos Lane, Erasmus Powell
Dubois, Perry, Spencer, part of Warrick	Thomas Vandeveer
Fayette	Allen Crisler
Floyd	Moses Kirkpatrick
Franklin	George L. Murdock, James B. Ray
Gibson	William Prince
Greene, Morgan, Owen	Eli Dixon
Harrison	John N. Dunbar,[2] John Tipton
Jackson	James Braman
Jefferson	Copeland P. J. Arion, Israel T. Canby
Jennings	Zenas Kimberly
Knox	Benjamin V. Beckes, General Washington Johnston
Lawrence	John Milroy
Monroe	David H. Maxwell
Orange	Charles Dewey, Alexander Wallace
Parke and Vigo	Joseph Shelby
Pike	John Johnson
Posey	Charles I. Battell
Randolph	John Wright
Ripley	Joseph Bentley
Scott	William D. Clark
Sullivan	John Benefield
Switzerland	William B. Chamberlain, Samuel Merrill
Union	Thomas Brown
Vanderburgh, and part of Warrick	Hugh M. Donaghe
Washington	Samuel Milroy, Noah Wright
Wayne	Jeremiah Cox, Joseph Holman, Loring A. Waldo

Senators Elected[3]

District	
Bartholomew, Jackson, Scott	William Graham
Crawford and Harrison	James B. Slaughter
Daviess, Knox, Martin	Frederick Shoults
Dubois, Perry, Spencer, part of Warrick	Daniel Grass
Fayette and Union	John Conner
Franklin	William B. Laughlin
Greene, Owen, Pike, Sullivan, Vigo	Thomas H. Blake
Jefferson and Jennings	Brooke Bennett
Posey, Vanderburgh, Warrick	Elisha Harrison
Washington	Marston G. Clark

1 The members of the House and Senate had been reapportioned by an act of January 2, 1821; the membership in the House was increased to forty-three and to sixteen in the Senate. *Laws of Indiana,* 1820-21, pp. 87-90. See Appendix, below, for new districts.

2 Dunbar died November 24 or 25, during the first week of the Assembly. David G. Mitchell was elected in his place and was seated December 8, 1821. *House Journal,* 1821-22, pp. 67, 174.

3 Senators Conner, Blake, Graham, Grass, Bennett, and Clark were considered as representing new districts under the reapportionment act, and drew lots to determine their terms. Blake and Conner drew one-year terms; Clark and Bennett, two-year; and Grass and Graham, three-year. *Senate Journal,* 1820-21, p. 89.

August 5, 1822

Representatives Elected

Seventh Session, December 2, 1822—January 11, 1823

District	
Bartholomew	Charles DePauw
Clark	William G. Armstrong, Isaac Howk
Crawford	Henry Green
Daviess and Martin	William H. Routt
Dearborn	Horace Bassett, Ezekiel Jackson, Pinckney James
Dubois, Perry, Spencer, part of Warrick	John Daniel
Fayette	Oliver H. Smith
Floyd	Alexander S. Burnett
Franklin	John E. Bush, William McCleery
Gibson	David Robb

Greene, Morgan, Owen, part of Putnam	Eli Dixon
Harrison	Peter Mauck, Dennis Pennington
Jackson	William Marshall
Jefferson	Nathaniel Hunt, Milton Stapp
Jennings	William A. Bullock
Knox	Benjamin V. Beckes, General Washington Johnston
Lawrence	Joseph Glover
Monroe	Joshua H. Lucas
Orange	John G. Clendenin, Jacob Moulder
Parke and Vigo	Lucius H. Scott
Pike	John Johnson
Posey	William Casey
Randolph	John Wright
Ripley	Joseph Bentley
Scott	William D. Clark
Sullivan	Henry D. Palmer
Switzerland	John Dumont, Linus Scoville
Union	Sylvanus Everts
Vanderburgh and part of Warrick	Joseph Lane
Washington	Ezra Childs (or Child), Noah Wright
Wayne	Robert Hill, John Jordan, Isaac Julian

District	Senators Elected
Clark and Floyd	John H. Thompson[1]
Dearborn	John Gray
Dubois, Perry, Spencer, part of Warrick	Daniel Grass
Fayette and Union	Lewis Johnson
Franklin	James B. Ray
Greene, Owen, Parke, Putnam, Sullivan, Vigo	John Jenckes
Lawrence, Monroe, Orange	Samuel Chambers[2]
Ripley and Switzerland	George Craig

[1] Thompson was elected to fill out the unexpired term of Joseph Bartholomew who had resigned on April 22, 1822. *Executive Proceeding, 1816-1836,* 215.

[2] Chambers was elected to fill out the unexpired term of James Gregory. *Ibid.*

August 4, 1823

Representatives Elected

Eighth Session, December 1, 1823—January 31, 1824

District	
Bartholomew	Benjamin Irwin
Clark	William G. Armstrong, Reuben W. Nelson
Crawford	Elisha Tadlock
Daviess and Martin	James G. Read
Dearborn	Benjamin I. Blythe, David Bowers, Samuel Jelley
Decatur, Henry, Rush, Shelby	Thomas Hendricks
Dubois, Perry, Spencer, part of Warrick	David Edwards
Fayette	James Brownlee
Floyd	Alexander S. Burnett
Franklin	George L. Murdock, David Oliver
Gibson	John Milburn
Greene, Morgan, Owen	Eli Dixon
Hamilton, Johnson, Madison, Marion	James Paxton
Harrison	Dennis Pennington, John Zenor
Jackson	William Marshall
Jefferson	Copeland P. J. Arion, David Hillis
Jennings	William A. Bullock
Knox	John Law, James B. McCall
Lawrence	Vinson Williams
Monroe	David H. Maxwell
Montgomery, Putnam, unorganized territory	Amos Robertson

Orange	John G. Clendenin, Ezekiel S. Riley
Parke and Vigo	Thomas H. Blake
Pike	John Johnson
Posey	John Schnee
Randolph	John Wright
Ripley	Robert Kennedy
Scott	William D. Clark
Sullivan	Henry D. Palmer
Switzerland	Ralph Cotton, Stephen C. Stevens
Union	Sylvanus Everts
Vanderburgh, and part of Warrick	Robert M. Evans
Washington	Ezra Childs (or Child), Alexander Huston
Wayne	Robert Hill, William Jones, Abel Lomax

Senators Elected

District	
Clark and Floyd	John H. Thompson
Decatur, Hamilton, Henry, Johnson, Madison Marion, Rush, Shelby	James Gregory
Jefferson and Jennings	Milton Stapp
Lawrence, Monroe, Orange	Samuel Chambers
Pike and Gibson	Isaac Montgomery
Randolph and Wayne	James Rariden
Washington	Samuel Milroy

August 2, 1824

Representatives Elected

Ninth Session, January 10—February 12, 1825

District	
Allen and Randolph	Daniel Worth
Bartholomew	Benjamin Irwin
Clark	William G. Armstrong, Reuben W. Nelson
Crawford	Elisha Tadlock
Daviess and Martin	James G. Read
Dearborn	Horace Bassett, Ezekiel Jackson, Abel C. Pepper

County	Representative
Decatur, Henry, Rush, Shelby	Thomas Hendricks
Dubois, Perry, Spencer, part of Warrick	David Edwards
Fayette	Newton Claypool
Floyd	John K. Graham
Franklin	David Oliver, Noah Noble
Gibson	David Robb
Greene, Morgan, Owen	Daniel Harris
Hamilton, Johnson, Madison, Marion	John Conner
Harrison	Benjamin Hurst, Thomas Posey
Jackson	Obadiah Crane
Jefferson	David Hillis, Nathan B. Palmer
Jennings	John Walker
Knox	Benjamin V. Beckes, Daniel Langton
Lawrence	William Erwin
Monroe	David H. Maxwell
Montgomery, Putnam, unorganized territory	Amos Robertson
Orange	John G. Clendenin, Alexander Wallace
Parke, Vermillion, Vigo	James Farrington
Pike	John Johnson
Posey	James H. Richardson
Ripley	John Richey
Scott	Jesse Jackson
Sullivan	Josiah Mann
Switzerland	Stephen C. Stevens, William Gard

Union	Thomas Brown
Vanderburgh, and part of Warrick	John McCreery
Washington	Alexander Huston, Robert McIntyre
Wayne	Eleazar Hiatt, Henry Hoover, Abel Lomax

District	Senators Elected
Bartholomew, Jackson, Scott	William Graham
Crawford and Harrison	Dennis Pennington
Daviess, Knox, Martin	John Ewing
Dubois, Perry, Spencer, part of Warrick	Daniel Grass
Posey, Vanderburgh, and part of Warrick	Thomas Givens

August 1, 1825

Representatives Elected

Tenth Session, December 5, 1825—January 21, 1826

District	
Allen and Randolph	Daniel Worth
Bartholomew	Philip Sweetser
Clark	Isaac Howk, John Lemon
Clay, Greene, Morgan, Owen	John Sims
Crawford	David Stewart
Daviess and Martin	William Wallace
Dearborn	Thomas Guion, Ezekiel Jackson, Abel C. Pepper
Decatur, Henry, Rush, Shelby	Thomas R. Stanford
Dubois, Perry, Spencer	John Daniel
Fayette	Newton Claypool
Floyd	Alexander S. Burnett
Franklin	John Reid, Noah Noble[1]
Gibson	Robert M. Evans

Hamilton, Johnson, Madison, Marion	James Paxton
Harrison	Joseph Paddacks, Thomas Posey
Hendricks, Montgomery, Putnam and other territory	Amos Robertson
Jackson	William Marshall
Jefferson	David Hillis, Nathan B. Palmer
Jennings	John Walker
Knox	Benjamin V. Beckes, James T. Moffatt
Lawrence	Vinson Williams
Monroe	John Ketcham
Orange	John G. Clendenin, Ezekiel S. Riley
Parke, Vermillion, Vigo	James Blair
Pike	John Johnson
Posey	James H. Richardson
Ripley	Merit S. Craig
Scott	Moses Gray
Sullivan	George Boon
Switzerland	William Gard, William C. Keen
Union	John B. Rose
Vanderburgh and Warrick	Thomas Fitzgerald
Washington	Ezra Childs (or Child), William Baird
Wayne	Samuel Hannah, Caleb Lewis, Abel Lomax

District	Senators Elected
Clark and Floyd	John K. Graham[2]
Clay, Greene, Hendricks, Montgomery, Morgan, Owen, Parke, Putnam, Sullivan, Vermillion, Vigo	John M. Colman
Dearborn	John Watts

Decatur, Hamilton, Henry, Johnson, Madison, Marion, Rush, Shelby	James Gregory
Fayette and Union	Ross Smiley
Franklin	David Oliver
Ripley and Switzerland	William Cotton
Washington	John De Pauw[3]

[1] Noble resigned following his appointment as receiver of public moneys in the Indianapolis Land Office early in December. Samuel Lewis was elected in his place and took his seat on December 13, 1825. *Executive Proceedings, 1816-1836,* 352.

[2] Graham was elected to serve out the term of John H. Thompson who was elected lieutenant governor. *Ibid.,* 352.

[3] De Pauw was elected to serve out the term of Samuel Milroy who moved to Carroll County. *Ibid.*

August 7, 1826

Representatives Elected

Eleventh Session, December 4, 1826—January 27, 1827

District	
Allen and Randolph	Samuel Hanna
Bartholomew	Philip Sweetser
Clark	Isaac Howk, John Lemon, Joseph Work
Clay and Putnam	George Piercy
Crawford	Seth M. Levenworth
Daviess and Martin	James G. Read
Dearborn	Ezra Ferris, Horace Bassett, Ezekial Jackson, Johnson Watts
Decatur	Doddridge Alley
Dubois and Pike	John Johnson
Fayette	Newton Claypool, Martin M. Ray
Floyd	Alexander S. Burnett
Fountain, Montgomery, and other territory	Henry Ristine
Franklin	Samuel Lewis, John T. McKinney
Gibson	Walter Wilson
Greene and Owen	Eli Dixon

Hamilton, Henry, Madison	Elisha Long
Harrison	Benjamin Hurst, Harbin H. Moore, James B. Slaughter
Hendricks, Morgan, and other territory	Thomas J. Matlock
Jackson	William Marshall
Jefferson	David Hillis, John L. Spann
Jennings	William A. Bullock
Johnson and Shelby	Lewis Morgan
Knox	Benjamin V. Beckes, General Washington Johnston
Lawrence	Lewis Roberts
Marion	Morris Morris
Monroe	John Ketcham
Orange	John G. Clendenin, Alexander Wallace
Parke and Vermillion	Joseph M. Hayes
Perry and Spencer	John Daniel
Posey	James H. Richardson
Ripley	Merit S. Craig
Rush	Charles Test
Scott	Moses Gray
Sullivan	George Boon
Switzerland	Stephen C. Stevens, William B. Chamberlain
Union	Thomas Brown
Vanderburgh & Warrick	Thomas Fitzgerald
Vigo	John Jackson
Washington	Alexander Little, Abner Martin, Absalom Sargeant
Wayne	William Elliott, Henry Hoover, Caleb Lewis, Abel Lomax

District	Senators Elected[1]
Allen, Henry, Randolph, Rush	Amaziah Morgan
Clark and Floyd	John S. Simonson
Dubois, Gibson, Pike	Isaac Montgomery

Fountain, Montgomery, Parke, Putnam, Vermillion	Amos Robertson
Greene, Monroe, Owen	David H. Maxwell
Hamilton, Hendricks, Madison, Marion	Calvin Fletcher
Jefferson and Jennings	Israel T. Canby
Lawrence and Orange	John Milroy
Washington	Marston G. Clark
Wayne	James Rariden

[1] Under the new apportionment act of January 19, 1826, the number of senators was increased from sixteen to twenty, and the number of representatives from forty-three to fifty-eight. Senators from the four new districts drew by lot the following terms: Maxwell and Robertson, one year; Fletcher, two; Morgan, three. *Laws of Indiana,* 1825-26, pp. 5-6; *Senate Journal,* 1826-27, p. 5.

August 6, 1827

Representatives Elected

Twelfth Session, December 3, 1827—January 24, 1828

District	
Allen and Randolph	Samuel Hanna
Bartholomew	Benjamin Irwin
Clark	Isaac Howk, John Lemon, Joseph Work
Clay and Putnam	George Piercy
Crawford	Seth M. Levenworth
Daviess and Martin	James G. Read
Dearborn	Horace Bassett, Joel Decoursey, Ezekiel Jackson James T. Pollock
Decatur	Thomas Hendricks
Dubois and Pike	John Johnson
Fayette	Newton Claypool
Floyd	John K. Graham
Fountain, Montgomery, and other territory	John Beard
Franklin	John Reid, John T. McKinney
Gibson	Walter Wilson
Greene and Owen	Thomas F. G. Adams

Hamilton, Henry, Madison	Elisha Long
Harrison	Harbin H. Moore, James B. Slaughter
Hendricks, Morgan, and other territory	Thomas J. Matlock
Jackson	William Marshall
Jefferson	John L. Spann, Milton Stapp
Jennings	Ezra F. Pabody
Johnson and Shelby	John Smiley
Knox	Samuel Judah, Thomas McClure
Lawrence	Lewis Roberts
Marion	George L. Kinnard
Monroe	Enos Blair
Orange	John G. Clendenin, Alexander Wallace
Parke and Vermillion	Eliphalet Allen
Perry and Spencer	Isaac Veatch
Posey	Samuel Annable
Ripley	Merit S. Craig
Rush	William Newell
Scott	Arthur Watts
Sullivan	George Boon
Switzerland	William Campbell, Stephen C. Stevens
Union	Thomas Brown, Joseph Hanna[1]
Vanderburgh & Warrick	Charles M. Johnson
Vigo	Nathaniel Huntington
Washington	John De Pauw, Alexander Little, Hugh McPheeters
Wayne	William Elliott, John Jones, Abel Lomax, William Steele

District	Senators Elected
Bartholomew, Jackson, Scott	William Graham
Crawford, Perry, Spencer	John Daniel
Daviess, Knox, Martin	John Ewing
Fountain, Montgomery, Parke, Putnam, Tippecanoe, Vermillion	James Blair

Greene, Monroe, Owen	David H. Maxwell
Harrison	Daniel C. Lane
Posey, Vanderburgh and Warrick	Thomas Givens

[1] Hanna resigned on September 13 following his election in August. William Lewis was elected in his place. *Executive Proceedings, 1816-1836,* 352.

August 4, 1828

Representatives Elected

Thirteenth Session, December 1, 1827—January 24, 1828

District	
Allen and Randolph	Daniel Worth
Bartholomew	Newton C. Jones[1]
Clark	Isaac Howk, John Lemon, Joseph Work
Clay and Putnam	Joseph Orr
Crawford	Seth M. Levenworth
Daviess and Martin	James G. Read
Dearborn	Horace Bassett, George H. Dunn, James T. Pollock, Arthur St. Clair
Decatur	Thomas Hendricks
Dubois and Pike	James Ritchie
Fayette	Samuel C. Sample, Marks Crume
Floyd	Isaac Stewart
Fountain, Montgomery, & adj. area	Robert Taylor
Franklin	Daniel St. John, David Wallace
Gibson	David Robb
Greene and Owen	John M. Young
Hamilton, Henry, Madison	Elisha Long
Harrison	Robert F. Bell, Dennis Pennington, James B. Slaughter
Hendricks, Morgan, and other territory	Thomas J. Matlock
Jackson	William Marshall

Jefferson	David Hillis, Nathan B. Palmer
Jennings	Ezra F. Pabody
Johnson and Shelby	Sylvan B. Morris
Knox	Samuel Judah, John C. Reiley
Lawrence	Vinson Williams
Marion	George L. Kinnard
Monroe	Enos Blair
Orange	James Lynd, John B. Moyer
Parke and Vermillion	Eliphalet Allen
Perry and Spencer	Samuel Frisbie
Posey	John Y. Welborn
Ripley	Merit S. Craig
Rush	William J. Brown
Scott	James Goodhue
Sullivan	George Boon
Switzerland	John F. Dufour, John Dumont
Union	James Leviston
Vanderburgh and Warrick	William Trafton
Vigo	Nathaniel Huntington[2]
Washington	Ezra Childs (or Child), Robert McIntyre, Hugh McPheeters
Wayne	William Elliott, John Finley, Abel Lomax, William Steele

District	Senators Elected
Clay, Sullivan, Vigo	William C. Linton
Carroll, Hamilton, Hancock, Hendricks, Madison, Marion	Calvin Fletcher
Dearborn	John Watts
Decatur, Johnson, Morgan, Shelby	James Gregory
Fayette and Union	Newton Claypool
Franklin	John T. McKinney
Jefferson and Jennings	John Sering[3]
Ripley and Switzerland	Stephen C. Stevens

[1] Jones died shortly after his election to the House, and Philip Sweetser was elected in his place on October 10. *Executive Proceedings, 1816-1836,* p. 353.

[2] Huntington died of yellow fever at New Orleans on September 29, 1828. Demas Deming was elected in his place. *Ibid.*

[3] Sering was elected to serve out the term of Israel T. Canby who resigned to become a candidate for governor. *Ibid.,* 352-53n.

August 3, 1829

Representatives Elected

Fourteenth Session, December 7, 1829—January 30, 1830

District	
Allen, Cass, and other territory	Anthony L. Davis
Bartholomew	William Herod
Carroll, Fountain, Montgomery Tippecanoe Warren	John Beard, Samuel Milroy[1]
Clark	Andrew Fite, Isaac Howk, Alexander F. Morrison
Clay and Putnam	John McNary
Crawford	Seth M. Levenworth
Daviess and Martin	James G. Read
Dearborn	Walter Armstrong, Horace Bassett, Thomas Guion, James T. Pollock
Decatur	Thomas Hendricks
Delaware and Randolph	Lemuel C. Jackson
Dubois and Pike	Thomas C. Stewart
Fayette	Marks Crume
Floyd	Jacob Bence
Franklin	Benjamin S. Noble, David Wallace
Gibson	Samuel Hall
Greene and Owen	Eli Dixon
Hamilton, Hancock, Henry, Madison	William Conner, Elisha Long

Harrison	Robert F. Bell, Dennis Pennington, James B. Slaughter
Hendricks, Morgan, and other territory	Curtis G. Hussey
Jackson	James Hamilton
Jefferson	David Hillis, James H. Wallace
Jennings	Ezra F. Pabody
Johnson and Shelby	Rezin Davis
Knox	John C. Reiley, General Washington Johnston
Lawrence	Pleasant Parks
Marion	George L. Kinnard
Monroe	John Ketcham
Orange	Thomas Coffin, John B. Moyer
Parke and Vermillion	John Gardner
Perry and Spencer	Richard Polke
Posey	William Casey
Ripley	Thomas Smith
Rush	William J. Brown
Scott	Jesse Jackson
Sullivan	George Boon
Switzerland	John Dumont, Samuel Jack
Union	James Leviston, Ross Smiley
Vanderburgh and Warrick	Robert M. Evans
Vigo	Thomas H. Blake
Washington	John Kingsbury, Alexander Little, Charles B. Naylor[2]
Wayne	John Finley, Henry Hoover, John Jones, James Rariden

District	Senators Elected
Allen, Cass, Delaware, Randolph	Daniel Worth
Carroll, Montgomery, Putnam, Tippecanoe	Joseph Orr
Clark and Floyd	John M. Lemon
Dubois, Gibson, Pike	David Robb
Jefferson and Jennings	John Sering

Henry and Rush	Amaziah Morgan
Lawrence and Orange	John G. Clendenin
Washington	John DePauw
Wayne	Abel Lomax

[1] Milroy resigned September 10, 1829, and Robert Johnson was elected in his place. *Executive Proceedings, 1816-1836,* 353.

[2] Naylor's election was contested by Ezekiel D. Logan and the House ruled in favor of Logan on December 10, 1829. *House Journal,* 1829-30, p. 55.

August 2, 1830

Returns for House of Representatives

Fifteenth Session, December 6, 1830—February 10, 1831

District — Candidates

	*John Beard	*Abel Claypool	Crooks	Davis	White
Carroll Fountain Montgomery[1] Tippecanoe Warren	388	314	274	150	62

	*Samuel H. Dowden	*Ezra Ferris	*Walter Armstrong	*James T. Pollock	Thomas Guion	James Walker[2]
Dearborn[1]	1387	1192	1190	1012	913	901

	*Marks Crume	*David Hankins	J. D. Thompson	A. Morgan
Fayette[1]	792	756	568	354

	*Alexander Worth	Lewis Mastin	Gideon Johnson	Solomon Dunnegan	John W. Cox
Hendricks[3] Morgan	223	304	20	19	3

	*David Hillis	*James H. Wallace	R. Hopkins	C. Kinnear	William Powell	Jacob Jackson
Jefferson[1]	922	780	595	558	110	90

	*John Smiley	Rezin Davis	John Hendricks
Johnson Shelby[1]	114	476	316

	*John C. Reiley	*John Decker	Ebenezer Welton	Joseph Chambers	Joseph Roseman
Knox[4]	598	507	445	342	45

	*Alexander W. Russell	Robert Hanna
Marion[1]	682	552

	*John Owen (or Owens)	John Hite	Craven P. Hester
Monroe[1]	343	309	307

	*William S. Bussell	William J. Brown	Marinus Willett
Rush[1]	729	508	123

	*John Dumont	*George Craig	Scott	John F. Dufour	Charles F. Krutz	Beal[6]
Switzerland[5]	639	231	221	220	205	198

	*Amory Kinney	John Jenckes
Vigo[1]	485	323

	*Hugh McPheeters	*Rudolphus Schoonover	*Ezekiel D. Logan	Woodbridge Parker	William Shanks	Charles B. Naylor[7]
Washington[1]	1317	1057	961	546	406	380

	*John Finley	*Eli Wright	*Henry Hoover	*William Elliott	William Steele	John Jones[8]
Wayne[1]	1560	1501	1439	1158	1121	1068

Representatives Elected for Whom No Returns Have Been Found

District	
Allen, Cass and adjoining territory	Joseph Holman
Bartholomew and adjoining territory	William Herod
Clark	Isaac Howk, John E. Roe, Joseph Work
Clay and Putnam	John McNary

Crawford	Zebulon Levenworth
Daviess and Martin	James G. Read
Decatur	Thomas Hendricks
Delaware and Randolph	David Seamans
Dubois and Pike	Thomas C. Stewart
Floyd	Jacob Bence
Franklin	John Reid, David Wallace
Gibson	Samuel Hall
Greene and Owen	James Galletly
Hamilton, Hancock, Henry, Madison and adjoining territory	Thomas Bell, Elisha Long
Harrison	George Bentley, Joseph Paddacks, John Zenor
Jackson	James Hamilton
Jennings	Henry L. Soper
Lawrence	Pleasant Parks
Orange	Thomas Coffin, James Lynd
Parke and Vermillion	John Gardner
Perry and Spencer	John Pitcher
Posey	William Casey
Ripley	William Skeen
Scott	Alexander Lowry
Sullivan	George Boon
Union	Thomas Brown
Vanderburgh and Warrick	Jay Morehouse[9]

1 Indianapolis *Indiana Journal,* August 11, 1830.

2 In addition to candidates listed for Dearborn County, Davis Weaver received 591 votes, William Tucker, 293.

3 *History of Hendricks County, Indiana* . . . (Inter-State Publishing Co., Chicago, 1885), 302.

4 Vincennes *Western Sun,* August 14, 1830.

5 Lawrenceburg *Indiana Palladium,* August 9, 1830.

6 In addition to the candidates listed for Switzerland County, Buch received 73 votes, McHenry, 78.

7 In addition to the candidates listed for Washington County, John Dover received 182 votes, Alexander Huston, 168.

8 In addition to the candidates listed for Wayne County, William Searce received 908 votes, Joseph Lewis, 776, and Marinus Willett, 170.

9 Morehouse died of yellow fever at New Orleans on October 15, 1830. Joseph Lane was elected in his place and was seated on December 27. Warrick County Election Return, October, 1830; *House Journal,* 1830-31, pp. 178-79.

Returns for Senate

District	Candidates	
	*William Graham	Philip Sweetser
Bartholomew[1]	225	587
Jackson[1]	559	154
Scott[1]	266	181
Total	1050	922
	*Joseph Orr	John B. Chapman
Carroll County (Deer Creek Township)[2]	60	29
Clinton		
Montgomery[1]	267	350
Putnam		
Tippecanoe		
	*John Ewing	Wilson Lagow
Daviess[3]	422	169
Knox[3]	702	264
Martin[3]	227	78
Total	1351	511
	*James Whitcomb	John Ketcham
Greene[1]	382	183
Monroe[1]	551	456
Owen[1]	442	75
Total	1375	714

	*Dennis Pennington	John F. Bell	John W. Payne
Harrison[1]	792	372	320

Senators Elected for Whom No Returns Have Been Found

District	
Crawford, Perry, Spencer	Samuel Frisbie
Fountain, Parke, Vermillion, Warren	James Blair
Posey, Vanderburgh, Warrick	Thomas Givens

1 Indianapolis *Indiana Journal,* August 11 and 18, 1830.

2 James H. Stewart, *Recollections of the Early Settlement of Carroll County, Indiana* (Cincinnati, 1872), 292.

3 Vincennes *Western Sun,* August 14, 1830.

August 1, 1831

Returns for House of Representatives

Sixteenth Session, December 5, 1831—February 3, 1832

District	Candidates					
	*David V. Culley	*William Flake	*Warren Tebbs	Matthias Haines	Ezra Ferris	M. Stewart[2]
Dearborn[1]	1084	1017	901	791	772	676

District	Candidates	
	*Lewis Mastin	John Hannah
Hendricks[3]	369	236

District	Candidates			
	*James H. Cravens	*Edward R. Maxwell	David Hillis	James H. Wallace
Jefferson[4]	799	770	760	630

District	Candidates				
	*David S. Bonner	*John Decker	Joseph Chambers	John F. Snapp	James Thorn
Knox[5]	469	398	376	330	243

District	Candidates	
	*Henry Brady	Samuel G. Mitchell
Marion[6]	677	571

District	Candidates	
	*Theodore C. Cone[8]	William C. Linton
Vigo[7]	524	468

Representatives Elected for Whom No Returns Have Been Found

District	
Allen, Elkhart, St. Joseph	Samuel Hanna
Bartholomew	Jesse Ruddick
Boone, Hamilton, and adjoining territory	William Conner
Carroll and Cass	Walter Wilson
Clark	Benjamin Ferguson, Thomas J. Henley
Clay	Jared Peyton
Clinton and Montgomery	Jacob Angle, John Nelson
Crawford	David Griggs
Daviess and Martin	William Wallace
Decatur	Doddridge Alley

Delaware and adjoining territory	Elias Murray
Dubois and Pike	George H. Proffit
Fayette	Manlove Caldwell, Marks Crume
Floyd	Harbin H. Moore, William Williams
Fountain	Thomas Clawson, William Crumpton
Franklin	Benjamin S. Noble, John Reid
Gibson	John Hargrove
Greene	George Baber
Hancock and Madison	Thomas Bell
Harrison	Joseph Paddacks, James B. Slaughter
Henry	Thomas R. Stanford
Jackson	Jesse B. Durham
Jennings	John Vawter
Johnson	John Smiley
Lawrence	Hugh L. Livingston, Pleasant Parks
Monroe	William Hite
Morgan	John W. Cox
Orange	James Lynd, John B. Moyer
Owen	Robert M. Wooden
Parke	William P. Bryant
Perry and Spencer	Richard Polke
Posey	William Casey
Putnam	James Secrest, Alexander C. Stevenson
Randolph	Andrew Aker
Ripley	Joseph Robinson
Rush	William Frame, Marinus Willett
Scott	John Harrod
Shelby	Sylvan B. Morris
Sullivan	John W. Davis
Switzerland	William Cotton
Tippecanoe	Aaron Finch, William Heaton
Union	Jeremiah Grover, John B. Rose
Vanderburgh and Warrick	Joseph Lane
Vermillion	John Gardner, Eli Reynolds
Warren	Samuel B. Clark
Washington	Ezekiel D. Logan, Henry P. Thornton
Wayne	Richard Henderson, Henry Hoover, John Jones, William Steele

1 Lawrenceburg Indiana *Palladium,* August 6, 1831.

2 In addition to the candidates listed for Dearborn County, J. Murray received 139 votes.

[3] *History of Hendricks County* (1885), 302.

[4] Madison *Indiana Republican*, August 4, 1831.

[5] Vincennes *Western Sun*, August 6, 1831.

[6] Indianapolis *Indiana Journal*, August 6, 1831.

[7] Terre Haute *Western Register*, August 6, 1831.

[8] Cone died December 19. At the special election held January 2, 1832, to choose his successor, Elisha M. Huntington received 280 votes, John F. Cruft, 167, James T. Moffatt, 125, and Ralph Wilson, 80. *Ibid.*, December 24, 1831, and January 7, 1832.

Returns for Senate[1]

District	Candidates	
	*Levi Jessup	Willis G. Conduit
Boone[2]	107	46
Hendricks[2]	326	295
Morgan[2]	347	433
Total	780	774
	*James Farrington	George Boon
Clay[3]	100	155
Sullivan		
Vigo[3]	753	243
	*James T. Pollock	George H. Dunn
Dearborn[4]	1081	824
	*Calvin Fletcher	George L. Kinnard
Hamilton[5]	232	66
Marion[5]	549	704
Total	781	770
	*Joseph M. Hayes	Arthur Patterson
Parke[3]	631	624

Senators Elected for Whom No Returns Have Been Found

District	
Bartholomew and Johnson	William Herod
Carroll, Cass, Tippecanoe	Othniel L. Clark
Clinton and Montgomery	John Beard
Decatur and Shelby	Thomas Hendricks

Fayette and Union	James Leviston
Fountain	Benjamin F. Wallace
Franklin	Enoch McCarty
Hancock, Henry, Madison	Elisha Long
Ripley and Switzerland	John Dumont

1 A new apportionment act had been passed January 30, 1831, which increased the number of senators and senatorial districts from twenty-three to thirty. The number of representatives was increased from sixty-one to seventy-five. Senators from the new districts were classified by lot according to Article III of the Constitution: Hayes and Long drew first class or one-year terms; Herod and Jessup second class or two-year terms; Beard, Clark, and Wallace third class or three-year terms. *Senate Journal,* 1831-32, p. 8.

2 Indianapolis *Indiana Journal,* August 13, 1831.

3 Terre Haute *Western Register,* August 6, 1831.

4 Lawrenceburg *Indiana Palladium,* August 6, 1831.

5 Indianapolis *Indiana Journal,* August 6, 1831.

August 6, 1832

Returns for House of Representatives

Seventeenth Session, December 3, 1832—February 4, 1833

District	Candidates			
	*George Crawford	Elisha Egbert	William Bissell	Richard L. Britton
Allen				
Elkhart[1]	113	20	89	......
LaGrange				
LaPorte				
St. Joseph[1]	104	45	5	11

	*John H. Goodbar	*Jesse Carter	Jacob Angle	John Nelson	Robert Smith
Clinton[2]	33	298	132	94	3
Montgomery[2]	754	328	477	412	5
Total	787	626	609	506	8

	*George H. Dunn	*David V. Culley	*Oliver Heustis	Matthias Haines	Samuel H. Dowden	Thomas Howard
Dearborn[3]	1203	1159	1069	1053	999	983

	*Lewis Mastin	Alexander Little	John C. Julien	Gideon Wilson
Hendricks[4]	362	195	171	64

	*James H. Cravens	*Nathan B. Palmer	Edward R. Maxwell
Jefferson[5]	1163	1088	1082

	*John Vawter	William A. Bullock
Jennings[6]	414	257

	*David S. Bonner (W)	Samuel Tomlinson
Knox[7]	505	488

	*Robert Hanna	Henry Brady	Samuel G. Mitchell	Scattering
Marion[8]	658	402	238	15

	*William Bradley	Nathaniel Cotton	Daniel Kelso	George Craig
Switzerland[9]	421	292	189	108

Representatives Elected for Whom No Returns Have Been Found

District	
Bartholomew	Jesse Ruddick
Boone, Hamilton, and adjoining territory	Austin Davenport
Carroll and Cass	Walter Wilson
Clark	Benjamin Ferguson, Thomas J. Henley, John C. Parker
Clay	Jared Peyton
Crawford	Zebulon Levenworth
Daviess and Martin	Erasmus H. McJunkin, William Wallace
Decatur	William Fowler
Delaware and adjoining territory	David Ribble
Dubois and Pike	George H. Proffit
Fayette	Allen Crisler, Marks Crume

Floyd	Harbin H. Moore
Fountain	Abel Claypool, Edward A. Hannegan
Franklin	John Reid, John Roop
Gibson	John Hargrove
Greene	Drury B. Boyd
Hancock and Madison	Thomas Bell
Harrison	David G. Mitchell, John W. Payne
Henry	Thomas R. Stanford
Jackson	James Hamilton
Johnson	Joab Woodruff
Lawrence	Hugh L. Livingston, William B. Slaughter
Monroe	James Parks
Morgan	John W. Cox
Orange	Shadrach R. A. Carter, James Lynd
Owen	Robert M. Wooden
Parke	William P. Bryant, Richard Pruitt
Perry and Spencer	Mason J. Howell
Posey	Richard Daniel
Putnam	John McNary, Lewis H. Sands
Randolph	William Edwards
Ripley	William Skeen
Rush	Joseph Lowe, Nathaniel Smith
Scott	Elisha G. English
Shelby	Rezin Davis
Sullivan	John W. Davis
Tippecanoe	Aaron Finch, Morgan Shortridge
Union	Zachariah Ferguson, William Watt
Vanderburgh and Warrick	Joseph Lane
Vermillion	James Osborn
Vigo	Elisha M. Huntington
Warren	James H. Buell
Washington	Gustavus Clark, Rudolphus Schoonover
Wayne	Abner M. Bradbury, Caleb Lewis, James Rariden, William Steele

1 South Bend *St. Joseph Beacon,* August 8, 1832.
2 Crawfordsville *Record,* August 7, 1832.
3 Lawrenceburg *Palladium,* July 28, August 11, 1832.
4 *History of Hendricks County* (1885), 302.
5 Madison *Indiana Republican,* August 9, 1832.
6 *Ibid.,* August 16, 1832.
7 Vincennes *Western Sun,* August 11, 1832.
8 Indianapolis *Indiana Journal,* August 11, 1832.
9 Printer's Retreat *Weekly Messenger,* August 14, 1832.

Returns for Senate

District	*Samuel Hanna	Pleasant Harris	J. Smith
Allen[1]	676	429	645
Delaware			
Elkhart[1]	37	157	16
Randolph			
St. Joseph[1]	66	97	8

District	*David Hillis	Williamson Dunn
Jefferson[2]	1412	420

Senators Elected for Whom No Returns Have Been Found

District	
Clark and Floyd	John M. Lemon
Dubois, Gibson, Pike	David Robb
Hancock, Henry, Madison	Elisha Long
Lawrence and Orange	Samuel Chambers
Parke	Hugh F. Feeny
Rush	Amaziah Morgan
Washington	Ezekiel D. Logan
Wayne	David Hoover

[1] South Bend *St. Joseph Beacon,* August 8, 22, 1832.
[2] Madison *Indiana Republican,* August 9, 1832.

August 5, 1833

Returns for House of Representatives

Eighteenth Session, December 2, 1833—February 3, 1834

District	*David H. Colerick	George Crawford	Anthony Defrees	William N. Hood	William Suttenfield	Hughes
Allen[1]	444	386	222	103	31	10
Elkhart[1]	165	128	......	8	......	......
LaGrange						
LaPorte[1]	20	102	14	......	2	......
St. Joseph[1]	81	52	115	......	2	......

	*Austin Davenport	Robert L. Hannaman
Boone Hamilton[2]	136	296

	*Gillis McBean	Philip Pollard	J. M. Ewing
Carroll Cass[3]	302	113	1

	*George H. Dunn	*David Guard	*Thomas Guion	Oliver Heustis	Alfred J. Cotton	Warren Tebbs
Dearborn[4]	1437	1180	1113	848	838	655

	*Frederick Leslie	*George P. R. Wilson	John Zenor	Thomas Craig	George Arnold
Harrison[5]	1023	654	630	158	149

	*Thomas Nichols	Christian C. Nave	James Anderson	Gideon Wilson
Hendricks[6]	327	276	203	96

	*Nathan B. Palmer	*James H. Wallace	Edward R. Maxwell	George W. Bantz	Samuel Welch
Jefferson[7]	891	762	628	254	238

	*Samuel Smith, Jr.	*John F. Snapp	Samuel Emison	Samuel Judah	William Raper
Knox[8]	634	599	498	249	125

	*Henry Brady	William Sanders	Matthias T. Nowland	John Eccles	Samuel Frazier
Marion[9]	913	377	250	33	17

	*Rees Hardesty	*George Piercy	Henry Secrest	W. Buckhemor	Gardner
Putnam[2]	908	612	505	476	239

	*Daniel Kelso	Samuel Fallis	Charles F. Krutz	John P. Lillard	Solomon Washer	Wilson B. Benefiel
Switzerland[10]	262	220	190	190	132	78

	*Abner M. Bradbury	*Abel Thornberry	*William Steele	*John Jones	Henry Hoover	Abel Lomax[12]
Wayne[11]	1536	1511	1485	1425	1225	1191

Representatives Elected for Whom No Returns Have Been Found

District	
Bartholomew	William P. Kiser
Clark	Samuel J. Stewart, John H. Thompson
Clay	William Yocum
Clinton and Montgomery	Jacob Angle, David Vance
Crawford	Zebulon Levenworth
Daviess and Martin	David McDonald
Decatur	William Fowler
Delaware and adjoining territory	David Kilgore
Dubois and Pike	William M. Wright
Fayette	Marks Crume, Caleb B. Smith
Floyd	Prindowell M. Dorsey, William Williams
Fountain	Thomas J. Evans, Lawson B. Hughes
Franklin	Benjamin S. Noble, John Reid
Gibson	John Hargrove
Greene	George Baber
Hancock and Madison	John Foster
Henry	Thomas R. Stanford
Jackson	Richard Beem
Jennings	William C. Bramwell
Johnson	Joab Woodruff
Lawrence	John Brown, Absalom Fields
Monroe	Paris C. Dunning
Morgan	Grant Stafford
Orange	Shadrach R. A. Carter, Joel Vandeveer
Owen	George W. Moore
Parke	Joseph A. Wright
Perry and Spencer	Mason J. Howell
Posey	Jesse R. Craig
Randolph	William Edwards
Ripley	Thomas Smith
Rush	Samuel Bigger, Marinus Willett

Scott	Elisha G. English
Shelby	Rezin Davis
Sullivan	James De Pauw
Tippecanoe	Thomas B. Brown, Loyal Fairman
Union	William H. Bennett, Zachariah Ferguson
Vanderburgh and Warrick	John A. Brackenridge
Vermillion	Miles Gookins, Isaac Pearson
Vigo	Elisha M. Huntington
Warren	Samuel B. Clark
Washington	Henry C. Monroe, Woodbridge Parker

1 South Bend *St. Joseph Beacon,* August 10, 17, 1833; Election Returns, LaPorte and St. Joseph counties, Archives Division.

2 Indianapolis *Indiana Democrat,* August 10, 1833.

3 *Cass County Times,* August 8, 1833.

4 Lawrenceburg *Palladium,* August 10, 1833. In addition to the candidates listed for Dearborn County, Henry Hopkins received 37 votes, John Fryer, Sr., 54.

5 Election Returns, Harrison County Courthouse.

6 *History of Hendricks County* (1885), 303.

7 Madison *Indiana Republican,* August 8, 1833.

8 Vincennes *Western Sun,* August 17, 1833.

9 Indianapolis *Indiana Journal,* August 10, 1833.

10 Printer's Retreat *Weekly Messenger,* August 10, 17, 1833.

11 Richmond *Palladium,* August 10, 1833.

12 In addition to the candidates listed for Wayne County, John Erwin received 1041 votes, S. Pierce 888, J. Martin 222, Z. W. Pendleton 182, and J. P. Gunkle 88.

Returns for Senate

District	Candidates	
	*William Wallace	Henry M. Shaw
Daviess[1]	447	267
Knox[1]	453	666
Martin[1]	217	149
Total	1117	1082
	*David V. Culley	Johnson Watts
Dearborn[2]	1218	970
	*Alexander F. Morrison	Austin W. Morris
Hamilton[3]	214	223
Marion[3]	804	794
Total	1018	1017

	*John W. Payne	George Bentley
Harrison[4]	1052	247

	*Lewis Mastin	C. G. Hussey
Boone		
Hendricks[5]	608	294
Morgan		

	*Andrew C. Griffith	John Vawter	Jesse Jackson
Jackson[6]	753	172	37
Jennings[6]	25	586	120
Scott[6]	109	121	320
Total	887	679	477

	*Daniel Sigler	L. M. Knight
Putnam[7]	1062	515

Senators Elected for Whom No Returns Have Been Found

District	
Bartholomew and Jennings	Zachariah Tannehill[8]
Clark and Floyd	David W. Daily[9]
Crawford, Perry, Spencer	George B. Thompson
Dubois, Gibson, Pike	Elisha Embree[10]
Fountain	Frederick C. Paine[11]
Greene, Monroe, Owen	James Whitcomb
Posey, Vanderburgh, Warrick	Charles I. Battell
Vermillion and Warren	Stephen S. Collett

1 Vincennes *Western Sun,* August 17, 1833.

2 Lawrenceburg *Palladium,* August 10, 1833. Culley was elected to fill out the unexpired term of James T. Pollock who resigned as senator on February 22, 1833. *Executive Proceedings, 1816-1836,* 354n.

3 Indianapolis *Indiana Journal,* August 10, 1833. Morrison was elected to fill out the term of Calvin Fletcher who resigned his seat in the Senate on January 26, 1833. *Executive Proceedings, 1816-1836,* 354.

4 Election Returns, Harrison County Courthouse.

5 *History of Hendricks County* (1885), 303.

6 Madison *Indiana Republican,* August 15, 1833.

7 Indianapolis *Indiana Democrat,* August 10, 1833.

8 Tannehill was elected to fill out the term of William Herod who resigned as senator on April 4, 1833. *Executive Proceedings, 1816-1836,* 354-55n.

[9] Daily was elected to fill out the term of John M. Lemon who resigned as senator on May 23, 1833, to become receiver of public moneys in the LaPorte Land Office. *Ibid.*, 355.

[10] Embree was elected to fill out the term of David Robb who resigned as senator on April 13, 1833, to become register of the LaPorte Land Office. *Ibid.*

[11] Paine was elected to fill out the term of Benjamin F. Wallace who resigned as senator on April 10, 1833. *Ibid.*

August 4, 1834

Returns for House of Representatives

Nineteenth Session, December 1, 1834—February 9, 1835

District — Candidates

District	*Nelson H. Torbet	*James Walker	*Thomas Howard	Alfred J. Cotton	David Guard	Isaac Caldwell
Dearborn[1]	1333	1330	1257	869	857	711

District	*Caleb B. Smith	*Marks Crume	J. A. Wilson
Fayette[2]	1075	922	483

District	*Robert McIntyre	*Thomas J. Evans	Isaac Martin	William Worthington
Fountain[3]	1130	879	477	263

District	*John M. Johnston	*James Conwell	B. S. Noble	Joseph Bennett	C. W. Hutchen	James Halsey
Franklin[4]	920	580	432	410	133	111

District	*Frederick Leslie	*Geo. P. R. Wilson	Thomas Craig	George Arnold	Jesse Weatherly
Harrison[5]	837	671	540	531	23

District	*Christian C. Nave	Thomas Nichols	William Naylor	James Anderson	John Dunn	Henry H. Marvin
Hendricks[6]	270	268	176	171	50	21

District	*James H. Wallace	*Joseph G. Marshall	John Smock	William C. Sullivan	Robert Kinnear
Jefferson[7]	919	846	583	421	382

District	*Henry M. Shaw	John F. Snapp	Robert N. Carnan
Knox[8]	517	381	253

	*Jonathan A. Liston	Samuel Miller	Benjamin McCarty	Pleasant Harris
LaPorte[9]	77	182	155	52
St. Joseph				

	*Jeremiah Johnson	Archibald C. Reed	Andrew Robe	M. T. Nowland
Marion[10]	780	764	137	26

	*Enos Lowe	*Paton Wilson	James Strange	J. McKinney	S. M. McCorkle	W. W. Crooks
Parke[11]	636	545	495	269	223	187

	*Thomas Smith	Hezekiah Shook	Merit S. Craig
Ripley[12]	355	288	266

	*Samuel Bigger	*Marinus Willett	R. Hackleman
Rush[2]	1543	1446	455

	*Daniel Kelso	John Pavy	P. H. Banta	Scattering
Switzerland[13]	585	374	72	2

	*John S. Newman	*Joseph Curtis	*Abner M. Bradbury	*Martin M. Ray	Abel Thornberry	Joseph V. Gregg[15]
Wayne[14]	1890	1765	1749	1591	1176	1018

Representatives Elected For Whom No Returns Have Been Found

District	
Allen, Huntington, and adjoining territory	William Rockhill
Bartholomew	Jacob Cook

Boone, Hamilton, and adjoining territory	Robert L. Hannaman
Carroll, Cass, Miami, White	Chauncy Carter
Clark	William G. Armstrong, Daniel Bower, Eli McCalley
Clay	Daniel Harris
Clinton and Montgomery	Jacob Angle, Thomas M. Curry
Crawford	Joseph N. Phelps
Daviess and Martin	Patrick M. Brett, Josiah Culbertson
Decatur	Samuel Bryan
Delaware and adjoining territory	David Kilgore
Dubois and Pike	William M. Wright
Elkhart, LaGrange, and adjoining territory	John B. Chapman
Floyd	Levi McDougle
Gibson	John Hargrove
Greene	Joseph P. Storm
Hancock and Madison	Thomas Bell
Henry	Thomas R. Stanford
Jackson	John F. Carr
Jennings	John Vawter
Johnson	Joab Woodruff
Lawrence	Pleasant Parks, Richard W. Thompson
Monroe	Paris C. Dunning
Morgan	Grant Stafford
Orange	Shadrach R. A. Carter, Joel Vandeveer
Owen	George W. Moore
Perry and Spencer	Mason J. Howell
Posey	George S. Green
Putnam	James Gaddes, Rees Hardesty
Randolph	Zachariah Puckett
Scott	Isaac Hoagland
Shelby	Jacob Shank
Sullivan	Joseph Latshaw
Tippecanoe	James Davis, Benjamin Henkle
Union	William H. Bennett, James R. Mendenhall
Vanderburgh and Warrick	John A. Brackenridge
Vermillion	Joseph Schooling
Vigo	Ralph Wilson

Warren	James Gregory
Washington	Levi P. Lockhart, Robert Strain

[1] Lawrenceburg *Indiana Palladium,* August 9, 1834.
[2] Connersville *Watchman,* August 8, 1834.
[3] Covington *Western Constellation,* August 8, 1834.
[4] Brookville *Indiana American,* August 8, 1834.
[5] Election Returns, Harrison County Courthouse.
[6] *History of Hendricks County* (1885), 303.
[7] Madison *Republican and Banner,* August 7, 1834.
[8] Vincennes *Western Sun,* August 9, 1834.
[9] LaPorte County Election Returns, Archives Division.
[10] Indianapolis *Indiana Journal,* August 9, 1834.
[11] Covington *Western Constellation,* August 22, 1834.
[12] Ripley County Election Returns, Archives Division.
[13] Printer's Retreat *Weekly Messenger,* August 8, 1834.
[14] Richmond *Palladium,* August 9, 1834.
[15] In addition to the candidates listed for Wayne County, Lewis McLane received 759 votes, Jonathan Shaw, 75, Robert Chapman, 56.

Returns for Senate

District	Candidates	
	*Othniel L. Clark	Samuel Milroy
Carroll[1]	220	380
Cass[1]	356	113
Miami[1]	64	27
Tippecanoe[1]	929	547
White[1]	46	31
Total	1615	1098

	*John Beard	David Vance	John H. Goodbar
Clinton[2]	266	185	21
Montgomery	655	546	134
Total	921	731	155

	*Daniel Plummer	Walter Armstrong
Dearborn[2]	1417	844

	*William Caldwell	Ross Smiley
Fayette[2]	862	622
Union[2]	670	590
Total	1532	1212

	*John Hamilton	Abel Claypool	Frederic C. Paine
Fountain[3]	597	427	398

	*John Reid
Franklin[4]	1109

	*Henry Brady	John W. Reding
Hamilton[5]	264	261
Marion[5]	978	769
Total	1242	1030

	*John Dumont	James H. Cravens	A. Sebastian
Ripley[6]	327	517	109
Switzerland[7]	402	345	129

Senators Elected for Whom No Returns Have Been Found

District	
Clay, Sullivan, Vigo	George Boon
Decatur and Shelby	William Fowler
Delaware and Randolph	Andrew Aker
Washington	Henry W. Hackett[8]

1 Connersville *Watchman,* August 22, 1834. The Indianapolis *Indiana Journal* of August 16 gives the Carroll County vote as 272 for Clark and 345 for Milroy.

2 Indianapolis *Indiana Journal,* August 16, 1834.

3 Covington *Western Constellation,* August 8, 1834.

4 Brookville *Indiana American,* August 8, 1834.

5 Indianapolis *Indiana Journal,* August 9, 1834.

6 Ripley County Election Returns, Archives Division. The Ripley County clerk noted the returns for the General Assembly at the bottom of his official report on the vote for governor and lieutenant governor. Either his figures for the senatorial candidates were in error or the newspaper's report of the Switzerland County vote was wrong; otherwise Cravens would have been elected rather than Dumont.

7 Printer's Retreat *Weekly Messenger,* August 8, 1834.

8 Hackett was elected to fill out the term of Ezekiel D. Logan who had resigned on May 17, 1834, because of ill health. *Executive Proceeding, 1816-1836,* 355-56n.

August 3, 1835

Returns for House of Representatives

Twentieth Session, December 7, 1835—February 8, 1836

District	*Gillis McBean	Chauncy Carter
Carroll[1]	313	183
Cass[1]	319	309
Miami[1]	134	89
White[1]	48	49
Total	814	630

District	*Henry Ristine	*Henry Lee	Thomas M. Curry	Edwin Winship	Ross
Clinton Montgomery[2]	776	688	777	271	68

District	*Henry Walker	*Thomas Howard	*Milton Gregg	William Conaway	James P. Millikan	Warren Tebbs
Dearborn[2]	1283	1272	1220	1208	1196	1189

District	*James Collins	*Shepherd Whitman	William Williams	Levi McDougall
Floyd[2]	755	578	537	103

District	*Thomas J. Evans	*William Templeton	C. S. Winans	Jonathan Burch	John Ward
Fountain[3]	980	488	429	358	319

District	*John M. Johnston	*Enoch McCarty	C. W. Hutchens
Franklin[2]	910	777	629

District	*George P. R. Wilson	*John Zenor	William Armstrong	Thomas Craig	George Arnold	Abraham Carr
Harrison[4]	635	632	430	402	316	20

District	*Christian C. Nave	James Anderson	Job Osborn
Hendricks[5]	541	380	154

	*Milton Stapp	*John Chambers	Joseph G. Marshall	Samuel Welch	Charles I. Cosby
Jefferson[6]	1132	1113	1053	248	85

	*Robert N. Carnan	*John Myers	George Calhoun (or Calhound)
Knox[7]	894	677	495

	*Jonathan A. Liston	Charles W. Cathcart (D)	Samuel Miller
LaPorte[8]	134	433	212
St. Joseph			

	*Austin W. Morris	A. C. Reed	Robert Hanna
Marion[9]	967	652	212

	*William H. Craig	Shell
Morgan[2]	372	239

	*George K. Steele	Paton Wilson
Parke[2]	818	713

	*Daniel Harrow	*John C. Chiles	John McNary	Sinclair	James Duffield	Harris[10]
Putnam[2]	751	733	698	588	453	309

	*Alfred Posey	*Marinus Willett	Wm. P. Rush
Rush[2]	1365	1307	1086

	*Joseph C. Eggleston	Alexander Sebastian	Joshua Hicks	James M. Cotton	Thomas W. Butler	William Scott
Switzerland[11]	602	196	140	84	4	3

	*Thomas B. Brown	*James Davis	Andrew Ingram	John Pettit
Tippecanoe[2]	854	822	691	165

	*Stephen B. Gardner	*Hiram B. Cole	Joseph Schooling	Isaac Pearson	W. C. Doncarlos	A. Morehead
Vermillion[3]	600	337	312	297	248	145

	*Marston G. Clark	*Robert Strain	Levi P. Lockhart	Coffin	Rudolphus Schoonover
Washington[2]	888	726	718	691	424

	*Joseph Curtis	*Richard J. Hubbard	*Martin M. Ray	*Daniel Clark	Abner M. Bradbury	Joseph V. Gregg[13]
Wayne[12]	1963	1895	1734	1511	1497	1268

Representatives Elected for Whom No Returns Have Been Found

District	
Allen, Huntington, and adjoining territory	Lewis G. Thompson
Bartholomew	Thomas G. Lee
Boone, Hamilton, and adjoining territory	Robert L. Hannaman
Clark	William G. Armstrong, John C. Huckleberry
Clay	Daniel Harris
Crawford	Joseph N. Phelps
Daviess and Martin	Lewis Jones
Decatur	Samuel Bryan
Delaware and Grant	David Kilgore
Dubois and Pike	Benjamin Edmonston
Elkhart, LaGrange, and adjoining territory	Ebenezer M. Chamberlain
Fayette	Philip Mason, Caleb B. Smith
Gibson	Smith Miller
Greene	Joseph P. Storm
Hancock and Madison	Leonard Bardwell
Henry	David Macy
Jackson	John F. Carr

Jennings	John Vawter
Johnson	John S. Thompson
Lawrence	Noah Boone, Richard W. Thompson
Monroe	Paris C. Dunning
Orange	John Murray, Joel Vandeveer
Owen	George W. Moore
Perry and Spencer	Mason J. Howell
Posey	Jesse R. Craig
Randolph	William Edwards
Ripley	Thomas Smith
Scott	Jesse Jackson
Shelby	John Walker
Sullivan	Seth Cushman
Union	William H. Bennett, William Watt
Vanderburgh and Warrick	Christopher C. Graham
Vigo	Elisha M. Huntington
Warren	James H. Buell

1 Logansport *Canal Telegraph,* August 8, 15, 1835.

2 Indianapolis *Indiana Journal,* August 14, 1835.

3 Covington *Western Constellation,* August 8, 1835.

4 Election Returns, Harrison County Courthouse.

5 *History of Hendricks County* (1885), 303.

6 Madison *Republican and Banner,* August 6, 1835.

7 Vincennes *Western Sun,* August 15, 1835.

8 Jasper Packard, *History of LaPorte County, Indiana . . .* (LaPorte, 1876), 233.

9 Indianapolis *Indiana Journal,* August 7, 1835.

10 In addition to candidates listed for Putnam County, George Piercy received 141 votes and Davis, 110.

11 Printer's Retreat *Weekly Messenger,* August 8, 1835.

12 Richmond *Palladium,* August 8, 1835.

13 In addition to the candidates listed for Wayne County, John Jones received 1025 votes.

Returns for Senate

District	Candidates	
	*David H. Colerick (D)	William G. Ewing
Allen		
Elkhart		
Huntington		
LaGrange		
LaPorte[1]	293	277
St. Joseph		
Wabash		

	*David W. Daily	P. M. Dorsey	Leslie
Clark			
Floyd[2]	30	1024	40

	*Henry M. Shaw	Patrick M. Brett
Daviess[3]	490	278
Knox[3]	710	369
Martin[3]	176	216
Total	1376	863

	*David Hillis
Jefferson[4]	1906

	*Austin M. Puett	Enos Lowe	William T. Noel
Parke[2]	629	592	325

	*Amaziah Morgan	Joseph Lowe
Rush[2]	1315	818

	*Henry W. Hackett	Wright
Washington[2]	915	820

	*William Elliott	Henry Hoover
Wayne[2]	1547	1439

Senators Elected for Whom No Returns Were Found

District	
Dubois, Gibson, Pike	Thomas C. Stewart
Franklin	John Reid[5]
Hancock, Henry, Madison	Thomas Bell
Lawrence and Orange	Samuel Chambers
Posey, Vanderburgh, Warrick	William Casey[6]

1 Packard, *History of LaPorte County,* 233.

2 Indianapolis *Indiana Journal,* August 14, 1835.

3 Vincennes *Western Sun,* August 8, 1835. Shaw was elected to fill the vacancy caused by the death of William Wallace.

4 Madison *Republican and Banner,* August 6, 1835. Hillis was the only candidate.

5 Reid died August 14, a few days after the election. James Conwell was elected in his place on October 17. *Executive Proceedings, 1816-1836,* 356.

6 Casey was elected to fill out the unexpired term of Charles I. Battell who had been appointed president judge of the Fourth Judicial Circuit. *Ibid.*

August 1, 1836

Returns for House of Representatives

Twenty-first Session, December 5, 1836—February 6, 1837

District	Candidates		
	*John Burk (W)	Joel Grover	William Vance
Adams[1] Huntington Jay Wells	3	6	40

District	*John P. Dunn (D)	*Abel C. Pepper (D)	*Pinckney James (W)	*David Guard (W)	George P. Buell	James Walker[3]
Dearborn[2]	1378	1303	1176	1115	1099	988

District	*Thomas J. Evans (W)	*William Templeton[5]	E. Wade
Fountain[4]	1026	1157	460

District	*Enoch McCarty (W)	*Rufus Haymond (W)	R. Winchell	S. Wiley	Joseph Bennett	F. Alger
Franklin[6]	781	726	724	277	210	97

District	*William A. Porter (W)	*John Zenor (W)	Thomas Craig	William Applegate
Harrison[7]	1109	935	621	105

District	*Thomas Nichols (W)	William T. Matlock	Edward Railsback
Hendricks[8]	507	482	104

District	*Joseph G. Marshall (W)	*Milton Stapp (W)	*John Chambers (D)	John Smock	William Powell	John McCoy
Jefferson[9]	1275	1151	904	660	90	......

	*John Myers (D)	Hiram Decker (W)
Knox[10]	688	645

	*Joel Long (D)	Stephen Marsters
Kosciusko Marshall[11] Starke	32	102

	*Austin W. Morris (W)	*Robert Hanna (W)	Alexander F. Morrison	A. B. Strong	W. Rector
Marion[12]	1169	980	805	627	129

	*William Berry (D)	Craven P. Hester	Jesse Brandon
Monroe[13] Part of Brown	730	582	6

	*Thomas M. Curry (W)	*Henry Lee (D)	Isaac Naylor	John Nelson
Montgomery[14]	804	704	670	571

	*Benjamin McCarty (W)	J. R. C. Brown (D)
Porter[15] Newton	138	115

	*Joseph C. Eggleston (D)	Daniel Kelso
Switzerland[2]	650	263

	*John W. Odell (W)	*Thomas B. Brown (D)	Thomas Watson	H. Ensminger
Tippecanoe[16]	911	844	826	748

	*William Watt (D)	*William H. Bennett (W)	James Osborn	James W. Crist
Union[17]	649	553	458	431

	*Lewis Burnes (D)	*John Hoobler (D)	Miles Gookins	Castleman	Stokes
Vermillion[18]	651	547	479	294	128

	*Daniel Mace (W)	Luther Tillotson	M. Cox	H. Ounghst
Warren[19] Part of Jasper	379	245	121	19

	*Joseph Curtis (W)	*Lot Bloomfield (W)	*Richard J. Hubbard (W)	*Nathan Smith (W)	William M. Doughty	Cornelius Ratliff
Wayne[20]	2006	1998	1957	1709	1158	920

Representatives Elected for Whom No Returns Have Been Found

District	
Allen	William Rockhill (D)
Bartholomew and part of Brown	Thomas G. Lee (D), John McKinney (D)
Boone	Abner H. Longley (D)
Carroll	Albert G. Hanna (D)
Cass	Graham N. Fitch (D)
Clark	William G. Armstrong (W), Benjamin Ferguson (W)
Clay	Jesse J. Burton (D)
Clinton	Edwin Winship (W)
Crawford	Isaac Sands (W)
Daviess	James Breeze (W)
Decatur	James Elder (W)
DeKalb, LaGrange, Noble, Steuben	Thomas Gale (W)
Delaware	William Vanmetre (W)
Dubois and Pike	George H. Proffit (W)
Elkhart	John Jackson (D)

Fayette	Marks Crume (W), Caleb B. Smith (W)
Floyd	Henry P. Thornton (W)
Fulton and Miami	William N. Hood (W)
Gibson	Smith Miller (D)
Grant and Wabash	Josiah L. Wines (W)
Greene	Joseph P. Storm (D)
Hamilton	William Conner (W)
Hancock	Thomas D. Walpole (W)
Henry	Richard Henderson (W), David Macy (W)
Jackson	William Marshall (D)
Jasper, Pulaski, White	Robert Newell (W)
Jennings	Ezra F. Pabody (W)
Johnson	James Lusk (D)
LaPorte	Leo H. T. Maxson (D)
Lawrence	Noah Boone (D), Vinson Williams (D)
Madison	John H. Cook (W)
Martin	John Reiley (D)
Morgan	Hiram Matthews (W)
Orange	Joel Vandeveer (D)
Owen	Delana R. Eccles (D)
Parke	George K. Steele (D), Joseph A. Wright (D)
Perry	Joshua B. Huckeby (W)
Posey	Robert D. Owen (D)
Putnam	John W. Cunningham (W), Isaac Mahan (W), John S. Talbott (D)
Randolph	Zachariah Puckett (W)
Ripley	Hezekiah Shook (D)
Rush	Alfred Posey (W), Benjamin F. Reeve (W), William P. Rush (W)
St. Joseph	Thomas D. Baird (W)
Scott	Samuel S. Heath (D)
Shelby	Edward Gird (D), Erasmus Powell (W)
Spencer	Mason J. Howell (D)
Sullivan	Joseph Briggs (W), Samuel Brown (D)
Vanderburgh	William T. T. Jones (W)
Vigo	Thomas Dowling (W), William Wines (D)

Warrick	Christopher C. Graham (D)
Washington	John DePauw (D), Robert Strain (D)

[1] Election Returns, Adams County Courthouse, Decatur.

[2] Printer's Retreat *Weekly Messenger,* August 6, 1836.

[3] In addition to the candidates listed for Dearborn County, Thomas Guion received 972 votes; Daniel Roberts, 962.

[4] Covington *Western Constellation,* August 5, 1836.

[5] Templeton died a day or so before the election but news of his death did not reach the voters in time to prevent his election. At an election held October 3 to fill the vacancy, Robert McIntyre, Democrat, received 649 votes and Peter H. Patterson, 317. *Ibid.,* October 7, 1836.

[6] Brookville *Indiana American,* August 5, 1836.

[7] Election Returns, Harrison County Courthouse, Corydon.

[8] *History of Hendricks County* (1885), 303.

[9] Madison *Republican and Banner,* August 10, 1836.

[10] Vincennes *Western Sun,* August 6, 1836.

[11] Donald McDonald, *A Twentieth Century History of Marshall County Indiana* (2 vols. Chicago, 1908), 2:366.

[12] Indianapolis *Indiana Journal,* August 6, 1836.

[13] Bloomington *Post,* August 5, 1836.

[14] Crawfordsville *Record,* August 6, 1836.

[15] Weston A. Goodspeed and Charles Blanchard (eds.), *Counties of Porter and Lake Indiana* (Chicago, 1882), 72.

[16] Lafayette *Free Press,* August 5, 1836.

[17] Liberty *Star and Banner,* August 6, 1836.

[18] Covington *Western Constellation,* August 19, 1836.

[19] *Ibid.,* August 12, 1836.

[20] Richmond *Palladium,* August 6, 1836.

Returns for Senate[1]

District	Candidates	
	*Thomas C. Moore (D)	Samuel Judah
Daviess[1a]	545	347
Knox[1a]	580	708
Martin[1a]	327	72
Total	1452	1127
	*Newton Claypool (W)	M. R. Hull
Fayette[2]	Maj. of 192	
Union[2]	381	461
	*David G. Mitchell	George P. R. Wilson
Harrison[3]	743	729

	*Alexander Little (W)	Lewis Mastin
Hendricks[4]	673	467

	*Simon Turman (D)	James Gregory	Asaph Hill	W. H. H. Scott
Part of Jasper				
Vermillion[5]	377	37	385	329
Warren	231	513	38	25

	*Gustavus A. Everts (W)	David Evans (D)
Part of Jasper		
LaPorte[6]	468	467
Porter[7]	133	125
Pulaski		
White		

	*Jonathan A. Liston (W)	Lot Day
Kosciusko		
Marshall[8]	68	65
St. Joseph		
Starke		

	*Paris C. Dunning (D)	Eli P. Farmer
Monroe[9]	759	530

	*Abner M. Bradbury (W)	Henry Hoover
Wayne[10]	1703	1127

Senators Elected for Whom No Returns Have Been Found

District	
Bartholomew and Jennings	John Vawter (W)
Boone and Hamilton	Bicknell Cole (W)
Carroll and Clinton	Samuel Milroy (D)
Cass, Fulton, Miami	George W. Ewing (D)
Crawford, Perry, Spencer	George B. Thompson (W)
DeKalb, Elkhart, LaGrange, Noble, Steuben	George Crawford (W)

Delaware and Randolph	Andrew Kennedy (D)[11]
Floyd	James Collins (W)
Grant, Huntington, Jay, Wabash	Ezra S. Trask (D)
Greene and Owen	David M. Dobson (D)
Henry	Thomas R. Stanford (W)
Jackson and Scott	Isaac Hoagland (W)
Johnson	John S. Thompson (W)
Lawrence	Richard W. Thompson (W)
Morgan	Grant Stafford (W)
Posey, Vanderburgh, Warrick	William Casey (D)
Putnam	Daniel Sigler (W)
Ripley	Thomas Smith (D)
Shelby	John Walker (W)

[1]By the new apportionment act of January 13, 1836, the number of senatorial districts was increased to forty-six, with one senator to each district excepting one. *Laws of Indiana,* 1835-36 (gen.), pp. 3-5. Fifteen of the senatorial districts were considered as new districts. Senators from these districts drew terms as follows—one year: Collins, Everts, Ewing, Liston, and Milroy; two years: Dobson, Smith, Stafford, Thompson of Lawrence; three years: Cole, Crawford, Stanford, Thompson of Johnson, Trask, and Walker. Wayne County was given two senators; Bradbury, the second senator, drew a two-year term. *Senate Journal,* 1836-37, p. 8.

[1a] Vincennes *Western Sun,* August 6, 1836.

[2] Liberty *Star and Banner,* August 6, 1836. Claypool was elected to fill the vacancy created by the resignation of William Caldwell. *Executive Proceedings, 1816-1836,* 357.

[3] Election Returns, Harrison County Courthouse, Corydon.

[4] *History of Hendricks County* (1885), 303.

[5] Covington *Western Constellation,* August 12, 1836.

[6] Packard, *History of LaPorte County,* 233.

[7] Goodspeed and Blanchard (eds.), *Counties of Porter and Lake,* 72.

[8] McDonald, *History of Marshall County,* 2:366.

[9] Bloomington *Post,* August 5, 1836.

[10] Richmond *Palladium,* August 6, 1836.

[11] Kennedy was elected to fill out the term of Andrew Aker who had resigned as senator on May 19, 1836. *Executive Proceedings, 1816-1836,* 356.

August 7, 1837

Returns for House of Representatives

Twenty-second Session, December 4, 1837—February 19, 1838

District	Candidates		
	*William Vance	George A. Tate	James W. Willer
Adams[1]	59	10	5
Huntington			
Jay			
Wells			

	*Job B. Eldridge	Graham N. Fitch
Cass[2]	472	446

	*George Arnold	*Abram Ferris	*Enoch W. Jackson	*Alexander E. Glenn	Jacob W. Egelston	Pinckney James[4]
Dearborn[3]	1859	1650	1549	1535	1372	1162

	*William T. Matlock	Christian C. Nave
Hendricks[5]	784	557

	*Samuel Judah	*Jonathan P. Cox	Samuel Emison	William Mieure	Archibald McKee	William Patterson
Knox[6]	639	571	487	482	81	49

	*Jeremiah Hamell (W)	A. L. Ball (D)
Lake[7]	65	70
Porter		

	*Alexander F. Morrison	*Robert Hanna	Douglass Maguire	John H. Newland
Marion[8]	1479	1305	1233	200

	*William Berry	John Ketcham
Part of Brown		
Monroe[9]	593	427

	*James M. Cotton	I. W. Robinson	Royal F. North	Bela Hedrick
Switzerland[10]	860	323	184	10

	*Achilles Williams	*Richard J. Hubbard	*Nathan Smith	*Joseph C. Hawkins	Henry Hoover	Thomas Tyner[12]
Wayne[11]	2215	1718	1701	1390	1181	1083

Representatives Elected for Whom No Returns Have Been Found

District	
Allen	Lewis G. Thompson
Bartholomew and part of Brown	Thomas G. Lee, Zachariah Tannehill
Boone	Joseph E. Hocker
Carroll	Samuel Milroy
Clark	Benjamin Ferguson, Thomas J. Henley, Henry Hurst
Clay	Samuel H. Smydth
Clinton	Andrew Major
Crawford and Dubois	Aaron B. McCrilles
Daviess and Martin	Abner Davis
Decatur	James Blair
DeKalb, LaGrange, Noble, Steuben	David B. Herriman
Delaware	William G. Brenner[13]
Elkhart	Ebenezer M. Chamberlain
Fayette	Marks Crume, Wilson Thompson
Floyd	Shepherd Whitman
Fountain	James P. Carleton, Thomas J. Evans
Franklin	Rufus Haymond, Redin Osborn
Fulton and Miami	William N. Hood
Gibson	Smith Miller
Grant and Wabash	Josiah L. Wines
Greene	Drury Boyd
Hamilton	Jacob Robbins
Hancock	Thomas D. Walpole
Harrison	George P. R. Wilson, John Zenor
Henry	David Macy, Miles Murphy
Jackson	John F. Carr
Jasper, Pulaski, White	William M. Kenton
Jefferson	Joseph G. Marshall, Milton Stapp
Jennings	Ezra F. Pabody
Johnson	Benjamin S. Noble
Kosciusko, Marshall, Starke	Aaron M. Perine
LaPorte	Charles McClure
Lawrence	Melchert Helmer, Vinson Williams
Madison	Henry Wyman
Montgomery	John Bryce, Henry S. Lane, Henry Ristine

Morgan	John Sims
Orange	Joel Vandeveer
Owen	Basil Champer
Parke	Jeptha Garrigus, William T. Noel
Perry	Robert G. Cotton
Pike	George H. Proffit
Posey	Robert Dale Owen
Putnam	John W. Cunningham, James Gaddes
Randolph	Zachariah Puckett
Ripley	Hezekiah Shook
Rush	Benjamin Boon, Benjamin F. Reeve, Ward W. Williams
St. Joseph	John A. Hendricks
Scott	John E. Roe
Shelby	Thomas R. E. Davis[14], William J. Peaslee
Spencer	Mason J. Howell
Sullivan	Samuel Brown, William R. Hadden
Tippecanoe	Samuel A. Huff, Thomas Watson
Union	William H. Bennett, James Leviston
Vanderburgh	William T. T. Jones
Vermillion	Lewis Burnes, John Porter
Vigo	Thomas Dowling, William Wines
Warren and part of Jasper	James Gregory
Warrick	Christopher C. Graham
Washington	Samuel Huston, Henry Monroe

1 Election Returns, Adams County Courthouse, Decatur.

2 Logansport *Herald,* August 10, 1837.

3 Rising Sun *Times,* August 12, 1837.

4 In addition to the candidates listed for Dearborn County, John Neal received 925 votes; Nathaniel L. Squibb, 636; John Cundell, 182.

5 *History of Hendricks County* (1885), 303.

6 Vincennes *Western Sun,* August 12, 1837.

7 Goodspeed and Blanchard (eds.), *Counties of Porter and Lake,* 447.

8 Indianapolis *Indiana Journal,* August 12, 1837.

9 Bloomington *Post,* August 11, 1837.

10 Vevay *Village Times,* August 10, 1837.

11 Richmond *Palladium,* August 19, 1837.

12 In addition to the candidates listed for Wayne County, Caleb Lewis received 951 votes, John Jones 835, Joseph Morrow 826, George Holman 431, and A. W. Bowers 29.

13 A writ was issued November 28, 1837, for a special election to fill the vacancy created by Brenner's death. John Richey (or Richie) was elected on December 9 and took his seat on December 18. *Executive Proceedings, 1816-1836,* 357.

14 A writ was issued August 21, 1837, for a special election to fill the vacancy created by Davis' death. Joseph B. Nickoll was elected in his place. *Ibid.*

Returns for Senate

District	Candidates		
	*George W. Ewing	Cyrus Taber	Nicholas D. Grover
Cass[1]	470	237	211
Fulton[1]	65	37	8
Miami[1]	190	36	36
	*Johnson Watts	Mark McCracken	Moses Hornaday
Dearborn[2]	1515	1329	86
		*Charles W. Cathcart (D)	John H. Bradley (W)
Part of Jasper			
Lake[3]		86	49
LaPorte[4]		467	507
Porter			
Pulaski			
White			
		*Henry Brady	Austin W. Morris
Marion[5]		1216	1163
	*Martin R. Green	James H. Scott	Daniel Kelso
Switzerland[6]	1113	188	51

Senators Elected for Whom No Returns Have Been Found

District	
Carroll and Clinton	Aaron Finch
Clay, Sullivan, Vigo	James T. Moffatt
Decatur	James Morgan
Delaware and Randolph	Andrew Kennedy
Fayette and Union	William Watt
Floyd	Preston F. Tuley
Fountain	Jesse Bowen
Franklin	David Mount
Jefferson	Williamson Dunn[7]

Kosciusko, Marshall, St. Joseph, and Starke	Thomas D. Baird
Montgomery	Othniel L. Clark
Tippecanoe	John Beard

[1] Logansport *Herald,* August 10, 1837. The votes for Fulton and Miami counties may not be complete.
[2] Rising Sun *Times,* August 12, 1837.
[3] Goodspeed and Blanchard (eds.), *Counties of Porter and Lake,* 447.
[4] Packard, *History of LaPorte County,* 234.
[5] Indianapolis *Indiana Journal,* August 12, 1837.
[6] Vevay *Village Times,* August 10, 1837.
[7] Elected to complete the term of David Hillis.

August 6, 1838

Returns for House of Representatives

Twenty-third Session, December 3, 1838—February 18, 1839

District	Candidates	
	*William Vance (W)	J. F. Merrill
Adams[1]	138	5
Blackford		
Huntington		
Jay		
Wells		
Whitley		

	*Job B. Eldridge (W)	Nicholas D. Grover	Jordan Vigus	Samuel Ward
Cass[2]	367	140	124	12

	*Nathaniel Fields (W)	*Henry Hurst (W)	Thomas J. Henley (D)	John S. Simonson (D)
Clark[3]	1003	981	908	888

	*Samuel Sands (D)	William Course
Crawford[3]	400	263

	*William Conaway	*Jacob W. Egelston	*Ebenezer Dumont	*George Arnold	E. W. Jackson	John Tait, Jr.[5]
Dearborn[4]	1366	1158	1122	1111	998	906

	*David B. Herriman (D)	Joshua T. Hobbs	Joseph B. Allison	Oliver C. Ward	Drusus Nichols
DeKalb[6] LaGrange Noble Steuben	44	30	11	11	3

	*David Kilgore (W)	John Richey
Delaware[7]	754	325

	*Isaac Stewart (D)	Henry P. Thornton (W)
Floyd[3]	792	704

	*George P. R. Wilson (W)	*Nathaniel Albertson (D)	John Zenor (W)	William A. Porter (W)	Ignatius Mattingly (W)	George Arnold (D)
Harrison[3]	882	819	673	580	245	180

	*Samuel Brenton (W)	Samuel A. Verbrike	Archibald Alexander
Hendricks[7]	621	380	362

	*Joseph G. Marshall (W)	*Michael G. Bright (D)	John Smock (W)	John Hunt (D)	Timothy Barber
Jefferson[3]	1389	1322	853	579	84

	*Samuel Judah (W)	Jonathan P. Cox
Knox[8]	Elected by a large majority	

	*Charles McClure (D)	A. L. Osborn (W)
LaPorte[9]	783	311

	*James Johnson (D)	*Robert Hanna	Douglass Maguire	Alexander Wilson
Marion[10]	1385	1240	1156	1038

	*George H. Johnston (D)	James H. King	Jesse Rader
Monroe[11]	774	649	8

	*Jonathan Williams	W. Landers	S. Dunigan
Morgan[10]	681	470	401

	*William A. Bowles (D)	Meacham (W)
Orange[7]	maj. of 44	

	*James M. Cotton (W)	Elwood Fisher
Switzerland[3]	629	547

	*Joseph Morrow (W)	*Caleb Lewis (W)	*Caleb B. Jackson (W)	*Richard J. Hubbard (W)	William R. Foulke	Smith Hunt[13]
Wayne[12]	1861	1795	1722	1603	1591	1561

Representatives Elected for Whom No Returns Have Been Found

District	
Allen	Lewis G. Thompson (W)
Bartholomew and Brown	Thomas G. Lee (D), Williamson Terrell (W)
Boone	John H. Nelson (D)
Carroll	Samuel Milroy (D)
Clay	Samuel Howe Smydth (W)
Clinton	Andrew Major (D)
Daviess	John Flint
Decatur	Abram Hendricks (W)
Dubois and Pike	George H. Proffit (W)
Elkhart	Samuel T. Clymer (W)
Fayette	Philip Mason (W), John Willey (W)

Fountain	Thomas J. Evans (W), Joseph McCormack (D)
Franklin	Abner McCarty (W), John A. Matson (W)
Fulton and Miami	Alexander Wilson (W)
Gibson	James Devin (W)
Grant and Wabash	Josiah L. Wines (W)
Greene	John F. Allison (W)
Hamilton	Francis B. Coggswell
Hancock	Joseph Chapman (D)
Henry	Robert M. Cooper (W), Jesse H. Healey (W)
Jackson	John F. Carr (D)
Jasper (part), Pulaski, White	William M. Kenton
Jasper (part) and Warren	James Gregory (W)
Jennings	John L. Spann (W)
Johnson	Berrian Reynolds (D)
Kosciusko, Marshall, Starke	Aaron M. Perine (D)
Lake and Porter	George Cline (D)
Lawrence	George W. Carr (D), Melchert Helmer (W)
Madison	Henry Wyman (D)
Martin	John Reiley (D)
Montgomery	James R. M. Bryant (W), John Bryce (D)
Owen	Basil Champer (W)
Parke	William T. Noel, Austin M. Puett
Perry	Robert G. Cotton (W)
Posey	Robert Dale Owen (D)
Putnam	John C. Chiles (W), John McNary, James Townsend
Randolph	Miles Hunt (W)
Ripley	John Glass (D)
Rush	John W. Alley (W), Jesse Morgan (W), William P. Rush (W)
St. Joseph	Elisha Egbert (W)
Scott	William Truelock (W)
Shelby	William J. Peaslee (W), Erasmus Powell (D)

Spencer	William Jones (W)
Sullivan	George Boon (D), Samuel Brown (D)
Tippecanoe	James Earl, John Pettit
Union	Joseph Anderson, Erasmus Rose
Vanderburgh	Joseph Lane (D)
Vermillion	James Blair (W), William P. Dole (W)
Vigo	George W. Cutter, Amory Kinney
Warrick	Christopher C. Graham
Washington	Valentine Baker (D), Henry C. Monroe (D), Woodbridge Parker (D)

1 Election Returns, Adams County Courthouse, Decatur.

2 Logansport *Herald,* August 9, 1838; Logansport *Canal Telegraph,* August 11, 1838.

3 Leavenworth *Arena,* August 9 and 16, 1838.

4 Lawrenceburg *Political Beacon,* August 11, 1838.

5 In addition to the candidates listed for Dearborn County, George P. Buell received 816 votes; S. H. Dowden, 765; Oliver Heustis, 631; John Lawrence, 561; Charles Dashiell, 258; Abraham Ferris, 228; James Murray, 142.

6 *History of DeKalb County, Indiana* . . . (Inter-State Publishing Co., Chicago, 1885), 316.

7 Election Returns, August, 1838, Archives Division.

8 Vincennes *Western Sun,* August 11, 1838.

9 *History of LaPorte County, Indiana* . . . (Chas. C. Chapman & Co., 1880), 540.

10 Indianapolis *Indiana Journal,* August 11, 1838.

11 Bloomington *Post,* August 10, 1838.

12 Richmond *Indiana Palladium,* August 11, 1838.

13 In addition to the candidates listed for Wayne County, Warner M. Leeds received 1553 votes and William Locke, 1427.

Returns for Senate

District	Candidates		
	*William G. Ewing (W)	David H. Colerick	Thomas W. Sweeney
Adams[1]	105	21	17
Allen			
Wells			

District		*William G. Armstrong (W)	Lemuel Ford (D)
Clark[2]		1032	826

District	*Copeland P. J. Arion (W)	Williamson Dunn (W)	Samuel Welch (D)
Jefferson[2]	851	823	617

	*Grant Stafford (W)	J. W. Cox
Morgan[3]	775	773

	*Ezekiel S. Riley (W)	Joel Vandeveer
Orange[4]	maj. of 106	

	*Nathan Smith (W)	*Achilles Williams (W)	David Hoover	William Elliott
Wayne[5]	1880	1655	1635	1551

Senators Elected for Whom No Returns Have Been Found

District	
Dubois, Gibson, Pike	John Hargrove
Grant, Huntington, Jay, Wabash	James Trimble (D)
Greene and Owen	David M. Dobson (D)
Hancock and Madison	Thomas Bell (W)
Lawrence	Gustavus Clark (W)
Parke	William P. Bryant (W)
Ripley	Thomas Smith (D)
Rush	Joseph Lowe (D)
Washington	Henry W. Hackett (D)

1 Election Returns, Adams County Courthouse, Decatur.
2 Leavenworth *Arena,* August 16, 1838.
3 Indianapolis *Indiana Journal,* August 11, 1838.
4 Election Returns, August, 1838, Archives Division.
5 Richmond *Indiana Palladium,* August 11, 1838.

August 5, 1839
Returns for House of Representatives
Twenty-fourth Session, December 2, 1839—February 24, 1840

District	Candidates				
	*Lewis W. Purviance (D)	William Vance	D. Bennett	Jacob Bosworth	W. W. Perssuant
Adams[1]	8	66	63	12	4
Huntington					
Jay					
Wells					
Whitley					

	*Henry B. Milroy (D)	Albert L. Holmes
Carroll[2]	616	583

	*Graham N. Fitch (D)	Nicholas D. Grover (W)
Cass[3]	516	366

	*Samuel Sands (D)	George A. Brown
Crawford[4]	383	244

	*William Lanius (D)	*William Conaway (D)	*Amos Lane (D)	*William Perry (D)	William R. Cole	Jacob W. Egelston[6]
Dearborn[5]	1923	1705	1698	1464	1318	1217

	*David B. Herriman (D)	Asa Brown
DeKalb[7]	72	84
LaGrange		
Noble		
Steuben[8]	78	113

	*Elisha Long (D)	*Redin Osborn (D)	George Holland	William Anderson
Franklin[9]	1152	932	833	724

	*Alexander Wilson (W)	Joseph Holman	William M. Reyburn (W)
Fulton[10]	69	63	81
Miami[10]	170	171	102
Total	239	234	183

	*Nathaniel Albertson (D)	*John Zenor (W)	William M. Saffer (D)	Frederick Leslie (W)
Harrison[4]	1102	916	860	813

	*Samuel Judah (W)	*Jonathan P. Cox (W)	John Myers	James Johnson	Samuel Langton
Knox[11]	745	572	525	518	302

	*Sylvanus Everts (W)	W. A. Place (D)
LaPorte[12]	683	554

	*James Johnson (D)	*Philip Sweetser (W)	Alexander Wilson	William Moore
Marion[13]	1221	1095	931	403

	*Joseph Campbell (W)	Willis A. Gorman (D)
Monroe[2]	764	749

	*William Jones	Smith
Perry[4]	467	223
Spencer[4]	471	308
Total	938	531

	*Elijah Bell (W)	G. Chambers	Thomas C. Stewart
Pike[4]	363	243	136

	*Elwood Fisher (D)	Daniel Kelso	Eden Edwards	Isaiah W. Robinson (D)
Switzerland[14]	778	441	352	32

	*Joseph S. Jenckes (W)	*George W. Cutter (W)	Johnson McWhinney
Vigo[15]	1236	1227	490

Representatives Elected for Whom No Returns Have Been Found

District	
Allen	Lewis G. Thompson (W)
Bartholomew and Brown	Benjamin F. Arnold (D), Eliakim Hamlin (D)
Boone	John H. Nelson (D)

Clark	Thomas J. Henley (D), James G Read (D)
Clay	John Osborn (W)
Clinton	Samuel C. Dunn (W)
Daviess and Martin	John Flint (W)
Decatur	Martin Jamison (W)
Delaware	Abraham Buckles (D)
Dubois	Benjamin Edmonston (D)
Elkhart	Matthew Rippey (D)
Fayette	Matthew R. Hull (D), Samuel W. Parker (W)
Floyd	Isaac Stewart (D)
Fountain	Joseph McCormack (D), James P. Carleton (D)
Gibson	Smith Miller (D)
Grant and Wabash	James S. Shively (D)
Greene	John F. Allison (W)
Hamilton	Francis B. Coggswell (D)
Hancock	John Foster (D)
Hendricks	James F. Beckett (W)
Henry	Ralph Berkshire (W), Robert M. Cooper (W)
Jackson	William Shields (D)
Jasper, Pulaski, White	John B. Wilson (D)
Jefferson	John Hunt, Jr. (D), George Robinson (W), Charles Woodard (W)
Jennings	John L. Spann (D)
Johnson	Fabius M. Finch (W)
Kosciusko, Marshall, Starke	Amzi L. Wheeler (D)
Lawrence	Robert M. Carleton (D), Hugh Hamer (W)
Madison	Willis G. Atherton (W)
Montgomery	Henry Lee (D), John Nelson (D), Abijah O'Neall (W)
Morgan	John Eccles (D)
Orange	William A. Bowles (D)
Owen	George W. Moore (D)
Parke	Robert Clark (D), Jeptha Garrigus (D)
Posey	Matthew R. Southard (W)
Putnam	Joseph F. Farley (D), Edward W. McGaughey (W)

Randolph	Miles Hunt (W)
Ripley	Joseph Robinson (W)
Rush	Jesse Morgan (W), Osmyn Robinson (D), Thomas Worster (D)
St. Joseph	Leonard Rush (W)
Scott	Elisha G. English (D)
Shelby	Balis Coats (W), William W. McCoy (D)
Sullivan	Justus Davis (D), William R. Hadden (D)
Tippecanoe	William M. Porter (D), James White (D)
Union	William H. Bennett (W), James Osborn (D)
Vanderburgh	William Brown Butler (W)
Vermillion	Joseph Moore (D), John Gardner
Warren	William G. Montgomery (W)
Warrick	Alpha Frisbie (D)
Washington	Henry C. Monroe (D), John I. Morrison (D)
Wayne	William Baker (D), Caleb B. Jackson (W), Lewis Burke (W), Morris Lancaster (W)

---

1 Election Returns, Adams County Courthouse, Decatur.

2 Election Returns, August, 1839, Archives Division.

3 Logansport *Herald,* August 6, 1839; Logansport *Telegraph,* August 10, 1839.

4 Leavenworth *Arena,* August 8 and 15, 1839.

5 Aurora *Dearborn County Democrat,* August 8, 1839; Lawrenceburg *Political Beacon,* August 10, 1839.

6 In addition to the candidates listed for Dearborn County, Enoch W. Jackson received 927 votes and Joel Lynn, 702.

7 *History of DeKalb County* (1885), 316.

8 *History of Steuben County* (1885), 321.

9 Brookville *Indiana American,* August 9, 1839.

10 Peru *Gazette,* August 10, 1839.

11 Vincennes *Western Sun,* August 17, 1839.

12 *History of LaPorte County* (1880), 540.

13 Indianapolis *Indiana Journal,* August 9, 1839.

14 Vevay *Times,* August 10, 1839.

15 Terre Haute *Wabash Enquirer,* August 16, 1839.

Returns for Senate

District	Candidates	
	*G. Burton Thompson (W)	James R. E. Goodlet
Crawford[1]	560	116
Perry[1]	375	291
Spencer[1]	333	386
Total	1268	793

	*Robert N. Carnan (W)	Josiah Culbertson
Daviess		
Knox[2]	1153	276
Martin		

	*Ebenezer M. Chamberlain (D)	Elias Baker
DeKalb[3]	67	86
Elkhart		
LaGrange		
Noble		
Steuben[4]	78	115

	*Henry Kinzer (D)	George P. R. Wilson (W)	Dennis Pennington (W)	George Bentley (W)
Harrison[5]	875	657	391	42

	*William Berry (D)	John Ketcham
Monroe[6]	875	680

	*James H. Cravens (W)	William Brown
Ripley[7]	maj. of 156	

Senators Elected for Whom No Returns Have Been Found

District	
Bartholomew and Jennings	Zachariah Tannehill (D)
Boone and Hamilton	Jacob Angle (W)

Blackford, Grant, Huntington, Jay, Wabash	John Foster (D)
Hendricks	Christian C. Nave (W)
Henry	Jehu T. Elliott (W)
Jackson and Scott	John F. Carr (D)
Jasper (part), Vermillion, Warren	James Blair (W)
Johnson	Samuel Herriott (W)
Parke	Joseph A. Wright (D)
Posey, Vanderburgh, Warrick	Joseph Lane (D)
Putnam	Alexander C. Stevenson (W)
Shelby	Joseph B. Nickoll (D)
Tippecanoe	Thomas Smiley (D)

1 Leavenworth *Arena,* August 15, 1839.

2 Vincennes *Western Sun,* August 17, 1839.

3 *History of DeKalb County* (1885), 316.

4 *History of Steuben County* (1885), 321.

5 Leavenworth *Arena,* August 8, 1839.

6 Election Returns, August, 1839, Archives Division.

7 Aurora *Dearborn County Democrat,* October 31, 1839. Cravens was elected to fill the vacancy created by Thomas Smith's election to Congress.

August 3, 1840

Returns for House of Representatives

Twenty-fifth Session, December 7, 1840—February 15, 1841

District	Candidates	
	*Morrison Rulon (D)	Nathan B. Hawkins
Adams[1]	127	150
Blackford		
Huntington		
Jay		
Wells		
Whitley		
	*Samuel Hanna (W)	Joseph Sinclair
Allen[2]	516	507
	*James Butler (W)	Spear S. Tipton (W)
Cass[3]	567	374

	*James G. Sloan (W)	Samuel Sands
Crawford[4]	396	379

	*Isaac Dunn (W)	*John B. Clark (W)	*Abijah North (W)	*William R. Cole (W)	John P. Dunn	Mark McCracken[6]
Dearborn[5]	1817	1805	1796	1789	1672	1665

	*John B. Howe (W)	Madison Marsh
DeKalb[7]	92	122
LaGrange		
Noble		
Steuben[8]	209	185

	*Eleazer Coffeen (W)	Abraham Buckles (D)
Delaware[2]	764	546

	*Aaron B. McCrillus (W)	Thomas C. Stewart
Dubois[4]	[majority 52]	
Pike[4]	[majority 94]	

	*John A. Matson (W)	*James Conwell (W)	George G. Shoup	Joseph Bennett
Franklin[9]	1194	1150	1088	1072

	*William M. Reyburn (W)	Benjamin Henton
Fulton[10]	207	125
Miami[10]	280	277
Total	487	402

	*James Sweetser (W)	James S. Shively
Grant[10]	431	342
Wabash[10]	291	189
Total	722	531

Harrison[4]	*John Zenor (W) 1250	*Frederick Leslie (W) 1221	Nathaniel Albertson 952	Sandbach 912

Hendricks[11]	*Samuel Brenton (W) 1150	H. M. Voorees 707

Jasper Pulaski[12] White	*Robert Newel (W) 61	John B. Wilson 56

Jefferson[13]	*Samuel Goodnow (W) 1684	*George Robinson (W) 1678	*Charles Woodard (W) 1645	Gamaliel Taylor 1088	John Hunt, Jr. 1069	John Chambers 1066

Knox[14]	*Samuel Judah (W) 935	Andrew Berry 696	William Patterson 2

Lake[15] Porter	*Seneca Ball (W) 108	William K. Talbott (D) 127

LaPorte[16]	*Daniel Brown (W) 963	W. A. Place (D) 809

Madison[2]	*Willis G. Atherton (W) 663	Henry Wyman 532	Archibald Cooney 185

Marion[17]	*Philip Sweetser (W) 1685	*Israel Harding (W) 1678	Corson Vickers (D) 1318	Alexander F. Morrison (D) 1312

	*David Byers (D)	Eli P. Farmer (W)
Monroe[2]	909	731

	*Frederick Connor (W)	Axton (D)
Perry[4]	470	229

	*Daniel Harrow (W)	*John M. Colman (W)	*John C. Chiles (W)	Joseph F. Farley	George Piercy	Hillis
Putnam[18]	1574	1505	1493	1275	1271	1152

	*Jesse Morgan (W)	*Joseph Peck (W)	*James M. Ross (W)	John W. Alley	Osmyn Robinson	Jethro S. (?) Folger
Rush[19]	1577	1571	1563	1237	1215	1212

	*William Jones (W)	Daniel Brown (D)
Spencer[2]	571	333

	*George Boon (D)[20]	William R. Hadden
Sullivan[18]	849	416

	*Hosier J. Durbin (W)	Elwood Fisher (D)
Switzerland[21]	1052	834

	*Othniel L. Clark (W)	*Morgan Shortridge (W)
Tippecanoe[2]	1524	1518

	*John Russell (W)	*William Kyle (W)	Joseph Moore	William Caldwell
Vermillion[2]	844	825	659	651

	*James Farrington (W)	*Thomas Dowling (W)	*Joseph Jenckes (W)	William Ray of Riley
Vigo[18]	1454	1406	1385	667

	*William Shanks or Shank (W)	*Rudolphus Schoonover (W)	Poor	McMahan	Wright[23]
Washington[22]	1387	1381	1071	1210	895

District	Representatives Elected for Whom No Returns Have Been Found
Bartholomew and Brown	Tunis Quick (W), Williamson Terrell (W)
Boone	John Chrisman (D)
Carroll	James McCulley (D)
Clark	Thomas J. Henley (D), James G. Read (D)
Clay	Jesse J. Burton (D)
Clinton	Martin Z. Saylor (W)
Daviess	Samuel Howe Smydth (W)
Decatur	James Blair (W)
Elkhart	Matthew Rippey (D)
Fayette	Philip Mason (W), Caleb B. Smith (W)
Floyd	Jacob Miller (W)
Fountain	Solomon Clark (D), Davis Newel (D)
Gibson	Isaac Montgomery (W)
Greene	James S. Freeman (W)
Hamilton	Jacob Robbins (W)
Hancock	Thomas D. Walpole (W)
Henry	David C. Shawhan (W), Thomas R. Stanford (W)
Jackson	Ezekiel L. Dunbar (D)
Jennings	Presley Welch (W)
Johnson	James Ritchey (D)
Kosciusko, Marshall, Starke	Peter L. Runyan (W)
Lawrence	George W. Carr (D), Hugh Hamer (W)
Martin	Aaron Houghton (W)
Montgomery	Joshua Harrison (W), John Wilson (W)

Morgan	Perry M. Blankenship (W)
Orange	William A. Bowles (D)
Owen	Basil Champer (W)
Parke	Andrew Foote (W), James Kerr (W)
Posey	William Casey (D)
Randolph	Smith Elkins (W)
Ripley	Henry J. Bowers (W)
St. Joseph	John D. Defrees (W)
Scott	Aaron Rawlings (W)
Shelby	Joshua B. Lucas (D), William W. McCoy (D)
Union	John L. Burgess (W), John B. Rose (W)
Vanderburgh	William Brown Butler (D)
Warren	William G. Montgomery (W)
Warrick	Christopher C. Graham (D)
Wayne	Daniel Bradbury (W), Allen Hiatt (W), Morris Lancaster (W), Daniel Stratton (W)

1 Election Returns, Adams County Courthouse, Decatur.

2 Election Returns, August, 1840, Archives Division.

3 Logansport *Telegraph,* August 8, 1840.

4 Leavenworth *Arena,* August 6 and 13, 1840.

5 Aurora *Dearborn County Democrat,* September 3, 1840.

6 In addition to the candidates listed for Dearborn County, John D. Johnson received 1662 votes; Daniel Taylor, 1636.

7 *History of DeKalb County* (1885), 317.

8 *History of Steuben County* (1885), 321.

9 Brookville *Indiana American,* August 7, 1840. Matson resigned by December 22, 1840. Shoup was elected in his place and was seated January 13, 1841. Recommendations, Appointments, Resignations file, Archives Division.

10 Peru *Gazette,* August 8, 1840.

11 Indianapolis *Indiana Journal,* August 20, 1840.

12 *Counties of White and Pulaski* (F. A. Battey & Co., Chicago, 1883), 475.

13 Madison *Courier,* August 8, 1840.

14 Vincennes *Western Sun,* August 8, 1840.

15 Goodspeed and Blanchard (eds.), *Counties of Porter and Lake,* 448.

16 *History of LaPorte County* (1880), 540.

17 Indianapolis *Indiana Journal,* August 8, 1840.

18 Terre Haute *Enquirer,* August 12, 1840.

19 Rushville *Whig,* August 8, 1840.

20 Boon died January 10, 1841. Ransom W. Akin was elected to succeed him and was seated February 1. *House Journal,* 1840-41, pp. 320, 551.

21 Vevay *Times,* August 13, 1840.

22 Salem *Washington Republican,* August 8, 1840.

23 In addition to the candidates listed for Washington County, Markwell received 132 votes and Cauble 100 votes.

Returns for Senate

District	Candidates	
	*Williamson Wright (W)	Chauncy Carter (D)
Cass[1]	553	445
Fulton[1]	205	131
Miami[1]	294	270
Total	1052	846

	*James T. Moffatt (W)	Wilson
Clay		
Sullivan[2]	391	924
Vigo[2]	1411	614

	*Johnson Watts (W)	Abel C. Pepper
Dearborn[3]	1823	1653

	*David Mount (W)	Thomas Pursel
Franklin[4]	1192	1084

	*Sylvanus Everts (W)	Charles W. Cathcart (D)
Jasper (part)		
Lake[5]	101	141
LaPorte[6]	1013	765
Porter		
Pulaski[7]	60	57
White		

	*Robert Hanna (W)	Henry Brady
Marion[8]	1657	1348

	*Joseph C. Eggleston (W)	Martin R. Green (D)
Switzerland[9]	1047	850

	*Samuel Hoover (W)
Tippecanoe[10]	1502

Senators Elected for Whom No Returns Have Been Found

District	
Carroll and Clinton	Horatio J. Harris (D)
Decatur	James Morgan (W)
Delaware and Randolph	Michael Aker (W)
Fayette and Union	Samuel W. Parker (W)
Floyd	James Collins (W)
Fountain	Absalom Mendenhall
Kosciusko, Marshall, St. Joseph	Thomas D. Baird (W)
Montgomery	John Beard (W)
Parke	Samuel H. McCord
Posey, Vanderburgh, Warrick	Gaines H. Roberts
Wayne	Charles H. Test (W)

1 Peru *Gazette,* August 8, 15, 22, 1840.
2 Terre Haute *Enquirer,* August 12, 1840.
3 Aurora *Dearborn County Democrat,* September 3, 1840.
4 Brookville *Indiana American,* August 7, 1840.
5 Goodspeed and Blanchard (eds.), *Counties of Porter and Lake,* 448.
6 *History of LaPorte County* (1880), 540.
7 *Counties of White and Pulaski,* 475.
8 Indianapolis *Indiana Journal,* August 8, 1840.
9 Vevay *Times,* August 13, 1840.
10 Election Returns, August 1840, Archives Division.

August 2, 1841

Returns for House of Representatives

Twenty-sixth Session, December 6, 1841—January 31, 1842

District	Candidates		
	*Robert D. Tisdale (W)	Morrison Rulon	Josephus Martin
Adams[1]	189	134	7
Jay			

District			
		*Andrew L. Robinson (D)	William George
Carroll[2]		761	637

District			
	*Nicholas D. Grover (W)	J. C. Douglass	John Ritchey
Cass[3]	642	269	119

	*Richard A. Clements	James McDonald (W)
Daviess[4]	620	525

	*Ethan A. Brown (D)	*James P. Millikan (D)	*James Rand (D)	George Cornelius (W)	John B. Piatt (W)	Jonathan Blasdel (W)
Dearborn[5]	1966	1799	1781	1440	1341	1300

	*Madison Marsh (D)	Seth W. Murray
DeKalb[6]	159	118
Steuben[7]	205	193
Total	364	311

	*William M. Saffer (D)	*Frederick Leslie (W)	William A. Porter	George P. R. Wilson
Harrison[8]	898	832	819	753

	*Joseph G. Marshall (W)	*Samuel Goodnow (W)	*Archibald Lawrence (D)	John McCoy	Charles Woodard	H. Troutwine[10]
Jefferson[9]	1352	1234	1012	716	547	544

	*John Myers (D)	Samuel Judah
Knox[11]	653	588

	*John Thompson (D)	James Latta
LaGrange[12]	Maj. of 33	
Noble[12]	263	193

	*Joseph W. Chapman (D)	*John H. Bradley (W)	A. Blackburn (W)	Gustavus A. Everts (W)
LaPorte[13]	851	698	506	323

	*Israel Harding (W)	*William J. Brown (D)	Austin W. Morris (W)
Marion[14]	1652	1414	1110

	*Jeptha Garrigus	*Pratt Frink	Andrew Foote	Doggett
Parke[4]	1174	1120	1075	658

	*Pleasant A. Hackleman (W)	*William C. Robinson (W)	Wm. P. Rush (Ind W)	Thompson (Ind W)
Rush[15]	1253	1110	1071	703

	*John W. Davis (D)	*Justus Davis (D)	Burr McGrew	Samuel Ledgerwood
Sullivan[4]	1193	622	409	271

	*James P. Ellis (W)	*Elizur Deming (W)	John Pettit	James W. Wilson	Wm. Farnsworth
Tippecanoe[16]	1167	1149	1137	824	218

	*John Hoobler (D)	William Kile
Vermillion[4]	693	507

	*John Hodges (W)	*William Wines (D)	Joseph S. Jenckes	William Gannon	Samuel Wheeler	Harrison Hamilton
Vigo[4]	1300	1032	959	183	37	21

	*George May (D)	*Henry C. Monroe (D)	Samuel Huston	Sugg
Washington[17]	1541	910	871	173

	*Daniel Strattan (W)	*William R. Foulke (W)	*Daniel Sinks (W)	Caleb Lewis	Andrew F. Scott	John Jones[19]
Wayne[18]	1543	1496	1463	1446	1281	1210

Representatives Elected for Whom No Returns Have Been Found

District	
Allen	Marshall S. Wines (D)
Bartholomew	Tunis Quick (W)
Benton, Jasper, Pulaski, White	William Coon (D)
Blackford, Huntington, Wells	Elias Murray (W)
Boone	John Chrisman (D)
Brown and Monroe	Willis A. Gorman (D)
Clark	Thomas J. Henley (D), John S. Simonson (D)
Clay	Francis B. Yocum (D)
Clinton	Martin Z. Sayler (D)
Crawford	John Edwards (W)
Decatur	James Saunders (W)
Delaware	Goldsmith C. Gilbert (W)
Dubois	John Poulson (D)
Elkhart	William B. Mitchell (D)
Fayette	Miner Meeker (W), Wilson Thompson (D)
Floyd	John S. Davis (W)
Fountain	Edward A. Hannegan (D)
Franklin	John T. Cooley (D), George G. Shoup (D)
Fulton and Marshall	William Rannells (W)
Gibson	Joseph Devin (W)
Grant	James S. Shively (D)
Greene	John F. O'Neal (D)
Hamilton	Francis B. Coggswell (D), William D. Rooker (W)
Hancock	Joseph Chapman (D), James P. Foley (W)
Hendricks	William Townsend (W)
Henry	Robert M. Cooper (W), Joel Reed (W)
Jackson	Ezekiel L. Dunbar (D)
Jennings	James Goodhue (W)
Johnson	James Ritchey (D)
Kosciusko and Whitley	Peter L. Runyan
Lake and Porter	Lewis Warriner (D)

Lawrence	Ralph G. Norvell (D), John J. Barnett (W)
Madison	Thomas McAllister (D)
Martin	Cager Peek (D)
Miami and Wabash	Daniel R. Bearss (W)
Montgomery	John Barnett (W), John Nelson (D), Henry T. Snook (D)
Morgan	Francis A. Matheny (D)
Orange	Henry Lingle (D)
Owen	Martin Snoddy (D)
Perry	Robert G. Cotton (W)
Pike	Alvan T. Whight (D)
Posey	Arza Lee (W)
Putnam	Albert G. Hutton (D), George Pearcy, Jr. (D)
Randolph	Robert W. Butler (D)
Ripley	Henry J. Bowers (W)
St. Joseph	John D. Defrees (W)
Scott	Aaron Rawlings (W)
Shelby	John Hendricks
Spencer	John Proctor (W)
Switzerland	Samuel Howard (W)
Union	Daniel Ogden (W), Jeremiah S. Williamson (W)
Vanderburgh	Amos Clark (W)
Warren	William G. Montgomery (W)
Warrick	Christopher C. Graham (D)

[1] Election Returns, Adams County Courthouse, Decatur.

[2] Election Returns, August, 1841, Archives Division. Returns of Carrollton Township, Carroll County, were received too late to be included. They were: Robinson, 41; George, 27.

[3] Logansport *Telegraph,* August 7, 1841.

[4] Terre Haute *Wabash Courier,* August 7 and 14, 1841.

[5] Wilmington *Dearborn County Register,* August 7, 1841.

[6] *History of DeKalb County* (1885), 317.

[7] *History of Steuben County* (1885), 321.

[8] Election Returns, Harrison County Courthouse, Corydon.

[9] Madison *Courier,* August 7, 1841.

[10] In addition to the candidates listed for Jefferson County, Samuel Welch received 455 votes; James W. Hinds, 418; Allan E. Arion, 259; H. E. Parton, 238; William B. Settle, 111.

[11] Vincennes *Western Sun,* August 7, 1841.

[12] Goshen *Democrat,* August 12, 19, 1841.

[13] *History of LaPorte County* (1880), 541.

[14] Indianapolis *Indiana Journal,* August 4, 1841.

15 Rushville *Whig,* August 6, 1841.

16 Lafayette *Journal & Free Press,* August 11, 1841.

17 Salem *Washington Republican,* August 11, 1841.

18 Centerville *Wayne County Record,* August 11, 1841.

19 In addition to the candidates listed for Wayne County, Samuel Johnson received 389 votes; Josiah Bell, 369; Daniel Winder, 360; George W. Whitman, 7.

Returns for Senate[1]

District	Candidates	
	*Joseph Sinclair (D)	Charles W. Ewing
Adams[2]	147	182
Allen		
Huntington		
Wells		

District		
	*Abner Davis (D)	Elias S. Terry
Daviess[3]	577	576
Martin[3]	maj. of 150	

District		
	*David B. Herriman (D)	John B. Howe
DeKalb[4]	177	99
LaGrange[5]		maj. of 28
Noble[5]	263	189
Steuben[6]	206	194

District			
	*Jesse D. Bright (D)	Williamson Dunn	Shadrach Wilber
Jefferson[7]	1089	881	553

District		
	*Nathaniel West (D)	William Hannaman (W)
Marion[8]	1284	1052

District		
	*Benjamin F. Reeve (Ind. Whig)	Jesse Morgan (W)
Rush[9]	1125	1085

District		
	*William Shanks (D)	Poor
Washington[10]	1092	727

	*Lewis Burke (W)	*David Hoover (D)	William Elliott	Charles H. Test	Pusey Grave	Silas H. Beeson
Wayne[11]	1544	1537	1259	1254	442	299

Senators Elected for Whom No Returns Have Been Found

District	
Benton, Jasper, Pulaski, Warren, White	Zebulon Sheets (W)
Clark	James G. Read (D)
Crawford and Orange[12]	Isaac Sands (W)
Dubois, Gibson, Pike	Smith Miller (D)
Fountain	Solomon Hetfield[13]
Greene and Owen	David M. Dobson (D)
Hancock and Madison	Thomas D. Walpole (W)
Lawrence	George W. Carr (D)
Montgomery	Robert C. Gregory[14] (W)
Morgan	Parmenter M. Parks (D)
Parke	Hugh J. Bradley (W)
Posey and Vanderburgh	John Pitcher (W)
Ripley	William T. S. Cornett (W)

[1] The State had been redistricted by the last General Assembly. See below, 404-5. The three districts composed of Daviess and Martin counties, Benton, Jasper, Pulaski, Warren, and White counties, and DeKalb, LaGrange, Noble, and Steuben counties were considered as new districts and the senators from those districts, Abner Davis, Zebulon Sheets, and David B. Herriman, drew lots to determine the length of their terms. Davis drew the three-year term, Herriman, two years, and Sheets, one. *Senate Journal,* 1841-42, p. 5.

[2] Election Returns, Adams County Courthouse, Decatur.

[3] Terre Haute *Wabash Courier,* August 14, 1841.

[4] *History of DeKalb County* (1885), 317.

[5] Goshen *Democrat,* August 12 and 19, 1841.

[6] *History of Steuben County* (1885), 321.

[7] Madison *Courier,* August 7, 1841.

[8] Indianapolis *Indiana Journal* (semiweekly), September 29, 1841. West was elected to fill the vacancy caused by the resignation of Robert Hanna on July 31, 1841. Executive Proceedings, 1837-1845, in Archives Division.

[9] Rushville *Whig,* August 6, 1841.

[10] Salem *Washington Republican,* August 11, 1841.

[11] Centerville *Wayne County Record,* August 11, 1841.

[12] In the redistricting of the state for the election of senators, Crawford and Orange were joined to make a district whereas Orange had formerly been a district by itself and Crawford together with Perry and Spencer formed a district. G. Burton Thompson, senator from the latter district, who still had another year to serve, resigned on July 1, 1841. Perry and Spencer counties

were joined to Warrick to form a district and Gaines H. Roberts who had formerly represented Posey, Vanderburgh, and Warrick was shifted to the new district without a re-election. This left Posey and Vanderburgh to form a district and John Pitcher was elected to represent it in the Senate. The Senate apparently did not consider any of these as new districts. See above, note 1.

13 Hetfield was elected on November 20 to fill out the unexpired term of Absalom Mendenhall who resigned on October 8 because of ill health. Executive Proceedings, 1837-1845, p. 693, and Resignations file, Archives Division.

14 Gregory was elected to fill out the term of John Beard, who resigned April 26, 1841.

August 1, 1842

Returns for House of Representatives

Twenty-seventh Session, December 5, 1842—February 13, 1843

District	Candidates		
	*Nathan B. Hawkins (W)	Elisha E. Parret (D)	Josephus Martin
Adams[1]	149	207	68
Jay			
		*Marshall S. Wines (D)[3]	T. Johnson
Allen[2]		614	532
		*Andrew L. Robinson (D)	Thomas Stirlin
Carroll[4]		831	491
		*Chauncy Carter (D)	Job B. Eldridge (W)
Cass[5]		531	519
		*Enos Beal (W)	Madison Marsh (D)
DeKalb[6]		89	186
Steuben[7]		271	174
Total		360	360
		*John Jackson (D)	Thomas G. Harris (Ind)
Elkhart[8]		715	572
			*John Hargrove (D)
Gibson[4]			maj. of 6

	*Frederick Leslie (W)	*George P. R. Wilson (W)	William M. Saffer (D)	John Bence	David Stucker	Joseph Avery
Harrison[9]	774	771	694	631	92	88

	*Henry H. Marvin (W)	Benjamin S. Logan
Hendricks[10]	786	779

	*Samuel Goodnow (W)	*David Hillis (W)	Archibald Lawrence (D)	H. Troutwine (D)
Jefferson[11]	1317	1278	1143	581

	*John Myers (D)	George Leech
Knox[12]	824	748

	*William Mitchell (W)	John Thompson (D)
LaGrange[8]	maj. of 122	
Noble[8]	252	238

	*John Francis (W)	*John H. Bradley (W)	John Chapman	A. B. Brown
LaPorte[13]	854	839	770	29

	*Thomas Johnson (D)	*William J. Brown (D)	Thomas J. Todd (W)	Obadiah Harris (W)
Marion[14]	1353	1345	1332	1324

	*Gabriel Swihart (D)	A. Holderman (W)
Miami[15]	339	319
Wabash		

	*Alvan T. Whight (D)	C. F. White (W)
Pike[4]	524	252

	*James Denny (W)	*John H. Roberts (D)	*John Reel (W)	J. H. Farmer	David Wills	Elias Neff
Putnam[16]	1460	1397	1377	1238	1213	570

	*George W. Brown (D)	*Joseph Lowe (D)	*George B. Tingley (W)	Samuel Barrett	Orange H. Neff	William C. Robinson
Rush[17]	1343	1326	1259	1057	860	654

	*Hugh C. Flannegan (W)	George C. Merrifield
St. Joseph[8]	673	550

	*Isaac Shelby (W)	*William L. Leyman (D)	William Sims	Elisha G. Layne
Tippecanoe[18]	1246	1235	1223	1218

	*William Brown Butler (W)	J. W. Lilleston (W)	Goodsell (D)
Vanderburgh[19]	369	354	224

	*Allen Hiatt (W)	*Daniel Strattan (W)	*William R. Foulke (W)	Henry Hoover (D)	Othniel Beeson (D)	William Brown (D)
Wayne[20]	1806	1759	1763	1195	1192	1164

Representatives Elected for Whom No Returns Have Been Found

District	
Bartholomew	Aquilla Jones (D)
Benton, Jasper, Pulaski, White	Ira Brown (D)
Blackford, Huntington, Wells	William Prilliman (D)

Boone	John Chrisman (D), Jonathan H. Rose (D)
Brown and Monroe	Willis A. Gorman (D), John M. Sluss (W)
Clark	Thomas J. Henley (D), John S. Simonson (D)
Clay	John B. Nees (D)
Clinton	Andrew Major (D)
Crawford	John Edwards (W)
Daviess	Richard A. Clements (W)
Dearborn	Ethan Allen Brown (D), John Lewis (D), James P. Millikan (D)
Decatur	David Montague (W)
Delaware	Goldsmith C. Gilbert (W)
Dubois	Benjamin R. Edmonston (D)
Fayette	Newton Claypool (W), Miner Meeker (W)
Floyd	Nathaniel Moore (D)
Fountain	Joseph McCormick (D), John Stewart (D)
Franklin	John P. Cooley (D), George G. Shoup (D)
Fulton, Marshall, Starke	Amzi L. Wheeler (D)
Grant	John Dunn (D)
Greene	John F. O'Neal (D)
Hamilton	Allen Sumner (W)
Hancock	Joseph Mathers (W)
Henry	Isaac Parker (W), Simon Summers (W)
Jackson	Ezekiel L. Dunbar (D)[21]
Jennings	Dewitt C. Rich (W)
Johnson	Franklin Hardin (D)
Kosciusko and Whitley	Abraham Cuppy (D)
Lake and Porter	Adam S. Campbell (D)
Lawrence	Ralph G. Norvell (D)
Madison	John Davis (W), Robert N. Williams (W)
Martin	Cager Peek (D)
Montgomery	John Nelson (D), Henry T. Snook (D)
Morgan	Francis A. Matheny (D)
Orange	Henry Lingle (D)
Owen	George W. Moore (D)

Parke	William G. Coffin (W), George K. Steele (W)
Perry	Joshua B. Huckeby (W)
Posey	Arza Lee (W)
Randolph	Robert W. Butler (D)
Ripley	Henry J. Bowers (W)
Scott	Elisha G. English (D)
Shelby	Fletcher Tevis (D)
Spencer	John Proctor (W)
Sullivan	John W. Davis (D)
Switzerland	Perret Dufour (D)
Union	James Osborn (D)
Vermillion	William Bales (W)
Vigo	John Hodges (W), Septer Patrick (W), John Strain (W)
Warren	Nathaniel Butterfield (W)
Warrick	Isham Fuller (D)
Washington	Valentine Baker (D), Ezekiel D. Logan (D)

1 Election Returns, Adams County Courthouse, Decatur.

2 Fort Wayne *Sentinel,* August 6, 1842.

3 Wines died September 20 at Attica and Lewis G. Thompson was elected to serve in his place. Election Returns, Archives Division.

4 Election Returns, August, 1842, Archives Division.

5 Logansport *Telegraph,* August 13, 1842.

6 *History of DeKalb County* (1885), 317.

7 *History of Steuben County* (1885), 321. The political affiliation of the candidates was given in the Fort Wayne *Sentinel,* August 6, 1842. Since there was a tie, the decision of which one should serve was determined by lot.

8 Goshen *Democrat,* August 4 and 11, 1842.

9 Election Returns, Harrison County Courthouse, Corydon.

10 *History of Hendricks County* (1885), 304.

11 Madison *Courier,* August 6, 1842.

12 Vincennes *Western Sun,* August 6, 1842.

13 Packard, *History of LaPorte County,* 236.

14 Indianapolis *Indiana Journal,* August 10, 1842.

15 Peru *Democrat,* August 6, 1842.

16 Greencastle *Visiter,* August 10, 1842. In addition to the candidates listed, A. B. Denton received 562 votes.

17 Rushville *Whig,* August 5, 1842.

18 Lafayette *Tippecanoe Journal and Lafayette Free Press,* August 4, 1842.

19 Evansville *Indiana Statesman,* August 8, 1842.

20 Centerville *Wayne County Record,* August 10, 1842. In addition to the candidates listed, Isaiah Osborn received 238 votes; H. B. Payne, 199; Elihu Cox, 220. They were labeled Abolitionists.

21 Dunbar's death was announced in the House on December 31. Samuel P. Mooney was elected to succeed him and was seated January 21, 1843. *House Journal,* 1842-43, pp. 252, 447.

Returns for Senate

District	Candidates	
	*James Hodge (W)	Joseph S. Buckles (D)
Delaware[1]	655	587
Grant		

District		
	*William B. Mitchell (D)	Samuel T. Clymer (Ind)
Elkhart[2]	763	543
Kosciusko[2]	432	474
Whitley[2]	119	117
Total	1314	1131

District		
	*Dennis Pennington (W)	Nathaniel Albertson (D)
Harrison[3]	802	797

District		
	*Archibald Alexander (W)	William Townsend
Hendricks[4]	771	757

District		
	*John Ewing (W)	Robert N. Carnan
Knox[5]	911	615

District	
	*William Casey (D)[7]
Posey	
Vanderburgh[6]	438

District		
	*Edward W. McGaughey (W)	Albert G. Hutton
Putnam[8]	1379	1334

Senators Elected for Whom No Returns Have Been Found

District	
Bartholomew and Jennings	Zachariah Tannehill (D)
Benton, Jasper, Pulaski, Warren, White	James H. Buell (W)

Boone and Hamilton	Mark A. Duzan (D)
Brown and Monroe	Eli P. Farmer (W)
Daviess and Martin	Samuel Howe Smydth[9]
Fulton, Marshall, St. Joseph	John D. Defrees[10]
Henry	Thomas R. Stanford (W)
Jackson and Scott	John F. Carr (D)
Johnson	James Ritchey (D)
Perry, Spencer, Warrick	Robert G. Cotton (W)
Shelby	John Y. Kennedy[11]
Switzerland	Daniel Kelso (W)[12]
Tippecanoe	John W. Odell (W)[13]
Vermillion	Stephen S. Collett (W)

1 G. W. H. Kemper, *A Twentieth Century History of Delaware County, Indiana* (2 vols. Chicago, 1908), 1:528.

2 Goshen *Democrat,* August 4, 11, 1842.

3 Election Returns, Harrison County Courthouse, Corydon.

4 *History of Hendricks County* (1885), 304.

5 Vincennes *Western Sun,* August 6, 1842.

6 Evansville *Indiana Statesman,* August 5, 1842. Elected without opposition.

7 The resignation of William Casey, senator elect from Posey and Vanderburgh counties, was presented to the Senate by the Governor on December 6. He said he had not ordered an election to choose a successor because another individual claimed to be elected. The matter was referred to the committee on elections but no report of the committee was found. John Pitcher was also representing the district in the Senate. *Senate Journal,* 1842-43, pp. 10-11.

8 Greencastle *Visiter,* August 10, 1842.

9 The resignation of Samuel Howe Smydth, senator elect, was presented to the Senate on December 15. *Senate Journal,* 1842-43, pp. 73-74. He died May 10, 1843, in Marseilles, France. Indianapolis *Indiana State Sentinel,* August, 1843. There is no record of an election to fill the vacancy. Abner Davis also represented this district in the Senate.

10 Defrees was elected to serve out the term of Thomas D. Baird whose death occurred September 6, 1842. Election Returns, September and October, 1842.

11 There is no record in the House Journal of anyone serving from Shelby County in this session, but Kennedy's name is among the list of representatives printed in the Indianapolis *Indiana Journal* (weekly), August 16, 1842. The House Journal shows a Mr. Kennedy voting.

12 Kelso was elected to fill out the unexpired term of Joseph C. Eggleston who had resigned on July 13, 1842. Executive Proceedings, 1837-45.

13 Odell was elected to fill out the unexpired term of Samuel Hoover who had resigned on February 25, 1842. *Ibid.*

August 7, 1843

Returns for House of Representatives

Twenty-eighth Session, December 4, 1843—January 15, 1844

District	Candidates	
	*Samuel S. Mickle (D)	Zachariah Smith
Adams[1]	229	225
Jay		

District		
	*Lucian P. Ferry (D)	M. Sweetser (W)
Allen[2]	723	658

District		
	*David McConnell (D)	H. Robinson
Benton[3]		maj. of 11
Jasper		
Pulaski[4]	96	97
White		

District	
	*Peter Kemmer (or Keimer) (D)
Blackford[5]	maj. of 373
Huntington	
Wells	

District		
	*Andrew L. Robinson (D)	Thomas M. Curry
Carroll[6]	777	639

District			
	*Jacob Helwig (D)	Benjamin Alton	Alexander Chapin
DeKalb[7]	264	232	......
Steuben[8]	196	213	49
Total	460	445	49

District		
	*Joseph Cowan (D)	Violett (W)
Elkhart[9]	812	694

	*Franklin McRae (D)	*William M. Saffer (D)	Andrew M. Jones	Joseph Cromwell
Harrison[10]	1082	1007	921	832

	*Stephen Lee (W)	*Isaac Chambers (D)	*Benjamin Tevis (W)	Charles Woodard	Archibald Lawrence	George W. Cross
Jefferson[11]	1475	1443	1431	1408	1341	1166

	*James D. Williams (D)	Abner T. Ellis
Knox[12]	872	761

	*Joshua T. Hobbs (W)	Jewett
LaGrange[9]	maj. of 120	
Noble[9]	255	330

	*William Allen (W)	*Ferdinand Roberts (W)	Charles W. Cathcart	James Bradley
LaPorte[13]	828	797	736	693

	*Obadiah Harris (W)	*John Sutherland (W)	Livingston Dunlap (D)	Nathaniel Bolton (D)
Marion[14]	1585	1566	1557	1462

	*Arza Lee (W)	Robert Wilson
Posey[15]	853	678

	*William D. Allen (D)	*John H. Roberts (D)	James Denny	Isaac Matkins
Putnam[16]	1584	1420	1187	1192

	*Thomas M. Smith (D)	William McKay (W)	William Burrows (W)
Spencer[17]	388	384	60

	*Thomas T. Wright (D)	Coffin (W)
Switzerland[18]	1026	801

	*Daniel Miller (W)	J. W. Lilleston	G. W. Finch	Joseph Huey
Vanderburgh[19]	408	321	268	8

	*Henry Hostetter (D)	William Bales
Vermillion[6]	694	597

	*Samuel Hannah (W)	*David P. Holloway (W)	*John W. Williamson (W)	Caleb Lewis (D)	Jacob Brooks (D)	Jesse Meek (D)
Wayne[20]	1606	1589	1462	1441	1403	1142

Representatives Elected for Whom No Returns Have Been Found

District	
Bartholomew	Heman H. Barbour (D)
Boone	Benjamin Boone (D)
Brown and Monroe	Willis A. Gorman (D)
Cass	George W. Blakemore (W)
Clark	James S. Athon (D), John S. Simonson (D)
Clay	John B. Nees (D)
Clinton	Ephraim Byers (D)
Crawford	Huston Miller (D)
Daviess and Martin	Silas L. Halbert (D)
Dearborn	Pinckney James (W), David Macy (W), Richard N. Spicknall (D)
Decatur	David Montague (W)
Delaware	Goldsmith C. Gilbert (W)
Dubois	Benjamin R. Edmonston (D)
Fayette	Samuel W. Parker (W), Henry Simpson (W)

Floyd	George J. Wolf (W)
Fountain	John R. Jones (D)
Franklin	James R. Jones (D), Joel Palmer (D)
Fulton and Marshall	Joseph Robbins (D)
Gibson	William Montgomery (D)
Grant	Samuel L. Woolman (W)
Greene	John F. O'Neal (D)
Hamilton	Haymond W. Clark (W), William W. Conner (W)
Hancock	Joseph Chapman (D), James P. Foley (W)
Hendricks	Samuel A. Verbrike (W)
Henry	Robert J. Huddleston (W), Joel Reed (W)
Jackson	Samuel P. Mooney (D)
Jennings	DeWitt C. Rich (W)
Johnson	Franklin Hardin (D)
Kosciusko and Whitley	Abraham Cuppy (D)
Lake and Porter	Alexander McDonald (D)
Lawrence	William Burton (D), Ralph G. Norvell (D)
Madison	Thomas McAllister (D)
Miami and Wabash	Daniel R. Bearss (W)
Montgomery	Philip E. Engle (D), James H. Harrison (W), James Seller (W)
Morgan	Francis A. Matheny (D)
Orange	William A. Bowles (D)
Owen	George W. Moore (D)
Parke	William G. Coffin (W), James Kerr (W)
Perry	Arnold Elder (D)
Pike	Robert Logan (D)
Randolph	Edward Edger (D), Royston Ford (W)
Ripley	Meshack Hyatt (W)
Rush	Samuel Barrett (W), Jesse Morgan (W)
St. Joseph	Harris E. Hurlbut (W)
Scott	David McClure (D)
Shelby	Augustus C. Handy (D)
Sullivan	Thomas Turman (D)
Tippecanoe	Samuel F. Clark (D), Philip Foresman (W), Isaac Shelby (W)
Union	Charles Nutter (W)

Vigo	Thomas Dowling (W), Caleb Garrett (W), John Hodges (W)
Warren	Leroy Gregory (W)
Warrick	Isham Fuller (D)
Washington	John Kelly (D), Ezekiel D. Logan (D)

1 Election Returns, Adams County Courthouse, Decatur.

2 Fort Wayne *Sentinel,* August 12, 1843.

3 Goshen *Democrat,* August 31, 1843.

4 *Counties of White and Pulaski,* 476.

5 Fort Wayne *Sentinel,* August 26, 1843. Blackford was called the banner Democratic county of the Tenth District.

6 Election Returns, Archives Division.

7 *History of DeKalb County* (1885), 317.

8 *History of Steuben County* (1885), 322.

9 Goshen *Democrat,* August 17, 1843.

10 Election Returns, Harrison County Courthouse, Corydon.

11 Madison *Courier,* August 12, 1843.

12 Vincennes *Western Sun,* August 12, 1843. The vote in Knox County does not include the returns from Decker township.

13 Packard, *History of LaPorte County,* 236.

14 Indianapolis *Indiana State Journal,* August 9, 1843.

15 Evansville *Indiana Statesman,* September 2, 1843.

16 Greencastle *Visiter,* August 10, 1843.

17 Evansville *Journal,* August 24, 1843.

18 Vevay *Indiana Palladium,* August 12, 1843.

19 Evansville *Indiana Statesman,* August 12, 1843. The Goshen *Democrat,* September 7, 1843, said Lilleston had publicly renounced his allegiance to the Whigs.

20 Centerville *Wayne County Record,* August 16, 1843. In addition to the candidates listed, Andrew Meredith received 431 votes; Pusey Grave, 428; Timothy L. Garrigus, 384, all designated as Abolitionists.

Returns for Senate

District	Candidates	
	*Andrew Major (D)	Stephen Sims
Carroll[1]	777	634
Clinton		
	*David B. Herriman (D)	William Mitchell
DeKalb[2]	293	212
LaGrange[3]	maj. of 60	
Noble[3]	334	280
Steuben[4]	241	235

	*John D. Defrees (W)	Amzi L. Wheeler
Fulton[5]	maj. of 31	
Marshall[5]		maj. of 163
St. Joseph[5]	maj. of 161	
Total	maj. of 29	

	*Shadrach Wilber (D)	Williamson Dunn (W)
Jefferson[6]	1413	1383

	*John Ewing (W)	John Myers	Loudermilk
Knox[7]	712	685	147

	*Thomas J. Todd (W)	Alexander F. Morrison (D)
Marion[8]	1571	1507

	*Albert G. Hutton (D)	John C. Chiles
Putnam[9]	1395	1245

	*David Henry (W)	Daniel Kelso (Ind)
Switzerland[10]	916	915

Senators Elected for Whom No Returns Have Been Found

District	
Blackford, Jay, Randolph	Isaac F. Wood (D)
Cass, Miami, Wabash	William M. Reyburn (W)
Clay, Sullivan, Vigo	Ransom W. Akin (D)
Dearborn	George P. Buell (D)
Decatur	James Morgan (W)
Fayette and Union	James Leviston (D)
Floyd	John S. Davis (W)
Fountain	C. V. Jones (D)
Franklin	George Berry (D)
LaPorte, Lake, Porter	Joseph W. Chapman (D)

Montgomery	Frederick Moore (W)
Tippecanoe	Godlove S. Orth (W)

1 Election Returns, Archives Division.

2 *History of DeKalb County* (1885), 317.

3 Goshen *Democrat,* August 17, 1843.

4 *History of Steuben County* (1885), 322.

5 Goshen *Democrat,* August 17, 1843.

6 Madison *Courier,* August 12, 1843. Wilber was elected to fill out the unexpired term of Jesse D. Bright who had resigned on April 22 to run for the office of lieutenant governor. Executive Proceedings, 1837-1845.

7 Vincennes *Western Sun,* August 12, 1843. Ewing had resigned as senator on April 3, 1843, after serving one year.

8 Indianapolis *Indiana State Journal,* August 9, 1843.

9 Greencastle *Visiter,* August 10, 1843. Hutton was elected to fill the vacancy created by the resignation of Edward McGaughey who was a candidate for representative in Congress.

10 Vevay *Indiana Palladium,* August 12, 1843. Henry's election was contested by Kelso. The Senate committee to which the dispute was referred spent considerable time reviewing the case but failed to agree; consequently neither man was seated. *Senate Journal,* 1843-44, pp. 39-40, 253-331, 379-86.

August 5, 1844

Returns for House of Representatives[1]

Twenty-ninth Session, December 2, 1844—January 13, 1845

District	Candidates		
	*Robert Huey (D)	Nathan B. Hawkins	Eli Davis
Adams[2]	268	199	0
Jay	364	293	14
Total	632	492	14

	*Samuel Stophlet (W)	Nathaniel A. Woodward
Allen	761	755

	*William Herod (W)	Heman H. Barbour
Bartholomew	1011	989

	*Gideon S. Brecount (D)	Henry Robertson
Benton		
Jasper		
Pulaski		
White	219	254

	*Jared Darrow (D)	Sylvanus Church
Blackford	210	62
Huntington	291	216
Wells	247	158
Total	748	436

	*John Duzan (D)	*Harvey G. Hazelrigg (W)	John Richey	Frederick Lowe
Boone	890	864	858	825

	*Silvanus Manville (D)	James Taggart, Jr.
Brown	314	183

	*Andrew L. Robinson (D)	John Lowe
Carroll	847	711
Richardville (Howard)		

	*George W. Blakemore (W)	William S. Palmer
Cass	709	621

	*John S Simonson (D)	*Thomas J. Howard (D)	James Robertson	Obadiah Knowland
Clark	1396	1383	1087	407

	*Allen T. Rose (D)	Ira Allen
Clay	543	404

	*James Hill (D)	Samuel D. Maxwell
Clinton	741	662

	*Jonathan R. Brown (D)	James G. Sloan
Crawford	424	372

	*James P. McGaughey (W)	Jesse Morgan
Daviess	764	666

	*Oliver Heustis (D)	*John Lewis (D)	*William Lanius (D)	Benjamin Plummer	William Hinkson	John Tait, Jr.[4]
Dearborn	1942	1931	1928	1584	1552	1544
Ohio[3]	190	189	193	204	202	204
	2132	2120	2121	1788	1754	1748

	*Joseph Robinson (W)	James M. Talbott
Decatur	1224	998

	*Jacob Helwig (D)	Arial Walden	Suldoon M. Clark (?)
DeKalb	304	244	......
Steuben	241	222	34

	*John Tomlinson (W)	Thomas Collins (D)
Delaware	884	684

	*Silas Davis (D)	Andrew F. Kelso
Dubois	368	[not given]

	*Joseph Cowan (D)	Sapington B. Kyler
Elkhart	873	691

	*Newton Claypool (W)	*Samuel Little (W)	Wilson Thompson	William Marks
Fayette	951	967	789	817

	*George J. Wolf (W)	John Jones
Floyd	958	952

	*John R. Jones (D)	Curtis Newell
Fountain	1166	780

	*David G. Hannah (D)	*Joel Palmer (D)	John H. Farquhar	James Conwell
Franklin[5]	1465	1451	1228	1141

	*William G. Pomeroy (W)	Amzi L. Wheeler	Abijah Hawley
Fulton	323	284	3
Marshall	204	236	40

	*William Montgomery (D)	Thomas J. Montgomery
Gibson	837	751

	*James S. Shively (D)	Joseph Morrow	Thomas Dean
Grant	418	252	199

	*Lovel H. Rousseau (W)	Frederick Slinkard (D)
Greene	775	729

	*William W. Conner (W)	William Garver	Jacob L. Pfaff
Hamilton	771	682	214
Tipton			

	*George Tague (D)	George Henry
Hancock	715	688

	*William T. Matlock (W)	Samuel C. Mitchell
Hendricks	1110	845

	*Isaac Parker (W)	*John W. Grubbs (W)	Miles Murphy	William Grose	Israel Evans	Walter Edgerton
Henry	1299	1246	971	923	175	147

	*Samuel P. Mooney (D)	Hugh A. Findley
Jackson	1203	230

	*Thomas L. Sullivan (W)	*Milton Stapp (W)	*David Hillis (W)	Isaac Chambers	Peter Jordan	Fleming Durham
Jefferson[6]	1707	1670	1657	1376	1261	1253

	*DeWitt C. Rich (W)	Joseph W. Ballard	James Hicklin
Jennings	1041	292	44

	*Franklin Hardin (D)	John Slater (Ind D)	John R. Slater	Scattering
Johnson	913	520	23	2

	*Daniel G. McClure (W)	John S. Benefiel
Knox[7]	1056	575

	*Stephen H. Colms	Abraham Cuppy
Kosciusko	587	508
Whitley	159	236
Total	746	744

	*William H. Nimmon (W)	Thomas I. Spaulding (D)
LaGrange[8]	maj. of 79	
Noble[8]	347	366

	*Samuel J. Anthony (D)	Alexander F. Brown
Lake	149	123
Porter[9]	271	268
Total	420	391

	*Andrew L. Osborn (W)	*John M. Barclay (W)	Samuel Treat	Thomas P. Armstrong	Willys Peck	Jesse Jones
LaPorte[10]	814	811	776	748	47	46

	*Lucian Q. Hoggatt (D)	William Duncan
Lawrence	1007	981

	*Thomas Bell (W)	*Thomas McAllister (D)	Evan Ellis	William Wilson
Madison	936	775	774	758

	*John M. Jamison (W)	*John L. Bruce (W)	Demas L. McFarland (D)	Ellis N. Shimer (D)
Marion	1699	1693	1589	1590

	*Cager Peek (D)	Thomas G. Brooks
Martin	435	280

	*John U. Pettit (D)	Stearns Fisher
Miami[11]	516	444
Wabash[8]	500	552
Total	1016	996

	*David Byers (D)	Austin Seward
Monroe	925	771

	*Francis H. Fry (W)	*Henry T. Snook (D)	Samuel C. Willson	James R. M. Bryant
Montgomery	1464	1459	1447	1400

	*Alexander B. Conduitt (W)	Alfred M. Delavan	William E. Carter
Morgan	1058	1052	15

	*Joel Vandeveer (D)	David Riley
Orange	857	511

	*Frederick Hauser (D)	Harlin Richards (W)
Owen	781	708

	*James Kerr (W)	*Hugh J. Bradley (W)	Daniel M. Morris	James Headley
Parke	1355	1354	1340	1338

	*Joshua B. Huckeby (W)	Harmon G. Barkwell
Perry	414	386

	*Alvan T. Whight (D)	Elijah Hammond
Pike	511	436

	*James C. Endicott (D)	Arza Lee
Posey	926	676

	*Alexander C. Stevenson (W)	*Ambrose D. Hamrick (W)	*David Wills (W)	John H. Roberts	Benjamin Walden	Thomas H. Clarke
Putnam	1563	1551	1540	1379	1379	1334

	*Royston Ford (W)	Jeremiah Smith	Ira Swain
Randolph	756	638	205

	*James Hinchman (W)	*George B. Tingley (W)	William Scruggs	William Moffitt
Rush	1518	1499	1283	1265

	*William Miller (W)	George C. Merrifield	Joseph Call
St. Joseph	805	638	55

	*Augustus C. Handy (D)
Shelby	1174

	*Thomas M. Smith (W)	Oliver Morgan (D)	William M. Hammond (W)
Spencer	422	316	129

	*Thomas T. Wright (D)	Alexander Sebastian
Switzerland[12]	1183	728

	*John W. Odell (W)	*Isaac Shelby (W)	*Philip Foresman (W)	Marks Crume	Samuel McCormick	Samuel F. Clark
Tippecanoe[13]	1484	1470	1468	1459	1426	1418

	*Charles Nutter (W)	Elijah Van Sandt	Maxwell
Union	641	610	49

	*James T. Walker (D)	William Olmstead (W)
Vanderburgh	600	515

	*Henry Hostetter (D)	Abner B. Small (W)
Vermillion	775	739

	*Caleb Garrett (Ind)	*John Hodges (Ind)	*David M. Jones (W)	Joseph S. Jenckes	Joseph C. Early
Vigo	1319	1288	1144	857	806

	*Leroy Gregory (W)	Robert E. Crocket
Warren[14]	635	332

	*Isham Fuller (D)	Lewis (D)
Warrick[15]	637	496

	*William Shanks (D)	*John Kelly (D)	Valentine Baker
Washington	1421	1399	891

	*Eli Wright (W)	*Joseph Lewis (W)	*Walter Legg (W)	Daniel B. Crawford	Jonathan Unthank	Isaiah Osborn	Philander Crocker
Wayne	2167	2175	2138	1286	335	317	315

Representatives Elected for Whom No Returns Were Found

District	
Harrison	Frederick Leslie (W), George P. R. Wilson (W)
Ripley	David Boardman (W)
Scott	David McClure (D)
Sullivan	Thomas Turman (D)

[1] Beginning with the election in 1844, the returns for members of the General Assembly are much more complete because of an act passed in 1843 which required the county clerks to include these votes along with others reported to the Secretary of State. The returns published in the present volume for the elections from 1844 through 1851 have been compiled from the original returns in the Secretary of State files, Archives Division, unless otherwise indicated.

[2] Election Records, Adams County Courthouse, Decatur.

[3] Rising Sun *Blade,* August 17, 1844.

[4] In addition to the candidates listed, Roger Ide received thirty-eight votes and Aaron Pursell, thirty-six.

[5] Brookville *Indiana American,* August 9, 1844.

[6] Madison *Courier,* August 10, 1844. Illness prevented Hillis from serving.

[7] Vincennes *Western Sun,* August 24, 1844.

[8] Indianapolis *Indiana State Journal,* August 17, 1844.

[9] In addition to the candidates listed here, Porter County gave nine votes to Aaron Servis and one to George L. Zabriskie.

[10] The returns from Scipio Township, LaPorte County, received too late to be included, were: Osborn, 96; Barclay, 97; Treat, 72; Armstrong, 69; Peck and Jones, 6 each.

[11] Peru *Observer,* August 10, 1844.

[12] Vevay *Indiana Palladium,* August 10, 1844.

[13] In addition to the candidates listed for Tippecanoe County, Henry Moon received thirty-one votes, Lewis Falls and Reuben Baker, thirty-two each.

[14] In addition to the candidates listed for Warren County, Moses J. Lincoln received two votes and John Stephenson, one.

[15] New Harmony *Indiana Statesman,* August 17, 1844.

Returns for Senate

District	Candidates	
	*William Rockhill (D)	Lot S. Bayliss
Adams	263	206
Allen	812	705
Huntington	297	223
Wells	253	168
Total	1625	1302

	*James G. Read (D)	William G. Armstrong
Clark	1392	1069

	*Huston Miller (D)	Isaac Sands
Crawford	378	468
Orange	952	768
Total	1330	1236

	*Abner Davis (D)[1]	Richard A. Clements
Daviess	689	759
Martin	466	262
Total	1155	1019

	*Benjamin R. Edmonston (D)	James Devin
Dubois	426	227
Gibson	854	781
Pike	498	472
Total	1778	1480

	*Matthew Rippey (D)[2]	John W. Violette (Violett)
Elkhart	886	679
Kosciusko	523	583
Whitley	229	167
Total	1638	1429

	*John F. Allison (W)	John F. Oneal (D)
Greene	775	768
Owen	746	747
Total	1521	1515

	*Andrew Jackson (D) (D)	Thomas D. Walpole (W) (W)
Hancock	723	648
Madison	839	799
Total	1562	1447

	*Samuel Goodnow (W)	Archibald Lawrence (Ind.)	Thomas Jones (Liberty)
Jefferson[3]	1689	1292	37

	*Hugh Hamer (W)	George W. Carr (D)
Lawrence	995	976

	*Parmenter M. Parks (D)	Algernon S. Griggs	Eli J. Sumner
Morgan	1078	1034	16

	*David Henry (W)	Daniel Kelso (D)
Ohio		
Switzerland[4]	998	925

	*William G. Coffin (W)	William P. Bryant
Parke	1340	1333

	*Joseph Lane (D)	William C. Pelham (W)	John W. Lilleston (D)
Posey	1039	571	1
Vanderburgh	632	482	3

	*Jesse Morgan (W)	Gabriel C. McDuffie
Rush	1504	1265

	*William P. Dole (W)[5]	William Utter
Vermillion	758	738

	*Ezekiel D. Logan (D)	Isaiah Peugh
Washington	1277	1080

	*David P. Holloway (W)	*Abner M. Bradbury (W)	Charles Burroughs	Hiram P. Bennett
Wayne	2034	2090	1384	1255

Senator Elected for Whom No Return Was Found

District	
Ripley	Henry J. Bowers (W)

[1] On October 2, 1844, a writ was issued for a special election to fill the vacancy caused by Davis' death. At this election, held November 4, Elijah Chapman received 444 votes and Aaron Houghton, 339, in Martin County. No return was found for Daviess County, but Chapman received a majority of the votes in the district and was seated. Martin County Election Returns, Archives Division; Executive Proceedings, 1837-1845, p. 694.

2 Rippey was elected to fill the vacancy caused by the death of William B. Mitchell.

3 Madison *Courier,* August 10, 1844.

4 Vevay *Indiana Palladium,* August 10, 1844.

5 Dole was elected to fill out the unexpired term of Stephen S. Collett, deceased.

August 4, 1845†

Returns for House of Representatives

Thirtieth Session, December 1, 1845—January 20, 1846

District	Candidates	
	*Samuel S. Mickle (D)	Anthony Pitman
Adams[1]	267	192
Jay	299	305
Total	566	497
	*Christian Parker (W)	Franklin P. Randall (D)
Allen	849	757
	*Ephraim Arnold (D)	Samuel B. McKeehan
Bartholomew	1049	895
	*William Coon (D)	Elijah Eldridge
Benton		
Jasper		
Pulaski	125	135
White	218	225
	*Robert B. Turner (D)	John D. Pulse
Blackford	187	81
Huntington[2]	maj. of 31	
Wells		
	*Harvey G. Hazelrigg (W)	Hiram Blackstone (D)
Boone	788	734
	*Jacob B. Lowe	Frederick F. Butler
Brown		
Monroe	1026	472

	*Henry P. Tedford (D)	Philip Waters
Carroll	745	504
Richardville (Howard)		

	*Cyrus Taber (D)	Horace P. Biddle
Cass	684	623

	*John S. Simonson (D)	*John D. Ferguson (W)	James Robertson (D)	George Greene	Thomas W. Prather
Clark	1266	1114	1016	999	86

	*Wilson Seawright (D)	Joseph Baum	Martin Burton	William Shuck
Clinton[3]	574	30	27	15

	*Daniel A. McRae (W)	Jonathan R. Brown (D)
Crawford	448	413

	*Richard A. Clements (W)	Thomas Gootee	Jesse Morgan
Daviess	763	550	64
Martin	250	370	16
Total	1013	920	80

	*George Cornelius (W)	*Richard D. Slater (D)	James H. Lane (D)	*William Lanius (D)	Daniel Baldridge (D)	Farrington Barricklow (D)[4]
Dearborn	1493	1304	1207	1082	861	858
Ohio[5]	403	329	348	359	99	144
Total	1896	1633	1555	1441	960	1002

	*William J. Robinson (W)	Royal P. Cobb (D)	William B. Lewis
Decatur	981	909	97

	*Clark Powers	Enos Beall	Samuel Barre
DeKalb	317	236	14
Steuben	278	313	22
Total	595	549	36

	*George W. Lemmons (D) (Lemonds)	John Donnell (D)
Dubois	438	239

	*Samuel T. Clymer (D)	George Crawford	M. H. Rollin
Elkhart	720	593	31

	*Miner Meeker (W)	*William Stewart (W)	John Caldwell	Nathaniel McClure
Fayette[6]	989	975	797	767

	*John Jones (D)	Jacob T. Smith
Floyd	969	865

	*John Bowman (D)	*Hugh S. Scott (D)	Finley L. Maddox	Curtis Newell	Charles Tyler	David Brier
Fountain	940	882	799	162	160	2

	*Spencer Wiley (D)	*E. D. Crookshank (D)	James H. Lee	Abraham Lee	Samuel Shirk	Elihu Lonsberry
Franklin[7]	1325	1312	94	63	62	43

	*Anthony F. Smith (W)	Joseph Robbins	Abijah Hawley
Fulton	299	220	1
Marshall	200	238	42
Total	499	458	43

	*Samuel Hall (W)	Smith Miller (D)
Gibson	676	675

	*Joseph Morrow (W)	John Foster	John Dunn	Ira Hollingsworth
Grant	414	339	142	58

	*Lovell H. Rousseau (W)	Albert G. Skinner (D)
Greene	893	750

	*Carter T. Jackson (D)	*Robert P. Kimberlin (D)	James A. Groves	Stephen Carey	Elihu Picket	Francis Ellingwood
Hamilton[8]	715	610	450	419	214	165
Tipton	139	110	80	64	......	1
Total	854	720	530	483	214	166

	*George Henry (W)	*Reuben A. Riley (D)	Joseph Chapman	David S. Gooding	William A. Franklin	Thomas G. Butler
Hancock	663	656	600	584	68	52

	*William A. Porter (W)	*Dennis Pennington (W)	Franklin McRae (D)	William M. Saffer (D)
Harrison	1213	1185	1098	1053

	*Jonathan S. Harvey (W)	Henry H. Marvin	Calvin A. Jessup
Hendricks	945	750	55

	*Samuel Coffin (W)	*Marble S. Cameron (W)	George C. McCune	Emory Southwick	Alfred H. Hiatt	William W. Bowman
Henry	1246	1235	839	508	399	207

	*Samuel P. Mooney (D)
Jackson	919

	*Thomas Wise (W)	*John Chambers (Ind. D)	*Milton Stapp (W)	John Smock (W)	Shadrach Wilber (Ind.)	Benjamin Tevis (Ind.)
Jefferson[9]	1506	1467	1422	1394	1277	1205

	*Allen Hill (W)	Parley Hill (D)
Jennings	773	683

	*Daniel Webb (D)	John Slater	John R. Smock	F. M. Finch
Johnson	878	543	22	1

	*Robert N. Carnan (W)	James D. Williams (D)	Matthias Berry
Knox	869	777	4

	*David Rippey (D)	Stephen H. Colms	Danforth A. Hurlbut	Scott Barber
Kosciusko	591	609	13	......
Whitley	257	191	......	1
Total	848	800	13	1

	*Thomas H. Wilson (D)	Joseph Foos	Henry J. Cushman
LaGrange	469	532	67
Noble	450	366	4
Total	919	898	71

	*Alexander McDonald (D)	Aaron Litle	Charles L. Stockton	Lewis Warriner
Lake	194	98	9	1
Porter	244	321	30	......
Total	438	419	39	1

	*George W. Carr (D)	*John Edwards (W)	John J. Barnett	David S. Lewis (D)	James Baty
Lawrence	1042	969	968	927	42

	*Nathaniel B. Webber (D)	*Young E. R. Wilson (D)	Henry B. Evans	Obadiah Harris	Simon Smock	Simon B. Boardman
Marion	1502	1498	1402	1385	45	43

	*Benjamin Henton (D)	Alphonso A. Cole	A. D. Seward
Miami	566	527	......
Wabash	549	549	25
Total	1115	1076	25

	*Samuel Herron (D)	*John Nelson (D)	*Henry T. Snook (D)	William Carson	Christian Coon	Martin Bowers
Montgomery[10]	1297	1296	1290	1210	1193	1187

	*Alexander B. Conduit (W)	Alfred M. Delavan (D)	Eli J. Sumner
Morgan	977	964	38

	*George W. Moore (D)	James Eson
Owen	810	437

	*William R. Nofsinger (D)	*James Kerr (W)	Johnson Webster	James McCampbell
Parke	1338	1334	1294	1285

	*George B. Thompson (W)	William G. Ewing
Perry	385	384

	*Robert Logan (D)	Elijah Bell	Andrew B. Chambers
Pike	473	351	20

	*James C. Endicott (D)	John B. Gardiner	Arza Lee
Posey	812	621	156

	*James B. Brumfield (W)	*Henry Secrest (D)	John Cowgill (W)	James H. Farmer (D)
Putnam	1482	1481	1464	1359

	*Royston Ford (W)	Robert W. Butler	David Semans
Randolph	713	674	191

	*William Blackwell (W)	Robert W. Fisk	Ebenezer Ridlin
Ripley	967	812	64

	*James Hinchman (W)	*Robert S. Cox (W)	Reuben D. Logan	William Scruggs	Jonathan Gray	James Paxton
Rush	1346	1339	1211	1175	35	32

	*Thomas S. Stanfield (W)	Augustine P. Richardson	Joseph Call
St. Joseph	700	590	102

	*Samuel Davis (D)	Matthew Henning
Scott	455	454

	*James M. Sleeth (D)	Henry T. Gaines
Shelby	1118	994

	*Wilson Huff (W)	Allen Gentry	Thomas M. Smith
Spencer	494	442	192

	*John H. Wilson (D)	*Silas Osborn (D)	Thomas Marks	Jesse P. Hill	William Price	Allen McBride
Sullivan	796	714	635	396	139	134

	*Edward Burns (D)	Scott Carter
Switzerland	932	903

	*William L. Leyman (D)	*Samuel McCormick (D)	Othniel L. Clark	William Potter	Luther Jewett	William W. Robinson
Tippecanoe	1404	1381	1218	1175	54	46

	*William Watt (D)	*Ambrose S. Ruby (W)	Thomas Cason	James Osbon	Thomas Maxwell	Ephraim Dorton
Union	675	675	632	601	64	60

	*Conrad Baker (W)	Barney Royston
Vanderburgh	630	572

	*Thomas Dowling (W)	*Grafton F. Cookerly (W)	John Hodges	William D. Griswold	George W. Ball	Noah Eversole
Vigo	1265	883	849	546	348	76

	*Colbrath Hall (W)	Wesley Clark
Warren[11]	713	372

	*Isham Fuller (D)	John Lynn	James Woods
Warrick[12]	532	480	14

	*William Shanks (D)	*Henry C. Monroe (D)	Arvin Wright	Levi McDougal
Washington	1399	1301	973	145

	*Joseph Lewis (W)	*Walter Legg (W)	*George W. Julian (W)	Joseph Holman	John Lacy	Allen W. Lewis
Wayne[13]	1895	1873	1810	1165	1010	413

Representatives Elected for Whom No Returns Were Found

District	
Clay	Francis B. Yocum (D)
Delaware	John Tomlinson (W)
LaPorte	J. S. Carter (D), Andrew L. Osborn (W)
Madison	Evan Ellis (D)
Orange	Joel Vandeveer (D)
Vermillion	William P. Dole (W)

† See note 1, p. 286, above.

1 Election Returns, Adams County Courthouse, Decatur.

2 Fort Wayne *Sentinel,* August 9, 1845.

3 In addition to the candidates listed for Clinton County, N. Gaskill received eight votes, John Fisher received six, and James Hill, five.

4 In addition to the candidates listed, David G. Rabb, Whig, received 682 votes in Dearborn, and 295 in Ohio County; C. Bird Pate received 67 in Dearborn and five in Ohio; Dearborn also gave 28 votes each to James Wymond and Thomas Smith, 27 to Thomas Purcel, and 22 to George Heustis.

5 Brookville *Indiana American,* August 15, 1845. This paper also carries an explanation of why Lanius was elected rather than Lane who received a larger vote. The act creating Ohio County provided that one of the three representatives elected jointly by Dearborn and Ohio should reside in the latter county. Since Cornelius, Slater, and Lane were all residents, of Dearborn, Lanius of Ohio County, was given preference over Lane.

6 In addition to the candidates listed for Fayette County, Samuel Darter received 20 votes and James Tuttle, 18.

7 In addition to the candidates listed for Franklin County, William S. Geyer received 25 votes; Isaac Goble, 11; T. B. Scoby, 8; Charles Misner, 6; Henry McBride, 5; Freeman Alger, 4; J. O. (?) St. John, Robert John, R. Templeton, two each; Isaac Burkholder, William McClure, E. H. Jolliff, E. Serring, R. H. Cullum, and William Kahill, one each.

8 In addition to the candidates listed, Hamilton County gave 119 votes to William Frost and 16 votes to William Stoops.

9 Madison *Courier,* August 9, 1845. In addition to the candidates listed, Archibald Lawrence received 188 votes; Samuel C. Daily, 160; John Brazelton, 118; ——— Hoyt, 70; and Daniel Nelson, 64. Most of these were running as candidates of the Liberty party.

10 In addition to the candidates listed for Montgomery County, Widdows P. Moore received 7 votes; Joseph Carder and James Campbell, 6 each.

11 In addition to the candidates listed for Warren County, James H. Robbins and Isaac High received eight votes each, and William G. Montgomery received one vote.

12 In addition to the candidates listed for Warrick County, David W. Beason received two votes, and Andrew Williams received one.

13 In addition to the candidates listed for Wayne County, Joseph Curtis received 376 votes, and Joseph Quigg, 347.

Returns for Senate

District	Candidates	
	*Heman H. Barbour (D)	DeWitt C. Rich
Bartholomew	1072	852
Jennings	658	794
Total	1730	1646

	*William G. Montgomery (W)	Ebenezer Lucas	John K. Lovejoy
Benton			
Jasper			
Pulaski	137	128	......
Warren	687	462	5
White	227	221	1

	*William W. Conner (W)	George Bowman (D)	Jacob L. Pfaff
Boone	709	740	43
Hamilton	670	623	199
Tipton	102	99	......
Total	1481	1462	242

	*William Berry (D)	Isaac Samsel
Brown		
Monroe	1206	235

	*Richard Winchell (W)	Andrew J. Harlan (D)	Daniel Worth	Isaac Schooly
Delaware				
Grant	451	420	97	89

	*Abraham Cuppy (D)	James Banta	W. R. Ellis	Dr. Matchett
Elkhart	824	571	2	1
Kosciusko	595	610	......	......
Whitley	279	165	......	......
Total	1698	1346	2	1

	*William G. Pomeroy (W)[1]	Merrill Williams	George S. Harris
Fulton	279	249	5
Marshall[2]	207	215	41
St Joseph	718	587	90
Total	1204	1051	136

	*John Zenor (W)	Nathaniel Albertson (D)	George Bentley
Harrison	1195	1098	27

	*Samuel A. Verbrike (W)	Jeremiah Depew	William Townsend	Christian C. Nave	Henry Morgan
Hendricks	820	680	153	89	41

	*Eli Murphey (W)	George B. Rogers
Henry	1225	954

	*Elisha G. English (D)	John B. Rust
Jackson	808	493
Scott	454	416
Total	1262	909

	*Franklin Hardin (D)	John Ritchey	John Smiley	B. Applegate
Johnson	1059	54	6	1

	*Abner T. Ellis (W)	John Decker	John Ewing
Knox	811	549	355

	*Mason J. Howell (D)	Robert G. Cotton
Perry	291	499
Spencer	493	631
Warrick	821	272
Total	1605	1402

	*Ambrose D. Hamrick (W)	John H. Roberts (D)
Putnam	1481	1446

	*Augustus C. Handy (D)	John Hendricks
Shelby	1084	871

Senator Elected for Whom No Return Was Found

District	
Vermillion	Isaac Chenowith (W)

[1] Pomeroy was elected to fill the vacancy caused by John D. Defrees' removal from the district. Resignations file, 1845, in Archives Division.

[2] In addition to the candidates listed, Marshall County gave seven votes to Seth Hussey and one vote to Zelson S. Cleaveland.

August 3, 1846†

Returns for House of Representatives

Thirty-first Session, December 7, 1846—January 28, 1847

District	*John H. Deam (D)	William H. Parmelee
Adams	296	168
Wells	236	151
Total	532	319

District	*Christian Parker (W)	Nelson McLain
Allen	769	734

District	*Samuel Decker (D)	Abraham Snethen (W)	John K. Lovejoy	Lemuel Shortridge
Benton				
Jasper[1]	[166]	[134]	......	......
Pulaski	154	134	......	......
White	258	245	5	1

District	*William Jones (D)	Joseph Holiday (D)	William T. Shull	Enoch Bowden	William McDowell
Blackford					
Jay[2]	193	249	139	34	21

District	*Stephen Neal (D)	Samuel S. Strong	Alexander B. Clark
Boone	725	680	37

District	*William M. Mason (D)	Allen S. Anderson	Cornelius W. Tucker
Brown	235	200	20

District	*Albert G. Hanna (D)	Thomas Thompson
Carroll	772	755

	*Hervey Brown (W)	*William S. Palmer (D)	Charles D. Murray	Theophilus Bryant
Cass	804	778	675	638
Richardville (Howard)[3]	173	223	184	211
Total	977	1001	859	849

	*Thomas Carr (D)	*John D. Ferguson (W)	James Darough	John B. Beggs	Matthew Clegg	John F. Willey
Clark	1031	1027	962	559	267	235

	*John Lewis (D)	George Donham	David Thomas
Clay	408	394	26

	*James F. Suit (W)	Wilson Seawright	Daniel D. Lightner
Clinton	696	596	15
Tipton	97	129	......
Total	793	735	15

	*David S. Huffstetter (D)	*Simon S. Monk (D)	John Baker
Crawford	415	398	454
Orange	1016	895	709
Total	1431	1293	1136

	*Zachariah Walker (W)	Hiram Palmer	John P. Davis (or Daviess)
Daviess	657	449	188
Martin	144	273	291
Total	801	722	479

	*John D. Johnson (D)	*Alvin G. Tebbs (D)	Charles Dashiell	Daniel Baldridge	Richard Abbott
Dearborn	1813	1372	1261	543	24

	*David B. Wheeler[4]	William P. Means	Stephen Sabin	Scattering
DeKalb	346	235	5	2
Steuben	389	271	26	1
Total	725	506	31	3

	*John Trimble (W)	Jeremiah Dynes (D)	Andrew Herrod (D)	Henry Balton (W)	Johiel Graham (D)
Delaware	558	443	110	76	34

	*George W. Lemonds (D)	Benjamin T. Goodman
Dubois	351	345

	*Asa A. Norton (D)	Thomas G. Harris
Elkhart	792	723

	*William Stewart (W)	Robert N. Taylor	Jonathan Eyestone
Fayette	967	749	20

	*George May (D)	Thomas Chesnut	William H. Mallory	Presley L. McKinney
Fountain	879	701	156	36

	*E. D. Crookshank (D)	*Spencer Wiley (D)	Hadley D. Johnson	Scattering
Franklin	1451	1441	1031	12

	*James O. Parks (D)	John L. Westervelt (W)	David Vanvactor
Fulton	266	271	1
Marshall[5]	322	284	33
Total	588	555	34

	*Smith Miller (D)	Lewis Wilson
Gibson	689	629

	*Andrew J. Harlan (D)	James Sweet	Henley James
Grant	410	395	219

	*John Jones, Jr. (D)
Greene	845

	*Jesse Lutz (W)	*Samuel Jennison (D)	Samuel H. Colip	Carah W. Harrison	William Stoops	Elihu Pickett	Francis Ellingwood
Hamilton	701	685	684	656	178	171	22

	*Andrew F. Hatfield (D)	Elijah S. Cooper
Hancock	632	585

	*William A. Porter (W)	Ulerick H. Hon	Jacob L. Kintner	Robert B. Pennington
Harrison	1081	840	107	7

	*Jonathan S. Harvey (W)	Samuel C. Mitchell	Joseph Williams	James Dugan
Hendricks	1042	668	58	11

	*James Gilleece (D)	John Housman
Huntington	275	292
Whitley	256	234
Total	531	526

	*Meedy W. Shields (D)	Abraham Love
Jackson[6]	731	523

	*William Hendricks (W)	*Thomas Wise (W)	*Fabius Hull (W)	John Brazelton	John Smock	Shadrach Wilber
Jefferson	1529	1516	1366	1334	981	718

	*Allen Hill (W)	Parley Hill	Joseph W. Ballard	James M. Stott
Jennings	646	576	98	55

	*Gilderoy Hicks (W)	James Ritchey	Isaac Smock	William Magill
Johnson	745	706	9	1

	*Robert N. Carnan (W)	Horace B. Shepherd	John S. Benefiel
Knox	1015	358	73

	*Stephen H. Colms (W)	Joseph W. Fallingsly
Kosciusko	720	492

	*John Y. Clark (W)	Delavan Martin	Aaron Thompson
LaGrange	527	516	48

	*Harvey E. Woodruff (D)	Alfred Williams	Michael Steichelman	H. S. Adams	Scattering
Lake	208	3	18	0	10
Porter	319	49	0	13	4
Total	527	52	18	13	14

	*Samuel Stewart (W)	*Franklin W. Hunt (W)	Jacob G. Sleight (D)	William Wright (D)	T. N. West	George Sawin
LaPorte[7]	942	939	865	852	62	58

	*George W. Carr (D)	John Edwards
Lawrence	968	960

	*William Young (D)	Robert N. Williams	John Kelsay
Madison	698	630	23

	*Samuel Harding (W)	*Samuel V. B. Noel (W)	*William J. Moore (W)	Thomas W. Council	Daniel Moore	Joseph Johnson
Marion[8]	1597	1587	1559	1541	1471	1448

	*George W. Holman (D)	Samuel Jameson
Miami	571	525

	*Francis H. Fry (W)	*Sherman Hostetter (W)	David A. Shannon	Chilion Johnson
Montgomery	1446	1408	1361	1318

	*Isaac W. Tackitt (D)	Cyrus Whetzel	Eli J. Sumner
Morgan	976	942	41

	*Thomas H. Wilson (D)	Anson Greenman
Noble	521	431

	*John Tait, Jr. (W)	Perret Dufour	Nicholas Vineyard
Ohio	571	146	57
Switzerland	761	762	231
Total	1332	908	288

	*James W. Dobson (D)
Owen	881

	*William R. Nofsinger (D)	*James Kerr (W)	William Tinbrook	Aquilla Justus
Parke	1260	1232	1231	1198

County				
Perry	*George B. Thompson (W) 498	Joshua Huckeby 262		
Pike	*Robert Logan (D) 488	Warner L. Scott 361		
Posey	*John Hall (D) 861	*Magnus T. Carnahan (D) 760	Alvin P. Hovey 627	Adam Lichtenberger 535
Putnam	*Henry Secrest (D) 1424	*David Scott (W) 1377	Alexander S. Farrow 1350	Alexander D. Billingsley 1241
Randolph	*James Griffis (W) 844	Simeon H. Lucas 718	Daniel Hill 156	
Ripley	*James H. Cravens (W) 841	Elliott Roszell 672	Samuel Hall 104	
Rush	*William Thomas (W) 1360	*John M. Hudelson (W) 1343	Alexander Innis 1223	John McMillan 1203
St. Joseph	*Thomas S. Stanfield (W) 742	Augustine P. Richardson 700	Charles Badger 72	
Scott	*Horatio N. Holland (W) 450	David McClure 426		
Shelby	*James M. Sleeth (D) 1065	William Hacker 919		
Spencer	*Wilson Huff (W) 548	James Proctor 448		

	*Benjamin Wolfe (D)	*Silas Osborn (D)	George W. Stewart	John Marks
Sullivan	770	693	643	598

	*Thomas Smiley (D)	*Philip McCormick (W)	William Farnsworth	Samuel Favorite	Wesley Henkle	Lawson Abbott
Tippecanoe	1484	1469	1394	1419	60	62

	*James Yaryan (W)	John S. Reid	Elihu Talbut
Union	628	612	35

	*Charles I. Battell (W)	James T. Walker	Wilks Reagin
Vanderburgh	601	372	54

	*William P. Dole (W)	William A. Lawlis (or Lawlyes)
Vermillion	718	585

	*John Dowling (W)	*William K. Edwards (W)	Cephas S. Holden	Grafton F. Cookerly	Jonathan Rogers	Joel Kester
Vigo	1007	869	720	706	221	178

	*Jacob D. Cassatt (W)	Gabriel Swihart	A. D. Seward	Alexander Jackson
Wabash	662	637	21	2

	*Colbrath Hall (W)	Lawrence Kinison	James Donahey
Warren[9]	591	9	2

	*Cyrus L. Dunham (D)	*Thomas Green (W)	William Shanks	John Sowder	Levi McDougal
Washington	1154	1149	1105	534	139

	*Robert M. Gordon (W)	*Jacob B. Julian (W)	*Solomon Meredith (W)	*William S. Addleman (W)	Francis King	John Martindale	Daniel B. Crawford
Wayne[10]	1896	1844	1714	1630	1263	1246	1219

Representatives Elected for Whom No Returns Were Found

District	
Bartholomew	Ephraim Arnold (D)
Decatur	Philander Hamilton (W)
Floyd	Jacob Anthony (W)
Henry	John Powell (W), Simon Summers (W)
Monroe[11]	John Eller
Warrick	Isham Fuller (D)

† See note 1, p. 286, above.

[1] Logansport *Democratic Pharos,* August 12, 1846. Thirteen other votes cast in Jasper County were scattered among unlisted candidates.

[2] In addition to the candidates listed, Jay County gave Theophilus Wilson one vote and Lewis Milligan one vote.

[3] Logansport *Telegraph,* August 15, 1846.

[4] A special election was held November 16, 1846, to fill the vacancy caused by Wheeler's death. George W. Balding, Whig, was elected, receiving 176 votes in DeKalb County. William P. Means received 33 votes, Abner Windsor, nine, and Luther Keep, five. No return was found for Steuben County.

[5] Marshall County also gave Jacob K. Hupp one vote.

[6] In addition to the candidates listed for Jackson County, Sterling Vaughn received ten votes, David Harrison, seven, and Michael Elliott, three.

[7] *History of LaPorte County* (1880), 541.

[8] In addition to the candidates listed for Marion County, Samuel Rhorer received 37 votes, David G. Boardman, 36, and Henry Brewer, 35.

[9] In addition to the candidates listed for Warren County, James H. Robbins and C. Haywood each received one vote.

[10] In addition to the candidates listed for Wayne County, Joseph Curtis received 332 votes, Allen W. Lewis, 327, Joseph Quigg, 318, and Joseph Williams, 313.

[11] John S. Watts, Whig, was elected at a special election held November 28, 1846, to fill the vacancy caused by the death of John Eller who had been elected in August. Secretary of State file, folder 249, in Archives Division.

Returns for Senate

District	Candidates		
	*Dixon Milligan (W)	Theophilus Wilson	David Simmons (or Semans)
Blackford			
Jay[1]	315	319	12
Randolph	690	852	158

	*Philip Waters (D)	James W. Wilson	Solomon C. Start
Carroll	728	674	31
Clinton	649	596	30
Total	1377	1270	61

	*Cyrus Taber (D)	John P. Baker
Cass	713	743
Pulaski	162	129
Richardville (Howard)[2]	211	199
Total	1086	1071

	*James H. Henry (D)	James T. Moffatt
Clay	562	360
Sullivan	1072	372
Vigo	827	1245
Total	2461	1977

	*Richard A. Clements (W)[3]	Cager Peek	Francis P. Bradley
Daviess	823	238	216
Martin	260	322	95
Total	1083	560	311

	*James P. Millikan (D)	William B. McCullough
Dearborn	1628	1126

	*Madison Marsh	William H. Nimmon	Reuben Bement
DeKalb	367	202	11
Noble	481	476	0
Steuben	371	278	25
Total	1219	956	36

	*Henry Simpson (W)	Ross Smiley	Matthew R. Hull
Fayette	964	780	20
Union	640	613	54
Total	1604	1393	74

	*Joseph Coats (D)	William Piatt	Finley L. Maddox	Samuel W. Richey
Fountain	1037	567	236	41

	*George Berry (D)	Ezra L. Bourne	John Burk
Franklin	1656	12	1

	*Lot Day (D)	William G. Pomeroy	George Holloway
Fulton	272	262	1
Marshall	348	269	41
St. Joseph	718	715	75
Total	1338	1246	117

	*Andrew L. Osborn (W)	John M. Lemon (D)	Robert Stewart
Lake	139	172	3
LaPorte	997	798	62
Porter	303	285	25
Total	1439	1255	90

	*William Stewart (D)	Robert Hanna	Henry W. Depuy
Marion	1574	1517	36

	*John Beard (W)	John Nelson
Montgomery	1472	1311

	*Martin R. Green (D)	John A. Beal	Daniel Kelso
Ohio	470	177	170
Switzerland	783	737	290
Total	1253	914	460

	*William Hamilton Stockwell (D)
Posey	1388
Vanderburgh	968
Total	2356

	*Godlove S. Orth (W)	John S. Berryhill	Andrew Hoover
Tippecanoe	1485	1413	46

Senators Elected for Whom No Returns Were Found

District	
Decatur	Joseph Robinson (W)
Floyd	John S. Davis (W)

1 William Milligan received two votes in Jay County.

2 Logansport *Telegraph*, August 15, 1846.

3 Clements was elected to fill out the term of Elijah Chapman, resigned.

August 2, 1847†

Returns for House of Representatives

Thirty-second Session, December 6, 1847—February 17, 1848

District	*David McDonald (D)	William A. Bugh
Adams	234	326
Wells	341	192
Total	575	518

	*Christian Parker (W)	*Peter Keiser (D)	Andrew Wakefield	Matthew P. Montgomery
Allen	917	885	838	787

	*Charles Jones (D)	John F. Jones	Hugh Ferry
Bartholomew	1034	848	6

	*David McConnell (D)	Rufus Brown
Benton		
Jasper	214	172
Pulaski	160	132
White	283	266

	*Joseph W. Holliday (W)[1]	Robert Huey (D)
Blackford	204	125
Jay	maj. of 9	

	*Stephen Neal (D)	*Hiram Blackstone (D)	Wesley Smith	Andrew Boone	T. J. McCorkle
Boone	738	657	633	614	35

	*Jacob B. Lowe (D)
Brown	
Monroe	1410

	*Thomas Thompson (W)	Henry P. Tedford
Carroll	848	737

	*Corydon Richmond (W)	J. H. Kern
Cass	803	733
Howard		

	*John H. Sullivan (D)	*Thomas Carr (D)	John F. Willey (W)	Obadiah Knowland (W)	Drummond (Ind D)	Mathes (W)
Clark[2]	1292	1282	913	681	123	94

	*Elias Bowling (W)	Delana E. Williamson	John Lewis
Clay	386	383	274

	*Thomas Kennard (D)	Zachariah B. Gentry
Clinton	628	545
Tipton	138	73
Total	766	618

	*John Coble (W)	John W. Rice
Crawford	529	454

	*Elias S. Terry (W)	David P. Zeliff	Zachariah Walker
Daviess	721	510	241

	*George W. Lane (D)	*Richard D. Slater (D)	Hamilton Conaway	Richard Freeland
Dearborn	1619	1609	1353	903

	*John P. Widney (D)	William Huff	Robert Stewart	Wesley Park
DeKalb[3]	376	351	0	1
Steuben	425	381	6	0
Total	801	732	6	1

	*Samuel Orr (W)	Warren Stewart	John H. Ellis
Delaware	756	431	254

	*Benjamin T. Goodman (D)	George W. Lemonds
Dubois	524	289

	*Horace H. Hall (D)	John Rorer	N. F. Brodrick
Elkhart	823	188	162

	*Thomas D. Hankins (W)	*Samuel Little (W)	Samuel Miller	Richard R. Nuzum
Fayette	956	904	831	818

	*John B. Winstandley (D)	William Underhill
Floyd	1063	1061

	*Solomon Hetfield (D)	Davis Newell	Hugh S. Scott
Fountain[4]	1305	482	23

	*Aaron B. Line (D)	*John B. Campbell (D)	Edwin Barrow	Eliphalet Barber
Franklin	1441	1432	1100	1066

	*John J. Shryock (D)	John H. Staley	William Mason
Fulton	341	385	1
Marshall	259	265	49
Starke			

	*George W. Thompson (W)	Silas M. Holcomb
Gibson	808	743

	*Andrew J. Harlan (D)	William Lomax	Robert Wilson
Grant	478	333	175

	*Stephen H. Lockwood (W)	John Yarnall
Greene	892	829

	*Samuel H. Colip (W)	Earl S. Stone	Jacob L. Pfaff
Hamilton	781	662	162

	*David S. Gooding (W)	James W. Hervey	Elihu Coffin
Hancock	678	636	7

	*William A. Porter (W)	Franklin McRae
Harrison[5]	1271	1059

	*Jonathan S. Harvey (W)	Jeremiah Depew	Solomon Rushton
Hendricks[6]	1028	773	33

	*Henry Swihart (W)	Joseph H. Pratt (D)	Smith Rambo
Huntington	373	390	0
Whitley	313	281	1
Total	686	671	1

	*John L. Ford (D)	Andrew Robertson
Jackson	717	448

	*Fabius Hull (W)	*John Chambers (D)	Lemuel C. Janes	Daniel Nelson
Jefferson[7]	1822	1647	1385	122

	*Isaiah M. Norris (D)	William B. Griffin	Hume Sturgeon
Johnson	1015	613	57

	*James D. Williams (D)	George D. Hay
Knox	836	743

	*James S. Frazier (W)	Elijah Horton
Kosciusko	750	600

	*William H. Nimmon (W)	George W. Sheldon	George Gale
LaGrange	689	639	40
Noble	488	524	0
Total	1177	1163	40

	*Alexander McDonald (D)	Harlow S. Orton
Lake	219	187
Porter	333	356
Total	552	543

	*Franklin W. Hunt (W)	*Myron H. Orton (W)	William Taylor (D)	J. G. Sleight (D)
LaPorte[8]	1015	960	938	868

	*Samuel W. Short (D)	John J. Barnett
Lawrence	981	925

	*Samuel Harding (W)	*Hervey Brown (W)	George A. Chapman	Thomas W. Council	S. B. Boardman	James Hayworth
Marion	1598	1562	1489	1476	13	14

	*John P. Davis (W)	John Mosier	Samuel Blades
Martin	395	377	47

	*Alphonso A. Cole (W)	George W. Holman
Miami[9]	[93 majority]	
Wabash	810	788

	*Ambrose W. Armstrong	*John W. Dimmitt (D)	Allen Harrison	Absalom Kirkpatrick	John B. Johnson	Elijah Brown
Montgomery	1434	1357	1311	1239	29	23

	*Oliver R. Dougherty (W)	Isaac W. Tackitt	William Chambers
Morgan	1111	935	19

	*Samuel F. Covington (D)	*Charles T. Jones (D)	John A. Beal	James S. Jelley	William H. Black
Ohio[10]	562	426	359	204	25
Switzerland	898	1067	992	511	11
Total	1560	1493	1351	715	36

	*James Danner (D)	Michael Mavity	William Key
Orange	785	317	14

	*James W. Dobson (D)	Jefferson H. Woodsmall
Owen	823	679

	*William Tinbrook (D)	*Addison L. Roache (D)	Samuel Davis	Peter J. Stryker
Parke	1415	1382	1348	1302

	*Erastus Sacket (W)	William L. Connor
Perry	642	120

	*James C. Graham (W)	James R. Withers
Pike	470	456

	*Felix Mills (D)	*Adam Lichtenberger (D)	John Hall	Magnus T. Carnahan	Urbane Williams
Posey	1020	948	723	592	142

	*William A. McKenzie (W)	*William Albin (W)	James M. Hanna	Alexander Dunnington
Putnam	1529	1521	1426	1377

	*Asahel Stone (W)	*Henry H. Neff (W)	Daniel B. Miller	Robert W. Butler	Daniel Hill	Benjamin Prickett
Randolph	780	757	741	736	94	62

	*David Criswell (W)	John Sunman	Jacob Jolly
Ripley	1005	869	1

	*John M. Hudelson (W)	*William C. Robinson (W)	William S. Hall	David McKee
Rush	1495	1485	1305	1285

	*William Miller (W)	Norman Eddy	George S. Harris	Abel A. Whitlock
St. Joseph	694	646	42	1

	*Alonzo A. Morrison (W)	Thomas Beavers	Joshua W. Read	Matthew Gillespie
Scott	518	352	57	4

	*William Major (D)	Daniel A. Hart	Smith Wingate
Shelby	1046	838	119

	*Thomas F. DeBruler (W)	Alexander Britton
Spencer	645	361

	*Benjamin Wolfe (D)	Silas Osborn
Sullivan	847	743

	*Thomas Smiley (D)	*John Doyle (D)	*Philip McCormick (W)	Isaac Shelby	Albert S. White	Rufus Lockwood
Tippecanoe[11]	1422	1407	1352	1351	1296	1182

	*Daniel Trembly (D)	Benjamin Miller	Saban Haworth
Union	671	635	75

	*James E. Blythe (W)	Nathaniel J. James
Vanderburgh	630	579

	*William P. Dole (W)	William A. Lawlyes
Vermillion	777	650

	*Cephas S. Holden	*Amory Kinney (W)	*Grafton F. Cookerly	John Dowling	John Hodges	Joseph Cooper
Vigo[12]	1052	930	896	863	739	464

	*James R. M. Bryant (W)	Colbrath Hall	Jefferson D. Hillis
Warren	639	252	54

	*Cyrus L. Dunham (D)	*George May (D)	Thomas Green	Henry C. Monroe	Thomas Morgan
Washington	1501	1400	1090	689	43

	*David Commons (W)	*Robert Gordon (W)	*Solomon Meredith (W)	*Stephen B. Stanton (W)	D. B. Crawford
Wayne[13]	2153	2049	1865	1816	1314

Representatives Elected for Whom No Returns Were Found

District	
Decatur	Philander Hamilton (W)
Henry	Marble S. Cameron (W),[14] Samuel Coffin (W)
Jennings	Hiram Prather (W)
Madison	Robert N. Williams (W)[15]
Warrick	Isham Fuller (D)

† See note 1, p. 286, above.

1 For some reason Holliday did not serve in the House of Representatives. Instead, at a special election held in December, Morrison Rulon was chosen to serve in his place. Blackford County Election Returns, December, 1847.

2 Madison *Courier,* August 7, 1847.

3 *History of DeKalb County* (1885), 319.

4 The returns from Wabash Township, received too late to be included in the tabulation, gave Hetfield 153; Newell 18.

5 Harrison County Records, Archives Division.

6 In addition to the candidates listed for Hendricks County, Henry G. Todd received two votes and Edmund Clark, one.

7 Madison *Courier,* August 7, 1847.

8 *History of LaPorte County* (1880), 541.

9 Indianapolis *Indiana State Journal,* August 21, 1847.

10 In addition to the candidates listed for Ohio County, James Wymond received five votes and J. Harris, four.

11 In addition to the candidates listed for Tippecanoe County, Daniel B. Crouse received sixty-five votes, Job Haigh, fifty-one, and Samuel A. Davis, fifty-four.

12 In addition to the candidates listed for Vigo County, Joseph James received 362 votes and William Naylor 352.

13 In addition to the candidates listed for Wayne County, A. W. Lewis received 255 votes, Joseph Williams, 248, Joseph Curtis, 242, and H. B. Payne, 226.

14 Cameron died on October 28, 1847. At a special election held November 27, 1847, to fill the vacancy, Jesse W. Baldwin received 714 votes and Henry Bigler, 437. Henry County Election Return, November, 1847.

15 The House Journal gives the name as Ruel N. Williams.

Returns for Senate

District / Candidates

	*Franklin P. Randall (D)	David Angel
Adams	315	244
Allen	967	776
Wells	265	284
Total	1547	1304

	*James G. Read (D)	John D. Ferguson
Clark	1269	1198

	*David S. Huffstetter (D)
Crawford	429
Orange	1028
Total	1457

	*Aaron Houghton (W)	Josiah Culbertson
Daviess	851	653
Martin	514	378
Total	1365	1031

	*Smith Miller (D)	James W. Cockrum
Dubois	543	281
Gibson	777	765
Pike	480	465
Total	1800	1511

	*Delavan Martin (D)	Thomas G. Harris	Joseph Cowan	James P. Wicker
Elkhart[1]	759	583	1	0
LaGrange	605	732	0	15
Total	1364	1315	1	15

	*William M. McCarty (D)[2]	Thomas Kennedy
Franklin	1423	1059

	*Lovell H. Rousseau (W)	John F. Oneal
Greene	961	778
Owen	921	692
Total	1882	1470

	*Thomas D. Walpole	John Templin	Samuel Tyson
Hancock	664	648	8
Madison	765	748	16
Total	1429	1396	24

	*Elias Murray[3] (W)	David Rippey
Huntington	390	377
Kosciusko	742	614
Whitley	298	300
Total	1430	1291

	*Samuel Goodnow (W)	William Ford
Jefferson[4]	1630	1531

	*Michael A. Malott (D)	John Edwards
Lawrence	1009	920

	*Jacob D. Cassatt (W)	John U. Pettit (D)
Miami		
Wabash	847	756

	*Alexander B. Conduit (W)	Wesley White	Eli J. Sumner
Morgan	1098	939	18

	*Enoch R. James (D)	John Gregg
Posey	1731	0
Vanderburgh	1119	6
Total	2850	6

	*William T. S. Cornett (W)	Isaiah W. Robinson
Ripley	998	880

	*Asahel W. Hubbard (W)	Archibald Kennedy
Rush	1491	1309

	*John I. Morrison (D)	Nathan Kimball
Washington	1488	1136

	*David P. Holloway (W)	Caleb Lewis	Nathan Johnson
Wayne	1910	1193	233

1 The votes from Middlebury Township, Elkhart County, were received too late to be included. They were: Martin, 79; Harris, 72.

2 McCarty was elected to fill the vacancy occasioned by George Berry's appointment as surgeon in the United States Army.

3 Goodnow died September 16, 1848. William Hendricks, Jr., was elected to fill out his term.

4 Madison *Courier,* August 7, 1847.

August 7, 1848†

Returns for House of Representatives

Thirty-second Session, December 4, 1848—January 5, 1849

District	Candidates	
	*Samuel Decker (D)	William W. Carson (W)
Adams Wells	418	248

	*Christian Parker (W)
Allen	915

	*Heman H. Barbour (D)	*Charles Jones (D)	Richard M. Kelly	John Essex
Bartholomew	1184	1202	1061	973

	*Roland Hughes (D)	Turner A. Knox	Scattering
Benton	82	58	......
Jasper	224	143	......
Pulaski	193	69	1
White	814	589	3
Total	1313	859	4

	*George S. Howell (D)	Jacob M. Haynes	James Marquis	Daniel W. McNeal
Blackford	255	101	......	......
Jay	334	347	13	7
Total	589	448	13	7

	*Lorenzo C. Dougherty (D)	Joseph Davis
Boone	909	705

	*Patterson C. Parker (D)	William S. Roberts
Brown	404	240

	*James Odell (D)	Enoch Rinehart	William Potter
Carroll	991	841	79

	*George W. Blakemore (W)	George B. Walker
Cass	866	791
Howard		

	*James G. Caldwell (D)	*John C. Huckleberry (D)	Charles E. Walker	Arvin Wright
Clark	1216	1188	1030	667

	*John T. Alexander (D)	George G. McKinley
Clay	638	532

	*Alexander M. Young (D)	*James Hill (D)	Samuel D. Maxwell	John Cooper	John Q. A. Perrin	James Forsee
Clinton	873	844	756	499	112	34
Tipton	196	183	157	119	......	69
Total	1069	1027	913	618	112	103

	*John W. Rice (W)	*John W. Gillum (D)	Lewis F. Perry	John Barnett
Crawford	547	615	391	381
Orange	990	820	885	128
Total	1537	1435	1276	509

	*Benjamin Goodwin (W)	James S. Morgan	John M. Williams	Joseph Warner	Coleman C. Wallace[1]
Daviess	532	350	149	220	58
Martin	193	210	350	33	5
Total	725	560	499	253	63

	*John D. Johnson (D)	*Alvin J. Alden (D)	*George M. Lozier (D)	Servetus Tufts	John Ryman
Dearborn[2]	2046	1731	1538	1385	1038

	*Reuben J. Dawson (D)	Cyrus G. Luce
DeKalb	586	343
Steuben	344	355
Total	930	698

	*Samuel Orr (W)	James Hodge	George W. Garst
Delaware	1043	770	393

	*Benjamin R. Edmonston (D)
Dubois	600

	*Matthew Rippey (D)	*Lavinius Pierce (D)	Joseph H. Leeper	David Zook
Elkhart	985	906	827	743

	*Thomas D. Hankins (W)	Thomas J. Crisler
Fayette	951	746

	*John B. Winstandley (D)	Blaine Marshel
Floyd	1129	1006

	*Finley L. Maddox (D)	Isaac Colman
Fountain	1092	840

	*John B. Campbell (D)	*Aaron B. Line (D)	Daniel Wolf	Samuel Goudie
Franklin	1387	1346	877	849

	*Enos S. Tuttle (W)	Albert G. Deavitt	Moses N. Leeland
Fulton	325	329	0
Marshall	399	358	15
Total	724	687	15

	*James W. Cockrum (W)	James Hudelson (D)
Gibson[3]	831	783

	*Andrew J. Harlan (D)	James A. Stretch	Joseph Johnson
Grant	702	622	15

	*John Yarnall[4]	John W. Ferguson
Greene	913	889

	*Griffin M. Shaw (D)	Samuel H. Colip	John H. Brumfield
Hamilton	777	772	330

	*Reuben A. Riley (D)	Elijah S. Cooper
Hancock	749	719

	*George P. R. Wilson (W)	Philip Zenor
Harrison	1252	1035

	*David Wade (W)	James Parks	Henry G. Todd
Hendricks	1079	914	1

	*William A. Rifner (W)	*Martin L. Bundy (W)	Jeremiah Veach	Emery Southwick	John Darr	Richard J. Hubbard
Henry	1219	1192	883	856	383	176

	*Samuel Jones (D)	Henry Swihart
Huntington	446	440
Whitley	345	343
Total	791	783

	*John L. Ford (D)	William Robertson
Jackson	980	6

	*William M. Dunn (W)	*Henry Jackman (W)	Thomas Brunton
Jefferson	1841	1812	1274

	*Smith Vawter (W)	John L. Spann	Parley Hill
Jennings	968	680	29

	*Cyrus M. Allen (W)	John B. Irvin
Knox	1276	374

	*James S. Frazier (W)	Daniel Shoemaker	Daniel Whitinger
Kosciusko	786	676	28

	*Elijah A. Webster (W)	David B. Herriman	Richard Green
LaGrange	686	621	17
Noble	557	593	1
Total	1243	1214	18

	*Benjamin N. Spencer (D)	Andrew B. Price	Thomas H. Fifield
Lake	197	141	1
Porter	376	358	29
Total	573	499	30

	*Willard A. Place (D)	*Franklin W. Hunt (W)	Alexander H. Robinson	Amasa Ainsworth
LaPorte	1097	961	956	951

	*George W. Carr (D)	Creed Y. Wilson
Lawrence	1051	905

	*Townsend Ryan (D)	Robert N. Williams
Madison	850	818

	*James P. Drake (D)	*Henry Brady (D)	*Arthur S. Vance (W)	Samuel V. B. Noel (W)	Samuel Harding (W)	Powell Howland (D)
Marion	1826	1753	1749	1745	1734	1729

	*Nathan O. Ross (D)	Burrel L. Daniels (W)
Miami	743	717

	*Samuel H. Buskirk (D)	Edward Borland
Monroe	987	872

	*Henry T. Snook (D)	*David D. Nicholson (D)	Sherman Hostetter	John Wilson	Scattering
Montgomery	1471	1471	1457	1456	6

	*Oliver R. Dougherty (W)	Reuben Griffitt	William J. Manker
Morgan	1151	1026	23

	*Daniel Kelso (D)	John Tait	John J. Marsh
Ohio	469	428	1
Switzerland[5]	1026	1040	0
Total	1495	1468	1

	*David M. Dobson (D)	Samuel Pickens
Owen	874	827

	*Samuel A. Duvall (Ind. D.)	*John Meacham (Ind. D)	Peter Warner	James M. Crooks
Parke	1514	1477	1344	1298

	*Robert G. Cotton (W)	Job Hatfield	Harmon G. Barkwell
Perry	500	405	44

	*James R. Withers (D)	James C. Graham (W)
Pike[6]	531	489

	*Hamilton S. Casselberry (D)	*Felix Mills (D)	Philip D. Wilson
Posey	1284	1008	603

	*Archibald Johnston (W)	*Dillard C. Donnohue (W)	William Long	Isaiah Wright
Putnam	1663	1452	1440	1380

	*Isaac F. Wood (D)	Ralph M. Pomeroy	Ira Swain
Randolph	906	884	258

	*Richard Kelley (W)	Jesse L. Holman (D)
Ripley	1113	1004

	*John M. Hudelson (W)	*Robert S. Cox (W)	John S. Campbell	John Boyd
Rush	1388	1373	1355	1

	*William Miller (W)	Abel A. Whitlock
St. Joseph	834	752

	*Hezekiah S. Smith (D)	George K. Hester
Scott	478	475

	*Thomas A. Hendricks (D)	Nathan Earlywine
Shelby	1384	994

	*John W. Graham (W)	William B. Richardson
Spencer	580	529

	*Benjamin Wolfe (D)	*Silas Osborn (D)	Orson Willard	Justus Davis	Joseph Dilly
Sullivan[7]	864	699	549	516	297

	*John Doyle (D)	*Peter Goldsberry (D)	Philip McCormick	Jethro Wade	Robert Brackenridge	Jesse B. Lutz
Tippecanoe	1401	1362	912	811	796	576

	*George C. Starbuck (W)	Daniel Trembly
Union	714	653

	*Nathaniel J. James (D)	Nathan Rowley
Vanderburgh	694	641

	*Robert J. Gessie (W)	Charles Trowbridge
Vermillion	782	755

	*Thomas Dowling (W)	*William K. Edwards (W)	Grafton F. Cookerly (D)
Vigo	1263	1221	910

	*William T. Ross (D)	Daniel M. Cox
Wabash	859	830

	*James R. M. Bryant (W)	Joab White	Scattering
Warren	747	154	6

	*Abram Chambers	Alpha Frisbie (D)
Warrick	637	580

	*William Thompson (D)	*James A. Cravens (D)	John C. Townsend	Levi McDougal
Washington	1267	1259	1089	848

	*Jacob B. Julian (W)	*Stephen B. Stanton (W)	*David Commons (W)	*Solomon Meredith (W)	John Brown	Thomas Means
Wayne	2196	2093	2055	1945	1734	1369

	Joseph Holman	John Bradbury	Allen W. Lewis	Joseph Curtis	Joseph Williams	William Dulan
Wayne (cont.)	1362	1288	571	304	259	147

Representatives Elected for Whom No Returns Were Found

District	
Decatur	James Morgan (W)
Johnson	Gilderoy Hicks (D)

† See note 1, p. 286, above.

1 In addition to the candidates listed, John P. Davis received four votes in Daviess County and two in Martin.

2 Lawrenceburg *Indiana Register,* August 12, 1848. In addition to the candidates listed for Dearborn County, Daniel A. Rowland received 735 votes, Levi Boyd, 574, and Mason J. Cloud, 338.

[3] Princeton *Democrat Clarion,* August 12, 1848.

[4] At a special election held on November 9, 1848, Richard H. Rousseau (W) was elected in place of Yarnall. Greene County Election Return, November, 1848.

[5] Rising Sun *Indiana Whig,* August 19, 1848.

[6] Vincennes *Western Sun & General Advertiser,* August 12, 1848.

[7] In addition to the candidates listed for Sullivan County, Jesse P. Hill received 56 votes and Thomas Marks, 22.

Returns for Senate

District	Candidates	
	*William Herod (W)	Zachariah Tannehill
Bartholomew	1062	1175
Jennings	959	733
Total	2021	1908

District	*William G. Montgomery (W)	Thomas J. Finney	Benjamin Henkle	William H. Salter
Benton	66	74	6	......
Jasper	146	188	14	2
Warren	657	373	90	......
White				

District	*William Garver (D)	Harvey G. Hazelrigg	Jacob L. Pfaff	Israel S. Pfaff
Boone	843	851	28	5
Hamilton	775	815	293	......
Tipton	218	156	3	......
Total	1836	1822	324	5

District	*Thomas M. Adams (D)
Brown	668
Monroe	1758
Total	2426

District	*Joseph S. Buckles (D)
Delaware	713
Grant	

	*William A. Porter (W)	George Bentley
Harrison	1297	748

	*Jonathan S. Harvey (W)	James M. Gregg	Thomas Nichols
Hendricks	1075	892	10

	*George Evans	Robert M. Cooper
Henry	1345	1109

	*Henry Day (W)	Lampden P. Milligan
Huntington	436	460
Kosciusko	774	696
Whitley	323	365
Total	1533	1521

	*Elisha G. English (D)	Aaron Hubbard
Jackson	896	516
Scott	479	492
Total	1375	1008

	*Franklin Hardin (D)
Johnson[1]	elected without opposition

	*Abner T. Ellis (W)	James D. Williams
Knox	971	748

	*William P. Dole (W)	Addison L. Roache
Parke	1431	1445
Vermillion	846	689
Total	2277	2134

	*Christopher C. Graham (D)	John A. Brackenridge
Perry	390	568
Spencer	508	621
Warrick	906	412
Total	1804	1601

	*Ambrose D. Hamrick (W)	Jacob Durham
Putnam	1575	1433

	*James M. Sleeth (D)	Martin M. Ray
Shelby	1351	1052

[1] Lafayette *Courier,* August 11, 1848.

August 6, 1849†

Returns for House of Representatives

Thirty-fourth Session, December 3, 1849—January 21, 1850

District Candidates

	*Samuel S. Mickle (D)	John Grim	William Henderson	Joshua R. Randall	Scattering
Adams	426	190	117	......	4
Wells	387	75	92	62	1
Total	813	265	209	62	5

	*Ochmig Bird (D)	Charles M. Muhler
Allen	1055	571

	*Gideon B. Hart (D)	*Thomas Essex (D)	Richard M. Kelly	Joseph Hiner	James Anderson	Hugh Ferry
Bartholomew	1212	1126	976	717	17	10

	*William H. Salter (D)	William Kearns (or Kerns)
Benton	87	76
Jasper	204	222
Pulaski[1]	[84 majority]	
White	303	262

	*Robert Huey (D)	Whipple Cook
Blackford	346	69
Jay	397	284
Total	743	353

	*Lorenzo C. Dougherty (D)	James M. Workman
Boone	893	786

	*Lemuel Gentry (D)	John Ketcham
Brown	400	217
Monroe	855	953
Total	1255	1170

	*Samuel Weaver (D)	A. G. Moore	Scattering
Carroll	769	724	5

	*Charles D. Murray (W)	Thomas S. Shepherd
Cass	947	925
Howard		

	*Francis B. Yocom (D)	George Donham
Clay	599	473

	*Ephraim Byers (D)	Samuel D. Maxwell
Clinton	816	846
Tipton	224	171
Total	1040	1017

	*John Landiss (D)	Nehemiah Tower
Crawford	525	439

	*Benjamin Goodwin (W)	James S. Morgan
Daviess	842	485

	*Joseph F. Watkins (D)	*Daniel Conaway (D)	Levi Boyd
Dearborn	1800	1586	1024

	*William J. Robinson (W)	Samuel Todd
Decatur	1238	1198

	*Edward R. May (D)	John Tatman
DeKalb[2]	564	258
Steuben	335	474
Total	899	732

	*Samuel Orr (W)	Jeremiah Dynes
Delaware	828	758

	*Henry W. Barker (D)
Dubois	626

	*Charles M. Stone (W)	Thomas T. Courtney
Fayette	1023	779

	*Joshua P. Farnsley (D)	George J. Wolf	Alexander Hamilton
Floyd	1175	1035	1

	*Andrew M. Carnahan (W)	Philip P. Myer
Fountain	1051	933

	*Andrew J. Ross (D)	*John Cleaver (D)	Joseph Bennett	Daniel Wolf
Franklin	1349	1241	1158	986

	*Hugh Miller (D)	Timothy Barber	Charles Cromstorn
Fulton	716	185	......
Marshall	442	319	28
Starke			

	*Silas M. Holcomb (D)	James W. Cockrum (W)
Gibson[3]	927	830

	*John W. Dodd (D)	James Lewis	Stephen D. Ayres	George F. Dunn	David Jay	Silas Braffet
Grant	491	365	158	126	85	55

	*Andrew Humphreys (D)	Marcus H. Shryer
Greene	1027	888

	*Thomas Harvey (D)	*William Stoops (D)	Levi Haines	Stephen Casey
Hamilton	1028	995	795	737

	*John Alley (D)	Noble P. Howard
Hancock	727	673

	*George P. R. Wilson (W)	Frederick W. Mathis
Harrison	1134	1050

	*Samuel A. Russell (W)	Jacob C. Faught	John Reynearson	James Kersey	Richard R. Hall	D. Kersey
Hendricks[4]	644	559	327	205	33	2

	*John S. Cotton (D)	David Ridgway
Huntington	363	353
Whitley	347	305
Total	710	658

	*Samuel T. Wells (D)	John R. Hamilton
Jackson	824	716

	*John H. Bowen (W)	*William C. Hillis (W)	*Alexander C. Thom (W)	John A. Hendricks	David D. McClelland
Jefferson[5]	2019	1917	1805	1496	1007

	*Hiram Prather (W)	Morris Wildey	Addison Davis	Wm. S. Tiffany
Jennings	758	689	105	59

	*Gilderoy Hicks (D)	John McCorkle
Johnson	1181	674

	*Horace B. Shepard (W)	John H. Massey
Knox	729	722

	*William C. Graves (W)	Samuel D. Hall
Kosciusko	864	729

	*Rufus D. Keeney (W)	Ara C. Van Ornum
LaGrange	643	532
Noble	529	633
Total	1172	1165

	*Lewis Warriner (D)	George A. Woodbridge
Lake	264	186
Porter	441	350
Total	705	536

	*William Millikan (W)	*Alexander H. Robinson (W)	Willard A. Place	Jacob R. Hall
LaPorte	1073	1063	989	981

	*George W. Carr (D)	Felix L. Raymond
Lawrence	1186	684

	*Evan Ellis (D)	Robert N. Williams
Madison	974	803

	*William Robson (D)	*Isaac W. Hunter (D)	Samuel Merrill	John Burk
Marion	1941	1901	1829	1812

	*William E. Niblack (D)	Oliver P. Pierce
Martin	750	136

	*Alphonso A. Cole (W)	John A. Graham (D)	Michael Black
Miami	755	846	0
Wabash	788	674	219
Total	1533	1510	219

	*James F. Harney (D)	*William Campbell (W)	Mahlon D. Manson	Dennis G. Pottinger	Jehu Kenworthy	George W. McKenn
Montgomery	1344	1336	1321	1317	345	329

	*Alfred M. Delavan (D)	Parmenter M. Parks
Morgan	1304	1065

	*John W. Wright (W)	*John W. Spencer (D)	John Littlefield	John Tait, Jr.
Ohio	411	443	408	404
Switzerland	1097	1047	1033	979
Total	1508	1490	1441	1383

	*William F. Sherrod (D)	James Southern
Orange	967	763

	*James F. Miller (W)	William M. Franklin	Jefferson Wampler
Owen	868	863	1

	*Samuel H. Johnston (D)	*Andrew Tinbrook (W)	Alexander Buchanan	William Tinbrook
Parke	1366	1334	1322	1244

	*Frederick Connor	Major C. Barkwell	Russell G. Tift
Perry	442	281	202

	*James R. Withers (D)	Josiah Chappell
Pike	598	453

	*Magnus T. Carnahan (D)	*George W. Thomas (D)	James Davis	James Endicott	James Lafferty	John M. Grimes
Posey[6]	991	857	785	437	359	172

	*William D. Allen (D)	*Higgins Lane (W)	Elijah McCarty	Loyd Glazebrook	Abiather Crane
Putnam	1548	1492	1446	1256	163

	*Elza Lank (W)	*James Brown (D)	Edward Edger (D)	Ebenezer Tucker
Randolph	863	746	740	683

	*Hiram Knowlton (W)	Ebenezer Redlon	James Vanosdol	William Blackwell
Ripley	917	465	402	4

	*Greenberry Rush (W)	*Henry B. Hill (W)	Nehemiah Hayden	Jethro S. Folger	George Wiltse
Rush	1527	1526	1503	1443	9

	*Mark Whinery (W)	Lot Day	Ricketson Burroughs	Norman Eddy
St. Joseph	972	815	1	1

	*Dr. Alonzo A. Morrison (W)	Samuel S. Crowe
Scott	524	504

	*George W. Brown (D)	Henry H. Trimble
Shelby	1352	763

	*William B. Richardson	John W. Graham (W)
Spencer[7]	532	553
Jackson Township	68	42
Total	600	595

	*James K. O'Haver (D)	*James H. Weir (W)	Benjamin Wolfe	John Marks	William C. McBride
Sullivan	796	735	695	642	283

	*Thomas H. O'Neal (W)	*Isaac Shelby (W)	*Alexander L. Patterson (D)	John A. Wilstach	Peter Goldsberry	Jacob Benedict
Tippecanoe	1367	1351	1200	1195	1190	1168

	*James Leviston (D)	John F. Benwell (?)
Union	727	504

	*William R. Greathouse (D)	Cyrus K. Drew	James Wood
Vanderburgh	718	404	30

	*Robert J. Gessie (W)	Benjamin Wittenmyer
Vermillion	762	757

	*William K. Edwards (W)	*Linas A. Burnett (W)	Robert Wharry	James S. Freeman	John Adams
Vigo	1412	1062	822	490	54

	*Robert A. Chandler (D)	Seth St. John
Warren	554	477

	*Armer Reed (W)	Eldrid Hopkins	Isham Fuller
Warrick	482	456	369

	*James A. Cravens (D)	*John L. Menaugh	William Strain
Washington	1549	1529	934

	*Isaac Beard (D)	*James Elder (D)	*Oliver Butler (W)	William M. Laughlin	George W. Whitman	John B. Stitt
Wayne	1808	1742	1697	1685	1637	1602

Representatives Elected for Whom No Returns Were Found

District	
Clark	James S. Athon (D), James G. Caldwell (D)
Elkhart	Joseph H. Defrees (W), Michael C. Dougherty (D)
Henry	Simon Summers (W), Samuel W. Stewart (W)

† See note 1, p. 286, above.

1 Logansport *Democratic Pharos,* August 15, 1849.

2 In addition to the candidates listed, DeKalb County gave one vote each to Edward Fosdick and Timothy R. Dickinson.

3 Vincennes *Western Sun and General Advertiser,* August 11, 1849. The returns for Gibson County were complete except for one township which was expected to give a majority of twelve to twenty for the Democrats.

4 In addition to the candidates listed for Hendricks County, J. C. Kersey, John Pearson, and C. C. Nave received one vote each.

5 In addition to the candidates listed for Jefferson County, John Quinn received 659 votes and Richard A. Brown received 350.

6 In addition to the candidates listed for Posey County, James R. Casseboom received 49 votes.

7 The Spencer County clerk reported the vote as 553 for Graham and 532 for Richardson and gave the former a certificate of election. Richardson contested Graham's election, asserting that the vote of Jackson Township had been rejected because the judges of the election in that township had failed to sign the return. The House committee ruled the vote should be counted and seated Richardson. *House Journal,* 1849-50, pp. 5, 29-30.

Returns for Senate

District	Candidates		
	*Jacob Brugh (D)	Zachariah Puckett	Thomas Leedom
Blackford	277	104	1
Jay	363	265	......
Randolph	761	600	......
Total	1401	969	1

	*Thomas Kinnard (D)	Philip Waters	Scattering
Carroll	786	680	2
Clinton	749	797	......
Total	1535	1477	2

	*George B. Walker (D)	John P. Baker
Cass	897	982
Howard[1]		[14 majority]
Pulaski[1]	[110 majority]	

	*James M. Hanna (D)	Joseph W. Briggs
Clay	822	377
Sullivan	1112	597
Vigo	831	1468
Total	2765	2442

	*James P. Millikan (D)	Richard D. Slater (D)
Dearborn	1486	1137

	*James Morgan (W)	Robert H. Crawford
Decatur	1241	1233

	*Reuben J. Dawson (D)	Elijah H. Drake
DeKalb	493	326
Noble	582	569
Steuben	358	490
Total	1433	1385

	*John S. Reid (D)	John Yaryan
Fayette	933	948
Union	736	490
Total	1669	1438

	*John B. Winstandley (D)	Pleasant S. Shields
Floyd	1178	1067

	*Robert W. Lyon (D)	Simon Brown
Fountain	1064	889

	*George Berry (D)	George G. Shoup	Richard Bowin	Noah Miller	John D. Howland	John T. Misner
Franklin	1398	7	2	1	1	1

	*Norman Eddy (D)	William Miller	Lot Day
Fulton	464	421	0
Marshall	456	342	0
St. Joseph	884	904	1
Total	1804	1667	1

	*Abraham Teegarden (W)	William W. McCoy
Lake	184	270
LaPorte	1161	901
Porter	369	430
Total	1714	1601

	*Nicholas McCarty (W)	Henry Brady
Marion	1925	1831

	*Joseph Allen (D)	Abijah Oneall	Ephraim Rudisill
Montgomery	1355	1296	372

	*John Woods (D)	Scott Carter
Ohio	448	425
Switzerland	1150	1023
Total	1598	1448

	*John W. Odell (W)	John Lilly	Samuel A. Huff
Tippecanoe	1102	1023	411

1 Logansport *Democratic Pharos*, August 22, 1849.

August 5, 1850†

Returns for House of Representatives

Thirty-fifth Session, December 30, 1850—February 14, 1851

District	Candidates
	*Burket M. Elkins (D)
Adams[1]	maj. of 141
Wells[1]	maj. of 155

	*Ochmig Bird (D)	George Bullard (?)
Allen	1495	793

	*John M. Cowan (W)	Eli Brown
Benton	84	97
Jasper	257	256
Pulaski	424	197
White	964	871
Total	1729	1421

	*William T. Shull	Isaac Underwood
Blackford	300	90
Jay	439	499
Total	739	589

	*John H. Nelson (D)	*Henry M. Marvin (D)	Joseph Keath	Joseph F. Daugherty
Boone	1001	984	937	902

	*Thomas Thompson (W)	Albert G. Hanna
Carroll	910	899

	*Daniel D. Pratt (W)	Samuel L. McFadin
Cass[2]	1022	737
Howard[3]	[103 majority]	

	*George Schwartz (D)	*Thomas Carr (D)	Andrew J. Hay	Benjamin P. Fuller
Clark	1596	1326	966	344

	*Newton J. Jackson (D)	*James S. McClelland (D)	Martin W. Gentry	William Boyl	Scattering
Clinton	829	793	531	23	13
Tipton	503	291	108	......	......
Total	1332	1084	639	23	13

	*Nicholas Peckenpaugh (W)	Marcus Clark
Crawford	593	509

	*Benjamin Goodwin (W)	Francis Cassaday (D)	Jesse Morgan (D)	Gaylord G. Barton (D)
Daviess	642	390	118	97
Martin[4]	1076	534	314	231
Total	1718	924	432	328

	*Ebenezer Dumont (D)	*John B. Clark (W)	Alvin J. Alden	Levi Boyd	Alden H. Jumper
Dearborn	2070	1367	1300	505	54

	*Robert H. Crawford (D)	James Saunders
Decatur	1251	1127

	*John Stayner (D)	George R. Baker
DeKalb[5]	692	283
Steuben	309	478
Total	1001	761

	*Michael Thompson (W)	Abraham Dipboye	Daniel H. Andrews	William J. Moore
Delaware	750	484	364	199

	*Silas Davis	John Abel
Dubois	506	316

	*Milton Mercer (D)	John Jackson
Elkhart	1200	829

	*Charles M. Stone (W)	*John V. Lindsey (D)	Horatio Mason	Edward H. Barry
Fayette[6]	963	871	857	772

	*Ashbel P. Willard (D)	James C. Moodey
Floyd	1059	772

	*William K. Marquess (D)	John W. McKinney
Fountain	1052	959

	*Andrew J. Ross (D)	*Emanuel Withers (D)	Thornton F. Howe
Franklin[7]	1354	1515	785

	*William M. Patterson (D)	William G. Pomeroy
Fulton Marshall Starke	57	27

	*George B. Graff	Anderson F. Ely
Gibson	904	785

	*Joseph Morrow (W)	John W. Dodd
Grant	798	702

	*Andrew Humphreys (D)	Edmund E. Beazley
Greene	1035	896

	*William W. Conner (W)	George White
Hamilton	1054	691

	*Aaron Caylor (W)	John Alley
Hancock	783	729

	*John Simler (D)	Andrew M. Jones
Harrison	1035	832

	*George Fleece (W)	Samuel A. Russell
Hendricks	1154	836

	*Butler Hubbard (W)	*Russell Jordan (W)	Emory Southwick	Joel Reed
Henry	1485	1470	1438	1412

	*Henry Swihart (W)	Lambdin P. Milligan
Huntington Whitley[8]	369	354

	*John R. Hamilton (D)	Scattering
Jackson	1126	66

	*Howard Watts (W)	*J. W. Chapman (D)	John McCoy	B. F. Whitson	R. Wilkinson
Jefferson[9]	1576	1437	1211	227	154

	*Brannack Phillips (W)	Thomas Bland
Jennings	931	819

	*James Thorn (D)	John H. Massey
Knox	807	744

	*Benjamin Blue (D)	John Rogers
Kosciusko	863	651

	*John P. Jones (W)	Benjamin G. Bennett
LaGrange	689	627

	*William M. Harrison (D)	Jeremy Nixon
Lake Porter	268	270

	*William Millikan (W)	*James Bradley (D)	Jacob R. Hall	Alexander H. Robinson
LaPorte	971	954	939	905

	*George Isom (W)	Abraham J. Hostetler
Lawrence	1040	929

	*William Crim (D)	Joseph Hall
Madison	888	884

	*John Coburn (W)	*Percy Hosbrook (D)	*Benjamin Morgan (D)	Joseph W. Buchanon	Madison Webb	Fielding Beeler
Marion	1978	1959	1907	1824	1688	1595

	*Richard F. Donaldson (D)	John Rush (W)
Miami	887	824

	*Lemuel Gentry (D)	Zenas K. M. Hage	Jacob L. Pogue
Monroe	827	714	273

	*Thomas E. Harris (D)	*Robert W. McMakin (D)	Sherman Hostetter	William Campbell	E. P. Talbott
Montgomery	1561	1436	1421	1390	51

	*William P. Hammond (W)	Reuben Griffitt
Morgan	1138	265

	*Abraham Pancake	William H. Nimmon
Noble	691	595

	*Thomas Armstrong (D)	John S. Olmstead
Ohio	504	309
Switzerland	1083	638
Total	1587	947

	*John W. Rice (D)
Orange[4]	1001

	*John McKim (D)	J. B. Huckeby (W)	R. G. Tift (W)
Perry[10]	532	287	205

	*Silas M. Cox	*John Hall	Felix Mills	Elijah Lilleston	Andrew Cavett
Posey	1006	876	727	661	242

	*Elza Lank (W)	David Heaston
Randolph	1113	827

	*Luther Shook (D)	Harvey W. McCullough
Ripley	1136	1029

	*Davis Riley (D)	*Henry Haywood (W)	Greenberry Rush	John W. Macey
Rush[11]	1491	1369	1327	995

	*John Reynolds (W)	Abel A. Whitlock	Alphonso Wilson
St. Joseph	940	707	73

	*Samuel Davis (D)	Matthew Henning
Scott	547	469

	*George W. Brown (D)	Green B. McCarty	Septim G. Huntington
Shelby	1195	696	170

	*John Walls (W)	Thomas M. Smith	Benjamin Romine
Spencer	525	409	244

	*Alexander L. Patterson (D)	*Thomas H. O'Neal (W)	Lawrence B. Stockton	William Hawkins
Tippecanoe	1446	1430	1421	1028

	*William Watt (Ind. D)	Saban Haworth
Union	611	596

	*Isaac Hutchinson (D)	Theodore Venneman	Ira A. Fairchild	Isaac Wood	William F. Ledbetter
Vanderburgh	499	334	332	37	28

	*Benjamin Wittenmeyer (D)	Robert J. Gessie
Vermillion	780	770

Vigo[12]	*John P. Usher (W) 1645	*William K. Edwards (W) 1451	*William Goodman (W) 1228	Robert N. Hudson 1066	Linas A. Burnett 911	Zenas Smith 211

Warrick	*Eli Lewis 533	Armer Reed 416	Abram Chambers 343	Eldridge Hopkins 93

Washington	*Henry Painter (D) 1364	*James T. Campbell (D) 881	Thomas N. Jordan 866	Joseph Laughmiller 644	John Cole 9

Wayne	*Edmund Lawrence (W) 2061	*Joseph M. Bulla (W) 2032	*Miles Marshall (W) 1985	Isaac Beard 1860	Allen W. Lewis 1685	Noah W. Miner 1556

Representatives Elected for Whom No Returns Were Found

District	
Bartholomew	Callin McKinney (D)[13], Samuel A. Moore
Brown	Jonathan Watson (D)
Clay	Delana E. Williamson (D)
Johnson	Gilderoy Hicks (D)
Owen	William M. Franklin (D)
Parke	Gabriel Houghman (D), Isaac Robbins (W)
Pike	Perry Brown
Putnam	Archibald Johnston (W), Elijah McCarty (W)
Sullivan	John H. Wilson (D)
Wabash	Gabriel Swihart (D)
Warren	John Benson (D)

† See note 1, p. 286, above.
1 Fort Wayne *Sentinel*, August 10, 1850.

[2] Logansport *Democratic Pharos,* August 7, 1850.

[3] Logansport *Telegraph,* August 10, 1850.

[4] New Albany *Daily Ledger,* August 14, 1850.

[5] In addition to the candidates listed G. C. Mudget and E. R. May each received one vote in DeKalb County.

[6] In addition to the candidates listed for Fayette County, Samuel Little received one vote.

[7] In addition to the candidates listed for Franklin County, John Wynn and William Cumback each received one vote.

[8] In addition to the candidates listed, Whitley County gave two votes to Zenas Brown.

[9] Madison *Weekly Courier,* August 14, 1850.

[10] *The Economist* (Cannelton), August 10, 1850.

[11] In addition to the candidates listed for Rush County, Thomas Benton received one vote.

[12] Terre Haute *Wabash Courier,* August 10, 1850. In addition to the candidates listed for Vigo County, John Adams received 80 votes.

[13] Thomas Essex was elected at a special election held December 23, 1850, to fill the vacancy caused by the death of Callin McKinney who had been elected representative the previous August. Election Returns, 1850 (writ but no return).

Returns for Senate

District	Candidates	
	*Samuel S. Mickle (D)	Thomas W. Swinney
Adams[1]	maj. 77	
Allen	1253	1027
Wells[1]	maj. 294	
	*James S. Athon (D)	Burdet C. Pile
Clark	1447	793
	*Huston Miller (D)	Jesse T. Cox (Ind. D)
Crawford	479	578
Orange	966	682
Total	1445	1260
	*William E. Niblack (D)	Richard A. Clements (W)
Daviess	618	754
Martin[2]	1467	908
Total	2085	1662

	*Benjamin T. Goodman (Ind. D)	Henry W. Barker
Dubois	445	396
Gibson	831	532
Pike	317	597
Total	1593	1525

	*Joseph H. Defrees (W)	Jonathan Wyland
Elkhart		
LaGrange	700	627

	*Solon Turman[3]	George May
Fountain	763	706

	*Jesse J. Alexander (D)	Peter H. Roberts
Greene	1580	213
Owen		

	*John Hunt (D)	John H. Cook
Hancock	751	686
Madison	1104	831
Total	1855	1517

	*Joseph G. Marshall (W)
Jefferson[4]	2203

	*George G. Dunn (W)	Pleasant Parks
Lawrence	1116	938

	*Benjamin Henton (D)	Alphonso A. Cole
Miami	896	867
Wabash	1006	906
Total	1902	1773

	*Alfred M. Delavan (D)	Giles B. Mitchell
Morgan	1198	1052

	*Enoch R. James (D)	P. D. Wilson
Posey	1408	357
Vanderburgh	836	374
Total	2244	731

	*Hiram Knowlton (W)	Henry L. Gray
Ripley	1100	1081

	*Reuben D. Logan (D)	Benjamin F. Reeve	Joseph J. Amos
Rush	1418	1401	3

	*James A. Cravens (D)	John C. Thompson
Washington	1190	825

	*David P. Holloway (W)	James Elder
Wayne	2104	1710

1 Fort Wayne *Sentinel,* August 10, 1850.

2 New Albany *Daily Ledger,* August 14, 1850.

3 Turman was elected to fill out the unexpired term of Robert W. Lyon, deceased.

4 Madison *Weekly Courier,* August 14, 1850. Marshall was the only candidate.

August 4, 1851†

Returns for House of Representatives

Thirty-sixth Session, December 1, 1851—March 10, 1852, April 20—June 21, 1852

District	Candidates	
	*John Crawford (D)	Stephen R. Cowan
Adams	571	93

	*Isaac D. G. Nelson (D)
Allen	1936

	*Joseph Struble (D)	Samuel A. Moore
Bartholomew	1158	974

	*Solomon Hayes (D)	Henry Robertson	Scattering
Benton	85	106	0
White	432	341	14
Total	517	447	14

	*Joseph W. Holliday	Isaac Slater	William F. Jones
Blackford[1]	182	154	140

	*William Staton (W)	*William B. Beach (D)	Joseph Keath	Jeremiah Landers
Boone	850	829	808	797

	*William Taggart (D)	Silvanus Manville
Brown	378	357

	*Albert G. Hanna (D)	Thomas Thompson	Scattering
Carroll	910	749	2

	*William Z. Stuart (D)	T. H. Bringhurst
Cass	960	846

	*Thomas W. Gibson (D)	*Andrew J. Hay (W)	James G. Caldwell	John F. Willey
Clark	1284	1201	883	868

	*James F. Suit (W)	Zachariah B. Gentry
Clinton	786	667

	*Joel Ray	Samuel Pepper
Crawford	520	486

	*John Scudder (W)	Gaylord G. Barton
Daviess	823	695

	*William S. Holman (D)	*Oliver B. Torbet (D)	John B. Clark	John Godley
Dearborn	2075	1963	1381	861

	*Gilman C. Mudget	*George W. McConnell	Israel D. Morley	Wesley Park
DeKalb[2]	743	582	395	......
Steuben	501	475	488	26
Total	1244	1057	883	26

	*Michael Thompson (W)	Abraham Dipboye	Daniel H. Andrews	George Kilgore
Delaware	672	562	358	86

	*Henry W. Barker (D)	George W. Simmons	Edward Stephenson	Jacob Harmon
Dubois	516	147	142	101

	*Joseph Beane (D)	Milton Mercer
Elkhart	789	712

	*John V. Lindsey (D)	Archibald F. Martin
Fayette	867	857

	*Phineas M. Kent (D)	Dewitt C. Anthony
Floyd	1028	1020

	*Jacob Dice (D)	Edward A. Hannegan	William Piatt
Fountain	1165	977	80

	*Samuel Davis (W)	*Emanuel Withers (Ind. D)	Andrew J. Ross (D)	Robert Brundrett (D)
Franklin	1370	1340	1310	1158

	*James W. Cockrum (W)	S. M. Holcomb
Gibson[3]	932	867

	*Andrew Humphreys (D)	Richard H. Rousseau
Greene	1048	858

	*James H. Douthit (D)	Stephen Carey
Hamilton	818	743

	*John Foster (D)	Aaron Caylor (W)
Hancock	764	681

	*Thomas S. Gunn (W)	John Simler	Martin Byard	Thomas Patterson
Harrison	829	769	390	122

	*Ebenezer S. Watson (W)	Henry H. Marvin (W)	Harvey R. Barlow (W)
Hendricks	870	480	446

	*Isaac H. Morris (D)	William W. Williams
Henry	1558	1428

	*Nathaniel R. Lindsay (W)	Leonard Shoemaker	Jonathan D. Stratton
Howard	504	308	89
Tipton	272	296	5
Total	776	604	94

	*George McDowell (D)	John Studabaker
Huntington	682	633
Wells	485	365
Total	1167	998

	*Samuel T. Wells (D)	John R. Hamilton
Jackson	765	612

	*Adam M. C. Goudy	William H. Salter (D)
Jasper	427	218
Pulaski	150	264
Total	577	482

	*Francis F. Mayfield (W)	*John L. King (W)	John A. Hendricks	Howard Watts	Daniel Nelson
Jefferson[4]	1880	1846	1379	1142	53

	*Edward P. Hicks (W)	Morris Wildey
Jennings	959	859

	*Samuel Eccles (D)	J. B. Cobb (W)
Johnson[5]	762	544

	*James D. Williams (D)	John T. Freeland	John Ewing	John B. Dunning
Knox	607	569	505	91

	*Robert Geddes (W)	Alfred Wilcox
Kosciusko	873	776

	*Francis Henry (D)	John B. Howe
LaGrange	682	621

	*Alexander McDonald	Daniel Crumpacker
Lake	294	251

	*Franklin W. Hunt (W)	James Bradley
LaPorte	1337	778

	*Melchert Helmer (W)	James H. Anderson
Lawrence	1139	559

	*Thomas McAllister (D)	*Andrew Shanklin (W)	William A. Thompson	John C. Guston
Madison	1127	1052	769	191

	*Henry Brady (D)	*Isaac Smith (D)	Abraham A. Hammond (W)	Isaac B. Sandusky (W)
Marion[6]	1538	1472	1441	1250

	*Richard F. Donaldson (D)	James Parcels (W)
Miami	927	850

	*Samuel H. Buskirk (D)	Joseph G. McPheeters (W)	Hugh Marlin (D)
Monroe	894	694	199

	*Daniel C. Stover (D)	*Mahlon D. Manson (D)	James Rice	Samuel Herron	Thomas J. Scott
Montgomery	1491	1478	1411	1103	187

	*John Laverty (D)	William R. Harrison (W)
Morgan	1045	1026

	*Jerome Sweet (D)	Ephraim Walters
Noble	735	526

	*John W. Spencer (D)	*Samuel Porter (D)	Daniel Kelso	William M. French	James M. Cotton	William Woods[7]
Ohio	401	274	234	223	137	92
Switzerland	860	809	784	729	323	85
Total	1261	1083	1018	952	460	177

	*David S. Huffstetter (D)	William L. Spicely
Orange	1211	48

	*James W. Dobson (D)	Uriah A. V. Hester
Owen[8]	949	839

	*Elias G. Holladay (W)	S. F. Maxwell	Madison Lewis
Parke	991	967	91

	*Milton Walker (W)	Major C. Barkwell
Perry	542	509

	*James C. Graham	Levi Lockhart	Francis Slater
Pike	574	536	2

	*William M. Harrison (D)	John N. Skinner
Porter	499	433

	*Robert D. Owen (D)	*Urbin Marrs (W)	Felix Mills	James S. Carey	David T. Martle
Posey	1435	1031	963	55	19

	*Bradford Glazebrook (D)	Alexander S. Farrow (W)
Putnam	1328	1315

	*John Wilson (D)	William McQueen	Daniel Hill
Randolph	841	678	468

	*Hiram A. Hart (D)	Elias Conwell	Squire H. Knapp
Ripley[9]	946	768	205

	*Junius Beeson (D)	James M. Conner (W)	George Wiltse
Rush	1344	1338	61

	*Thomas S. Stanfield (W)	John Brownfield
St. Joseph	1033	847

	*William H. English (D)	Aaron Hubbard
Scott	555	486

	*William Major (D)
Shelby	1676

	*Thomas M. Smith (W)	John Walls	Martin B. Mason
Spencer	579	450	86

	*John W. Davis (D)	*Theopholis Chowning (D)	John Marks (D)	Joseph Dilly (D)	Elijah Milam (W)	Robert Lockridge (W)
Sullivan	1484	736	508	255	234	84

	*Godlove O. Behm (W)	Lawrence B. Stockton	Henry L. Ellsworth	John Little
Tippecanoe	1379	1219	119	2

Union	*James Leviston (D) 639	William Watt 583				
Vanderburgh	*Willard Carpenter (W) 637	Isaac Hutchinson 386	Granfill W. Hardin 249	James Wood 20		
Vermillion	*Henry Hostetter 836	John Collett 647				
Vigo	*Samuel B. Gookins (W) 1326	*Robert N. Hudson (W) 1209	Grafton F. Cookerly 994			
Warren	*James R. M. Bryant (W) 604	Ebenezer F. Lucas 538				
Warrick	*Eli Lewis (D) 893	Isham Fuller 415				
Washington	*Rudolphus Schoonover (D) 1583					
Wayne	*Edmund Lawrence (W) 2114	*John P. Doughty (W) 2067	*Joseph M. Bulla (W) 2053	John Weaver 1982	Nathan H. Raymond 1920	David W. Reed 1785
Whitley	*David B. Litchfield (D) 465	Josiah S. Brown 438				

Representatives Elected for Whom No Returns Were Found

District	
Clay	Oliver Cromwell (W), George Donham (D)

Decatur	John F. Stephens (W)
Fulton	Hugh Miller
Grant	Zimri Reynolds (D)
Jay	Robert Huey (D)
Marshall and Starke	Thomas Sumner (W)
Martin	Martin D. Crim (W)
Wabash	Calvin Cowgill (W)

† See note 1, p. 286, above.

[1] In addition to the candidates listed for Blackford County, Nelson D. Clouser received one vote.

[2] *History of DeKalb County* (1885), 320.

[3] Princeton *Democrat Clarion,* August 9, 1851.

[4] Madison *Daily Courier,* August 6, 1851.

[5] Indianapolis *Indiana State Sentinel* (weekly), August 14, 1851.

[6] Indianapolis *Daily Indiana State Journal,* August 7, 1851.

[7] In addition to the candidates listed, Ohio County gave 76 votes to John S. Roberts, 21 to James Fox and John M. Moody, and 4 to Stephen D. Baldwin. Switzerland County gave Roberts 280 votes, Baldwin 64, Fox 27, and Moody 7.

[8] In addition to the candidates listed for Owen County, Joseph G. Stevenson received one vote.

[9] In addition to the candidates listed for Ripley County, Samuel Thackery received one vote.

Returns for Senate, 1851

District	Candidates	
	*John L. Spann (D)	Smith Vawter
Bartholomew	1171	996
Jennings	858	1008
Total	2029	2004

	*Robert C. Kendall (W)	Alanson Jewett (or Anson)	Scattering
Benton	96	93	3
Jasper	329	356	......
Warren			
White	370	353	2

	*Lorenzo C. Dougherty (D)	William Bowers (W)
Boone	874	770
Hamilton	747	911
Tipton	436	110
Total	2057	1791

	*James S. Hester (D)	Pleasant L. D. Mitchell (D)
Brown	326	389
Monroe	842	730
Total	1168	1119

	*William M. Saffer (D)	Simeon K. Wolfe
Harrison	1041	1024

	*John Witherow (W)	Christian C. Nave
Hendricks	919	893

	*Ezekiel T. Hickman (D)	William A. Rifner
Henry	1548	1416

	*James R. Slack (D)	Ebenezer Thompson
Huntington	686	607
Wells	516	356
Total	1202	963

	*Frank Emerson (D)	John L. Ford
Jackson	765	658
Scott	496	452
Total	1261	1110

	*Thomas M. D. Longshore (D)	Elias Kizer	John H. Bond
Jay			
Randolph	863	734	382

	*Gilderoy Hicks (D)	Hart (Ind.)
Johnson[1]	993	201

	*Thomas Washburn (D)	Henry Swihart
Kosciusko	787	894
Noble	734	540
Whitley	473	435
Total	1994	1869

	*O. P. Davis (D)	William P. Cumings (W)
Parke	1069	1189
Vermillion[2]	898	610
Total	1967	1799

	*Job Hatfield (D)	David T. Laird
Perry	491	545
Spencer	586	685
Warrick	971	424
Total	2048	1654

	*Henry Secrest (D)	Oliver P. Badger (W)
Putnam	1586	1124

	*James M. Sleeth (D)
Shelby	1702

Senator Elected for Whom No Return Was Found

District	
Decatur	R. H. Crawford (D)

1 Indianapolis *Indiana State Sentinel* (weekly), August 14, 1851.
2 Perrysville *Eagle*, August 14, 1851.

CONSTITUTION

REFERENDUMS ON CALLING A CONSTITUTIONAL CONVENTION

Article VIII of the Constitution of 1816 provided that every twelfth year thereafter the voters should express their opinion on calling a convention to revise or amend the constitution. If a majority of voters were in favor of a revision, the Governor was to inform the General Assembly which should then provide for electing delegates to meet at a certain time and place. Instead of waiting until 1828 for the first referendum, the General Assembly of 1822-23 passed an act authorizing the voters at the August 1823 election to express their opinion. The second referendum was held in 1828 and the third in 1840 in accordance with the constitutional provision. The fourth in 1846 and the fifth in 1849 were provided for by special legislative acts. The response was favorable to calling a convention on the fourth referendum, but only about half of the voters had expressed an opinion. The question of calling a convention was warmly debated in the Assembly which met the following December, but the pro-convention members were outnumbered. Following the fifth referendum, the Assembly provided for the election of delegates to a convention to assemble in Indianapolis on October 7, 1850.

First Referendum, August 4, 1823[1]

County	For	Against
Bartholomew	48	131
Clark	[114]	[790]
Crawford	88	139
Dearborn	[75]	[1649]
Decatur	43	208
Dubois	[45]	[122]
Fayette	23	685
Floyd	113	318
Franklin	26	1056
Gibson	215	186
Greene	20	312
Hamilton	0	89
Harrison	208	736
Jefferson	[76]	[1046]

County	For	Against
Johnson	0	66
Knox	353	345
Lawrence	260	270
Marion	[56]	[268]
Martin	75	96
Montgomery	6	77
Morgan	16	172
Orange	468	132
Owen	33	183
Parke	[44]	[258]
Perry	[49]	[171]
Pike	50	170
Posey	321	309
Ripley	62	396
Rush	[27]	[305]
Shelby	16	225
Spencer	186	69
Sullivan	91	261
Switzerland	40	602
Vanderburgh	[196]	[34]
Vigo	56	282
Washington	233	1291
Wayne	72	1664
Total	3804	15,113

1 Compiled from the official election returns with the exception of the votes of Clark, Dearborn, Dubois, Jefferson, Marion, Parke, Perry, Rush, and Vanderburgh counties. The returns of Marion, Parke, and Rush are from the report of the Secretary of State in *House Journal,* 1823-24, pp. 52-53; those of Clark, Dearborn, and Jefferson are from the Indianapolis *Gazette,* September 2, 1823; those of Dubois and Perry are from the Corydon *Indiana Gazette,* September 3, 1823 (as given in Kettleborough (ed.), *Constitution Making,* 2:608); and the Vanderburgh return is from the Vincennes *Western Sun,* August 23, 1823. Some official returns were found that are not in the report of the Secretary of State. Also, there are some discrepancies in the figures given in the official returns and those reported by the Secretary of State. No returns were found for the following counties: Daviess, Henry, Jennings, Madison, Monroe, Putnam, Randolph, Scott, Union, and Warrick. The totals as reported by the Secretary of State were: for calling a convention, 2,601; against calling a convention, 11,991.

Second Referendum, August 4, 1828[2]

	For	Against
Allen		
Bartholomew	336	177
Carroll	37	81
Clark	563	770
Clay	12	74
Crawford	228	305
Daviess		
Dearborn	308	1779
Decatur	368	332
Dubois		
Fayette	123	973
Floyd	[197]	[474]
Fountain	131	342
Franklin	86	758
Gibson	222	341
Greene	120	351
Hamilton		
Hancock	2	104
Harrison	593	588
Henry	106	451
Hendricks		
Jackson		
Jefferson	[278]	[1081]
Jennings	106	461
Johnson	163	219
Knox	[603]	[261]
LaPorte		
Lawrence	477	78
Madison	26	158
Marion	324	577
Martin	185	101
Monroe	286	416
Montgomery	57	390
Morgan	273	296
Orange	318	568
Owen		
Parke	252	414
Perry	115	266
Pike	121	157

County	For	Against
Posey	460	378
Putnam	81	400
Randolph	147	182
Ripley		
Rush		
Scott	289	110
Shelby	187	447
Spencer	[194]	[138]
Sullivan	312	286
Switzerland	67	852
Tippecanoe[3]	47	198
Union		
Vanderburgh		
Vermillion	[74]	[395]
Vigo	[178]	[401]
Warren	17	108
Warrick	293	83
Washington	601	932
Wayne	644	1418
Total	10,607	19,671

[2] Compiled from the official election returns in the Archives Division with the exception of the votes of Floyd, Jefferson, Knox, Spencer, Vermillion, and Vigo counties which are from the Vincennes *Western Sun,* August 9 and 16, 1828. The Secretary of State gave the vote of only ten counties in his report on the referendum which is printed in *House Journal,* 1828-29, Appendix A. There are still a number of counties for which no returns have been found.

[3] Ten votes cast in Randolph Township, Tippecanoe County, against calling a convention were not included because they were not properly certified.

Third Referendum, August 3, 1840[4]

	For	Against
Adams		
Allen	39	664
Bartholomew	26	272
Benton		
Blackford	32	150
Boone		
Brown	112	196
Carroll	122	1047

Cass	17	173
Clark	146	1034
Clay	151	517
Clinton	78	459
Crawford		
Daviess	17	152
Dearborn	709	2406
Decatur	[318]	[1284]
DeKalb[5]	37	128
Delaware	132	1078
Dubois	[164]	[208]
Elkhart	143	586
Fayette	130	1520
Floyd	[56]	[852]
Fountain		
Franklin	180	1029
Fulton	37	284
Gibson	106	1319
Grant	74	571
Greene	132	525
Hamilton	348	1135
Hancock		
Harrison	194	1240
Hendricks	491	1350
Henry	153	2185
Huntington	25	198
Jackson	354	638
Jasper		
Jay		
Jefferson	244	1340
Jennings	114	875
Johnson	155	1229
Knox		
Kosciusko	49	470
LaGrange		
Lake	104	124
LaPorte	272	882
Lawrence	407	1207
Madison	218	491
Marion	268	1866
Marshall	33	290
Martin	173	380

County	For	Against
Miami	52	433
Monroe	293	1008
Montgomery	207	2366
Morgan	191	1681
Noble	54	179
Orange	430	1171
Owen	505	768
Parke	306	1961
Perry	55	446
Pike	109	634
Porter	99	200
Posey	126	1252
Pulaski		
Putnam		
Randolph	83	1079
Ripley		
Rush	345	2407
St. Joseph	126	657
Scott	167	600
Shelby	689	1326
Spencer	130	636
Steuben	203	151
Sullivan		
Switzerland	53	1438
Tippecanoe	276	1603
Union		
Vanderburgh	126	588
Vermillion	105	1269
Vigo	323	1454
Wabash	32	307
Warren	108	1007
Warrick	137	820
Washington	536	1812
Wayne	305	1937
Wells	12	171
White		
Whitley	55	105
Total	12,798	63,820

[4] Compiled from the official election returns in the Archives Division with the exception of the votes of Decatur, Dubois, and Floyd counties which are

from the report of the Secretary of State published in the Indiana *Documentary Journal,* 1840-41, No. 12, pp. 217-18. There are a number of discrepancies in the figures given here and those reported by the Secretary of State. His totals were: for a convention, 12,277; against, 61,721.

[5] The returns from Concord Township, DeKalb County, were received after the legal time limit and were reported separately. The vote was: for a convention, nine; against, 37. The Secretary of State included the vote in his report.

Fourth Referendum, August 3, 1846[6]

	For	Against
Adams	124	207
Allen	507	702
Bartholomew		
Benton	68	3
Blackford	130	20
Boone	268	288
Brown	159	244
Carroll	320	326
Cass	367	496
Clark	1042	238
Clay	21	25
Clinton	153	217
Crawford	47	184
Daviess	63	204
Dearborn	613	572
Decatur	516	1213
DeKalb	50	219
Delaware	759	295
Dubois	476	156
Elkhart	942	309
Fayette	484	778
Floyd	599	48
Fountain	1057	20
Franklin	1228	137
Fulton	323	145
Gibson		
Grant		
Greene	283	682
Hamilton	726	259
Hancock	668	376
Harrison	210	994

County	For	Against
Hendricks	323	684
Henry	308	794
[Howard] Richardville	41	84
Huntington		
Jackson	462	447
Jasper	106	132
Jay	69	288
Jefferson	1009	1381
Jennings	307	286
Johnson	729	261
Knox	402	430
Kosciusko	418	211
LaGrange	85	81
Lake	164	13
LaPorte	441	187
Lawrence	1313	410
Madison	724	398
Marion	604	1484
Marshall	580	3
Martin	116	142
Miami	315	241
Monroe	507	215
Montgomery	203	742
Morgan	306	596
Noble		
Ohio		
Orange	354	695
Owen	984	198
Parke	730	263
Perry	85	387
Pike	34	414
Porter	246	97
Posey	183	172
Pulaski	53	62
Putnam	1121	1194
Randolph	636	260
Ripley	237	1268
Rush	1099	1041
St. Joseph	423	348
Scott	62	187

Shelby	958	341
Spencer	439	435
Steuben	83	74
Sullivan	804	440
Switzerland		
Tippecanoe	1456	541
Tipton	48	101
Union		
Vanderburgh	20	92
Vermillion		
Vigo	701	960
Wabash	416	394
Warren		
Warrick	249	280
Washington	712	682
Wayne		
Wells	36	213
White	138	104
Whitley	150	284
Total	34,192	30,394

[6] Compiled from the official election returns in the Archives Division. A few returns were found that are not included in the report of the Secretary of State printed in the Indiana *Documentary Journal,* 1846-47, Part II, No. 7. Returns from some of the counties have not been found.

Fifth Referendum, August 6, 1849[7]

	For	Against
Adams	438	296
Allen	1130	483
Bartholomew	1025	897
Benton	102	61
Blackford	203	160
Boone	804	857
Brown	415	175
Carroll	887	607
Cass	990	575
Clark	1687	590
Clay	726	493
Clinton	827	778
Crawford	573	440

County	For	Against
Daviess	693	768
Dearborn	1087	1450
Decatur	1068	1328
DeKalb	555	156
Delaware	781	637
Dubois	547	259
Elkhart	1618	364
Fayette	1280	552
Floyd	1205	799
Fountain	1109	668
Franklin	1363	928
Fulton	512	366
Gibson	1150	602
Grant	632	573
Greene	976	952
Hamilton	1019	769
Hancock	1033	394
Harrison	1175	1022
Hendricks	782	982
Henry	1517	1261
Howard	504	379
Huntington	558	125
Jackson	917	652
Jasper	102	201
Jay	358	266
Jefferson	1338	1804
Jennings	532	988
Johnson	1155	635
Knox	901	490
Kosciusko	1097	404
LaGrange	819	233
Lake	393	66
LaPorte	1686	196
Lawrence	873	1076
Madison	759	1002
Marion	1609	1956
Marshall	545	155
Martin	302	467
Miami	749	707
Monroe	878	863

Montgomery	1198	1706
Morgan	1024	1279
Noble	916	215
Ohio	516	329
Orange	1106	715
Owen	1222	539
Parke	1476	1117
Perry	316	661
Pike	697	312
Porter	677	117
Posey	1492	545
Pulaski	187	130
Putnam	1577	1358
Randolph	1041	523
Ripley	596	1193
Rush	1656	1289
St. Joseph	1545	148
Scott	448	457
Shelby	1360	889
Spencer	552	569
Steuben	590	178
Sullivan	1114	555
Switzerland	1082	1057
Tippecanoe	1513	938
Tipton	215	179
Union	804	361
Vanderburgh	594	519
Vermillion	981	537
Vigo	1509	776
Wabash	971	579
Warren	538	526
Warrick	830	505
Washington	1630	979
Wayne	2439	954
Wells	401	278
White	292	265
Whitley	411	234
Total	81,500	57,418

[7] Compiled from the official election returns in the Archives Division. The figures agree with those given in the report of the Secretary of State in Indiana *Documentary Journal,* Part I, No. 3, pp. 81-82.

DELEGATES TO THE CONSTITUTIONAL CONVENTION OF 1850-51[1]

Election August 5, 1850

Returns for Representative Delegates

District	Candidates	
	*Erastus K. Bascom (D)	Greer
Adams[2]	514	328
Wells[3]	maj. of 293	

District		
	*Allen Hamilton (W)	Charles E. Sturgis
Allen	1272	1024

District		
	*Jonathan Harbolt (D)	A. M. C. Goudy
Benton	97	84
Jasper		
Pulaski		
White		

District		
	*Dixon Milligan	Edward G. Carroll
Blackford	70	320
Jay		

District		
	*Robert H. Milroy (D)	Philip Waters
Carroll	954	690

District		
	*George A. Gordon (D)	M. R. Wickersham
Cass[4]	855	875
Howard[4]	maj. of 138	

District				
	*Stephen Sims (W)	*Cornelius J. Miller (D)	Carter T. Jackson	John Young
Clinton				
Tipton	177	334	351	160

	*Edward R. May (D)	Wesley Park
DeKalb	697	300
Steuben	363	463
Total	1050	763

	*Benjamin R. Edmonston	Jacob Geiger
Dubois	463	442

	*Walter E. Beach (D)	E. M. Chamberlain
Elkhart[5]	1041	971

	*Henry P. Thornton (W)	Jacob Summers, Sr.
Floyd	933	900

	*Joseph Ristine (D)	David Brier
Fountain[6]	1123	1049

	*Samuel Hall	Frederick Bruner
Gibson	1261	256

	*George Tague (D)	Isaac Willett
Hancock	842	656

	*John Mathis (D)	Frederick Leslie	George P. R. Wilson
Harrison	1098	559	553

	*Christian C. Nave (D)	John Reynearson
Hendricks[7]	1085	922

	*William McKee Dunn (W)	*Michael G. Bright (D)	Moody Park
Jefferson[8]	1793	1531	1202

	*Edmund D. Taylor (D)	*John B. Niles (W)	Charles W. Cathcart	Alexander Blackburn
LaPorte	1002	993	931	839

	*John Davis (W)	William C. Fleming
Madison	1045	945

	*Douglass Maguire (W)	*Jacob Chapman (D)	*David Wallace (W)	Levi S. Todd	James Johnson	William Moore
Marion	1878	1868	1863	1845	1820	1685

	*John A. Graham (D)	William M. Reyburn
Miami	1140	567

	*Alexander B. Conduitt (W)	Isaac W. Tackitt
Morgan	1229	1042

	*Thompson P. Bicknell (W)	David B. Herriman
Noble	679	602

	*Daniel Kelso (D)	Perret Dufour (D)
Ohio	402	407
Switzerland	888	862
Total	1290	1269

	*William Holaday (Holliday)
Orange[9]	1387

	*Samuel Frisbie	R. G. Cotton
Perry[10]	479	478

	*Schuyler Colfax (W)	Albert G. Deavitt
St. Joseph	972	734

	*James Vanbenthusen (D)[11]	Nathan Lewis
Shelby	1085	1048

	*Wilson Huff (W)	W. Johnson	W. G. Thomas	J. Parker	R. Waer
Spencer[12]	664	285	122	68	41

	*John Pettit (D)	*Othniel L. Clark (W)	Lemuel Devault	Isaac Shelby
Tippecanoe[13]	1520	1410	1408	1368

	*Thomas Chenoweth (D)	T. C. W. Sale
Vermillion[14]	810	714

	*Cromwell W Barbour (W)	*Grafton F. Cookerly (D)	*Thomas I. Bourne (W)	E. Bowyer	William D. Griswold	John Hodges
Vigo[15]	1153	891	841	839	755	614

	*James R. M. Bryant (W)	Jehu George	Colbrath Hall	Jack Stinson
Warren	902	10	1	1

	*Christopher C. Graham
Warrick[16]	1268

	*Rudolphus Schoonover (D)	*Ezekiel D. Logan (D)	John H. Butler	James W. Martin
Washington	1357	1153	1127	541

	*John Beard (W)	*Othniel Beeson (D)	*James Rariden (W)
Wayne[17]	2068	1998	1862

Representative Delegates Elected for Whom No Returns Were Found

District	
Bartholomew	Smith Jones (D), Zachariah Tannehill (D)
Boone	Mark A. Duzan (D), William McLean (D)
Brown	Shadrach Chandler (D)
Clark	Jacob Fisher (D), Thomas Ware Gibson (D)
Clay	Francis B. Yocom (D)
Crawford	Samuel Pepper (W)
Dearborn	John D. Johnson (D), Johnson Watts (W)
Decatur	Joseph Robinson (W)
Delaware	David Kilgore (W)

Fayette	Ross Smiley (D), William W. Thomas (W)
Franklin	George G. Shoup (D), Spencer Wiley (D)
Fulton, Marshall, Starke	Amzi L. Wheeler (D)
Grant	Benoni C. Hogin (W)
Greene	Thomas Butler
Hamilton	Haymond W. Clark (W)
Henry	George H. Balingall (W), Daniel Mowrer (D)
Huntington and Whitley	Jacob Wunderlich
Jackson	Samuel P. Mooney (D)
Jennings	John L. Spann (D)
Johnson	Franklin Hardin (D)
Knox	Willis W. Hitt (W)
Kosciusko	James Garvin (D)
LaGrange	John B. Howe
Lake and Porter	Daniel Crumpacker (D)
Lawrence	Melchert Helmer (W)
Martin[18]	Thomas Gootee
Monroe	William C. Foster (D)
Montgomery	Horace E. Carter (D), David A. Shannon (D)
Owen	George W. Moore (D)
Parke	Samuel Davis (W), William R. Nofsinger (D)
Pike	Charles Alexander
Posey	Alvin P. Hovey (D), Robert Dale Owen (D)
Putnam	Oliver P. Badger (W), Alexander S. Farrow (W)
Randolph	Beattie McClelland (D)
Ripley	Henry J. Bowers (W)
Rush	William Bracken (D), Jefferson Helm (W)
Scott	Hezekiah S. Smith (D)
Sullivan	Benjamin Wolfe (D)
Union	Benjamin F. Brookbank
Vanderburgh	James E. Blythe (W)
Wabash	William Steele, Sr. (D)

[1] There were one hundred and fifty delegates; fifty were elected from the senatorial districts set up for the election of state senators and one hundred from the districts set up for the election of representatives to the General

Assembly. The returns are from the Secretary of State's file in Archives Division unless otherwise indicated. The political affiliations of the delegates are those indicated in the *Indiana State Sentinel* and *Indiana State Journal,* Indianapolis newspapers.

[2] Adams County Election Returns, Courthouse, Decatur.

[3] Fort Wayne *Sentinel,* August 10, 1850.

[4] Logansport *Democratic Pharos,* August 7, 14, 1850.

[5] Goshen *Democrat,* August 7, 1850.

[6] Covington *People's Friend,* August 10, 1850.

[7] *History of Hendricks County* (1885), 306.

[8] Madison *Weekly Courier,* August 14, 1850.

[9] New Albany *Daily Ledger,* August 14, 1850. Holaday was the only candidate. He resigned his seat in the Convention and was succeeded by William R. Johnson on January 18, 1851.

[10] *The Economist* (Cannelton), August 10, 1850.

[11] Vanbenthusen died on November 14, 1850, and was succeeded by James Elliott.

[12] *The Economist* (Cannelton), August 10, 1850.

[13] Lafayette *Courier* (daily), August 7, 1850.

[14] Perrysville *Eagle,* August 15, 1850.

[15] Terre Haute *Wabash Courier,* August 10, 1850. In addition to the candidates listed, Amory Kinney received 612 votes, William Ray, 505, Samuel W. Edmonds, 355, and William Naylor, 163.

[16] Newburgh *Warrick Democrat,* August 13, 1850.

[17] Centerville *Indiana True Democrat,* August 7, 1850.

[18] See below, note 15, p. 387.

Returns for Senatorial Delegates

District	Candidates	
	*James W. Borden (D)	Samuel Hanna
Adams[1]	526	324
Allen	1401	869
Wells		
	*Robert C. Kendall (W)	Robert A. Chandler
Benton	94	81
Jasper		
Warren		
White		
	*Nathan B. Hawkins (W)	Jeremiah Smith
Blackford	133	256
Jay		
Randolph		
	*Daniel Read (D)	Eli P. Farmer
Brown[2]	maj. of 311	
Monroe	891	786

	*Hiram Allen (W)	David Witherow
Carroll	965	7
Clinton		

	*Horace P. Biddle (W)	Robert Mehaffey
Cass[3]	939	835
Howard[3]	41	73
Pulaski[3]	74	92
Total	1054	1000

	*William R. Haddon (D)	Michael Combs
Clay		
Sullivan		
Vigo[12]	1022	1175

	*William F. Sherrod (D)	J. W. Gillum (W)
Crawford[4]		maj. of 117
Orange[4]	961	812

	*Robert Work (D)	Ephraim Walters	William Mitchell	Scattering
DeKalb	665	104	......	25
Noble	718	581	......	......
Steuben	457	......	12	......

	*Smith Miller
Dubois	435
Gibson	1309
Pike	

	*Joseph H. Mather (W)	John Moore
Elkhart[5]	1034	959
LaGrange		

	*Phineas M. Kent (D)	Alexander S. Burnett	Levi McDougle
Floyd	1004	679	51

		*Joseph Coats (D)	William H. Mallory (Free Soil)
Fountain[6]		1608	436

	*Hugh Miller (D)	Francis R. Tutt
Fulton Marshall St. Joseph Starke	710	1003

	*Thomas D. Walpole (W)	Reuben A. Riley	Orlando Craine (or Crane)
Hancock	748	634	121
Madison	933	862	130
Total	1681	1496	251

	*John Zenor (W)	William M. Saffer	William A. Porter
Harrison	715	669	425

	*Henry G. Todd (W)	A. Alexander
Hendricks[7]	1021	946

	*Elias Murray (W)	Elijah Horton
Huntington Kosciusko Whitley	832	621

	*Milton Gregg (W)	Joseph Woods
Jefferson	1550	1074

	*Samuel J. Anthony (D)	Aaron Litle (Little)
Lake LaPorte Porter	937	971

	*Alexander F. Morrison (D)	Robert Hanna
Marion	1848	1789

	*Harrison Kendall (D)	Job L. Knight (W)
Miami[8]	961	788
Wabash	1103	838
Total	2064	1626

	*James Crawford (W)	John Laverty
Morgan	1145	1137

	*Abel C. Pepper (D)	William Howe
Ohio	533	321
Switzerland	1062	887
Total	1595	1208

	*Oliver P. Davis (D)	George K. Steele (W)
Parke	1250	......
Vermillion[9]	945	602

	*John P. Dunn	John A. Brackenridge
Perry[10]	524	518
Spencer	635	652
Warrick[10]	837	571
Total	1996	1741

	*James Lockhart (D)	John Pitcher	A. L. Robinson
Posey	1328	583	20
Vanderburgh			

	*Thomas A. Hendricks (D)
Shelby	2040

	*Joel B. McFarland (D)	R. C. Gregory (W)
Tippecanoe[11]	1438	1398

	*John I. Morrison (D)
Washington	1469

	*John S. Newman (W)	Joseph Holman
Wayne[13]	2172	1724

Senatorial Delegates Elected for Whom No Returns Were Found

District	
Bartholomew and Jennings	Hiram Prather (W)
Boone, Hamilton, Tipton[14]	Albert Cole (W)
Clark	James G. Read (D)
Daviess	Elias S. Terry[15]
Dearborn	William S. Holman (D)
Decatur	James B. Foley (D)
Delaware and Grant	Walter March (D)
Fayette and Union	Daniel Trembly (D)
Franklin	George Berry (D)
Greene and Owen	David M. Dobson (D)
Henry	Isaac Kinley (D)
Jackson and Scott	John F. Carr (D)
Johnson	James Ritchey (D)
Knox	James Dick (D)
Lawrence	George W. Carr (D)
Montgomery	Henry T. Snook
Putnam	Alexander C. Stevenson (W)
Ripley	Thomas Smith (D)
Rush	Jesse Morgan (W)

1 Election Returns, Adams County Courthouse, Decatur.

2 Indianapolis *Indiana State Sentinel* (weekly), August 15, 1850.

3 Logansport *Democratic Pharos,* August 7, 14, 1850.

4 New Albany *Daily Ledger,* August 14, 1850.

5 Goshen *Democrat,* August 7, 1850.

6 Covington *People's Friend,* August 10, 1850.

7 *History of Hendricks County* (1885), 306.

8 Peru *Miami County Sentinel,* August 8, 1850.

9 Perrysville *Eagle,* August 15, 1850.

10 Newburgh *Warrick Democrat,* August 13 and 20, 1850.

11 Lafayette *Courier,* August 7, 1850.

12 Terre Haute *Wabash Courier,* August 10, 1850.

13 Centerville *Indiana True Democrat,* August 7, 1850.

14 The act calling the Convention provided that the voters of Hamilton County alone should elect the senatorial delegate in this district.

15 Terry resigned. Richard A. Clements was elected in his place and was seated on December 21, 1850. Daviess County did not elect a representative delegate. The regular apportionment law provided that Daviess and Martin counties should jointly elect one senator and one representative. The act calling the Convention provided that Daviess and Martin should each elect one delegate. In the Convention Journal the delegate from Daviess is listed as a senatorial delegate and the Martin County delegate as a representative delegate.

RATIFICATION OF THE CONSTITUTION OF 1851 AND THE NEGRO EXCLUSION CLAUSE

August 4, 1851[1]

County	Constitution		Exclusion Clause	
	For	Against	For	Against
Adams	643	39	541	120
Allen	1830	260	1775	261
Bartholomew	1753	318	1855	144
Benton	180	6	174	15
Blackford	438	12	414	26
Boone	1211	381	1248	187
Brown	596	116	686	39
Carroll	1405	179	1289	213
Cass	1431	185	1393	179
Clark	1873	359	2197	65
Clay	1056	113	1096	32
Clinton	1314	102	1117	146
Crawford	803	163	859	91
Daviess	1097	342	1168	97
Dearborn	2082	1049	2444	423
Decatur	1623	672	2012	213
DeKalb	710	95	461	415
Delaware	1261	388	1328	169
Dubois	803	20	739	2
Elkhart	905	257	486	786
Fayette	1411	218	1417	275
Floyd	1195	739	1711	113
Fountain	2017	161	1653	165
Franklin	2381	190	2331	184
Fulton	903	49	824	142
Gibson	1152	605	1575	131
Grant	1106	542	1005	596
Greene	1336	475	1331	115
Hamilton	1022	606	1035	577
Hancock	1358	76	1327	88

Harrison	1630	423	1898	75
Henry	2200	621	1931	802
Hendricks	1462	352	1410	328
Howard	687	258	592	346
Huntington	1046	210	961	168
Jackson	1429	130	1432	89
Jasper	609	10	496	64
Jay	845	113	587	337
Jefferson	2208	1009	2624	411
Jennings	1513	278	1552	168
Johnson	981	369	1172	101
Knox	984	661	1461	89
Kosciusko	1473	80	1179	319
LaGrange	1010	86	423	654
Lake	448	8	287	180
LaPorte	1769	132	1338	635
Lawrence	1232	546	1611	150
Madison	1518	324	1563	208
Marion	2112	740	2509	308
Marshall	790	18	587	278
Martin	571	246	725	76
Miami	1523	155	1483	239
Monroe	1244	423	1463	127
Montgomery	2140	688	2186	611
Morgan	1553	327	1371	309
Noble	530	390	541	340
Ohio	315	438	680	62
Orange	1263	184	1347	24
Owen	1531	215	1534	30
Parke	1635	509	1812	265
Perry	955	119	957	78
Pike	825	275	998	56
Porter	815	2	633	264
Posey	1465	420	1690	116
Pulaski	417	6	400	19
Putnam	2375	274	2466	96
Randolph	1245	773	964	1002
Ripley	1059	941	1408	384
Rush	2348	306	2268	331
St. Joseph	1603	104	952	861
Scott	784	92	913	66
Shelby	1693	242	1823	93

County	Constitution		Exclusion Clause	
	For	Against	For	Against
Spencer	930	300	1124	49
Starke	104	......	88	8
Steuben	787	88	257	592
Sullivan	1585	67	1514	88
Switzerland	966	942	1539	127
Tippecanoe	2377	183	1975	455
Tipton	540	26	533	36
Union	819	330	723	370
Vanderburgh	655	628	1017	159
Vermillion	1211	221	1337	38
Vigo	1820	235	1974	107
Wabash	1563	204	1447	286
Warren	1025	52	678	338
Warrick	1305	103	1350	34
Washington	1889	677	2171	388
Wayne	2756	1164	2380	1426
Wells	728	103	685	97
White	671	18	579	45
Whitley	769	83	739	62
Total	113,230	27,638	113,828	21,873

[1] Compiled from official election returns in the Archives Division. The Constitution provided that Article XIII in relation to Negroes and Mulattoes should be submitted to the voters for their approval or disapproval at the same time the Constitution was submitted for ratification. Section 1 of the article denied Negroes and Mulattoes the right to enter the state.

APPENDIX

ACTS FORMING AND ORGANIZING COUNTIES

Adams County: formation, February 7, 1835, effective on publication; organization, January 23, 1836, effective March 1.
Allen County: formation, December 17, 1823, effective April 1, 1824.
Bartholomew County: formation, January 8, 1821, effective February 12.
Benton County: formation, February 18, 1840, effective on passage.
Blackford County: formation, February 15, 1838, effective April 2; organization, January 29, 1839, effective on passage.
Boone County: formation, January 29, 1830, effective April 1.
Brown County: formation, February 4, 1836, effective April 1.
Carroll County: formation, January 7, 1828, effective May 1.
Cass County: formation, December 18, 1828, effective April 14, 1829.
Clark County: formation, February 3, 1801.
Clay County: formation, February 12, 1825, effective April 1.
Clinton County: formation, January 29, 1830, effective March 1.
Crawford County: formation, January 29, 1818, effective March 1.
Daviess County: formation, December 24, 1816, effective February 15, 1817.
Dearborn County: formation, March 7, 1803.
Decatur County: formation, December 31, 1821, effective March 4, 1822.
DeKalb County: formation, February 7, 1835, effective on publication; organization, January 14, 1837, effective May 1.
Delaware County: formation, January 26, 1827, effective April 1.
Dubois County: formation, December 20, 1817, effective February 1, 1818.
Elkhart County: formation, January 29, 1830, effective April 1.
Fayette County: formation, December 28, 1818, effective January 1, 1819.
Floyd County: formation, January 2, 1819, effective February 1.
Fountain County: formation, December 30, 1825, effective April 1, 1826.
Franklin County: formation, November 27, 1810, effective January 1, 1811.
Fulton County: formation, February 7, 1835, effective on publication; organization, January 23, 1836, effective April 1.
Gibson County: formation, March 9, 1813, effective April 1.
Grant County: formation, February 10, 1831, effective April 1.
Greene County: formation, January 5, 1821, effective February 5.
Hamilton County: formation, January 8, 1823, effective April 7.
Hancock County: formation, January 26, 1827, effective on passage; organization, December 24, 1827, effective March 1, 1828.
Harrison County: formation, October 11, 1808, effective December 1.
Hendricks County: formation, December 20, 1823, effective April 1, 1824.
Henry County: formation, December 31, 1821, effective June 1, 1822.
Howard County: formation (as Richardville County), January 15, 1844, effective on passage.
Huntington County: formation, February 2, 1832, effective on passage; organization, February 1, 1834, effective after publication in Indianapolis *Indiana Journal.*
Jackson County: formation, December 18, 1815, effective January 1, 1816.
Jasper County: formation, February 7, 1835, effective on publication; organization, February 17, 1838, effective March 15.
Jay County: formation, February 7, 1835, effective on publication; organization, January 30, 1836, effective March 1.
Jefferson County: formation, November 23, 1810, effective January 1, 1811.
Jennings County: formation, December 27, 1816, effective February 1, 1817.

Johnson County: formation, December 31, 1822, effective May 5, 1823.
Knox County: formation, June 20, 1790.
Kosciusko County: formation, February 7, 1835, effective on publication; organization, February 4, 1836, effective June 1.
LaGrange County: formation, February 2, 1832, effective April 1.
Lake County: formation, January 28, 1836, effective February 1; organization, January 18, 1837, effective February 15.
LaPorte County: formation, January 9, 1832, effective April 1.
Lawrence County: formation, January 7, 1818, effective March 16.
Madison County: formation, January 4, 1823, effective July 1.
Marion County: formation, December 31, 1821, effective April 1, 1822.
Marshall County: formation, February 7, 1835, effective on publication; organization, February 4, 1836, effective April 1.
Martin County: formation, January 17, 1820, effective February 1, 1820.
Miami County: formation, February 2, 1832, effective April 2, corrected by statute of January 30, 1833, effective on publication; organization, January 2, 1834, effective March 1.
Monroe County: formation, January 14, 1818, effective April 10.
Montgomery County: formation, December 21, 1822, effective March 1, 1823.
Morgan County: formation, December 31, 1821, effective February 15, 1822.
Newton County: formation, February 7, 1835, effective on publication; consolidated with Jasper County, 1839; re-created, December 8, 1859.
Noble County: formation, February 7, 1835, effective June 1; organization, February 6, 1836, effective March 1.
Ohio County: formation, January 4, 1844, effective March 1; organization, January 4, 1844, effective May 1.
Orange County: formation, December 26, 1815, effective February 1, 1816.
Owen County: formation, December 21, 1818, effective January 1, 1819.
Parke County: formation, January 9, 1821, effective April 2.
Perry County: formation, September 7, 1814, effective November 1.
Pike County: formation, December 21, 1816, effective February 1, 1817.
Porter County: formation, February 7, 1835, effective on publication; organization, January 28, 1836, effective February 1.
Posey County: formation, September 7, 1814, effective November 1.
Pulaski County: formation, February 7, 1835, effective on publication; organization, February 18, 1839, effective May 6.
Putnam County: formation, December 31, 1821, effective April 1, 1822.
Randolph County: formation, January 10, 1818, effective August 10.
Ripley County: formation, December 27, 1816; organization, January 14, 1818, effective April 10.
Rush County: formation, December 31, 1821, effective April 1, 1822.
St. Joseph County: formation, January 29, 1830, effective April 1.
Scott County: formation, January 12, 1820, effective February 1.
Shelby County: formation, December 31, 1821, effective April 1, 1822.
Spencer County: formation, January 10, 1818, effective February 1.
Starke County: formation, February 7, 1835, effective on publication; organization, January 15, 1850, effective on passage.
Steuben County: formation, February 7, 1835, effective on publication; organization, January 18, 1837, effective May 1.
Sullivan County: formation, December 30, 1816, effective January 15, 1817.
Switzerland County: formation, September 7, 1814, effective October 1.
Tippecanoe County: formation, January 20, 1826, effective March 1.
Tipton County: formation, January 15, 1844, effective on passage; organization, January 15, 1844, effective May 1.
Union County: formation, January 5, 1821, effective February 1.
Vanderburgh County: formation, January 7, 1818, effective February 1.

Vermillion County: formation, January 2, 1824, effective February 1.

Vigo County: formation, January 21, 1818, effective February 15.

Wabash County: formation, February 2, 1832, effective on passage, corrected by statute of January 30, 1833, effective on publication; organization, January 22, 1835, effective March 1.

Warren County: formation, January 19, 1827, effective March 1.

Warrick County: formation, March 9, 1813, effective April 1.

Washington County: formation, December 21, 1813; effective January 17, 1814.

Wayne County: formation, November 27, 1810, effective January 1, 1811.

Wells County: formation, February 7, 1835, effective on publication; organization, February 2, 1837, effective May 1.

White County: formation, February 1, 1834, effective April 1.

Whitley County: formation, February 7, 1835, effective on publication; organization, February 17, 1838, effective April 1.

GOVERNORS, 1816-1851

JONATHAN JENNINGS, November 7, 1816—September 12, 1822. Resigned following his election to Congress.

RATLIFF BOON, September 12—December 4, 1822. Completed Jennings' term.

WILLIAM HENDRICKS, December 4, 1822—February 12, 1825. Resigned upon his election to the United States Senate.

JAMES BROWN RAY, February 12—December 7, 1825. Completed Hendricks' term.

JAMES BROWN RAY, December 7, 1825—December 7, 1831.

NOAH NOBLE, December 7, 1831—December 6, 1837.

DAVID WALLACE, December 6, 1837—December 9, 1840.

SAMUEL BIGGER, December 9, 1840—December 6, 1843.

JAMES WHITCOMB, December 6, 1843—December 26, 1848. Resigned upon his election to the United States Senate.

PARIS C. DUNNING, December 26, 1848—December 5, 1849. Completed Whitcomb's term.

JOSEPH A. WRIGHT, December 5, 1849—January 12, 1857.

CONGRESS: APPORTIONMENT OF REPRESENTATIVES

The Federal constitution provided that representatives be apportioned among the several states according to their population; they were to be chosen by districts within the states, the boundaries of the districts being fixed by state law. The act of Congress, April 19, 1816, enabling the people of Indiana to form a state government, provided that until the 1820 Census was taken the state should be entitled to one representative in Congress.

1822-30

By Act of January 3, 1822, the state was divided into three districts:

First District		*Second District*	*Third District*
Daviess	Parke	Bartholomew	Dearborn
Dubois	Perry	Clark	Fayette
Gibson	Pike	Crawford	Franklin
Greene	Posey	Decatur	Henry
Knox	Putnam	Floyd	Randolph
Lawrence	Spencer	Harrison	Ripley
Martin	Sullivan	Jackson	Rush
Monroe	Vanderburgh	Jennings	Switzerland
Morgan	Vigo	Jefferson	Union
Orange	Warrick	Johnson	Wayne
Owen		Marion	
		Scott	
		Shelby	
		Washington	

1831-32

The organization of many new counties brought a reapportionment in 1831. The act of January 7 redistricted the state as follows:

First District		*Second District*	*Third District*
Carroll	Orange	Bartholomew	Allen
Clay	Owen	Boone	Dearborn
Clinton	Parke	Cass	Decatur
Daviess	Perry	Clark	Delaware
Dubois	Pike	Crawford	Fayette
Fountain	Posey	Elkhart	Franklin
Gibson	Putnam	Floyd	Grant
Greene	Spencer	Hamilton	Henry
Hendricks	Sullivan	Hancock	Randolph
Knox	Tippecanoe	Harrison	Ripley
Lawrence	Vanderburgh	Jackson	Rush
Martin	Vermillion	Jefferson	Switzerland
Monroe	Vigo	Jennings	Union
Montgomery	Warren	Johnson	Wayne
Morgan	Warrick	Madison	
		Marion	
		St. Joseph	
		Scott	
		Shelby	
		Washington	

1833-42

After the results of the 1830 Census were tabulated, Indiana's representation was increased to seven. The state was divided into seven districts by act of January 8, 1833.

First District

Crawford	Orange	Spencer
Dubois	Perry	Vanderburgh
Gibson	Pike	Warrick
Harrison	Posey	

Second District

Clay	Lawrence	Sullivan
Daviess	Martin	Vigo
Greene	Owen	
Knox	Putnam	

Third District

Clark	Jennings
Floyd	Scott
Jackson	Washington
Jefferson	

Fourth District

Dearborn	Ripley
Decatur	Rush
Franklin	Switzerland

Fifth District

Allen	Henry	Union
Delaware	Huntington	Wayne
Fayette	LaGrange	
Grant	Randolph	

Sixth District

Bartholomew	Hendricks	Monroe
Boone	Johnson	Morgan
Cass	Madison	Shelby
Hamilton	Marion	Wabash
Hancock	Miami	

Seventh District

Carroll	LaPorte	Tippecanoe
Clinton	Montgomery	Vermillion
Elkhart	Parke	Warren
Fountain	St. Joseph	

1843-51

Following the tabulation of the 1840 Census the state's representation was increased to ten. An act of February 9, 1843, divided the state into ten districts. Counties formed and organized after this date were assigned to various districts as indicated.

First District

Crawford	Orange	Spencer
Dubois	Perry	Vanderburgh
Gibson	Pike	Warrick
Harrison	Posey	

Second District

Crawford	Jefferson	Washington
Floyd	Jennings	
Jackson	Scott	

Third District

Dearborn	Ohio (after 1844)	Switzerland
Decatur	Ripley	
Franklin	Rush	

Fourth District

Fayette	Union
Henry	Wayne

Fifth District

Bartholomew	Johnson	Tipton (after 1844)
Brown	Madison	
Hamilton	Marion	
Hancock	Shelby	

Sixth District

Daviess	Martin	Sullivan
Greene	Monroe	
Knox	Morgan	
Lawrence	Owen	

Seventh District

Clay	Putnam
Hendricks	Vermillion
Parke	Vigo

Eighth District

Boone	Howard (after 1844)	Warren
Carroll	Montgomery	
Clinton	Tippecanoe	
Fountain		

Ninth District

Benton	Kosciusko	Marshall
Cass	Lake	Miami
Elkhart	LaPorte	St. Joseph
Fulton	Porter	Starke (after 1850)
Jasper	Pulaski	Wabash
		White

Tenth District

Adams	Grant	Randolph
Allen	Huntington	Steuben
Blackford	Jay	Wells
DeKalb	LaGrange	Whitley
Delaware	Noble	

GENERAL ASSEMBLY: APPORTIONMENT OF MEMBERS

Constitution of 1816, Art. XII, Sec. 9

Senatorial districts, one senator to each district

Clark
Dearborn
Franklin
Gibson
Harrison
Jackson, Orange, and Washington
Jefferson and Switzerland
Knox
Perry, Posey, and Warrick
Wayne

Representative districts

Clark—3
Dearborn—2
Franklin—3
Gibson—2
Harrison—3
Jackson—1
Jefferson—2
Knox—3
Orange—1
Perry—1
Posey—1
Switzerland—1
Warrick—1
Washington—2
Wayne—3

Act of January 2, 1821

Senatorial districts, one senator to each district

Bartholomew, Jackson, and Scott
Clark and Floyd
Crawford and Harrison
Daviess, Knox, and Martin
Dearborn
Dubois, Perry, Spencer, and Warrick
Fayette and Union
Franklin
Gibson and Pike
Greene, Owen, Sullivan, Vigo
Jefferson and Jennings
Lawrence, Orange, and Monroe
Posey, Vanderburgh, part of Warrick
Randolph and Wayne
Ripley and Switzerland
Washington

Representative districts

Bartholomew—1
Clark—2
Crawford—1
Daviess and Martin—1
Dearborn—3
Dubois, Perry, Spencer, part of Warrick—1
Fayette—1
Floyd—1
Franklin—2
Gibson—1
Greene, Owen, Morgan—1
Harrison—2
Jackson—1
Jefferson—2
Jennings—1
Knox—2
Lawrence—1
Monroe—1
Orange—2
Parke and Vigo—1
Pike—1
Posey—1
Randolph—1
Ripley—1
Scott—1
Sullivan—1
Switzerland—2
Union—1
Vanderburgh and part of Warrick—1
Washington—2
Wayne—3

Act of January 19, 1826

Senatorial districts, one senator to each district

Allen, Henry, Randolph, Rush
Bartholomew, Jackson, Scott, and adjoining territory
Clark and Floyd
Clay, Sullivan, Vigo
Crawford, Perry, Spencer
Daviess, Knox, Martin
Dearborn
Decatur, Johnson, Morgan, Shelby, and adjoining territory
Dubois, Gibson, Pike
Fayette and Union
Fountain, Montgomery, Parke, Putnam, Vermillion, and adjoining territory on the north
Franklin
Greene, Monroe, Owen
Hamilton, Hendricks, Madison, Marion, and adjoining territory
Harrison
Jefferson and Jennings
Lawrence and Orange
Posey, Vanderburgh, Warrick
Ripley and Switzerland
Washington
Wayne

Representative districts

Allen, Randolph, and adjoining territory—1
Bartholomew and adjoining territory—1
Clark—3
Clay and Putnam—1
Crawford—1
Daviess and Martin—1
Dearborn—4
Decatur—1
Dubois and Pike—1
Fayette and Union—1 each and 1 additional each year alternately, beginning with Fayette
Floyd—1
Fountain, Montgomery, and adjoining territory—1
Franklin—2
Gibson—1
Greene and Owen—1
Hamilton, Henry, Madison—1
Harrison—3
Hendricks, Morgan, and adjoining territory—1
Jackson—1
Jefferson—2
Jennings—1
Johnson and Shelby—1
Knox—2
Lawrence—1
Marion—1
Monroe—1
Orange—2
Parke and Vermillion—1
Perry and Spencer—1
Posey—1
Ripley—1
Rush—1
Scott—1
Sullivan—1
Switzerland—2
Vanderburgh and Warrick—1
Vigo—1
Washington—3
Wayne—4

Act of January 30, 1831

Senatorial districts, one senator to each district

Allen, Delaware, Elkhart, Randolph, St. Joseph
Bartholomew and Jennings
Boone, Hendricks, Morgan
Carroll, Cass, Tippecanoe
Clark and Floyd
Clay, Sullivan, Vigo
Clinton and Montgomery
Crawford, Perry, Spencer
Daviess, Knox, Martin
Dearborn
Decatur and Shelby
Dubois, Gibson, Pike
Fayette and Union
Fountain
Franklin
Greene, Monroe, Owen
Hamilton, Marion, and adjoining territory
Hancock, Henry, Madison
Harrison
Jackson, Jennings, Scott
Jefferson
Lawrence and Orange
Parke
Putnam
Ripley and Switzerland
Rush
Vanderburgh and Warrick
Vermillion and Warren
Washington
Wayne

Representative districts

Allen, Elkhart, St. Joseph—1
Bartholomew—1
Boone, Hamilton, and adjoining territory—1
Carroll and Cass—1
Clark—2 in 1831, 1833, 1835; 3 in 1832, 1834
Clay—1
Clinton and Montgomery—1
Crawford—1
Daviess and Martin—1 in 1831, 1833, 1835; 2 in 1832, 1834
Dearborn—3
Decatur—1
Delaware and adjoining territory—1
Dubois and Pike—1
Fayette—2
Floyd—1 in 1832, 1834; 2 in 1831, 1833, 1835
Fountain—2
Franklin—2
Gibson—1
Greene—1
Hancock and Madison—1
Harrison—2
Hendricks—1
Henry—1
Jackson—1
Jefferson—2
Jennings—1
Johnson—1
Knox—1 in 1832, 1834; 2 in 1831, 1833, 1835
Lawrence—1
Marion—1
Monroe—1
Morgan—1
Orange—2
Owen—1
Parke—1 in 1831, 1833, 1835; 2 in 1832, 1834
Perry and Spencer—1
Posey—1
Putnam—2
Randolph—1
Ripley—1
Rush—2
Scott—1
Shelby—1
Sullivan—1
Switzerland—1
Tippecanoe—2
Union—2
Vanderburgh and Warrick—1
Vermillion—1 in 1832, 1834; 2 in 1831, 1833, 1835
Vigo—1
Warren—1
Washington—2
Wayne—4

Act of January 13, 1836

Senatorial districts, one senator to each district[1]

Adams, Allen, Wells
Bartholomew and Jennings
Boone and Hamilton
Carroll and Clinton
Cass, Fulton, Miami
Clark
Clay, Sullivan, Vigo
Crawford, Perry, Spencer
Daviess, Knox, Martin
Dearborn
Decatur
DeKalb, Elkhart, LaGrange, Noble, Steuben
Delaware and Randolph
Dubois, Gibson, Pike
Fayette and Union
Floyd
Fountain
Franklin
Grant, Huntington, Jay, Wabash
Greene and Owen
Hancock and Madison
Harrison
Hendricks
Henry
Jackson and Scott
Jefferson
Johnson
Kosciusko, Marshall, St. Joseph, Starke
LaPorte, Newton, Porter, Pulaski, White, part of Jasper
Lawrence
Marion
Monroe
Montgomery
Morgan
Orange
Parke
Posey, Vanderburgh, Warrick
Putnam
Ripley
Rush
Shelby
Switzerland
Tippecanoe
Vermillion, Warren, part of Jasper
Washington
Wayne—2

1 With the exception of Wayne County, which was entitled to two senators.

Representative districts

Adams, Huntington, Jay, Wells—1
Allen—1
Bartholomew—2
Boone—1
Carroll—1
Cass—1
Clark—2 in 1836, 1838, 1839, 1840; 3 in 1837
Clay—1
Clinton—1
Crawford—1 in 1836, 1838, 1839, 1840; (with Dubois)—1 in 1837
Daviess—1 in 1836, 1838, 1840; (with Martin)—1 in 1837, 1839
Dearborn—4
Decatur—1
DeKalb, LaGrange, Noble, Steuben—1
Delaware—1
Dubois—1 in 1839; (with Pike)—1 in 1836, 1838, 1840; (with Crawford)—1 in 1837
Elkhart—1
Fayette—2
Floyd—1
Fountain—2
Franklin—2
Fulton and Miami—1
Gibson—1
Grant and Wabash—1
Greene—1
Hamilton—1
Hancock—1
Harrison—2
Hendricks—1
Henry—2
Jackson—1
Jasper, Pulaski, White—1
Jefferson—2 in 1837, 1838; 3 in 1836, 1839, 1840
Jennings—1
Johnson—1
Knox—1 in 1836, 1838, 1840; 2 in 1837, 1839
Kosciusko, Marshall, Starke—1
LaPorte—1
Lawrence—2
Madison—1
Marion—2
Martin—1 in 1836, 1838, 1840; (with Daviess)—1 in 1837, 1839
Monroe—1
Montgomery—2 in 1836, 1838, 1840; 3 in 1837, 1839
Morgan—1
Newton and Porter—1
Orange—1
Owen—1
Parke—2
Perry—1 in 1836, 1837, 1838, 1840; (with Spencer)—1 in 1839
Pike—1 in 1837, 1839; (with Dubois)—1 in 1836, 1838, 1840
Posey—1
Putnam—2 in 1837, 1839; 3 in 1836, 1838, 1840
Randolph—1
Ripley—1
Rush—3
St. Joseph—1
Scott—1
Shelby—2
Spencer—1 in 1836, 1837, 1838, 1840; (with Perry)—1 in 1839
Sullivan—1 in 1840; 2 in 1836, 1837, 1838, 1839
Switzerland—1
Tippecanoe—2
Union—2
Vanderburgh—1
Vermillion—2
Vigo—2 in 1836, 1837, 1838, 1839; 3 in 1840
Warren—1
Warrick—1
Washington—2 in 1836, 1837, 1839, 1840; 3 in 1838
Wayne—4

Act of January 16, 1841

Senatorial districts, one senator to each district[1]

Adams, Allen, Huntington, Wells
Bartholomew and Jennings
Benton, Jasper, Pulaski, Starke, Warren, and White
Blackford, Jay, Randolph
Boone and Hamilton
Brown and Monroe
Carroll and Clinton
Cass, Miami, Wabash
Clark
Clay, Sullivan, Vigo
Crawford and Orange
Daviess and Martin
Dearborn
Decatur
DeKalb, LaGrange, Noble, Steuben
Delaware and Grant
Dubois, Gibson, Pike
Elkhart, Kosciusko, Whitley
Fayette and Union
Floyd
Fountain
Franklin
Fulton, Marshall, St. Joseph
Greene and Owen
Hancock and Madison
Harrison
Hendricks
Henry
Jackson and Scott
Jefferson
Johnson
Knox
Lake, LaPorte, Porter
Lawrence
Marion
Montgomery
Morgan
Parke
Perry, Spencer, Warrick
Posey and Vanderburgh
Putnam
Ripley
Rush
Shelby
Switzerland
Tippecanoe
Vermillion
Vigo
Washington
Wayne—2

[1] With the exception of Wayne County which was entitled to two senators. The act also provided that in cases where one senatorial district had been attached to another, no election for senator should be held in the newly formed district until the term of service of the present senator had expired.

Representative districts

Adams and Jay—1
Allen—1
Bartholomew—1
Benton, Jasper, Pulaski, White—1
Blackford, Huntington, Wells—1
Boone—1 in 1841, 1843, 1845; 2 in 1842, 1844
Brown and Monroe—1 in 1841, 1843, 1845; 2 in 1842, 1844[2]
Carroll—1
Cass—1
Clark—2
Clay—1
Clinton—1
Crawford—1
Daviess—1 in 1841, 1842, 1844; (with Martin)—1 in 1843, 1845
Dearborn—3
Decatur—1
DeKalb and Steuben—1
Delaware—1
Dubois—1
Elkhart—1
Fayette—2
Floyd—1
Fountain—1 in 1841, 1843, 1844; 2 in 1842, 1845
Franklin—2
Fulton, Marshall, Starke—1
Gibson—1
Grant—1
Greene—1
Hamilton—1 in 1842, 1844; 2 in 1841, 1843, 1845
Hancock—1 in 1842, 1844; 2 in 1841, 1844, 1845
Harrison—2
Hendricks—1
Henry—2
Jackson—1
Jefferson—2 in 1842; 3 in 1841, 1843, 1844, 1845
Jennings—1
Johnson—1
Knox—1
Kosciusko and Whitley—1
LaGrange and Noble—1
Lake and Porter—1
LaPorte—2
Lawrence—1 in 1842, 1844; 2 in 1841, 1843, 1845
Madison—1 in 1841, 1843, 1845; 2 in 1842, 1844
Marion—2
Martin—1 in 1841, 1842, 1844; (with Daviess)—1 in 1843, 1845
Miami and Wabash—1
Montgomery—2 in 1842, 1844; 3 in 1841, 1843, 1845
Morgan—1
Orange—1
Owen—1
Parke—2
Perry—1
Pike—1
Posey—1
Putnam—2 in 1841, 1843, 1845; 3 in 1842, 1844
Randolph—1 in 1841, 1842, 1844, 1845; 2 in 1843
Ripley—1
Rush—2 in 1841, 1843, 1844, 1845; 3 in 1842
St. Joseph—1
Scott—1
Shelby—1
Spencer—1
Sullivan—1 in 1842, 1843, 1844; 2 in 1841, 1845
Switzerland—1
Tippecanoe—2 in 1841, 1842, 1845; 3 in 1843, 1844
Union—1 in 1842, 1843, 1844; 2 in 1841, 1845
Vanderburgh—1
Vermillion—1
Vigo—2 in 1841, 1845; 3 in 1842, 1843, 1844
Warren—1
Warrick—1
Washington—2
Wayne—3

[2] By an act of January 2, 1843, the general apportionment law of 1841 was amended to allow Brown and Monroe counties each to elect a representative in 1844.

Act of January 19, 1846

Senatorial districts, one senator to each district

Adams, Allen, Wells
Bartholomew and Jennings
Benton, Jasper, Warren, White
Blackford, Jay, Randolph
Boone, Hamilton, Tipton
Brown and Monroe
Carroll and Clinton
Cass, Howard, Pulaski
Clark
Clay, Sullivan, Vigo
Crawford and Orange
Daviess and Martin
Dearborn
Decatur
DeKalb, Noble, Steuben
Delaware and Grant
Dubois, Gibson, Pike
Elkhart and LaGrange (beginning in 1847
Fayette and Union
Floyd
Fountain
Franklin
Fulton, Marshall, St. Joseph, Starke
Greene and Owen
Hancock and Madison
Harrison
Hendricks
Henry
Huntington, Kosciusko, Whitley
Jackson and Scott
Jefferson
Johnson
Knox
Lake, LaPorte, Porter
Lawrence
Marion
Miami and Wabash (beginning in 1847)
Montgomery
Morgan
Ohio and Switzerland
Parke and Vermillion
Perry, Spencer, Warrick
Posey and Vanderburgh
Putnam
Ripley
Rush
Shelby
Tippecanoe
Washington
Wayne

Representative districts

Adams and Wells—1
Allen—1 in 1846, 1848, 1849, 1850; 2 in 1847
Bartholomew—1 in 1846, 1847; 2 in 1848, 1849, 1850
Benton, Jasper, Pulaski, White—1
Blackford and Jay—1
Boone—1 in 1846, 1848, 1849; 2 in 1847, 1850
Brown—1 in 1846, 1848, 1850; (with Monroe)—1 in 1847, 1849
Carroll—1
Cass and Howard—1 in 1847, 1848, 1849, 1850; 2 in 1846
Clark—2
Clay—1
Clinton and Tipton—1 in 1846, 1847, 1849; 2 in 1848, 1850
Crawford—1 in 1847, 1849, 1850; with Orange)—2 in 1846, 1848
Daviess—1 in 1847, 1849; (with Martin)—1 in 1846, 1848, 1850
Dearborn—3 in 1848; 2 in 1846, 1847, 1849, 1850
Decatur—1
DeKalb and Steuben—1
Delaware—1
Dubois—1
Elkhart—1 in 1846, 1847, 1850; 2 in 1848, 1849
Fayette—1 in 1846, 1848, 1849; 2 in 1847, 1850
Floyd—1
Fountain—1
Franklin—2
Fulton, Marshall, Starke—1
Gibson—1
Grant—1
Greene—1
Hamilton—1 in 1847, 1848, 1850; 2 in 1846, 1849
Hancock—1
Harrison—1
Hendricks—1
Henry—2
Huntington and Whitley—1
Jackson—1
Jefferson—2 in 1847, 1848, 1850; 3 in 1846, 1849
Jennings—1
Johnson—1
Knox—1

Kosciusko—1
LaGrange—1 in 1846, 1850; (with Noble)—1 in 1847, 1848, 1849
Lake and Porter—1
LaPorte—2
Lawrence—1
Madison—1
Marion—3 in 1846, 1848, 1850; 2 in 1847, 1849
Martin—1 in 1847, 1849; (with Daviess) —1 in 1846, 1848, 1850
Miami—1 in 1846, 1848, 1850; (with Wabash)—1 in 1847, 1849
Monroe—1 in 1846, 1848, 1850; (with Brown)—1 in 1847, 1849
Montgomery—2
Morgan—1
Noble—1 in 1846, 1850; (with LaGrange) 1 in 1847, 1848, 1849
Ohio and Switzerland—2 in 1847, 1849; 1 in 1846, 1848, 1850
Orange—1 in 1847, 1849, 1850; (with Crawford)—2 in 1846, 1848
Owen—1
Parke—2
Perry—1
Pike—1
Posey—2
Putnam—2
Randolph—1 in 1846, 1848, 1850; 2 in 1847, 1849
Ripley—1
Rush—2
St. Joseph—1
Scott—1
Shelby—1
Spencer—1
Sullivan—2 in 1846, 1848, 1849; 1 in 1847, 1850
Tippecanoe—2 in 1846, 1848, 1850; 3 in 1847, 1849
Union—1
Vanderburgh—1
Vermillion—1
Vigo—2 in 1846, 1848, 1849; 3 in 1847, 1850
Wabash—1 in 1846, 1848, 1850; (with Miami)—1 in 1847, 1849
Warren—1
Warrick—1
Washington—2
Wayne—4 in 1846, 1847, 1848; 3 in 1849, 1850

Act of February 13, 1851

Senatorial districts, one senator to each district

Adams and Allen
Bartholomew and Jennings
Benton, Jasper, Warren, White
Blackford, Delaware, Grant
Boone, Hamilton, Tipton
Brown and Monroe
Carroll and Clinton
Cass, Howard, Pulaski
Clark
Clay and Sullivan
Crawford and Orange
Daviess, Knox, Martin
Dearborn
Decatur
DeKalb and Steuben
Dubois, Gibson, Pike
Elkhart and LaGrange
Fayette and Union
Floyd
Fountain
Franklin
Fulton, Marshall, St. Joseph, and Starke
Greene and Owen
Hancock and Madison
Harrison
Hendricks
Henry
Huntington and Wells
Jackson and Scott
Jay and Randolph
Jefferson
Johnson
Kosciusko, Noble, Whitley
Lake, LaPorte, Porter
Lawrence
Marion
Miami and Wabash
Montgomery
Morgan
Ohio and Switzerland
Parke and Vermillion
Perry, Spencer, Warrick
Posey and Vanderburgh
Putnam
Ripley
Rush
Shelby
Tippecanoe
Vigo
Washington
Wayne

Representative districts

Adams—1
Allen—1
Bartholomew—1
Benton and White—1
Blackford—1
Boone—1 in 1852, 1853, 1855; 2 in 1851, 1854
Brown—1
Carroll—1
Cass—1
Clark—2 in 1851, 1853; 1 in 1852, 1854, 1855
Clay—2 in 1851, 1854; 1 in 1852, 1853, 1855
Clinton—1
Crawford—1
Daviess—1
Dearborn—2
Decatur—1
DeKalb and Steuben—2
Delaware—1
Dubois—1
Elkhart—1
Fayette—1
Floyd—1 in 1851, 1853, 1854; 2 in 1852, 1855
Fountain—1
Franklin—2
Fulton—1
Gibson—1
Grant—1
Greene—1
Hamilton—1
Hancock—1
Harrison—1
Henry—1 in 1851, 1853, 1855; 2 in 1852, 1854
Hendricks—1
Howard and Tipton—1
Huntington and Wells—1
Jackson—1
Jasper and Pulaski—1
Jay—1
Jefferson—2
Jennings—1
Johnson—1
Knox—1
Kosciusko—1
LaGrange—1
Lake—1
LaPorte—1
Lawrence—1
Madison—1 in 1852, 1853, 1855; 2 in 1851, 1854
Marion—2
Marshall and Starke—1
Martin—1
Miami—1
Monroe—1
Montgomery—1 in 1852, 1854; 2 in 1851, 1853, 1855
Morgan—1
Noble—1
Ohio and Switzerland—2
Orange—1
Owen—1
Parke—1
Perry—1
Pike—1
Porter—1
Posey—1 in 1852, 1853, 1855; 2 in 1851, 1854
Putnam—1 in 1851, 1854; 2 in 1852, 1853, 1855
Randolph—1
Ripley—1
Rush—1 in 1851, 1854; 2 in 1852, 1853, 1855
St. Joseph—1
Scott—1
Shelby—1
Spencer—1
Sullivan—2
Tippecanoe—1 in 1851, 1854; 2 in 1852, 1853, 1855
Union—1
Vanderburgh—1
Vermillion—1
Vigo—2 in 1851, 1854; 3 in 1852, 1853, 1855
Wabash—1
Warren—1
Warrick—1
Washington—1 in 1851, 1852, 1853, 1855; 2 in 1854
Wayne—3
Whitley—1

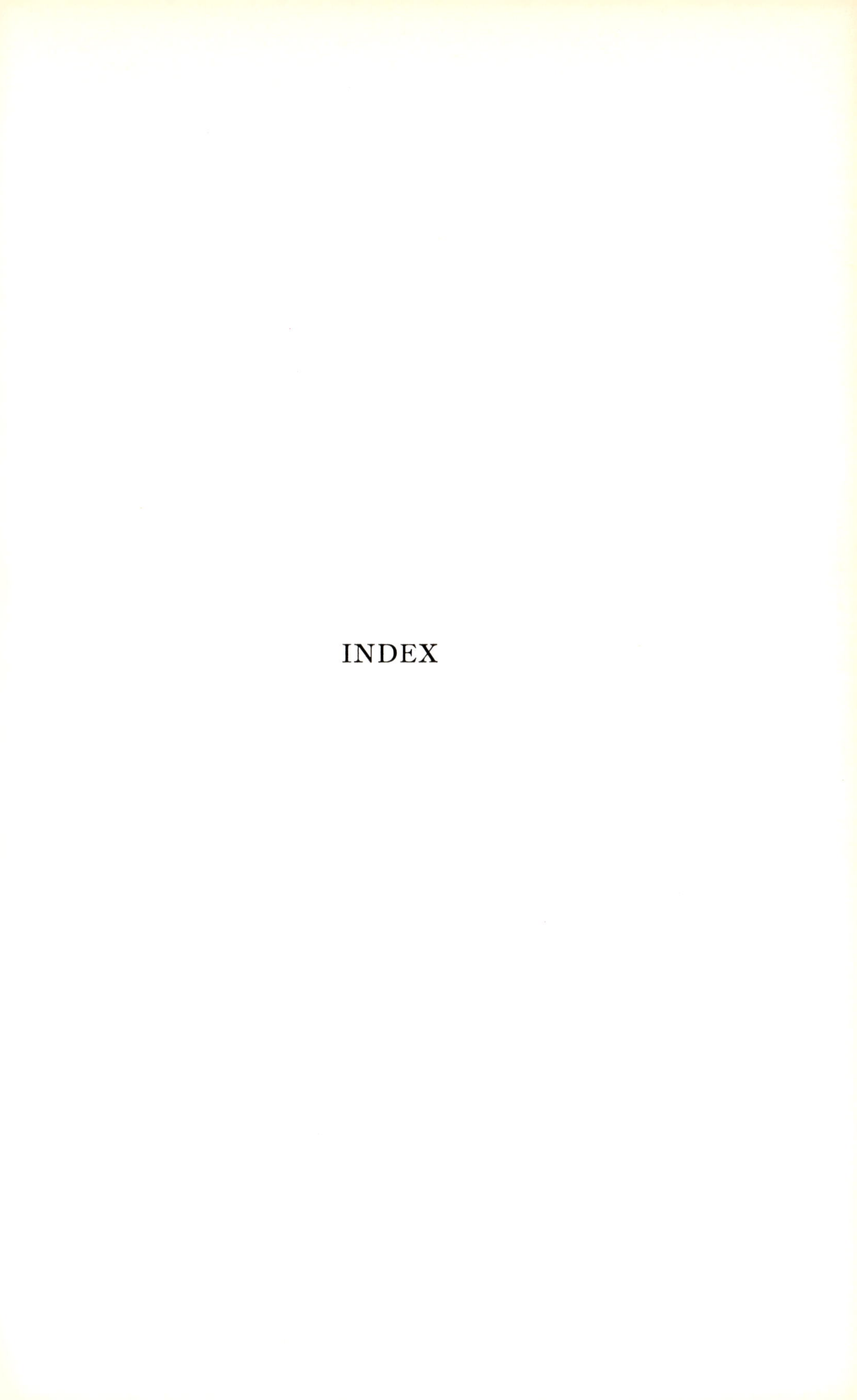

INDEX

INDEX

Asterisk (*) indicates election.

Abbott, Lawson, representative, Tippecanoe Co. (1846), 308.

Abbott, Richard, representative, Dearborn Co. (1846), 303.

Abel, John, representative, Dubois Co. (1850), 346.

Adams, Charles Francis, vice-president (1848), 63-67.

Adams, H. S., representative, Lake and Porter cos. (1846), 305.

Adams, John, representative, Vigo Co. (1849), 341; (1850), 352n.

Adams, John Quincy, president (1824), xvii-xviii, 8-9; (1828), 12-13.

Adams, Thomas F. G., representative, Greene and Owen cos. (1827), *198.

Adams, Thomas M., senator, Brown and Monroe cos. (1848), *332.

Addleman, William S., representative, Wayne Co. (1846), *309.

Ainsworth, Amasa, representative, La Porte Co. (1848), 328.

Aker, Andrew, representative, Randolph Co. (1831), *209; senator, Delaware and Randolph (1834), *223; resignation, 235n.

Aker, Michael, senator, Delaware and Randolph cos. (1840), *258.

Akin, Ransom W., representative, Sullivan Co. (1840), *256n; senator, Sullivan, etc. (1843), *277.

Albertson, Nathaniel, presidential elector (1848), *53-57; representative, U. S. Congress (1849), *118; representative, Harrison Co. (1838), *241; (1839), *246; (1840), 253; senator, Harrison Co. (1841), 270; (1845), 299.

Albin, William, representative, Putnam Co. (1847), *318.

Alden, Alvin J., representative, Dearborn Co. (1848), *325; (1850), 346.

Alexander, Archibald, representative, Hendricks Co. (1838), 241; senator (1842), *270; delegate, const. conv., 385.

Alexander, Charles, delegate, const. conv., Pike Co., *382.

Alexander, Jesse J., senator, Greene and Owen cos. (1850), *353.

Alexander, John T., representative, Clay Co. (1848), *324.

Alexander, Samuel, representative, Jefferson Co. (1816), *183.

Alger, Freeman, representative, Franklin Co. (1836), 229; (1845), 298n.

Allen, Cyrus M., representative, Knox Co. (1848), *327.

Allen, Eliphalet, representative, Parke and Vermillion cos. (1827), *199; (1828), *201.

Allen, Hiram, delegate, const. conv., Carroll and Clinton cos., *384.

Allen, Ira, representative, Clay Co. (1844), 279.

Allen, Joseph, senator, Montgomery Co. (1849), *344.

Allen, Peter, 138n; representative, Knox Co. etc. (1819), *186.

Allen, William, representative, La Porte Co. (1843), *273.

Allen, William D., representative, Putnam Co. (1843), *273; (1849), *340.

Alley, Doddridge, representative, Decatur Co. (1826), *196; (1831), *208.

Alley, John, representative, Hancock Co. (1849), *337; (1850), 347.

Alley, John W., representative, Rush Co. (1838), *243; (1840), 254.

Allison, John F., representative, Greene Co. (1838), *243; (1839), *248; senator, Greene and Owen (1844), *287.

Allison, Joseph B., representative, De Kalb Co. etc. (1838), 241.

Alton, Benjamin, representative, De Kalb and Steuben cos. (1843), 272.

Amos, Joseph J., senator, Rush Co. (1850), 354.

Anderson, Allen S., representative, Brown Co. (1846), 301.

Anderson, James, representative, Bartholomew Co. (1849), 334.

Anderson, James, representative, Hendricks Co. (1833), 215; (1834), 219; (1835), 224.

Anderson, James H., representative, Lawrence Co. (1851), 358.

Anderson, Joseph, representative, Union Co. (1838), *244.

Anderson, William, representative, Franklin Co. (1839), 246.

Andrew, Abraham P., presidential elector (1836), *21-24.

Andrews, Daniel H., representative, Delaware Co. (1850), 346; (1851), 356.

Angel, David, senator, Adams Co. etc. (1847), 321.

Angle, Jacob, representative, Clinton and Montgomery cos. (1831), *208; (1832), 211; (1833), *216; (1834), *221; senator, Boone and Hamilton cos. (1839), *250.

Annable, Samuel, representative, Posey Co. (1827), *199.

Anthony, Dewitt C., representative, Floyd Co. (1851), 356.

Anthony, Jacob, representative, Floyd Co. (1846), *309.

Anthony, Samuel J., representative, Lake and Porter cos. (1844), *282; delegate, const. conv., *385.

Anti-Masons, in presidential election (1832), xx-xxi, 20n.

Applegate, B., senator, Johnson Co. (1845), 300.

Applegate, William, representative, Harrison Co. (1836), 229.

Arion, Allan E., representative, Jefferson Co. (1841), 262n.

Arion, Copeland P. J., 165n; representative, Jefferson Co. (1821), *188; (1823), *191; senator (1838), *244.

Armstrong, Ambrose W., representative, Montgomery Co. (1847), *317.

Armstrong, Thomas, representative, Ohio and Switzerland cos. (1850), *349.

Armstrong, Thomas P., representative, La Porte Co. (1844), 282, 286n.

Armstrong, Walter, presidential elector (1832), *14-16; representative, Dearborn Co. (1829), *202; (1830), *204; senator (1834), 222.

Armstrong, William, representative, Harrison Co. (1835), 224.

Armstrong, William G., representative, Clark Co. (1822), *189; (1823), *191; (1824), *192; (1834), *220; (1835), *226; (1836), *231; senator (1838), *244; (1844), 286.

Arnold, Benjamin F., representative, Bartholomew and Brown cos. (1839), *247.

Arnold, Ephraim, representative, Bartholomew Co. (1845), *289; (1846), *309.

Arnold, George, representative, Dearborn Co. (1837), *236; (1838), *240.

Arnold, George, representative, Harrison Co. (1833), 215; (1834), 219; (1835), 224; (1838), 241.

Arnold, George B., 67n.

Atherton, Willis G., representative, Madison Co. (1839), *248; (1840), *253.

Athon, James S., representative, Clark Co. (1843), *274; (1849), *342; senator (1850), *352.

Avery, Joseph, representative, Harrison Co. (1842), 266.

Axton, ———, representative, Perry Co. (1840), 254.

Ayres, Stephen D., representative, Grant Co. (1849), 336.

Baber, George, representative, Greene Co. (1831), *209; (1833), *216.

Badger, Charles, representative, St. Joseph Co. (1846), 307.

Badger, Oliver P., senator, Putnam Co. (1851), 364; delegate, const. conv., *382.
Baird, Patrick, *see* Beard.
Baird, Thomas D., representative, St. Joseph Co. (1836), *232; senator, St. Joseph Co. etc. (1837), *240; (1840), *258; death, 271n.
Baird, William, representative, Washington Co. (1825), *195.
Baker, Conrad, representative, Vanderburgh Co. (1845), *296.
Baker, Elias, senator, De Kalb Co. etc. (1839), 250.
Baker, George R., representative, De Kalb and Steuben cos. (1850), 346.
Baker, John, representative, Crawford and Orange cos. (1846), 302.
Baker, John P., senator, Cass Co. etc. (1846), 310; (1849), 343.
Baker, Reuben, 286n.
Baker, Valentine, representative, Washington Co. (1838), *244; (1842), *269; (1844), 285.
Baker, William, representative, Wayne Co. (1839), *249.
Balding, George W., representative, De Kalb and Steuben cos. (1846), *309n.
Baldridge, Daniel, representative, Dearborn and Ohio cos. (1845), 290; (1846), 303.
Baldwin, Jesse W., representative, Henry Co. (1847), *320n.
Baldwin, Stephen D., representative, Ohio Co. (1851), 362n.
Bales, Asa, representative, U. S. Congress (1845), 111.
Bales, William, representative, Vermillion Co. (1842), *269; (1843), 274.
Balingall, George H., delegate, const. conv., Henry Co., *382.
Ball, A. L., representative, Lake and Porter cos. (1837), 236.
Ball, George W., representative, Vigo Co. (1845), 297.
Ball, Samuel, 67n.
Ball, Seneca, representative, Lake and Porter cos. (1840), *253.
Ballard, Joseph W., representative, Jennings Co. (1844), 282; (1846), 305.
Balton, Henry, representative, Delaware Co. (1846), 303.
Banta, James, senator, Elkhart Co. etc. (1845), 299.
Banta, P. H., representative, Switzerland Co. (1834), 220.
Bantz, George W., representative, Jefferson Co. (1833), 215.
Barber, Eliphalet, representative, Franklin Co. (1847), 315.
Barber, Scott, representative, Kosciusko and Whitley cos. (1845), 293.
Barber, Timothy, representative, Fulton Co. etc. (1849), 336.
Barber, Timothy, representative, Jefferson Co. (1838), 241.
Barbour, Cromwell W., delegate, const. conv., Vigo Co., *381.
Barbour, Heman H., representative, Bartholomew Co. (1843), *274; (1844), 278; (1848), *323; senator, Bartholomew and Jennings (1845), *298.
Barclay, John M., representative, La Porte Co. (1844), *282, 286n.
Bardon, Daniel (or David), 20n.
Bardwell, Leonard, representative, Hancock and Madison cos. (1835), *226.
Barker, Henry W., representative, Dubois Co. (1849), *336; (1851), *356; senator, Dubois Co. etc. (1850), 353.
Barkwell, Harmon G., representative, Perry Co. (1844), 283; (1848), 329.
Barkwell, Major C., representative, Perry Co. (1849), 339; (1851), 359.
Barlow, Harvey R., representative, Hendricks Co. (1851), 357.
Barnett, John, representative, Crawford and Orange cos. (1848), 325.
Barnett, John, representative, Montgomery Co. (1841), *262.
Barnett, John J., representative, Lawrence Co. (1841), *262; (1845), 294; (1847), 317.
Barre, Samuel, representative, De Kalb and Steuben cos. (1845), 291.

Barrett, Samuel, representative, Rush Co. (1842), 267; (1843), *275.

Barricklow, Farrington, representative, Dearborn and Ohio cos. (1845), 290.

Barrow, Edwin, representative, Franklin Co.(1847), 315.

Barry, Edward H., representative, Fayette Co. (1850), 346.

Bartholomew, Joseph, presidential elector (1816), *3; (1828), 12-13; representative, Clark Co. (1818), *185; senator, Clark Co. etc. (1820), *187; resignation, 190n.

Barton, Gaylord G., representative, Daviess and Martin cos. (1850), 346; Daviess Co. (1851), 355.

Bascom, Erastus K., delegate, const. conv., Adams and Wells cos., *378.

Bassett, A., 67n.

Bassett, Horace, representative, Dearborn Co. (1822), *189; (1824), *192; (1826), *196; (1827), *198; (1828), *200; (1829), *201.

Battell, Charles I., representative, Posey Co. (1820), *187; (1821), *188; Vanderburgh (1846), *308; senator, Vanderburgh Co. etc. (1833), *218; succeeded (1835), 228n.

Baty, James, representative, Lawrence Co. (1845), 294.

Baum, Joseph, representative, Clinton Co. (1845), 290.

Bayliss, Lot S., senator, Adams Co. etc. (1844), 286.

Beach, E., 67n.

Beach, Walter E., delegate, const. conv., Elkhart Co., *379.

Beach, William B., representative, Boone Co. (1851), *355.

Beal, ———, representative, Switzerland Co. (1830), 205.

Beal, John A., senator, Ohio and Switzerland cos. (1846), 312; representative (1847), 317.

Beall (Beal), Enos, representative, De Kalb and Steuben cos. (1842), *265; (1845), 291.

Beane, Joseph, representative, Elkhart Co. (1851), *356.

Beard, Isaac, representative, Wayne Co. (1849), *341; (1850), 351.

Beard, John, representative, Montgomery Co. etc. (1827), *198; (1829), *202; (1830), *204; senator (1831), *210, 211n; (1834), *222; (1837), *240; (1840), *258; resigned (1841), 265n; senator (1846), *311.

Beard, John, delegate, const. conv., Wayne Co., *381.

Beard, Patrick, senator, Wayne Co. (1816), *183, 184n; (1817), *185; (1820), *187.

Beardsley, E., 67n.

Beardsley, H. H., 67n.

Bearss, Daniel R., representative, Miami and Wabash cos. (1841), *262; (1843), *275.

Beason, David W., 298n.

Beavers, Thomas, representative, Scott Co. (1847), 319.

Beazley, Edmund E., representative, Greene Co. (1850), 347.

Beckes, Benjamin V., presidential elector (1828), *10-11; representative, Knox Co. (1821), *188; (1822), *190; (1824), *193; (1825), *195; (1826), *196.

Beckett, James F., representative, Hendricks Co. (1839), *248.

Beckford, Thomas, 52n.

Beecher, Lewis, presidential elector (1848), 67n.

Beeler, Fielding, representative, Marion Co. (1850), 349.

Beem, Richard, representative, Jackson Co. (1833), *216.

Beeson, Junius, representative, Rush Co. (1851), *360.

Beeson, Othniel, representative, Wayne Co. (1842), 267; delegate, const. conv., *381.

Beeson, Silas H., senator, Wayne Co. (1841), 264.

Beggs, Charles, representative, Clark Co. (1817), *184; (1818), *185.

Beggs, James, senator, Clark Co. (1816), *183, 184n; (1817), *185.

Beggs, John B., representative, Clark Co. (1846), 302.
Behm, Godlove O., representative, Tippecanoe Co. (1851), *360.
Bell, Elijah, representative, Pike Co. (1839), *247; (1845), 295.
Bell, John F., senator, Harrison Co. (1830), 207.
Bell, Josiah, representative, Wayne Co. (1841), 263n.
Bell, Robert F., representative, Harrison Co. (1828), *200; (1829), *203.
Bell, Thomas, representative, Madison Co. etc. (1830), *206; (1831), *209; (1832), *213; (1834), *221; (1844), *282; senator (1835), *228; (1838), *245.
Bement, Reuben, senator, De Kalb Co. etc. (1846), 311.
Benbow, William, 118n; presidential elector (1844), 48-52.
Bence, Jacob, representative, Floyd Co. (1829), *202; (1830), *206.
Bence, John, representative, Harrison Co. (1842), 266.
Benedict, Jacob, representative, Tippecanoe Co. (1849), 341.
Benefiel, John S., representative, Knox Co. (1844), 282; (1846), 305.
Benefiel (Benefield), Wilson B., representative, Switzerland Co. (1833), 215.
Benefield, John, representative, Sullivan Co. (1821), *188.
Bennett, Benjamin G., representative, La Grange Co. (1850), 348.
Bennett, Brooke, senator, Jefferson and Jennings cos. (1821), *189.
Bennett, D., representative, Adams Co. etc. (1839), 245.
Bennett, Hiram P., representative, U. S. Congress (1843), 106; senator, Wayne Co. (1844), 288.
Bennett, Joseph, representative, Franklin Co. (1834), 219; (1836), 229; (1840), 252; (1849), 336.
Bennett, William H., representative, Union Co. (1833), *217; (1834), *221; (1835), *227; (1836), *230; (1837), *238; (1839), *249.
Benson, John, representative, Warren Co. (1850), *351.
Bentley, George, representative, Harrison Co. (1830), *206; senator (1833), 218; (1839), 250; (1845), 299; (1848), 333.
Bentley, Joseph, representative, Ripley Co. (1821), *188; (1822), *190.
Benton, Thomas, representative, Rush Co. (1850), 352n.
Benwell, John F., representative, Union Co. (1849), 341.
Berford, William, 52n.
Berkshire, Ralph, representative, Henry Co. (1839), *248.
Berry, Andrew, representative, Knox Co. (1840), 253.
Berry, George, senator, Franklin Co. (1843), *277; (1846), *311; resignation (1847), 323n; senator (1849), *343; delegate, const. conv., *387.
Berry, Matthias, representative, Knox Co. (1845), 293.
Berry, William, representative, Brown and Monroe cos. (1836), *230; (1837), *236; senator (1839), *250; (1845), *299.
Berryhill, John S., senator, Tippecanoe Co. (1846), 312.
Bicknell, Thompson P., delegate, const. conv., Noble Co., *380.
Biddle, Horace P., presidential elector (1844), 43-47; representative, Cass Co. (1845), 290; delegate, const. conv., Cass Co. etc., *384.
Biddle, N., 132-33.
Bigelow, Jacob, representative, U. S. Congress (1843), 108.
Bigger, Samuel, governor (1840), *xxiii, 148-50n; (1843), 150-53n; representative, Rush Co. (1833), *216; (1834), *220; governor, decision on Clay Co. election return, 109n; term of service, 395.
Bigler, Henry, representative, Henry Co. (1847), 320n.
Billingsley, Alexander D., Putnam Co. (1846), 307.
Bird, Ochmig, representative, Allen Co. (1849), *334; (1850), *345.

Birney, James G., president (1840), xxiii, 37; (1844), 48-52.

Bissell, William, representative, Allen Co. etc. (1832), 211.

Black, Michael, 122n; representative, Miami and Wabash cos. (1849), 339.

Black, William H., representative, Ohio and Switzerland cos. (1847), 317.

Blackburn, Alexander, representative, La Porte Co. (1841), 259; delegate, const. conv., 379.

Blackford, Isaac, presidential elector (1824), 8-9; U. S. Senator (1818), 127; (1825), 127; (1826), 127; (1832), 129; governor (1825), xix, 138-39n; representative, Knox Co. (1816), *183; (1817), *184; resignation (1817), 185n.

Blackstone, Hiram, representative, Boone Co. (1845), 289; (1847), *313.

Blackwell, William, representative, Ripley Co. (1845), *295; (1849), 340.

Blades, Samuel, representative, Martin Co. (1847), 317.

Blair, Enos, representative, Monroe Co. (1827), *199; (1828), *201.

Blair, James, representative, Decatur Co. (1837), *237; (1840), *255.

Blair, James, representative, Vermillion Co. etc. (1825), *195; (1838), *244; senator (1827), *199; (1830), *207; (1839), *251.

Blake, James, presidential elector (1832), *14-16.

Blake, Thomas H., presidential elector (1816), *3; representative, U. S. Congress (1824), 77-78, 79-80; (1826), *80-81; (1828), 82-83; U. S. Senator (1831), 128; (1832), 129; (1838), xxii-xxiii, 132-33; representative, Vigo Co. etc. (1819), *186; (1823), *192; (1829), *203; senator (1821), *189, 189n.

Blakemore, George W., representative, Cass Co. (1843), *274; (1844), *279; Cass and Howard (1848), *324.

Blanchard, Jonathan, 67n.

Bland, Thomas, representative, Jennings Co. (1850), 348.

Blankenship, Perry M., representative, Morgan Co. (1840), *256.

Blasdel, Jonathan, representative, Dearborn Co. (1841), 259.

Bloomfield, Lot, representative, Wayne Co. (1836), *231.

Blue, Benjamin, representative, Kosciusko Co. (1850), *348.

Blythe, Benjamin I., representative, Dearborn Co. (1823), *191.

Blythe, James E., presidential elector (1848), 58-62, 67n; representative, Vanderburgh Co. (1847), *319; delegate, const. conv., *382.

Boardman, David, representative, Ripley Co. (1844), *285.

Boardman, David G., representative, Marion Co. (1846), 309n.

Boardman, Simon B., representative, Marion Co. (1845), 294; (1847), 317.

Boggs, John, 52n.

Bolton, Nathaniel, representative, Marion Co. (1843), 273.

Bond, John H., senator, Jay and Randolph cos. (1851), 363.

Bonner, David S., representative, Knox Co. (1831), *208; (1832), *212.

Boon, Benjamin, representative, Rush Co. (1837), *238.

Boon, George, presidential elector (1832), *14-16; (1840), 37n; representative, U. S. Congress (1833), 87-88; senator, U. S. Congress (1832), 129-30; representative, Sullivan Co. (1825), *195; (1826), *197; (1827), *199; (1828), *201; (1829), *203; (1830), *206; (1838), *244; (1840), *254; senator, Sullivan Co. etc. (1831), 210; (1834), *223; death (1840), 256n.

Boon, Ratliff, presidential elector (1828), *10-11; representative, U. S. Congress (1824), *77-78; (special, 1824), 80n; (1826), 80-81; (1828), *xx, 82-83; (1831), *xx, 84-85, 87n; (1833), *87; (1835), *90; (1837), 94; senator, U. S. Congress (1830), xx, 128; (1832), 129; (1836), 131; (1838), 132-33; lieutenant governor (1819), *159-60n; (1822), *160-61n; acting governor, xix, 395; representative, Warrick Co. (1816), *183; (1817), *184; senator (1818), *185; resignation (1819), 186n.

Boone, Andrew, representative, Boone Co. (1847), 313.

Boone, Benjamin, representative, Boone Co. (1843), *274.

Boone, John, representative, Harrison Co. (1816), *183.

Boone, Noah, representative, Lawrence Co. (1835), *227; (1836), *232.

Borden, James W., representative, U. S. Congress (1851), 126; delegate, const. conv., Adams, Allen and Wells cos., *383.

Borland, Edward, representative, Monroe Co. (1848), 328.

Bosworth, Jacob, representative, Adams Co. etc. (1839), 245.

Bourne, Ezra L., senator, Franklin Co. (1846), 311.

Bourne, Thomas I., delegate, const. conv., Vigo Co., *381.

Bowden, Enoch, representative, Blackford and Jay cos. (1846), 301.

Bowen, Jesse, senator, Fountain Co. (1837), *239.

Bowen, John H., representative, Jefferson Co. (1849), *337.

Bower, Daniel, representative, Clark Co. (1834), *221.

Bowers, A. W., representative, Wayne Co. (1837), 238n.

Bowers, David, representative, Dearborn Co. (1823), *191.

Bowers, Henry J., representative, Ripley Co. (1840), *256; (1841), *262; (1842), *269; senator (1844), *288; delegate, const. conv., *382.

Bowers, Martin, representative, Montgomery Co. (1845), 294.

Bowers, William, senator, Boone Co. etc. (1851), 362.

Bowin, Richard, senator, Franklin Co. (1849), 343.

Bowles, William A., presidential elector (1844), *38-42; representative, Orange Co. (1838), *242; (1839), *248; (1840), *256; (1843), *275.

Bowling, Elias, representative, Clay Co. (1847), *313.

Bowman, George, senator, Boone Co. etc. (1845), 299.

Bowman, John, representative, Fountain Co. (1845), *291.

Bowman, Levi R., representative, U. S. Congress (1847), 115.

Bowman, William W., representative, Henry Co. (1845), 293.

Bowyer, E., delegate, const. conv., Vigo Co., 381.

Boyd, Drury B., representative, Greene Co. (1832), *213; (1837), *237.

Boyd, John, representative, Rush Co. (1848), 330.

Boyd, Levi, representative, Dearborn Co. (1848), 331n; (1849), 335; (1850), 346.

Boyl, William, representative, Clinton and Tipton cos. (1850), 345.

Bracken, William, delegate, const. conv., Rush Co., *382.

Brackenridge, John A., presidential elector (1844), 43-47; representative, Vanderburgh and Warrick cos. (1833), *217; (1834), *221; senator, Warrick Co. etc. (1846), 333; delegate, const. conv., 386.

Brackenridge, Robert, representative, Tippecanoe Co. (1848), 330.

Bradbury, Abner M., representative, Wayne Co. (1832), *213; (1833), *216; (1834), *220; senator (1835), 226; (1836), *234, 235n; (1844), *288.

Bradbury, Daniel, representative, Wayne Co. (1840), *256.

Bradbury, John, representative, Wayne Co. (1848), 331.

Bradley, Francis P., senator, Daviess and Martin cos. (1846), 310.

Bradley, Hugh J., senator, Parke Co. (1841), *264; representative (1844), *283.

Bradley, James, representative, La Porte Co. (1843), 273; (1850), *348; (1851), *358.

Bradley, John H., presidential elector (1848), 63-67; senator, La Porte Co. etc. (1837), 239; lieutenant governor (1843), 173-75n; representative (1841), *259; (1842), *266.

Bradley, William, representative, Switzerland Co. (1832), *212.

Brady, Henry, representative, Marion Co. (1831), *208; (1832), 212; (1833), *215; (1848), *328; (1851), *358; senator (1834), *223; (1837), *239; (1840), 257; (1849), 344.

Braffet, Silas, representative, Grant Co. (1849), 336.

Braman, James, representative, Jackson Co. (1821), *188.

Bramwell, William C., representative, Jennings Co. (1833), *216.

Brandon, Jesse, representative, Monroe and Brown cos. (1836), 230.

Brazelton, John, representative, Jefferson Co. (1845), 298n; (1846), 305.

Brecount, Gideon S., representative, Benton Co. etc. (1844), *278.

Breeze, James, representative, Daviess Co. (1836), *231.

Brenner, William G., representative, Delaware Co. (1837), *237; death, 238n.

Brenton, Samuel, representative, U. S. Congress (1851), *126; representative, Hendricks Co. (1838), *241; (1840), *253.

Brett, Patrick M., representative, Daviess and Martin cos. (1834), *220; senator, Daviess Co. etc. (1835), 228.

Brewer, Henry, representative, Marion Co. (1846), 309n.

Brier, David, representative, U. S. Congress (1847), 116, 118n; (1851), 125; representative, Fountain Co. (1845), 291; delegate, const. conv., 379.

Briggs, Joseph, representative, Sullivan Co. (1836), *232; senator, Sullivan Co. etc. (1849), 343.

Bright, Jesse D., 178n; U. S. Senator (1845), *134; lieutenant governor (1843), *173-75n; senator, Jefferson Co. (1841), *263; resignation (1843), 278n.

Bright, Michael G., representative, Jefferson Co. (1838), *241; delegate, const. conv., *379.

Bringhurst, T. H., representative, Cass Co. (1851), 355.

Brison (Bryson), John, representative, Franklin Co. (1817), *184.

Britton, Alexander, representative, Spencer Co. (1847), 319.

Britton, Richard L., representative, Allen Co. etc. (1832), 211.

Brodrick, M. A., 67n.

Brodrick, N. F., 67n; representative, Elkhart Co. (1847), 314.

Brookbank, Benjamin F., delegate, const. conv., Union Co., *382.

Brooks, Jacob, representative, Wayne Co. (1843), 274.

Brooks, Thomas G., representative, Martin Co. (1844), 283.

Brown, A. B., representative, La Porte Co. (1842), 266.

Brown, Alexander F., representative, Lake and Porter cos. (1844), 282.

Brown, Asa, representative, Crawford Co. (1839), 246.

Brown, Daniel, representative, La Porte Co. (1840), *253.

Brown, Daniel, representative, Spencer Co. (1840), 254.

Brown, Eli, representative, Benton Co. etc. (1850), 345.

Brown, Elijah, representative, Montgomery Co. (1847), 317.

Brown, Ethan A., representative, Dearborn Co. (1841), *259; (1842), *268.

Brown, George A., representative, Crawford Co. (1839), 246.

Brown, George W., representative, Rush Co. (1842), *267.

Brown, George W., representative, Shelby Co. (1849), *340; (1850), *350.

Brown, Hervey, representative, Marion Co. (1847), *317.

Brown, Hervey, representative, Cass and Howard cos. (1846), *302.

Brown, Ira, representative, Benton Co. etc. (1842), *267.

Brown, J. R. C., representative, Porter and Newton cos. (1836), 230.

Brown, James, representative, Randolph Co. (1849), *340.

Brown, John, representative, Lawrence Co. (1833), *216.

Brown, John, representative, Wayne Co. (1848), 331.

Brown, Jonathan R., representative, Crawford Co. (1844), *279; (1845), 290.

Brown, Josiah S., representative, Whitley Co. (1851), 361.

Brown, Perry, representative, Pike Co. (1850), *351.

Brown, Richard A., representative, Jefferson Co. (1849), 342n.

Brown, Rufus, representative, Benton Co. etc. (1847), 313.

Brown, Samuel, representative, Sullivan Co. (1836), *232; (1837), *238; (1838), *244.

Brown, Simon, senator, Fountain Co. (1849), 343.

Brown, Thomas, representative, Union Co. (1821), *188; (1824), *194; (1826), *197; (1827), *199; (1830), *206.

Brown, Thomas B., representative, Tippecanoe Co. (1833), *217; (1835), *225; (1836), *230.

Brown, William, senator, Ripley Co. (1839), 250.

Brown, William, representative, Wayne Co. (1842), 267.

Brown, William J., representative, U. S. Congress (1843), *107; (1849), *119-20; representative, Rush Co. (1828), *201; (1829), *203; (1830), 205; Marion Co. (1841), *260; (1842), *266.

Brown, Zenas, representative, Whitley Co. (1850), 352n.

Brownfield, John, representative, St. Joseph Co. (1851), 360.

Brownlee, James, representative, Franklin Co. (1816), *183; Fayette Co. (1823), *191.

Bruce, John L., representative, Marion Co. (1844), *283.

Brugh, Jacob, senator, Blackford Co. etc. (1849), *342.

Brumfield, James B., representative, Putnam Co. (1845), *295.

Brumfield, John H., representative, Hamilton Co. (1848), 326.

Brundrett, Robert, representative, Franklin Co. (1851), 356.

Bruner, Frederick, delegate, const. conv., Gibson Co., 379.

Brunton, Thomas, representative, Jefferson Co. (1848), 327.

Bryan, Samuel, representative, Decatur Co. (1834), *221; (1835), *226.

Bryant, James R. M., representative, U. S. Congress (1843), 108; representative, Montgomery Co. (1838), *243; (1844), 283; Warren Co. (1847), *319; (1848), *331; (1851), *361; delegate, const. conv., *381.

Bryant, Theophilus, representative, Cass and Howard cos. (1846), 302.

Bryant, William P., representative, Parke Co. (1831), *209; (1832), *213; senator (1838), *245; (1844), 288.

Bryce, John, representative, U. S. Congress (1841), 104-5; U. S. Senator (1838), 132-33; representative, Montgomery Co. (1837), *237; (1838), *243.

Bryson, John, *see* Brison.

Buch, ———, representative, Switzerland Co. (1830), 206n.

Buchanan, Alexander, representative, Parke Co. (1849), 339.

Buchanon, Joseph W., representative, Marion Co. (1850), 349.

Buckhemor, W., representative, Putnam Co. (1833), 215.

Buckles, Abraham, representative, Delaware Co. (1839), *248; (1840), 252.

Buckles, Joseph S., senator, Grant and Delaware cos. (1842), 270; (1848), *332.

Buell, George P., representative, Dearborn Co. (1836), 229; (1838), 244n; senator (1843), *277.

Buell, James H., representative, Warren Co. (1832), *213; (1835), *227; senator, Warren Co. etc. (1842), *271.

Bufferm, John, 67n.

Bugh, William A., representative, Adams and Wells cos. (1847), 312.

Bulla, Joseph M., representative, Wayne Co. (1850), *351; (1851), *361.

Bullard (?), George, representative, Allen Co. (1850), 345.

Bullock, William A., representative, Jennings Co. (1822), *190; (1823), *191; (1826), *197; (1832), 212.

Bundy, Martin L., representative, Henry Co. (1848), *327.

Buntin, Robert, 3; representative, Knox Co. (1817), *185n; Knox and Sullivan (1818), *185.

Burch, Jonathan, representative, Fountain Co. (1835), 224.

Burgess, John L., representative, Union Co. (1840), *256.

Burk, John, representative, Adams Co. etc. (1836), *229.

Burk, John, 155n; senator, Franklin Co. (1846), 311.

Burk, John, representative, Marion Co. (1849), 338.

Burke, Lewis, representative, Wayne Co. (1839), *249; senator (1841), *264.

Burkholder, Isaac, representative, Franklin Co. (1845), 298n.

Burnes, Lewis, representative, Vermillion Co. (1836), *231; (1837), *238.

Burnett, Alexander S., presidential elector (1832), *14-16; lieutenant governor (1831), 165n; (1837), 168-70n; representative, Floyd Co. (1822), *189; (1823), *191; (1825), *194; (1826), *196; delegate, const. conv., 384.

Burnett, Linas A., representative, Vigo Co. (1849), *341; (1850), 351.

Burns, Edward, representative, Switzerland Co. (1845), *296.

Burroughs, Charles, senator, Wayne Co. (1844), 288.

Burroughs, Ricketson, representative, St. Joseph Co. (1849), 340.

Burrows, William, representative, Spencer Co. (1843), 273.

Burton, Jesse J., representative, Clay Co. (1836), *231; (1840), *255.

Burton, Martin, representative, Clinton Co. (1845), 290.

Burton, William, representative, Lawrence Co. (1843), *275.

Bush, John E., representative, Franklin Co. (1822), *189.

Buskirk, Samuel H., representative, Monroe Co. (1848), *328; (1851), *359.

Bussell, William S., representative, Rush Co. (1830), *205.

Butler, Frederick, representative, Brown and Monroe cos. (1845), 289.

Butler, James, representative, Cass Co. (1840), *251.

Butler, John, delegate, const. conv., Washington Co., 381.

Butler, Oliver, representative, Wayne Co. (1849), *341.

Butler, Ovid, presidential elector (1848), 63-67.

Butler, Robert W., representative, Randolph Co. (1841), *262; (1842) *269; (1845), 295; (1847), 318.

Butler, Thomas, delegate, const. conv., Greene Co., *382.

Butler, Thomas G., representative, Hancock Co. (1845), 292.

Butler, Thomas W., representative, Switzerland Co. (1835), 225.

Butler, William Brown, representative, Vanderburgh Co. (1839), *249; (1840), *256; (1842), *267.

Butler, William O., vice-president (1848), *53-57.

Butterfield, Nathaniel, representative, Warren Co. (1842), *269.

Byard, Martin, representative, Harrison Co. (1851), 357.
Byers, David, representative, Monroe Co. (1840), *254; (1844), *283.
Byers, Ephraim, representative, Clinton Co. (1843), *274; Clinton and Tipton (1849), *335.

Caldwell, Isaac, representative, Dearborn Co. (1834), 219.
Caldwell, James G., representative, Clark Co. (1848), *324; (1849), *342; (1851), 355.
Caldwell, John, representative, Fayette Co. (1845), 291.
Caldwell, Manlove, representative, Fayette Co. (1831), *209.
Caldwell, William, senator, Fayette and Union cos. (1834), *222; resignation (1836), 235n.
Caldwell, William, representative, Vermillion Co. (1840), 254.
Calhoun, John C., vice-president (1824), *4-5, 8-9; (1828), *10-11.
Calhound (Calhoun), George L., representative, Knox Co. (1835), 225.
Call, Jacob, representative, U. S. Congress (1824), 77-78; (special, 1824), *79-80.
Call, Joseph, representative, St. Joseph Co. (1844), 284; (1845), 296.
Call, William, 79n.
Cameron, Marble S., representative, Henry Co. (1845), *293; (1847), *320; death, 320n.
Campbell, Adam S., representative, Lake and Porter cos. (1842), *268.
Campbell, James, representative, Gibson Co. (1817), *184.
Campbell, James, 298n.
Campbell, James T., representative, Washington Co. (1850), *351.
Campbell, John B., representative, Franklin Co. (1847), *315; (1848), *326.
Campbell, John S., representative, Rush Co. (1848), 330.
Campbell, Joseph, representative, Monroe Co. (1839), *247.
Campbell, William, representative, Montgomery Co. (1849), *339; (1850), 349.
Campbell, William, representative, Switzerland Co. (1827), *199.
Canby, Israel T., 13n; U. S. Senator (1832), 129-30; governor (1828), xix, 140-41; representative, Jefferson Co. (1821), *188; senator, Jefferson and Jennings cos. (1826), *198; resignation, 201n.
Carder, Joseph, 298n.
Carey, James S., representative, Posey Co. (1851), 360.
Carey, Stephen, representative, Hamilton and Tipton cos. (1845), 292; Hamilton Co. (1851), 356.
Carleton, James P., representative, Fountain Co. (1837), *237; (1839), *248.
Carleton, Robert M., representative, Lawrence Co. (1839), *248.
Carnahan, Andrew M., representative, Fountain Co. (1849), *336.
Carnahan, Magnus T., representative, Posey Co. (1846), *307; (1847), 318; (1849), *340.
Carnan, Robert N., representative, Knox Co. (1834), 219; (1835), *225; (1845), *293; (1846), *305; senator, Knox Co. etc. (1839), *250; (1842), 270.
Carpenter, Willard, representative, Vanderburgh Co. (1851), *361.
Carr, Abraham, representative, Harrison Co. (1835), 224.
Carr, George W., 126n; presidential elector (1848), *53-57; representative, Lawrence Co. (1838), *243; (1840), *255; (1845), *294; (1846), *306; (1848), *328; (1849), *338; senator (1841), *264; (1844), 287; delegate, const. conv., *387.
Carr, John, presidential elector (1824), *4-5; representative, U. S. Congress (1831), *xx, 85-86; (1833), *88; (1835), *91; (1839), *98; (1841), 102.
Carr, John F., representative, Jackson Co. (1834), *221; (1835), *226;

Carr, John F. (Cont.)
(1837), *237; (1838), *243; senator, Jackson and Scott cos. (1839), *251; (1842), *271; delegate, const. conv., *387.

Carr, Samuel, governor (1819), 138n.

Carr, Thomas, representative, Clark Co. (1816), *183; (1817), *184.

Carr, Thomas, representative, Clark Co. (1846), *302; (1847), *313; (1850), *345.

Carroll, Edward G., delegate, const. conv., Blackford and Jay cos., 378.

Carson, William, representative, Montgomery Co. (1845), 294.

Carson, William W., representative, Adams and Wells cos. (1848), 323.

Carter, Chauncy, representative, Cass Co. etc. (1834), *221; (1835), 224; (1842), *265; senator (1840), 257.

Carter, Horace E., delegate, const. conv., Montgomery Co., *382.

Carter, J. S., representative, La Porte Co. (1845), *297.

Carter, Jesse, representative, Clinton and Montgomery cos. (1832), *211.

Carter, Scott, representative, Switzerland Co.(1845), 296; senator, Ohio and Switzerland cos. (1849), 344.

Carter, Shadrach R. A., representative, Orange Co. (1832), *213; (1833), *216; (1834), *221.

Carter, William E., representative, Morgan Co. (1844), 283.

Casey, Stephen, representative, Hamilton Co. (1849), 337.

Casey, William, representative, Posey Co. (1822), *190; (1829), *203; (1830), *206; (1831), *209; (1840), *256; senator, Posey Co. etc. (1835), *228, 228n; (1836), *235; (1842), *270; resignation, 271n.

Cason, Thomas, representative, Union Co. (1845), 296.

Cass, Lewis, president (1848), *53-57.

Cassaday, Francis, representative, Daviess and Martin cos. (1850), 346.

Cassatt, Jacob D., representative, Wabash Co. (1846), *308; senator, Wabash and Miami cos. (1847), *322.

Casseboom, James R., representative, Posey Co. (1849), 342n.

Casselberry, Hamilton S., representative, Posey Co. (1848), *329.

Casterline, Ziba, presidential elector (1844), 48-52.

Castleman, ——, representative, Vermillion Co. (1836), 231.

Caswell, Daniel J., presidential elector (1820), 3; representative, U. S. Congress (1824), 79.

Cathcart, Charles W., presidential elector (1844), *38-42; representative, U. S. Congress (1845), *112-13; (1847), *116-17 118n; representative, La Porte Co. (1835), 225; (1843), 273; senator, La Porte Co. etc. (1837), *239; (1840), 257; delegate, const. conv., 379.

Cauble, ——, representative, Washington Co. (1840), 256n.

Cavett, Andrew, representative, Posey Co. (1850), 349.

Caylor, Aaron, representative, Hancock Co. (1850), *347; (1851), 357.

Chamberlain, Ebenezer M., presidential elector (1848), *53-57; representative, U. S. Congress (1843), 108; representative, Elkhart Co. etc. (1835), *226; (1837), *237; senator (1839), *250; delegate, const. conv., 379.

Chamberlain, William B., representative, Switzerland Co. (1821), *188; (1826), *197.

Chambers, Abram, representative, Warrick Co. (1848), *331; (1850), 351.

Chambers, Andrew B., representative, Pike Co. (1845), 295.

Chambers, G., representative, Pike Co. (1839), 247.

Chambers, Isaac, representative, Jefferson Co. (1843), *273; (1844), 281.

Chambers, John, representative, Jefferson Co. (1835), *225; (1836),

*229; (1840), 253; (1845), *293; (1847), *316.

Chambers, Joseph, representative, Knox Co. (1830), 205; (1831), 208.

Chambers, Samuel, representative, Orange Co. (1817), *184; (1818), *185; (1819), *186; (1820), *187; senator, Orange Co. etc. (1822), *190, 190n; (1823), *192; (1832), *214; (1835), *228.

Chambers, William, representative, Morgan Co. (1847), 317.

Champer, Basil, representative, Owen Co. (1837), *238; (1838), *243; (1840), *256.

Chandler, Robert A., representative, Warren Co. (1849), *341; delegate, const. conv., Warren Co. etc., 383.

Chandler, Shadrach, delegate, const. conv., Brown Co., *381.

Chapin, Alexander, representative, De Kalb and Steuben cos. (1843), 272.

Chapman, Elijah, senator, Daviess and Martin cos. (1844), *288n; resigned, 312n.

Chapman, George A., representative, Marion Co. (1847), 317.

Chapman, J.W., representative, Jefferson Co. (1850), *348.

Chapman, Jacob, delegate, const. conv., Marion Co., *380.

Chapman, John, representative, La Porte Co. (1842), 266.

Chapman, John B., senator, Carroll Co. etc. (1830), 207; representative, Elkhart Co. etc. (1834), *221.

Chapman, Joseph, representative, Hancock Co. (1838), *243; (1841), *261; (1843), *275; (1845), 292.

Chapman, Joseph W., representative, La Porte Co. (1841), *259; senator (1843), *277.

Chapman, Robert, representative, Wayne Co. (1834), 222n.

Chappell, Josiah, representative, Pike Co. (1849), 340.

Chenoweth, Thomas, delegate, const. conv., Vermillion Co.,*381.

Chenowith, Isaac, senator, Vermillion Co. (1845), *300.

Chesnut, Thomas, representative, Fountain Co. (1846), 303.

Child (Childs), Ezra, representative, Washington Co. (1822), *190; (1823), *192; (1825), *195; (1828), *201.

Chiles, John C., representative, Putnam Co. (1835), *225; (1838), *243; (1840), *254; senator (1843), 277.

Chinn, Thomas, 82n.

Chowning, Theophilus, representative, Sullivan Co. (1851), *360.

Chrisman, John, representative, Boone Co. (1840), *255; (1841), *261; (1842), *268.

Church, Sylvanus, representative, Blackford Co. etc. (1844), 279.

Clark, Alexander B., representative, Boone Co. (1846), 301.

Clark, Amos, representative, Vanderburgh Co. (1841), *262.

Clark, Daniel, representative, Wayne Co. (1835), *226.

Clark, Edmund, representative, Hendricks Co. (1847), 320n.

Clark, Gustavus, representative, Washington Co. (1832), *213; senator, Lawrence Co. (1838), *245.

Clark, Haymond W., representative, Hamilton Co. (1843), *275; delegate, const. conv., *382.

Clark, John B., representative, Dearborn Co. (1840), *252; (1850), *346; (1851), 355.

Clark, John Y., representative, La Grange Co. (1846), *305.

Clark, Marcus, representative, Crawford Co. (1850), 346.

Clark, Marston G., presidential elector (1824), 6-7; (1836), *21-24; representative, Washington Co. (1820), *187; (1835), *226; senator (1821), *189, 189n; (1826), *198.

Clark, Othniel L., 109n; senator, Tippecanoe Co. etc. (1831),*210, 211n; (1834), *222, 223n; (1837), *240; representative, (1840), *254; (1845), 296; delegate, const. conv., *380.

Clark, Robert, representative, Parke Co. (1839), *248.
Clark, Samuel B., representative, Warren Co. (1831), *209; (1833), *217.
Clark, Samuel F., representative, Tippecanoe Co. (1843), *275; (1844), 284.
Clark, Solomon, representative, Fountain Co. (1840), *255.
Clark, Suldoon M., representative, De Kalb and Steuben cos. (1844), 280.
Clark, Wesley, representative, Warren Co. (1845), 297.
Clark, William D., representative, Scott Co. (1821), *188; (1822), *190; (1823), *192.
Clarke, Thomas H., representative, Putnam Co. (1844), 284.
Clawson, Thomas, representative, Fountain Co. (1831), *209.
Clay, Henry, president (1824), xvii-xviii, 6-7; (1832), xx, 18-20; (1844), 43-47.
Claypool, Abel, representative, Fountain Co. etc. (1830), *204; (1832), *213; senator (1834), 223.
Claypool, Newton, representative, Fayette Co. (1824), *193; (1825), *194; (1826), *196; (1827), *198; (1842), *268; (1844), *280; senator, Fayette and Union (1828), *201; (1836), *233.
Cleaveland, Zelson S., senator, Marshall Co. (1845), 300n.
Cleaver, John, representative, Franklin Co. (1849), *336.
Clegg, Matthew, representative, Clark Co. (1846), 302.
Clements, Richard A., representative, Daviess Co. (1841), *259; (1842), *268; (1845), *290; senator, Daviess and Martin cos. (1844), 287; (1846), *310; (1850), 352; delegate, const. conv., *387n.
Clendenin, John G., presidential elector (1836), *21-24; representative, U. S. Congress (1835), 90; representative, Orange Co. (1822), *190; (1823), *192; (1824), *193; (1825), *195; (1826), *197; (1827), *199; senator, Orange and Lawrence cos. (1829), *204.
Cline, George, representative, Lake and Porter cos. (1838), *243.
Cloud, Mason J., representative, Dearborn Co. (1848), 331n.
Clouser, Nelson D., representative, Blackford Co. (1851), 362n.
Clymer, Samuel T., representative, Elkhart Co. (1838), *242; (1845), *291; senator, Elkhart Co. etc. (1842), 270.
Coats, Balis, representative, Shelby Co. (1839), *249.
Coats, Joseph, senator, Fountain Co. (1846), *311; delegate, const. conv., *384.
Cobb, J. B., representative, Johnson Co. (1851), 358.
Cobb, James B., 93n.
Cobb, Royal P., representative, Decatur Co. (1845), 291.
Coble, John, representative, Crawford Co. (1847), *314.
Coburn, John, representative, Marion Co. (1850), *349.
Cockrum, James W., senator, Gibson Co. etc. (1847), 321; representative, Gibson Co. (1848), *326; (1849), 336; (1851), *356.
Coffeen, Eleazer, representative, Delaware Co. (1840), *252.
Coffin, ——, representative, Switzerland Co. (1843), 274.
Coffin, ——, representative, Washington Co. (1835), 226.
Coffin, Albert G., presidential elector (1848), 63-67.
Coffin, Elihu, representative, Hancock Co. (1847), 315.
Coffin, Samuel, representative, Henry Co. (1845), *293; (1847), *320.
Coffin, Thomas, representative, Orange Co. (1829), *203; (1830), *206.
Coffin, William G., representative, Parke Co. (1842), *269; (1843), *275; senator (1844), *288.

Coggswell, Francis B., representative, Hamilton Co. (1838), *243; (1839), *248; (1841), *261.

Cole, Albert B., delegate, const. conv., Boone Co. etc., *387.

Cole, Alphonso A., representative, Miami and Wabash cos. (1845), 294; (1847), *317; (1849), *339; senator (1850), 353.

Cole, Bicknell, senator, Boone and Hamilton cos. (1836), *234, 235n.

Cole, Hiram B., representative, Vermillion Co. (1835), *226.

Cole, John, representative, Washington Co. (1850), 351.

Cole, William R., representative, Dearborn Co. (1839), 246; (1840), *252.

Colerick, David H., representative, Allen Co. etc. (1833), *214; senator (1835), 227; (1838), 244.

Colfax, Schuyler, representative, U. S. Congress (1851), 125-26; delegate const. conv., St. Joseph Co., *380.

Colip, Jacob, 82n.

Colip, Samuel H., representative, Hamilton Co. (1846), 304; (1847), *315; (1848), 326.

Collett, John, representative, Vermillion Co. (1851), 361.

Collett, Stephen S., senator, Vermillion and Warren cos. (1833), *218; (1842), *271; death, 289n.

Collins, James, presidential elector (1844), 43-47; representative, Floyd Co. (1835), *224; senator (1836), *235, 235n; (1840), *258.

Collins, Thomas, representative, Delaware Co. (1844), 280.

Colman, Isaac, representative, Fountain Co. (1848), 326.

Colman, John M., senator, Putnam Co. etc. (1825), *195; representative, Putnam Co. (1840), *254.

Colms, Stephen H., representative, Kosciusko and Whitley cos. (1844), *282; (1845), 293; (1846), *305.

Colt, Erastus, 170n.

Combs, Michael, delegate, const. conv., Vigo Co., 384.

Commons, David, representative, Wayne Co. (1847), *320; (1848), *331.

Conaway, Daniel, representative, Dearborn Co. (1849), *335.

Conaway, Hamilton, representative, Dearborn Co. (1847), 314.

Conaway, William, representative, Dearborn Co. (1834), 224; (1838), *240; (1839), *246.

Conduit (Conduitt), Alexander B., 113n; representative, Morgan Co. (1844), *283; (1845), *295; senator (1847), *322; delegate, const. conv., *380.

Conduit, Willis G., senator, Boone Co. etc. (1831), 210.

Cone, Theodore C., representative, Vigo Co. (1831), *208; death, 210n.

Conner, James M., representative, Rush Co. (1851), 360.

Conner, John, senator, Franklin Co. (1816), *183, 184n; Fayette and Union (1821), *189, 189n; representative, Marion Co. etc. (1824), *193.

Conner, William, representative, Hamilton Co. etc. (1829), *202; (1831), *208; (1836), *232.

Conner, William W., representative, Hamilton Co. (1843), *275; (1844), *281; (1850), *347; senator (1845), *299.

Connor, Frederick, representative, Perry Co. (1840), *254; (1849), *339.

Connor, Samuel, representative, Perry Co. (1816), *183; (1817), *184; (1818), *185; (1820), *187, 187n.

Connor, William L., representative, Perry Co. (1847), 318.

Constitution of 1816, provisions, ix-xi, xxiv, 399; referendums on revision of, xxiv-xxv, 367-77n.

Constitution of 1851, Negro exclusion clause, vote on, xxv, 388-90; ratification, xxv, 388-90.

Constitutional Convention, 1850-51, apportionment of delegates, xxv, 382n-83; delegates, 378-87n.

Conwell, Elias, representative, Ripley Co. (1851), 360.

Conwell, James, 117n; representative, Franklin Co. (1834), *219; (1840), *252; (1844), 280; senator (1835), *228n.

Cook, Jacob, representative, Bartholomew Co. (1834), *220.

Cook, John H., representative, Madison Co. (1836), *232; senator, Hancock and Madison cos. (1850), 353.

Cook, Whipple, representative, Blackford and Jay cos. (1849), 334.

Cookerly, Grafton F., representative, U. S. Congress (1849), 120; representative, Vigo Co. (1845), *297; (1846), 308; (1847), *319; (1848), 330; (1851), 361; delegate, const. conv., *381.

Cooley, John P. (or T.), representative, Franklin Co. (1841), *261; (1842), *268.

Coon, Christian, representative, Montgomery Co. (1845), 294.

Coon, William, representative, Benton Co. etc. (1841), *261; (1845), *289.

Cooney, Archibald, representative, Madison Co. (1840), 253.

Cooper, A. C., 67n.

Cooper, Elijah S., representative, Hancock Co. (1846), 304; (1848), 327.

Cooper, John, representative, Clinton and Tipton cos. (1848), 325.

Cooper, Joseph, representative, Vigo Co. (1847), 319.

Cooper, Robert M., representative, Henry Co. (1838), *243; (1839), *248; (1841), *261; senator (1848), 333.

Cornelius, George, representative, Dearborn Co. (1841), 259; (1845), *290.

Cornett, William T. S., senator, Ripley Co. (1841), *264; (1847), *323.

Cosby, Charles I., representative, Jefferson Co. (1835), 225.

Cotton, Alfred J., representative, Dearborn Co. (1833), 215; (1834), 219.

Cotton, James M., representative, Switzerland Co. (1835), 225; (1837), *236; (1838), *242; (1851), 359.

Cotton, John S., representative, Huntington and Whitley cos. (1849), *337.

Cotton, Nathaniel, representative, Switzerland Co. (1832), 212.

Cotton, Ralph, representative, Switzerland Co. (1817), *184; (1818), *185; (1823), *192.

Cotton, Robert G., representative, Perry Co. (1837), *238; (1838), *243; (1841), *262; (1848), *329; senator (1842), *271; (1845), 300; delegate, const. conv., 380.

Cotton, William, senator, Switzerland Co. etc. (1819), *186; (1825), *196; representative (1831), *209.

Council, Thomas W., representative, Marion Co. (1846), 306; (1847), 317.

Counties, dates of formation and organization, 392-95.

Course, William, representative, Crawford Co. (1838), 240.

Courtney, Thomas T., representative, Fayette Co. (1849), 336.

Covington, Samuel F., representative, Ohio and Switzerland cos. (1847), *317.

Cowan, John M., representative, Benton Co. etc. (1850), *345.

Cowan, Joseph, representative, Elkhart Co. (1843), *272; (1844), *280; senator, Elkhart and LaGrange (1847), 321.

Cowan, Stephen R., representative, Adams Co. (1851), 354.

Cowgill, Calvin, representative, Wabash Co. (1851), *362.

Cowgill, John, representative, Putnam Co. (1845), 295.

Cox, Daniel M., representative, Wabash Co. (1848), 331.

Cox, Elihu, representative, Wayne Co. (1842), 269n.

Cox, Jeremiah, representative, Wayne Co. (1821), *188.

Cox, Jesse T., senator, Crawford and Orange cos. (1850), 352.

Cox, John W., representative, Hendricks and Morgan cos. (1830), 204; Morgan Co. (1831), *209; (1832), *213; senator (1838), 245.

Cox, Jonathan P., representative, Knox Co. (1837), *236; (1838), 241; (1839), *247.

Cox, M., representative, Warren and Jasper cos. (1836), 231.

Cox, Robert S., representative, Rush Co. (1845), *295; (1848), *330.

Cox, Sandford C., 113n.

Cox, Silas M., representative, Posey Co. (1850), *349.

Craig, George, senator, Ripley and Switzerland cos. (1822), *190; representative (1830), *205; (1832), 212.

Craig, Jesse R., representative, Posey Co. (1833), *216; (1835), *227.

Craig, Merit S., representative, Ripley Co. (1825), *195; (1826), *197; (1827), *199; (1828), *201; (1834), 220.

Craig, Thomas, representative, Harrison Co. (1833), 215; (1834), 219; (1835), 224; (1836), 229.

Craig, William H., representative, Morgan Co. (1835), *225.

Craine (or Crane), Orlando, delegate, const. conv., Hancock and Madison cos., 385.

Crane, Abiather, representative, Putnam Co. (1849), 340.

Crane, Obadiah, representative, Jackson Co. (1824), *193.

Cravens, James A., representative, Washington Co. (1848), *331; (1849), *341; senator (1850), *354.

Cravens, James H., 113n; presidential elector (1840), *29-32; (1848), 63-67; representative, U. S. Congress (1841), *103; governor (1849), 155-58; representative, Jefferson Co. (1831), xxiv, *208; (1832), *212; Ripley Co. (1846), *307; senator, Ripley and Switzerland cos. (1834), 223, 223n; Ripley Co. (1839), *250, 251n.

Cravens, John R., presidential elector (1848), 63-67.

Crawford, Daniel B., representative, Wayne Co. (1844), 285; (1846), 309; (1847), 320.

Crawford, George, representative, Elkhart Co. etc. (1832), *211; (1833), 214; (1845), 291; senator (1836), *234, 235n.

Crawford, James, delegate, const. conv., Morgan Co., *386.

Crawford, John, representative, Adams Co. (1851), *354.

Crawford, Robert H., senator, Decatur Co. (1849), 343; (1851), *364; representative (1850), *346.

Crawford, Thomas, representative, Jefferson Co. (1820), *187.

Crim, Martin D., representative, Martin Co. (1851), *362.

Crim, William, representative, Madison Co. (1850), *348.

Crisler, Allen, representative, Franklin Co. (1818), *185; (1819), *186; Fayette Co. (1821), *188; (1832), *212.

Crisler, Thomas J., representative, Fayette Co. (1848), 326.

Crist, James W., representative, Union Co. (1836), 230.

Criswell, David, representative, Ripley Co. (1847), *318.

Crocker, Philander, representative, Wayne Co. (1844), 285.

Crocket, Robert E., representative, Warren Co. (1844), 285.

Cromstorn, Charles, representative, Fulton Co. etc. (1849), 336.

Cromwell, Joseph, representative, Harrison Co. (1843), 273.

Cromwell, Oliver, representative, Clay Co. (1851), *361.

Crooks, ———, representative, Carroll Co. etc. (1830), 204.

Crooks, James M., representative, Parke Co. (1848), 329.

Crooks, W. W., representative, Parke Co. (1834), 220.

Crookshank, E. D., representative, Franklin Co. (1845), *291; (1846), *303.

Cross, George W., representative, Jefferson Co. (1843), 273.

Crouse, Daniel B., representative, Tippecanoe Co. (1847), 320n.

Crowe, Samuel S., representative, Scott Co. (1849), 340.

Crowsaw, Jacob, 105n.

Cruft, John F., representative, Vigo Co. (1831), 210n.

Crume, Marks, presidential elector (1832), *14-16; representative, Fayette Co. (1828), *200; (1829), *202; (1830), *204; (1831), *209; (1832), *212; (1833), *216; (1834), *219; (1836), *232; (1837), *237.

Crume, Marks, representative, Tippecanoe Co. (1844), 284.

Crumpacker, Daniel, representative, Lake Co. (1851), 358; delegate, const. conv., *382.

Crumpton, William, representative, Fountain Co. (1831), *209.

Culbertson, Josiah, representative, Daviess Co. etc. (1834), *221; senator (1839), 250; (1847), 321.

Culbertson, William, 153n.

Culley, David V., lieutenant governor (1834), 166-67n; representative, Dearborn Co. (1831), *208; (1832), *211; senator (1833), *217, 218n.

Cullum, R. H., 298n.

Cumback, William, representative, Franklin Co. (1850), 352n.

Cumings, William P., senator, Parke and Vermillion cos. (1851), 364.

Cundell, John, representative, Dearborn Co. (1837), 238n.

Cunningham, John W., representative, Putnam Co. (1836), *232; (1837), *238.

Cuppy, Abraham, representative, Kosciusko and Whitley cos. (1842), *268; (1843), *275; (1844), 282; senator, (1845), *299; death (1847), 323n.

Curry, Thomas M., representative, Clinton and Montgomery cos. (1834), *221; (1835), 224; Montgomery Co. (1836), *230; Carroll Co. (1843), 272.

Curtis, Joseph, representative, Wayne Co. (1834), *220; (1835), *226; (1836), *231; (1845), 298n; (1846), 309n; (1847), 320n; (1848), 331.

Cushman, Henry J., representative, La Grange and Noble cos. (1845), 294.

Cushman, Seth, representative, Sullivan Co. (1835), *227.

Cutter, George W., representative, Vigo Co. (1838), *244; (1839), *247.

Daily, David W., senator, Clark and Floyd cos. (1833), *218, 219n; (1835), *228.

Daily, Samuel C., representative, Jefferson Co. (1845), 298n.

Dallas, George M., vice-president (1844), *38-42.

Daniel, John, representative, Perry Co. etc. (1822), *189; (1825), *194; (1826), *197; senator (1827), *199.

Daniel, Richard, representative, Gibson Co. (1817), *184; (1818), *185; resignation, 186n; senator, Gibson Co. etc. (1820), *187; representative, Posey Co. (1832), *213.

Daniels, Burrel L., representative, Miami Co. (1848), 328.

Danner, James, representative, Orange Co. (1847), *317.

Darough, James, representative, Clark Co. (1846), 302.

Darr, John, representative, Henry Co. (1848), 327.

Darrow, Jared, representative, Blackford Co. etc. (1844), *279.

Darter, Samuel, 298n.

Dashiell, Charles, representative, Dearborn Co. (1838), 244n; (1846), 303.

Daugherty, Joseph F., representative, Boone Co. (1850), 345.

Davenport, Austin, representative, Boone Co. etc. (1832), *212; (1833), *215.

Davis, ———, representative, Carroll Co. etc. (1830), 204.

Davis, ———, representative, Putnam Co. (1835), 227n.

Davis, Aaron, 20n.

Davis, Abner, representative, Daviess and Martin cos. (1837), *237; senator (1841), *263, 264n, 271n; (1844), *287; death, 288n.

Davis, Addison, representative, Jennings Co. (1849), 337.

Davis, Anthony L., representative, Allen Co. etc. (1829), *202.

Davis, Eli, presidential elector (1844), 48-52; representative, Adams and Jay cos. (1844), 278.

Davis, James, representative, Posey Co. (1849), 340.

Davis, James, representative, Tippecanoe Co. (1834), *221; (1835), *225.

Davis, John, representative, Madison Co. (1842), *268; delegate, const. conv., *379.

Davis, John G., representative, U. S. Congress (1851),*124-25.

Davis (or Daviess), John P., representative, Daviess and Martin cos. (1846), 302; (1847), *317; (1848), 331n.

Davis, John S., presidential elector (1848), 58-62; representative U. S. Congress (1847), 114; representative, Floyd Co. (1841), *261; senator (1843), *277; (1846), *312.

Davis, John W., representative, U. S. Congress (1833), 87-88; (1835), *90-91; (1839), *97-98; (1841), 102, 105n; (1843), *107, 109n; (1845), *111-12; U. S. Senator (1832), 129-30; representative, Sullivan Co. (1831), *209; (1832), *213; (1841), *260; (1842), *269; (1851), *360.

Davis, Joseph, representative, Boone Co. (1848), 324.

Davis, Justus, representative, Sullivan Co. (1839), *249; (1841), *260; (1848), 330.

Davis, Oliver P., senator, Parke and Vermillion cos. (1851), *364; delegate, const. conv., *386.

Davis, Rezin, representative, Johnson and Shelby cos. (1829), *203; (1830), 204; (1832), *213; (1833), *217.

Davis, Samuel, representative, Franklin Co. (1851), *356.

Davis, Samuel, representative, Parke Co. (1847), 318; delegate, const. conv., *382.

Davis, Samuel, representative, Scott Co. (1845), *296; (1850), *350.

Davis, Samuel A., representative, Tippecanoe Co. (1847), 320n.

Davis, Samuel H., 67n, 118n.

Davis, Silas, representative, Dubois Co. (1844), *280; (1850), *346.

Davis, Thomas R. E., representative, Shelby Co. (1837), *238; death, 239n.

Dawson, Reuben J., representative, De Kalb Co. etc. (1848), *325; senator (1849), *343.

Day, Henry, senator, Huntington Co. etc. (1848), *333.

Day, Lot, senator, Marshall Co. etc. (1836), 234; (1846), *311; (1849), 344; representative (1849), 340.

Deam, John H., representative, Adams and Wells cos. (1846), *301.

Dean, Thomas, representative, Grant Co. (1844), 281.

Deavitt, Albert G., representative, Fulton and Marshall cos. (1848), 326; delegate, const. conv., St. Joseph Co., 380.

DeBruler, Lemuel, representative, U. S. Congress (1851), 122.

DeBruler, Thomas F., representative, Spencer Co. (1847), *319.

Decker, Hiram, presidential elector (1836), *21-24; representative, Knox Co. (1836), 230.

Decker, John, representative, Knox Co. (1830), *205; (1831), *208; senator (1845), 300.

Decker, Samuel, 126n; representative, Pulaski Co. etc. (1846), *301.

Decker, Samuel, representative, Adams and Wells cos. (1848), *323.

Decoursey, Joel, representative, Dearborn Co. (1827), *198.

Defrees, Anthony, representative, Allen Co. etc. (1833), 214.

Defrees, John D., representative, St. Joseph Co. (1840), *256; (1841), *262; senator, St. Joseph Co. etc. (1842), *271; (1843), *277; resignation, 300n.

Defrees, Joseph H., representative, Elkhart Co. (1849), *342; senator, Elkhart and La Grange cos. (1850), *353.

Delavan, Alfred M., representative, Morgan Co. (1844), 283; (1845), 295; (1849), *339; senator (1850), *353.

Deming, Demas, representative, Vigo Co. (1828), *202n.

Deming, Elizur, presidential elector (1844), 48-52; representative, U. S. Congress (1845), 112; (1851), 126n; governor (1843), xxiv, 150-53; representative, Tippecanoe Co. (1841), *260.

Deming, John J., presidential elector (1844), 48-52; representative in Congress (1845), 112-13.

Democratic party, beginning of, xxvii-xix, xx-xxi; in state and presidential elections, 1834-50, pp. xxii-xxiv.

Denny, James, representative, Putnam Co. (1842), *267; (1843), 273.

Denton, A. B., representative, Putnam Co. (1842), 269n.

De Pauw, Charles, representative, Bartholomew Co. (1822), *189.

De Pauw, James, representative, Sullivan Co. (1833), *217.

De Pauw, John, lieutenant governor (1819), 159-60n; senator, Washington Co. etc. (1816), *183, 184n; (1817), *185; resignation (1819), 186n; senator, Washington Co. (1825), *196, 196n; (1829), *204; representative (1827), *199; (1836), *233.

Depew, Jeremiah, senator, Hendricks Co. (1845), 299; representative (1847), 315.

Depuy, Henry W., senator, Marion Co. (1846), 311.

Devault, Lemuel, delegate, const. conv., Tippecanoe Co., 380.

Devin, James, representative, Gibson Co. (1838), *243; senator, Gibson Co. etc. (1844), 287.

Devin, Joseph, representative, Gibson Co. (1841), *261.

Dewey, Charles, representative, U. S. Congress (1822), 76; (1835), 91; U. S. Senator (1830), xx, 128; (1832), 129; (1838), 132-33; representative, Orange Co. (1821), *188.

Dice, Jacob, representative, Fountain Co. (1851), *356.

Dick, James, delegate, const. conv., Knox Co., *387.

Dickinson, Timothy R., representative, De Kalb Co. (1849), 342n.

Dilly, Joseph, representative, Sullivan Co. (1848), 330; (1851), 360.

Dimmitt, John W., representative, Montgomery Co. (1847), *317.

Dipboye, Abraham, representative, Delaware Co. (1850), 346; (1851), 356.

Dixon, Eli, representative, Greene Co. etc. (1821), *188; (1822), *190; (1823), *191; (1826), *196; (1829), *202.

Dobson, David M., representative, U. S. Congress (1847), 115-16, 118n; senator, Greene and Owen cos. (1836), *235, 235n; (1838), *245; (1841), *264; representative, Owen Co., (1848), *329; delegate, const. conv., *387.

Dobson, James W., representative, Owen Co. (1846), *306; (1847), *318; (1851), *359.

Dodd, John W., representative, Grant Co. (1849), *336; (1850), 347.

Doggett, ———, representative, Parke Co. (1841), 260.

Dole, William P., representative, Vermillion Co. (1838), *244; (1845),

297; (1846), *308; (1847), *319; senator (1844), *288; (1848), *333.

Donaghe, Hugh M., representative, Vanderburgh and Warrick cos. (1821), *188.

Donahey, James, representative, Warren Co. (1846), 308.

Donaldson, Richard F., representative, Miami Co. (1850), *349; (1851), *358.

Doncarlos, W. C., representative, Vermillion Co. (1835), 226.

Donham, George, representative, Clay Co. (1846), 302; (1849), 335; (1851), *361.

Donnell, John, representative, Dubois Co. (1845), 291.

Donnohue, Dillard C., representative, Putnam Co. (1848), *329.

Dorsey, Prindowell M., representative, Floyd Co. (1833), *216; senator, Clark and Floyd cos. (1835), 228.

Dorton, Ephraim, representative, Union Co. (1845), 296.

Dougherty, Lorenzo C., representative, Boone Co. (1848), *324; (1849), *335; senator, Boone Co. etc. (1851), *362.

Dougherty, Michael C., representative, Elkhart Co. (1849), *342.

Dougherty, Oliver R., representative, Morgan Co. (1847), *317; (1848), *329.

Doughty, John P., representative, Wayne Co. (1851), *361.

Doughty, William M., representative, Wayne Co. (1836), 231.

Douglas, Cyrus, 20n.

Douglass, J. C., representative, Cass Co. (1841), 258.

Douthit, James H., representative, Hamilton Co. (1851), *356.

Dover, John, representative, Washington Co. (1830), 206n.

Dowden, Samuel H., representative, Dearborn Co. (1830), *204; (1832), 211; (1838), 244n.

Dowling, John, representative, Vigo Co. (1846), *308; (1847), 319.

Dowling, Thomas, representative, Vigo Co. (1836), *232; (1837), *238; (1840), *255; (1843), *276; (1845), *297; (1848), *330.

Doyle, John, representative, Tippecanoe Co. (1847), *319; (1848), *330.

Drake, Elijah H., senator, De Kalb Co. etc. (1849), 343.

Drake, James P., representative, Marion Co. (1848), *328.

Drew, Cyrus K., representative, Vanderburgh Co. (1849), 341.

Drew, William C., senator, Fayette and Franklin cos. (1819), *186.

Drummond, ———, representative, Clark Co. (1847), 313.

Duffield, James, representative, Putnam Co. (1835), 225.

Dufour, John F., representative, Switzerland Co. (1828), *201; (1830), 205.

Dufour, Perret, representative, Switzerland Co. (1842), *269; (1846), 306; delegate, const. conv., 380.

Dugan, James, representative, Hendricks Co. (1846), 304.

Dulan, William, representative Wayne Co. (1848), 331.

Dumont, Ebenezer, representative, Dearborn Co. (1838), *240; (1850), *346.

Dumont, John, U. S. Senator (1838), 132-33; governor (1837), xxii, 145-48; representative, Switzerland Co. (1816), *183; (1822), *190; (1828), *201; (1829), *203; (1830), *205; senator, Ripley and Switzerland cos. (1831), *211; (1834), *223, 223n.

Dunbar, Ezekiel L., representative, Jackson Co. (1840), *255; (1841), *261; (1842), *268; death, 269n.

Dunbar, John N., representative, Harrison Co. (1819), *186; (1821), *188; death, 189n.

Duncan, William, representative, Lawrence Co. (1844), 282.

Dunham, Cyrus L., presidential elector (1848), *53-57; representative, U. S. Congress (1849), *118-19; (1851),

Dunham, Cyrus L. (Cont.)
*123; representative, Washington Co. (1846), *308; (1847), *320.

Dunigan, Solomon, *see* Dunnegan, Solomon.

Dunlap, Livingston, representative, Marion Co. (1843), 273.

Dunn, ———, 132-33.

Dunn, George F., representative, Grant Co. (1849), 336.

Dunn, George G., 113n, 126n; presidential elector (1844), 43-47; representative, U. S. Congress (1843), 107, 109n; (1847), *115-16, 118n; senator, Lawrence Co. (1850), *353.

Dunn, George H., representative, U. S. Congress (1835), 91; (1837), *95; (1839), 98; representative, Dearborn Co. (1828), *200; (1832), *211; (1833), *215; senator (1831), 210.

Dunn, Isaac, representative, Dearborn Co. (1840), *252.

Dunn, John, representative, Grant Co. (1842), *268; (1845), 292.

Dunn, John, representative, Hendricks Co. (1834), 219.

Dunn, John P., representative, Dearborn Co. (1836), *229; (1840), 252.

Dunn, John P., delegate, const. conv., Perry Co. etc., *386.

Dunn, Samuel C., representative, Clinton Co. (1839), *248.

Dunn, William McKee, representative, U. S. Congress (1849), 118-19; representative, Jefferson Co. (1848), *327; delegate, const. conv., *379.

Dunn, Williamson, representative, Jefferson Co. (1816), *183; (1817), *184; (1818), *185; (1819), *186; senator (1832), 214; (1837), *239; (1838), 244; (1841), 263; (1843), 277.

Dunnegan (Dunigan), Solomon, representative, Hendricks and Morgan cos. (1830), 204; Morgan Co. (1838), 242.

Dunning, John B., representative, Knox Co. (1851), 358.

Dunning, Paris C., presidential elector (1844), *38-42; lieutenant governor (1846), *175-78; acting governor, 395; representative, Monroe Co. (1833), *216; (1834), *221; (1835), *227; senator (1836), *234.

Dunnington, Alexander, representative, Putnam Co. (1847), 318.

Durbin, Hosier J., representative, Switzerland Co. (1840), *254.

Durham, Fleming, representative, Jefferson Co. (1844), 281.

Durham, Jacob, senator, Putnam Co. (1848), 334.

Durham, Jesse B., presidential elector (1828), *10-11; representative, Jackson Co. (1831), *209.

Duvall, Samuel A., representative, Parke Co. (1848), *329.

Duzan, John, representative, Boone Co. (1844), *279.

Duzan, Mark A., senator, Boone and Hamilton cos. (1842), *271; delegate, const. conv., Boone Co., *381.

Dynes, Jeremiah, representative, Delaware Co. (1846), 303; (1849), 336.

Earl, James, representative, Tippecanoe Co. (1838), *244.

Earle, Thomas, vice-president (1840), 37.

Early, Joseph C., representative, Vigo Co. (1844), 285.

Earlywine, Nathan, representative, Shelby Co. (1848), 330.

Eccles, Delana R., representative, Owen Co. (1836), *232.

Eccles, John, representative, Marion Co. (1833), 215.

Eccles, John, 113n; representative, Morgan Co. (1839), *248.

Eccles, Samuel, representative, Johnson Co. (1851), *358.

Eddy, Norman, representative, St. Joseph Co. (1847), 318; (1849), 340; senator (1849), *344.

Edger, Edward, representative, Randolph Co. (1843), *275; (1849), 340.

Edgerton, Walter, representative, Henry Co. (1844), 281.

Edmonds, Samuel W., delegate, const. conv., Vigo Co., 383n.

Edmonston, Benjamin R., representative, Dubois and Pike cos. (1835), *226; (1839), *248; (1842), *268; (1843), *274; (1848), *326; senator, Dubois Co. etc. (1844), *287; delegate, const. conv., *379.

Edwards, David, representative, Dubois Co. etc. (1823), *191.

Edwards, Eden, representative, Switzerland Co. (1839), 247.

Edwards, John, representative, Crawford Co. (1841), *261; (1842), *268.

Edwards, John, representative, Lawrence Co. (1845), *294; (1846), 306; senator (1847), 322.

Edwards, William, representative, Randolph Co. (1832), *213; (1833), *216; (1835), *227.

Edwards, William K., representative, Vigo Co. (1846), *308; (1848), *330; (1849), *341; (1850), *351.

Egbert, Elisha, representative, Allen Co. etc. (1832), 211; St. Joseph Co. (1838), *243.

Egelston, Jacob W., representative, Dearborn Co. (1837), 236; (1838), *240; (1839), 246.

Eggert, Adrian V., 105n.

Eggleston, Joseph C., representative, U. S. Congress (1845), 110-11; representative, Switzerland Co. (1835), *225; (1836), *230; senator (1840), *257; resignation (1842), 271n.

Elder, Arnold, representative, Perry Co. (1843), *275.

Elder, James, representative, Decatur Co. (1836), *231.

Elder, James, representative, Wayne Co. (1849), *341; senator (1850), 354.

Eldridge, Elijah, representative, Benton Co. etc. (1845), 289.

Eldridge, Job B., representative, Cass Co. (1837), *236; (1838), *240; (1842), 265.

Election campaigns, xi-xii, xvi.

Elections, method and procedure, x-xin, xii-xv; penalty for fraud, xv; failure in transmitting returns, xvi; Congressional, time of holding changed, xix-xx; special (1841), xx.

Elkins, Burket M., representative, Adams and Wells cos. (1850), *344.

Elkins, Smith, representative, Randolph Co. (1840), *256.

Eller, John, representative, Monroe Co. (1846), *309; death, 309n.

Ellingwood, Francis, representative, Hamilton and Tipton cos. (1845), 292; (1846), 304.

Elliott, James, delegate, const. conv., Shelby Co., *383n.

Elliott, Jehu T., senator, Henry Co. (1839), *251.

Elliott, Michael, representative, Jackson Co. (1846), 309n.

Elliott, William, representative, Wayne Co. (1826), *197; (1827), *199; (1828), *201; (1830), *205; senator (1835), *228; (1838), 245; (1841), 264.

Ellis, Abner T., representative, Knox Co. (1843), 273; senator (1845), *300; (1848), *333.

Ellis, Evan, representative, Madison Co. (1844), 282; (1845), *297; (1849), *338.

Ellis, James P., representative, Tippecanoe Co. (1841), *260.

Ellis, John H., representative, Delaware Co. (1847), 314.

Ellis, W. R., senator, Elkhart Co. etc. (1845), 299.

Ellsworth, Henry L., presidential elector (1848), 63 67; representative, Tippecanoe Co. (1851), 360.

Ellsworth, Henry W., presidential elector (1844), *38-42.

Ely, Anderson F., representative, Gibson Co. (1850), 347.

Embree, Elisha, representative, U. S. Congress (1847), *114; (1849), 118; senator, Gibson Co. etc. (1833), *218, 219n.

Emerson, Frank, senator, Jackson and Scott cos. (1851), *363.

Emison, Samuel, representative, Knox Co. (1833), 215; (1837), 236.

Endicott, James C., representative, Posey Co. (1844), *284; (1845), *295; (1849), 340.

Engle, Philip E., representative, Montgomery Co. (1843), *275.

English, Elisha G., representative, Scott Co. (1832), *213; (1833), *217; (1839), *249; (1842), *269; senator, Jackson and Scott cos. (1845), *300; (1848), *333.

English, William H., representative, Scott Co. (1851), *360.

Ensminger, representative, Tippecanoe Co. (1836), 230.

Erwin, John, representative, Wayne Co. (1833), 217n.

Erwin, William, representative, Lawrence Co. (1824), *193.

Eson, James, representative, Owen Co. (1845), 295.

Essex, John, representative, Bartholomew Co. (1848), 323.

Essex, Thomas, representative, Bartholomew Co. (1849), *334; (1850), *352n.

Evans, David, senator, La Porte Co. etc. (1836), 234.

Evans, George, senator, Henry Co. (1848), *333.

Evans, Henry B., 67n; representative, Marion Co. (1845), 294.

Evans, Israel, representative, Henry Co. (1844), 281.

Evans, Robert M., representative, U. S. Congress (1833), 87; representative, Gibson Co. (1819), *186; (1825), *194; Vanderburgh and Warrick (1823), *192; (1829), *203.

Evans, Thomas J., representative, U. S. Congress (1839), 100; representative, Fountain Co. (1833), *216; (1834), *219; (1835), *224; (1836), *229; (1837), *237; (1838), *243.

Eversole, Noah, representative, Vigo Co. (1845), 297.

Everts, Gustavus A., senator, La Porte Co. etc. (1836), *234, 235n; representative, La Porte Co. (1841), 259.

Everts, Sylvanus, presidential elector (1832), 17-20; representative, Union Co. (1822), *190; (1823), *192; La Porte Co. (1839), *247; senator, La Porte Co. etc. (1840), *257.

Ewing, Charles, senator, Adams Co. etc. (1841), 263.

Ewing, George W., presidential elector (1840), 37n; senator, Cass Co. etc. (1836), *234, 235n; (1837), *239.

Ewing, J. M., representative, Carroll and Cass cos. (1833), 215.

Ewing, John, representative, U. S. Congress (1833), *87-88; (1835), 90-91; (1837), 94; (1839), 97-98; U. S. Senator (1832), 129; senator, Knox Co. etc. (1824), *194; (1827), *199; (1830), *207; (1842), *270; (1843), *277, 278n; (1845), 300; representative (1851), 358.

Ewing, John, representative, Perry Co. (1819), *186; contests election, 187.

Ewing, Nathaniel, presidential elector (1820), *3.

Ewing, William G., representative, U. S. Congress (1847), 117; senator, Allen Co. etc. (1835), 227; (1838), *244.

Ewing, William G., representative, Perry Co. (1845), 295.

Eyestone, Jonathan, representative, Fayette Co. (1846), 303.

Fairchild, Ira A., representative, Vanderburgh Co. (1850), 350.

Fairman, Loyal, representative, Tippecanoe Co. (1833), *217.

Falley, Lewis, 52n.

Fallingsley, Joseph W., representative, Kosciusko Co. (1846), 305.

Fallis, Samuel, representative, Switzerland Co. (1833), 215.

Falls, Lewis, 286n.

Farley, Joseph F., representative, Putnam Co. (1839), *248; (1840), 254.

Farmer, Aaron, 20n.

Farmer, Eli P., representative, U. S. Congress (1845), 111-12; (1851), 124; senator, Monroe Co. (1836), 234; (1842), *271; representative (1840), 254; delegate, const. conv., 383.

Farmer, James H., representative, Putnam Co. (1842), 267; (1845), 295.
Farnsley, Joshua P., representative, Floyd Co. (1849), *336.
Farnsworth, William, representative, Tippecanoe Co. (1841), 260; (1846), 308.
Farquhar, John H., representative, Franklin Co. (1844), 280.
Farrington, James, representative, Vigo Co. etc. (1824), *193; (1840) *255; senator Vigo Co. etc. (1831), *210.
Farrow, Alexander S., representative, Putnam Co. (1846), 307; (1851), 360; delegate, const. conv., *382.
Faught, Jacob C., representative, Hendricks Co. (1849), 337.
Favorite, Samuel, representative, Tippecanoe Co. (1846), 308.
Feeny, Hugh F., senator, Parke Co. (1832), *214.
Feezler, William, 180n.
Ferguson, Benjamin, representative, Clark Co. (1816), *183; (1817), *184; (1831), *208; (1832), *212; (1836), *231; (1837), *237.
Ferguson, John D., representative, Clark Co. (1845), *290; (1846), *302; senator (1847), 321.
Ferguson, John W., representative, Greene Co. (1848), 326.
Ferguson, Zachariah, representative, Wayne Co. (1818), *185; Union Co. (1832), *213; (1833), *217.
Ferris, Abram (or Abraham), representative, Dearborn Co. (1837), *236; (1838), 244n.
Ferris, Ezra, representative, U. S. Congress (1822), 77; U. S. Senator (1816), 127; senator, Dearborn Co. (1816), *183, 184n; representative, (1820), *187; (1821), *188; (1826), *196; (1830), *204; (1831), 208.
Ferry, Hugh, representative, Bartholomew Co. (1847), 313; (1849), 334.
Ferry, Lucian P., 52n; representative, Allen Co. (1843), *272.
Fields, Absalom, representative, Lawrence Co. (1833), *216.
Fields, Nathaniel, representative, Clark Co. (1838), *240.
Fifield, Thomas, representative, Lake and Porter cos. (1848), 328.
Fillmore, Millard, vice-president (1848), 58-62.
Finch, Aaron, representative, Tippecanoe Co. (1831), *209; (1832), *213; senator, Carroll and Clinton cos. (1837), *239.
Finch, Fabius M., representative, Johnson Co. (1839), *248; (1845), 293.
Finch, G. W., representative, Vanderburgh Co. (1843), 274.
Findley, Abel, lieutenant governor (1816), 159.
Findley, Hugh A., representative, Jackson Co. (1844), 281.
Finley, John, representative, U. S. Congress (1835), 91-92; (1845), 111; representative, Wayne Co. (1828), *201; (1829), *203; (1830), *205.
Finney, Thomas J., senator, Benton Co. etc. (1848), 332.
Fisher, Elwood, representative, Switzerland Co. (1838), 242; (1839), *247; (1840), 254.
Fisher, Jacob, delegate, const. conv., Clark Co. *381.
Fisher, John, 297n.
Fisher, Stearns, representative, Miami and Wabash cos. (1844), 283.
Fisk, Robert W., representative, Ripley Co. (1845), 295.
Fitch, Graham N., presidential elector (1844), *38-42; (1848), *53-57; representative, U. S. Congress (1849), *121; (1851), *125-26; representative, Cass Co. (1836), *231; (1837), 236; (1839), *246.
Fite, Andrew, representative, Clark Co. (1829), *202.
Fitzgerald, Thomas, representative, Vanderburgh and Warrick cos. (1825), *195; (1826), *197.
Flake, William, representative, Dearborn Co. (1831), *208.
Flannegan, Hugh C., representative, St. Joseph Co. (1842), *267.

Fleece, George, representative, Hendricks Co. (1850), *347.
Fleming, William C., delegate, const. conv., Madison Co., 379.
Fletcher, Calvin, senator, Marion Co. etc. (1826), *198, 198n; (1828), *201; (1831), *210; resignation (1833), 218n.
Flint, John, representative, Daviess Co. (1838), *242; Daviess and Martin (1839), *248.
Floyd, Davis, representative, U. S. Congress (1822), 74-75; U. S. Senator (1816), 127; (1820), 127; lieutenant governor (1816), 159; representative, Harrison Co. (1816), *183.
Foley, James B., delegate, const. conv., Decatur Co., *387.
Foley, James P., representative, U. S. Congress (1845), 111; representative, Hancock Co. (1841), *261; (1843), *275.
Folger, Jethro S., (?), representative, Rush Co. (1840), 254; (1849), 340.
Foos, Joseph, representative, La Grange and Noble cos. (1845), 294.
Foote, Andrew, representative, Parke Co. (1840), *256; (1841), 260.
Ford, John L., representative, Jackson Co. (1847), *316; (1848), *327; senator, Jackson and Scott cos. (1851), 363.
Ford, Lemuel, senator, Clark Co. (1838), 244.
Ford, Royston, representative, Randolph Co. (1843), *275; (1844), *284; (1845), *295.
Ford, William, senator, Jefferson Co. (1847), 322.
Foresman, Philip, representative, Tippecanoe Co. (1843), *275; (1844), *284.
Forsee, James, representative, Clinton and Tipton cos. (1848), 325.
Fosdick, Edward, representative, DeKalb Co. (1849), 342n.
Foster, John, senator, Grant Co. etc. (1839), *251; representative, Grant Co. (1845), 292.
Foster, John, representative, Hancock and Madison cos. (1833), *216; (1839), *248; Hancock (1851), *357.
Foster, William C., delegate, const. conv., Monroe Co., *382.
Foulke, William R., representative, Wayne Co. (1838), 242; (1841), *260; (1842), *266.
Fowler, William, representative, Decatur Co. (1832), *211; (1833), *215; senator, Decatur and Shelby cos. (1834), *223.
Fox, James, representative, Ohio Co. (1851), 362n.
Frame, William, representative, Rush Co. (1831), *209.
Francis, John, representative, La Porte Co. (1842), *266.
Franklin, William A., representative, Hancock Co. (1845), 292.
Franklin, William M., representative, Owen Co. (1849), 339; (1850), *351.
Frazier, James S., representative, Kosciusko Co. (1847), *316; (1848), *327.
Frazier, Samuel, representative, Marion Co. (1833), 215.
Free Soil party, votes received by candidates for governor, xxiv, 155-58; in presidential election (1848), xxiv, 63-67.
Freeland, John T., representative, Knox Co. (1851), 358.
Freeland, Richard, representative, Dearborn Co. (1847), 314.
Freeman, James S., representative, Greene Co. (1840), *255; Vigo Co. (1849), 341.
Frelinghuysen, Theodore, vice-president (1844), 43-47.
French, William M., representative, Ohio and Switzerland cos. (1851), 359.
Frink, Pratt, representative, Parke Co. (1841), *260.
Frisbie, Alpha, representative, Warrick Co. (1839), *249; (1848), 331.
Frisbie, Samuel, representative, Perry Co. etc. (1828), *201; senator,

(1830), *207; delegate, const. conv., *380.

Frost, William, 298n.

Frush, J., 67n.

Fry, Francis H., representative, Montgomery Co. (1844), *283; (1846), *306.

Fryer, John, Sr., representative Dearborn Co. (1833), 217n.

Fuller, Benjamin P., representative, Clark Co. (1850), 345.

Fuller, Isham, representative, Warrick Co. (1842), *269; (1843), *276; (1844), *285; (1845), *297; (1846), *309; (1847), *320; (1849), 341; (1851), 361.

Gaddes, James, representative, Putnam Co. (1834), *221; (1837), *238.

Gail, Thomas, 52n.

Gaines, Henry T., representative, Shelby Co. (1845), 296.

Gale, George, representative, La Grange and Noble cos. (1847), 316.

Gale, Thomas, representative, De Kalb Co. etc. (1836), *231.

Galletly, James, representative, Greene and Owen cos. (1830), *206.

Gannon, William, representative, Vigo Co. (1841), 260.

Gard, William, representative, Switzerland Co. (1824), *193; (1825), *195.

Gardiner, John B., representative, Posey Co. (1845), 295.

Gardner, ——, representative, Putnam Co. (1833), 215.

Gardner, John, representative, Vermillion and Parke cos. (1829), *203; (1830), *206; Vermillion Co. (1831), *209; (1839), *249.

Gardner, Stephen B., representative, Vermillion Co. (1835), *226.

Garrett, Caleb, representative, Vigo Co. (1843), *276; (1844), *285.

Garrigus, Jeptha, representative, Parke Co. (1837), *238; (1839), *248; (1841), *260.

Garrigus, Timothy L., representative, Wayne Co. (1843), 276.

Garst, George W., representative, Delaware Co. (1848), 325.

Garver, William, representative, Hamilton and Tipton cos. (1844), 281; senator, Hamilton Co. etc. (1848), *332.

Garvin, James, delegate, const. conv., Kosciusko Co., *382.

Gaskill, N., 297n.

Geddes, Robert, representative, Kosciusko Co. (1851), *358.

Geiger, Jacob, delegate, const. conv., Dubois Co., 379.

General Assembly, elections, x, xxi, xxii, xxiii; members: term of office, ix; number and apportionment, ix-x, 399-408; qualifications, x; time of meeting, x; transmission of election returns, xiv, 286n. *See also* Senate.

Gentry, Allen, representative, Spencer Co. (1845), 296.

Gentry, Lemuel, representative, Monroe Co. (1849), *335; (1850), *349.

Gentry, Martin W., representative, Clinton and Tipton cos. (1850), 345.

Gentry, Zachariah B., representative, Clinton and Tipton cos. (1847), 314; Clinton Co. (1851), 355.

George, Jehu, delegate, const. conv., Warren Co. 381.

George, William, representative, Carroll Co. (1841), 258, 262n.

Gessie, Robert J., representative, Vermillion Co. (1848), *330; (1849), *341; (1850), 350.

Geyer, William S., 298n.

Gibson, Joseph, representative, Clark Co. (1820), *187.

Gibson, Thomas W., representative, Clark Co. (1851), *355; delegate, const. conv., *381.

Gilbert, Goldsmith C., representative, Delaware Co. (1841), *261; (1842), *268; (1843), *274.

Gilbert, John, presidential elector (1844), *38-42.

Gilleece, James, representative, Huntington and Whitley cos. (1846), *304.

Gillespie, Matthew, representative, Scott Co. (1847), 319.

Gillum, John W., representative, Crawford and Orange cos. (1848), *325; delegate, const. conv., 384.

Gird, Edward, representative, Shelby Co. (1836), *232.

Givens, Thomas, presidential elector (1832), *14-16; senator, Posey Co. etc. (1824), *194; (1827), *200; (1830), *207.

Glass, John, representative, Ripley Co. (1838), *243.

Glazebrook, Bradford, representative, Putnam Co. (1851), *360.

Glazebrook, Loyd, representative, Putnam Co. (1849), 340.

Glenn, Alexander E., representative, Dearborn Co. (1837), *236.

Glover, Joseph, representative, Lawrence Co. (1822), *190.

Goble, Isaac, 298n.

Godley, John, representative, Dearborn Co. (1851), 355.

Goldsberry, Peter, representative, Tippecanoe Co. (1848), *330; (1849), 341.

Goodbar, John H., representative, Clinton and Montgomery cos. (1832), *211; senator (1834), 222.

Goodhue, James, representative, Scott Co. (1828), *201; Jennings Co. (1841), *261.

Gooding, David S., representative, Hancock Co. (1845), 292; (1847), *315.

Goodlet, James R. E., representative, U. S. Congress (1833), 87; representative, Spencer Co. etc. (1839), 250.

Goodman, Benjamin T., representative, Dubois Co. (1846), 303; (1847), *314; senator, Dubois Co. etc. (1850), *353.

Goodman, William, representative, Vigo Co. (1850), *351.

Goodnow, Samuel, representative, Jefferson Co. (1840), *253; (1841), *259; (1842), *266; senator (1844), *287; (1847), *322.

Goodsell, ——, representative, Vanderburgh Co. (1842), 267.

Goodwin, Benjamin, representative, Daviess and Martin cos. (1848), *325; (1849), *335; (1850), *346.

Gookins, Miles, representative, Vermillion Co. (1833), *217; (1836), 231.

Gookins, Samuel B., representative, Vigo Co. (1851), *361.

Gootee, Thomas, representative, Daviess and Martin cos. (1845), 290; delegate, const. conv. (Martin Co.), *382.

Gordon, George A., delegate, const. conv., Cass and Howard cos., *378.

Gordon, Robert M., representative, Wayne Co. (1846), *309; (1847), *320.

Gorman, Willis A., representative, U. S. Congress (1849), *120; (1851), *124; representative, Monroe Co. (1839), 247; Brown and Monroe (1841), *261; (1842), *268; (1843), *274.

Goudie, James, representative, Franklin Co. (1818), *185; (1820), *187.

Goudie, Samuel, representative, Franklin Co. (1848), 326.

Goudy, Adam M. C., representative, Jasper and Pulaski cos. (1851), *357; delegate, const. conv., 378.

Governors, term, ix; succession in office, ix; list of, 395.

Graff, George B., representative, Gibson Co. (1850), *347.

Graham, Christopher C., representative, Vanderburgh and Warrick cos. (1835), *227; Warrick Co. (1836), *232; (1837), *238; (1838), *244; (1840), *256; (1841), *262; senator, Warrick Co. etc. (1848), *333; delegate, const. conv., *381.

Graham, James C., representative, Pike Co. (1847), *318; (1848), 329; (1851), *359.

Graham, Johiel, representative, Delaware Co. (1846), 303.

Graham, John A., representative, Miami and Wabash cos. (1849), 339;

delegate, const. conv. (Miami Co.), *380.

Graham, John K., representative, Clark Co. (1816), *183; (1824), *193; Floyd Co. (1827), *198; senator, Clark and Floyd cos. (1825), *195, 196n.

Graham, John W., representative, Spencer Co. (1848), *330; (1849), 340, 342n.

Graham, William, representative, U. S. Congress (1837), 94-95; (1839), 98; representative, Jackson Co. (1816), *183; (1817), *184; (1818), *185; (1819), *186; (1820), *187; senator, Jackson Co. etc. (1821), *189, 189n; (1824), *194; (1827), *199; (1830), *207.

Granger, Francis, vice-president, 21-24.

Grass, Daniel, senator, Warrick Co. etc. (1816), *183, 184n; (1821), *189, 189n; (1822), *190; (1824), *94; representative, Warrick Co. (1819), *186; (1820), *187.

Grave, Pusey, senator, Wayne Co. (1841), 264; representative (1843), 276n.

Graves, William C., representative, Kosciusko Co. (1849), *338.

Gray, D. W., 67n.

Gray, Henry L., senator Ripley Co. (1850), 354.

Gray, John, senator, Dearborn Co. (1819), *186; (1822), *190.

Gray, Jonathan, representative, Rush Co. (1845), 295.

Gray, Moses, representative, Scott Co. (1825), *195; (1826), *197.

Greathouse, William R., representative, Vanderburgh Co. (1849), *341.

Green, George S., representative, Posey Co. (1834), *221.

Green, Henry, representative, Harrison Co. (1820), *187; Crawford Co. (1821), *187; (1822), *189.

Green, Martin R., senator, Switzerland Co. (1837), *239; (1840), 257; Ohio and Switzerland (1846), *312.

Green, Richard, representative, La-Grange and Noble cos. (1848), 328.

Green, Thomas, representative, Washington Co. (1846), *308; (1847), 320.

Greene, George, representative, Clark Co. (1845), 290.

Greenman, Anson, representative, Noble Co. (1846), 306.

Greer, ——, delegate, const. conv., Adams and Wells cos., 378.

Gregg, James V., senator, Hendricks Co. (1848), 333.

Gregg, John, senator, Posey and Vanderburgh cos. (1847), 322.

Gregg, Joseph V., representative, Wayne Co. (1834), 220; (1835), 226.

Gregg, Milton, 105n; presidential elector (1848), 58-62; representative, Dearborn Co. (1835), *224; delegate, const. conv., Jefferson Co. *385.

Gregory, James, representative, U. S. Congress (1835), 92-93; lieutenant governor (1831), 164-65; senator, Washington Co. etc. (1820), *187; succeeded, 190n; senator, Shelby Co. etc. (1823), *192; (1825), *196; (1828), *201; Warren Co. etc. (1836), 234; representative, Warren Co. (1834), *221; (1837), *237; (1838), *243.

Gregory, Leroy, representative, Warren Co. (1843), *276; (1844), *285.

Gregory, Robert C., senator, Montgomery Co. (1841), *264; delegate, const. conv., Tippecanoe Co., 386.

Griffin, William B., representative, Johnson Co. (1847), 316.

Griffis, James, representative, Randolph Co. (1846), *307.

Griffith, Andrew C., senator, Jackson Co. etc. (1833), *218

Griffitt, Reuben, representative, Morgan Co. (1848), 329; (1850), 349.

Griggs, Algernon S., senator, Morgan Co. (1844), 288.

Griggs, David, representative, Crawford Co. (1831), *208.

Grim, John, representative, Adams and Wells cos. (1849), 334.

Grimes, John M., representative, Posey Co. (1849), 340.

Grimsley, Silas, 126n.

Griswold, William D., representative, Vigo Co. (1845), 297; delegate, const. conv., 381.

Grose, William, representative, Henry Co. (1844), 281.

Grover, Jeremiah, representative, Union Co. (1831), *209.

Grover, Joel, representative, Adams Co. etc. (1836), 229.

Grover, Nicholas D., senator, Cass Co. etc. (1837), 239; representative, Cass Co. (1838), 240; (1839), 246; (1841), *258.

Groves, James A., representative, Hamilton and Tipton cos. (1845), 292.

Grubbs, John W., representative, Henry Co. (1844), *281.

Guard, David, representative, Dearborn Co. (1833), *215; (1834), 219; (1836), *229.

Guion, Thomas, representative, Dearborn Co. (1825), *194; (1829), *202; (1830), 204; (1833), *215; (1836), 233n.

Gunkle, J. P., representative, Wayne Co. (1833), 217.

Gunn, Thomas S., representative, Harrison Co. (1851), *357.

Guston, John C., representative, Madison Co. (1851), 358.

Hacker, William, representative, Shelby Co. (1846), 307.

Hackett, Henry W., senator, Washington Co. (1834), *223, 223n; (1835), *228; (1838), *245.

Hackleman, Pleasant A., representative, U. S. Congress (1847), 114-15; representative, Rush Co. (1841), *260.

Hackleman, Robert, representative, Rush Co. (1834), 220.

Hadden, William R., representative, Sullivan Co. (1837), *238; (1839), *249; (1840), 254; delegate, const. conv., Sullivan Co. etc., *384.

Hage, Zenas K. M., representative, Monroe Co. (1850), 349.

Haigh, Jacob, representative, Tippecanoe Co. (1847), 320n.

Haines, Levi, representative, Hamilton Co. (1849), 337.

Haines, Matthias, representative, Dearborn Co. (1831), 208; (1832), 211.

Halbert, Silas L., representative, Martin Co. etc. (1843), *274.

Hall, Colbrath, representative, Warren Co. (1845), *297; (1846), *308; (1847), 319; delegate, const. conv., 381.

Hall, Horace H., representative, Elkhart Co. (1847), *314.

Hall, Jacob R., representative, La Porte Co. (1849), 338; (1850), 348.

Hall, John, representative, Posey Co. (1846), *307; (1847), 318; (1850), *349.

Hall, Joseph, representative, Madison Co. (1850), 348.

Hall, Richard R., representative, Hendricks Co. (1849), 337.

Hall, Samuel, U. S. Senator, (1838), 132-33; lieutenant governor (1840), *170-72n; representative, Gibson Co. (1829), *202; (1830), *206; (1845), *292; delegate, const. conv., *379.

Hall, Samuel, representative, Ripley Co. (1846), 307.

Hall, Samuel D., representative, Kosciusko Co. (1849), 338.

Hall, William S., representative, Rush Co. (1847), 318.

Halsey, James, representative, Franklin Co. (1834), 219.

Hamell, Jeremiah, representative, Lake and Porter cos. (1837), *236.

Hamer, Hugh, representative, Lawrence Co. (1839), *248; (1840), *255; senator, (1844), *287.

Hamilton, Alexander, representative, Floyd Co. (1849), 336.

Hamilton, Allen, delegate, const. conv., Allen Co., *378.

Hamilton, Harrison, representative, Vigo Co. (1841), 260.

Hamilton, James, representative, Jackson Co. (1829), *203; (1830), *206; (1832), *213.

Hamilton, John, senator, Fountain Co. (1834), *223.

Hamilton, John R., representative, Jackson Co. (1849), 337; (1850), *348; (1851), 357.

Hamilton, Philander, representative, Decatur Co. (1846), *309; (1847), *320.

Hamlin, Eliakim, representative, Bartholomew and Brown cos. (1839), *247.

Hammond, Abraham A., representative, Marion Co. (1851), 358.

Hammond, Elijah, representative, Pike Co. (1844), 284.

Hammond, H. C., U. S. Senator (1832), 129-30.

Hammond, William M., representative, Spencer Co. (1844), 284.

Hammond, William P., representative, Morgan Co. (1850), *349.

Hamrick, Ambrose D., representative, Putnam Co. (1844), *284; senator (1845), *300; (1848), *334.

Handy, Augustus C., representative, Shelby Co. (1843), *275; (1844), *284; senator (1845), *300.

Handy, Henry S., 84n.

Hankins, David, representative, Fayette Co. (1830), *204.

Hankins, Thomas D., representative, Fayette Co. (1847), *314; (1848), *326.

Hanna, Albert G., representative, Carroll Co. (1836), *231; (1846), *301; (1850), 345; (1851), *355.

Hanna, James M., presidential elector (1848), *53-57, 67n; representative, Putnam Co. (1847), 318; senator, Clay Co. etc. (1849), *343.

Hanna, Joseph, representative, Franklin Co. (1820), *187; Union Co. (1827), *199, 200n.

Hanna, Robert, 87n, 143n; U. S. Senator (1831), *134n; (1832), 129; representative, Marion Co. (1830), 205; (1832), *212; (1835), 225; (1836), *230; (1837), *236; (1838), *242; senator (1840), *257; resignation (1841), 264n; senator (1846), 311; delegate, const. conv., 385.

Hanna, Samuel, representative, Allen Co. etc. (1826), *196; (1827), *198; (1831), *208; (1840), *251; senator (1832), *214; delegate, const. conv., 383.

Hannah, David G., representative, Franklin Co. (1844), *280.

Hannah, John, representative, Hendricks Co. (1831), 208.

Hannah, Samuel, representative, Wayne Co. (1825), *195; (1843), *274.

Hannaman, Robert L., representative, Boone Co. etc. (1833), 215; (1834), *220; (1835), *226.

Hannaman, William, senator, Marion Co. (1841), 263.

Hannegan, Edward A., representative, U. S. Congress (1833), *89-90; (1835), *92-93; (1840 special), 101; U. S. Senator (1843), *134; (1848), 134; representative, Fountain Co. (1832), *213; (1841), *261; (1851), 356.

Hansell, John, 105n.

Harbolt, Jonathan, delegate, const. conv., Benton Co. etc., *378.

Hardesty, Rees, representative, Putnam Co. (1833), *215; (1834), *221.

Hardin, Franklin, representative, Johnson Co. (1842), *268; (1843), *275; (1844), *282; senator (1845), *300; (1848), *333; delegate, const. conv., *382.

Hardin, Granfill W., representative, Vanderburgh Co. (1851), 361.

Harding, Israel, representative, Marion Co. (1840), *253; (1841), *260.

Harding, Joseph S., 155n.

Harding, Samuel, representative, Marion Co. (1846), *306; (1847), *317; (1848), 328.

Harding, Stephen S., 118n; presidential elector (1844), 48-52; (1848), 67n; representative, U. S. Congress

Harding, Stephen S. (Cont.) (1847), 114-15; lieutenant governor (1843), 173-75; (1846), 175-78n.

Hargrove, John, representative, Gibson Co. (1831), *209; (1832), *213; (1833), *216; (1834), *221; (1842), *265; senator (1838), *245.

Harlan, Andrew J., presidential elector (1848), *53-57; representative, U. S. Congress (1849), *121-22; senator, Delaware and Grant cos. (1845), 299; representative (1846), *304; Grant Co. (1847), *315; (1848), *326.

Harmon, Jacob, representative, Dubois Co. (1851), 356.

Harney, James F., representative, Montgomery Co. (1849), *339.

Harrah, Daniel, *see* Harrow.

Harris, ———, representative, Putnam Co. (1835), 225.

Harris, Daniel, representative, Greene Co. etc. (1824), *193; Clay Co. (1834), *221; (1835), *226.

Harris, George S., senator, St. Joseph Co. etc. (1845), 299; representative, St. Joseph Co. (1847), 318.

Harris, Horatio J., senator, Carroll and Clinton cos. (1840), *258.

Harris, J., 320n.

Harris, Obadiah, representative, Marion Co. (1842), 266; (1843), *273; (1845), 294.

Harris, Pleasant, senator, Allen Co. etc. (1832), 214; representative, La Porte and St. Joseph cos. (1834), 220.

Harris, Thomas E., representative, Montgomery Co. (1850), *349.

Harris, Thomas G., representative, Elkhart Co. (1842), 265; (1846), 303; senator, Elkhart and La Grange (1847), 321, 323n.

Harrison, Allen, representative, Montgomery Co. (1847), 317.

Harrison, Carah W., representative, Hamilton Co. (1846), 304.

Harrison, Christopher, 145n; presidential elector (1824), 8-9; governor (1819), 137-38; lieutenant governor (1816), *xii, 159; (1819), 160n.

Harrison, David, representative, Jackson Co. (1846), 309n.

Harrison, Elisha, lieutenant governor (1825), 161-62n; representative, Warrick Co. (1818), *185; senator, Warrick Co. etc. (1819), *186, 186n; (1821), *189.

Harrison, James H., representative, Montgomery Co. (1843), *275.

Harrison, Joshua, representative, Montgomery Co. (1840), *255.

Harrison, William Henry, president (1836), *xxii, 21-24; (1840), *xxiii, 29-32.

Harrison, William M., representative, Lake and Porter cos. (1850), *348; Porter Co. (1851), *359.

Harrison, William R., representative, Morgan Co. (1851), 359.

Harrod, John, representative, Scott Co. (1831), *209. *See also* Herrod.

Harrow, Daniel, representative, Putnam Co. (1835), *225; (1840), *254.

Hart, ———, senator, Johnson Co. (1851), 363.

Hart, Daniel A., representative, Shelby Co. (1847), 319.

Hart, Gideon B., representative, Bartholomew Co. (1849), *334.

Hart, Hiram A., representative, Ripley Co. (1851), *360.

Harvey, Jonathan S., representative, Hendricks Co. (1845), *293; (1846), *304; (1847), *315; senator (1848), *333.

Harvey, Thomas, representative, Hamilton Co. (1849), *337.

Hatfield, Andrew F., representative, Hancock Co. (1846), *304.

Hatfield, Job, representative, Perry Co. (1848), 329; senator, Perry Co. etc. (1851), *364.

Hauser, Frederick, representative, Owen Co. (1844), *283.

Hawkins, John, presidential elector (1832), 17-20.

Hawkins, Joseph C., representative, Wayne Co. (1837), *236.

Hawkins, Nathan B., representative, Adams Co. etc. (1840), 251; (1842), *265; (1844), 278; delegate, Blackford Co. etc., *383.

Hawkins, William, representative, Tippecanoe Co. (1850), 350.

Hawley, Abijah, representative, Fulton and Marshall cos. (1844), 281; (1845), 292.

Haworth, Saban, representative, Union Co. (1847), 319; (1850), 350.

Hay, Andrew J., representative, Clark Co. (1850), 345; (1851), *355.

Hay, Andrew P., representative, Clark Co. (1819), *186; (1820), *187.

Hay, George D., representative, Knox Co. (1847), 316.

Hayden, Nehemiah, representative, Rush Co. (1849), 340.

Hayes, Joseph M., representative, U. S. Congress (1833), 89-90; representative, Parke and Vermillion cos. (1826), *197; senator, Parke Co. (1831), *210, 211n.

Hayes, Solomon, representative, Benton and White cos. (1851), *355.

Haymond, Rufus, 170n; representative, Franklin Co. (1836), *229; (1837), *237.

Haynes, Jacob M., representative, Blackford and Jay cos. (1848), 324.

Haywood, C., 309n.

Haywood, Henry, representative, Rush Co. (1850), *350.

Hayworth, James, representative, Marion Co. (1847), 317.

Hazelrigg, Harvey G., representative, Boone Co. (1844), *279; (1845), *289; senator, Boone Co. etc. (1848), 332.

Headley, James, representative, Parke Co. (1844), 283.

Healey, Jesse H., representative, Henry Co. (1838), *243.

Heaston, David, representative, Randolph Co. (1850), 350.

Heath, Robert, 113n.

Heath, Samuel S., representative, Scott Co. (1836), *232.

Heaton, William, representative, Tippecanoe Co. (1831), *209.

Hedrick, Bela, representative, Switzerland Co. (1837), 236.

Helm, Jefferson, delegate, const. conv., Rush Co., *382.

Helmer, Melchert, representative, Lawrence Co. (1837), *237; (1838), *243; (1851), *358; delegate, const. conv., *382.

Helwig, Jacob, representative, De Kalb and Steuben cos. (1843), *272; (1844), *280.

Henderson, Richard, representative, Wayne Co. (1831), *209; Henry Co. (1836), *232.

Henderson, Samuel, presidential elector (1832), 17-20.

Henderson, William, representative, Adams and Wells cos. (1849), 334.

Hendricks, Abram, representative, Decatur Co. (1838), *242.

Hendricks, John, representative, Johnson and Shelby cos. (1830), 204; Shelby Co. (1841), *262; senator (1845), 300.

Hendricks, John A., representative, Jefferson Co. (1849), 337; (1851), *357.

Hendricks, John A., representative, St. Joseph Co. (1837), *238.

Hendricks, Thomas, representative, Decatur Co. etc. (1823), *191; (1824), *193; Decatur Co. (1827), *198; (1828), *200; (1829), *202; (1830), *206; senator, Decatur and Shelby cos. (1831), *210.

Hendricks, Thomas A., representative, U. S. Congress (1851), *124; representative, Shelby Co. (1848), *330; delegate, const. conv., Shelby Co., *386.

Hendricks, William, presidential elector (1840), 33-36, 37n; representative, U. S. Congress (1816), *xii, xvii, 71; (1817), *xix, 71-72; (1818), *xix, 72-73; (1820), *xix, 73-74; resignation, 75n; U. S. Senator (1825), *xix, 127; (1830), *xx, 128; (1836), xxii, 131; (1838), 132-

Hendricks, William (Cont.) 33; (1843), 134; governor (1822), *138, 395.

Hendricks, William, Jr., representative, Jefferson Co. (1846), *305; senator (1848), *323n.

Henkle, Benjamin, representative, Tippecanoe Co. (1834), *221; senator, Benton Co. etc. (1848), 332.

Henkle, Wesley, representative, Tippecanoe Co. (1846), 308.

Henley, Thomas J., presidential elector, 33-36; representative, U. S. Congress (1843), *106; (1845), *110; (1847), *114; representative, Clark Co. (1831), *208; (1832), *212; (1837), *237; (1838), 240; (1839), *248; (1840), *225; (1841), *261; (1842), *268.

Henning, Matthew, representative, Scott Co. (1845), 296; (1850), 350.

Henry, David, senator, Switzerland Co. (1843), *277; election contested, 278n; (1844), *288.

Henry, Francis, representative, La Grange Co. (1851), *358.

Henry, George, representative, Hancock Co. (1844), 281; (1845), *292.

Henry, James H., senator, Clay Co. etc. (1846), *310.

Henton, Benjamin, representative, Fulton and Miami cos. (1840), 252; Miami and Wabash cos. (1845), *294; senator (1850), *353.

Herod, William, presidential elector (1840), *29-32; representative, U. S. Congress (special, 1837), 93; (1837), *96; (1839), 99-100; (1849), 119-20; representative, Bartholomew Co. (1829), *202n; (1830), *205; senator, Bartholomew and Johnson cos. (1831), *210, 211n; resignation (1833), 218n; representative, Bartholomew Co. (1844), *278; senator, Bartholomew and Jennings cos. (1848), *332.

Herriman, David B., representative, De Kalb Co. etc. (1837), *237; (1838), *241; (1839), *246; senator (1841), *263, 264n; (1843), *276; representative, La Grange and Noble cos. (1848), 328; delegate, Noble Co., 380.

Herriott, Samuel, senator, Johnson Co. (1839), *251.

Herrod, Andrew, representative, Delaware Co. (1846), 303.

Herron, Samuel, representative, Montgomery Co. (1845), *294; (1851), 359.

Hervey, James W., representative, Hancock Co. (1847), 315.

Hester, Craven P., representative, Monroe Co. (1830), 205; (1836), 230.

Hester, George K., representative, Scott Co. (1848), 330.

Hester, James S., senator, Brown and Monroe cos. (1851), *363.

Hester, Uriah A. V., representative, Owen Co. (1851), 359.

Hetfield, Solomon, representative, Fountain Co. (1847), *315, 320n; senator (1841), *264, 265n.

Heustis, George, representative, Dearborn and Ohio cos. (1845), 298n.

Heustis, Oliver, representative, Dearborn Co. (1832), *211; (1833), 215; (1838), 244n; (1844), *280.

Hiatt, Alfred H., representative, Henry Co. (1845), 293.

Hiatt, Allen, representative, Wayne Co. (1840), *256; (1842), *267.

Hiatt, Eleazar, representative, Wayne Co. (1824), *194.

Hicklin, James, representative, Jennings Co. (1844), 282.

Hickman, Ezekial T., senator, Henry Co. (1851), *363.

Hicks, Edward P., representative, Jennings Co. (1851), *358.

Hicks, Gilderoy, representative, Johnson Co. (1846), *305; (1848), *331; (1849), *338; (1850), *351; senator (1851), *363.

Hicks, Joshua, representative, Switzerland Co. (1835), 225.

High, Isaac, 298n.

Hill, Allen, representative, Jennings Co. (1845), *293; (1846), *305.

Hill, Asaph, senator, Jasper Co. etc. (1836), 234.

Hill, Daniel, representative, Randolph Co. (1846), 307; (1847), 318; (1851), 360.

Hill, Henry B., representative, Rush Co. (1849), *340.

Hill, James, representative, Clinton Co. (1844), *279; (1845), 297n; Clinton and Tipton cos. (1848), *325.

Hill, Jesse P., representative, Sullivan Co. (1845), 296; (1848), 332n.

Hill, Parley, representative, Jennings Co. (1845), 293; (1846), 305; (1848), 327.

Hill, Robert, representative, Wayne Co. (1817), *184; (1819), *186; (1822), *190; (1823), *192.

Hillis, ———, representative, Putnam Co. (1840), 254.

Hillis, David, lieutenant governor (1837), *168-70; representative, Jefferson Co. (1823), *191; (1824), *193; (1825), *195; (1826), *197; (1828), *201; (1829), *203; (1830), *204; (1831), 208; (1842), *266; (1844), 281; senator (1832), *214; (1835), *228.

Hillis, Jefferson D., representative, Warren Co. (1847), 319.

Hillis, William C., representative, Jefferson Co. (1849), *337.

Hinchman, James, representative, Rush Co. (1844), *284; (1845), *295.

Hinds, James W., representative, Jefferson Co. (1841), 262n.

Hiner, Joseph, representative, Bartholomew Co. (1849), 334.

Hinkson, William, representative, Dearborn and Ohio cos. (1844), 280.

Hite, John, representative, Monroe Co. (1830), 205.

Hite, William, representative, Monroe Co. (1831), *209.

Hitt, Willis W., delegate, const. conv., Knox Co., *382.

Hoagland, Isaac, representative, Scott Co. (1834), *221; senator, Jackson and Scott cos. (1836), *235.

Hobbs, Joshua T., representative, La Grange Co. etc. (1838), 241; (1843), *273.

Hocker, Joseph E., representative, Boone Co. (1837), *237.

Hodge, James, senator, Grant and Delaware cos. (1842), *270; representative, Delaware Co. (1848), 325.

Hodges, John, representative, Vigo Co. (1841), *260; (1842), *269; (1843), *276; (1844), *285; (1845), 297; (1847), 319; delegate, const. conv., 381.

Hogan, Edmund, representative, Gibson Co. (1816), *183; death, 184n.

Hoggatt, Lucian Q., representative, Lawrence Co. (1844), *282.

Hogin, Benoni C., delegate, const. conv., Grant Co., *382.

Hogue, Thomas, 67n.

Holaday (Holliday), William, delegate, const. conv., Orange Co., *380; resignation, 383n.

Holcomb, Silas M., representative, Gibson Co. (1847), 315; (1849), *336; (1851), 356.

Holden, Cephas S., representative, Vigo Co. (1846), 308; (1847), *319.

Holderman, A., representative, Miami Co. (1842), 266.

Holladay, Elias G., representative, Parke Co. (1851), *359.

Holland, George, representative, Franklin Co. (1839), 246.

Holland, Horatio N., representative, Scott Co. (1846), *307.

Holliday (Holiday), Joseph, representative, Blackford and Jay cos. (1846), 301; (1847), *313, 320n; (1851), 355.

Hollingsworth, Ira, representative, Grant Co. (1845), 292.

Holloway, David P., presidential elector (1848), 58-62; representative, Wayne Co. (1843), *274; senator (1844), *288; (1847), *323; (1850), *354.

Holloway, George, senator, Fulton Co. etc. (1846), 311.

Holman, George, representative, Wayne Co. (1837), 238n.

Holman, George W., representative, Miami Co. (1846), *306; Miami and Wabash cos. (1847), 317.

Holman, Jesse L., presidential elector (1816), *3; (1824), *8-9; (1848), 67n; U. S. Senator (1816), 127; (1820), 127; (1831), 128.

Holman, Jesse L., representative, Ripley Co. (1848), 329.

Holman, Joseph, representative, Wayne Co. (1816), *183; (1817), *184; (1819), *186; (1820), *187; (1821), *188; Allen and Cass cos. (1830), *205; Fulton and Miami cos. (1839), 246; Wayne Co. (1845), 297; (1848), 331; delegate, const. conv., 386.

Holman, William S., representative, Dearborn Co. (1851), *355; delegate, const. conv., *387.

Holmes, Albert L., presidential elector (1844), 43-47; representative, U. S. Congress (1845), 112; representative, Carroll Co. (1839), 246.

Hon, Ulerick H., representative, Harrison Co. (1846), 304.

Hoobler, John, representative, Vermillion Co. (1836), *231; (1841), *260.

Hood, William N., representative, Allen Co. etc. (1833), 214; Fulton and Miami (1836), *232; (1837), *237.

Hose, A., 67n.

Hoover, Andrew, senator, Tippecanoe Co. (1846), 312.

Hoover, David, senator, Wayne Co. (1832), *214; (1838), 245; (1841), *264.

Hoover, Henry, representative, Wayne Co. (1824), *194; (1826), *197; (1829), *203; (1830), *205; (1831), *209; (1833), 216; (1837), 236; (1842), 267; senator (1835), 228; (1836), 234.

Hoover, Samuel, senator, Tippecanoe Co. (1840), *257; resignation (1842), 271n.

Hopkins, Eldrid (Eldridge), representative, Warrick Co. (1849), 341; (1850), 351.

Hopkins, Henry, representative, Dearborn Co. (1833), 217n.

Hopkins, R., representative, Jefferson Co. (1830), 204.

Hornaday, Moses, senator, Dearborn Co. (1837), 239.

Horton, Elijah, representative, Kosciusko Co. (1847), 316; delegate, const. conv., 385.

Hosbrook, Percy, representative, Marion Co. (1850), *349.

Hostetler, Abraham J., representative, Lawrence Co. (1850), 348.

Hostetter, Henry, representative, Vermillion Co. (1843), *274; (1844), 285; (1851), *361.

Hostetter, Sherman, representative, Montgomery Co. (1846), *306; (1848), 328; (1850), 349.

Houghman, Gabriel, representative, Parke Co. (1850), *351.

Houghton, Aaron, representative, Martin Co. (1840), *255; senator, Daviess and Martin cos. (1844), 288n; (1847), *321.

House (Housh), Andrew, 20n.

Housman, John, representative, Huntington and Whitley cos. (1846), 304.

Hovey, Alvin P., representative, Posey Co. (1846), 307; delegate, const. conv., *382.

Howard, Noble P., representative, Hancock Co. (1849), 337.

Howard, Samuel, representative, Switzerland Co. (1841), *262.

Howard, Thomas, representative, Dearborn Co. (1832), 211; (1834), *219; (1835), *224.

Howard, Thomas J., representative, Clark Co. (1844), *279.

Howard, Tilghman A., 52n; presidential elector (1840), 33-36; representative, U. S. Congress (1839), *100; resignation, 101n; U. S. Senator (1832), 129; (1836), 131; (1838), 132-33; (1843), 134; governor (1840), xxiii, 148-50n.

Howe, John B., representative, La Grange Co. etc. (1840), *252; (1851), 358; senator (1841), 263; delegate, const. conv. *382.

Howe, Thornton F., representative, Franklin Co. (1850), 347.

Howe, William, delegate, const. conv., Ohio and Switzerland cos., 386.

Howell, George S., representative, Blackford and Jay cos. (1848), *324.

Howell, Mason J., representative, Spencer and Perry cos. (1832), *213; (1833), *216; (1834), *221; (1835), *227; Spencer Co. (1836), *232; senator, Spencer Co. etc. (1845), *300.

Howk, Isaac, representative, U. S. Congress (1831), 85-86; representative, Clark Co. (1822), *189; (1825) *194; (1826), *196; (1827), *198; (1828), *200; (1829), *201; (1830), *205; speaker of the House, xx.

Howland, John D., senator, Franklin Co. (1849), 343.

Howland, Powell, representative, Marion Co. (1848), 328.

Hoyt, ———, 298n.

Hubbard, Aaron, senator, Jackson and Scott cos. (1848), 333; representative, Scott Co. (1851), 360.

Hubbard, Asahel W., senator, Rush Co. (1847), *323.

Hubbard, Butler, representative, Henry Co. (1850), *347.

Hubbard, Richard J., representative, Wayne Co. (1835), *226; (1836), *231; (1837), *236; (1838), *242; Henry Co. (1848), 327.

Huckeby, Joshua B., representative, Perry Co. (1836), *232; (1842), *269; (1844), *283; (1846), 307; (1850), 349.

Huckleberry, John C., representative, Clark Co. (1835), *226; (1848), *324.

Huddleston, Robert J., representative, Henry Co. (1843), *275.

Hudelson, James, representative, Gibson Co. (1848), 326.

Hudelson, John M., representative, Rush Co. (1846), *307; (1847), *318; (1848), *330.

Hudson, Robert N., representative, Vigo Co. (1850), 351; (1851), *361.

Huey, Joseph, representative, Vanderburgh Co. (1843), 274.

Huey, Robert, representative, Adams and Jay cos. (1844), *278; Blackford and Jay cos. (1847), 313; (1849), *334; Jay Co. (1851), *362.

Huff, Samuel A., 126n; presidential elector (1848), 63-67; representative, Tippecanoe Co. (1837), *238; senator (1849), 344.

Huff, William, representative, De Kalb and Steuben cos. (1847), 314.

Huff, Wilson, representative, Spencer Co. (1845), *296; (1846), *307; delegate, const. conv., *380.

Huffstetter, David S., representative, Crawford and Orange cos. (1846), *302; senator (1847), *321; representative, Orange Co. (1851), *359.

Hughes, ———, representative, Allen Co. etc. (1833), 214.

Hughes, Lawson B., representative, Fountain Co. (1833), *216.

Hughes, Roland, representative, Benton Co. etc. (1848), *324.

Hughes, William, 52n.

Hull, Fabius, representative, Jefferson Co. (1846), *305; (1847), *316.

Hull, Matthew R., presidential elector (1844), 48-52; representative, U. S. Congress (1845), 111; senator, Fayette and Union cos. (1836), 233; (1846), 311; representative, Fayette Co. (1839), *248.

Humphreys, Andrew, representative, Greene Co. (1849), *337; (1850), *347; (1851), *356.

Hunt, Franklin W., representative, La Porte Co. (1846), *305; (1847), *316; (1848), *328; (1851), *358.

Hunt, John, senator, Hancock and Madison cos. (1850), *353.

Hunt, John, Jr., representative, Jefferson Co. (1838), 241; (1839), *248; (1840), 253.

Hunt, Miles, representative, Randolph Co. (1838), *243; (1839), *249.

Hunt, Nathaniel, representative, Jefferson Co. (1817), *184; (1818), *185; (1822), *190.

Hunt, Smith, representative, Wayne Co. (1838), 242.

Hunter, Isaac W., representative, Marion Co. (1849), *338.

Huntington, Elisha M., representative, Vigo Co. (1831), *210n; (1832), *213; (1833), *217; (1835), *227.

Huntington, Nathaniel, representative, Vigo Co. (1827), *199; (1828), *201; death, 202n.

Huntington, Septim G., representative, Shelby Co. (1850), 350.

Hupp, Jacob K., representative, Marshall Co. (1846), 309n.

Hurlbut, Danforth A., representative, Kosciusko and Whitley cos. (1845), 293.

Hurlbut, Harris E., representative, St. Joseph Co. (1843), *275.

Hurst, Benjamin, representative, Harrison Co. (1824), *193; (1826), *197.

Hurst, Henry, representative, Clark Co. (1837), *237; (1838), *240.

Hussey, Curtis G., representative, Hendricks Co. etc. (1829), *203; senator (1833), 218.

Hussey, Seth, senator, Marshall Co. (1845), 300n.

Huston, Alexander, representative, Washington Co. (1823), *192; (1824), *194; (1830), 206n.

Huston, Samuel, representative, Washington Co. (1837), *238; (1841), 260.

Hutchen, C. W., representative, Franklin Co. (1834), 219; (1835), 224.

Hutchinson, Isaac, representative, Vanderburgh Co. (1850), *350; (1851), 361.

Hutton, Albert G., representative, Putnam Co. (1841), *262; senator (1842), 270; (1843), *277, 278n.

Hyatt, Meshack, representative, Ripley Co. (1843), *275.

Ide, Roger, presidential elector (1844), 48-52; (1848), 67n; representative, Dearborn and Ohio cos. (1844), 286n.

Indiana, formation of state government, ix.

Ingram, Andrew, representative, Tippecanoe Co. (1835), 225.

Innis, Alexander, representative, Rush Co. (1846), 307.

Irvin, John B., representative, Knox Co. (1848), 327.

Irwin, Benjamin, representative, Bartholomew Co. (1823), *191; (1824), *192; (1827), *198.

Isom, George, representative, Lawrence Co. (1850), *348.

Jack, Samuel, representative, Switzerland Co. (1829), *203.

Jackman, Henry, representative, Jefferson Co. (1848), *327.

Jackson, Alexander, representative, Wabash Co. (1846), 308.

Jackson, Andrew, president (1824), *xvii-xviii, 4-5; (1828), *xx, 10-11; (1832), *xx, 14-15.

Jackson, Andrew, senator, Hancock and Madison cos. (1844), *287.

Jackson, Caleb B., representative, Wayne Co. (1838), *242; (1839), *249.

Jackson, Carter T., representative, Hamilton and Tipton cos. (1845), *292; delegate, const. conv., Clinton and Tipton cos., 378.

Jackson, Enoch W., representative, Dearborn Co. (1837), *236; (1838), 240; (1839), 249n.

Jackson, Ezekiel, representative, Dearborn Co. (1822), *189; (1824), *192; (1825), *194; (1826), *196; (1827), *198.

Jackson, Jacob, representative, Jefferson Co. (1830), 204.

Jackson, Jesse, presidential elector (1836), 25-28; representative, Scott Co. (1824), *193; (1829), *203; (1835), *227; senator, Scott Co. etc. (1833), 218.

Jackson, John, representative, Elkhart Co. (1836), *231; (1842), *265; (1850), 346.

Jackson, John, representative, Vigo Co. (1826), *197.

Jackson, Lemuel C., representative, Delaware and Randolph cos. (1829), *202.

Jackson, Nathan, representative, U. S. Congress (1837), *96-97n.

Jackson, Newton I., representative, Clinton and Tipton cos. (1850), *345.

James, Enoch R., senator, Posey and Vanderburgh cos. (1847), *322; (1850), *354.

James, Henley, representative, Grant Co. (1846), 304.

James, Joseph, representative, Vigo Co. (1847), 320n.

James, Nathaniel J., representative, Vanderburgh Co. (1847), 319; (1848), *330.

James, Pinckney, representative, Dearborn Co. (1822), *189; (1836), *229; (1837), *236; (1843), *274.

Jameson, Samuel, representative, Miami Co. (1846), 306.

Jamison, John M., representative, Marion Co. (1844), *283.

Jamison, Martin, representative, Decatur Co. (1839), *248.

Janes, Lemuel C., representative, Jefferson Co. (1847), 316.

Jay, David, representative, Grant Co. (1849), 336.

Jelley, James S., representative, Ohio and Switzerland cos. (1847), 317.

Jelley, Samuel, representative, Dearborn Co. (1819), *186; (1823), *191.

Jenckes, John, senator, Vigo Co. etc. (1822), *190; representative, Vigo Co. (1830), 205.

Jenckes, Joseph S., representative, Vigo Co. (1839), *247; (1840), *255; (1841), 260; (1844), 285.

Jennings, Jonathan, representative, U. S. Congress (1822), *xviii-xix, 74-75, *76-77; (1824), *78-79; (1826), *81-82; (1828), *xx, 83-84; (1831), 85-86; U. S. Senator (1825), 127; (1826), 127; (1831), 128; governor (1816, 1819), *xii, xvi, 137-38; term of service, 395.

Jennison, Samuel, representative, Hamilton Co. (1846), *304.

Jernegan, Joseph L., 122n; presidential elector (1848), 63-67.

Jessup, Calvin A., representative, Hendricks Co. (1845), 293.

Jessup, Levi, senator, Boone Co. etc. (1831), *210, 211n.

Jewett, ———, representative, La Grange and Noble cos. (1843), 273.

Jewett, Alanson (Anson), senator, Benton Co. etc. (1851), 362.

Jewett (or Jerrett, Spencett), David, 20n.

Jewett, Luther, representative, Tippecanoe Co. (1845), 296.

John, Enoch D., representative, Franklin Co. (1819), *186; (1820), *187.

John, Robert, 298n.

Johnson, Charles M., representative, Vanderburgh and Warrick cos. (1827), *199.

Johnson, Chilion, representative, Montgomery Co. (1846), 306.

Johnson, Gideon, representative, Hendricks and Morgan cos. (1830), 204.

Johnson, Hadley D., representative, Franklin Co. (1846), 303.

Johnson, James, representative, Marion Co. (1838), *242; (1839), *247; delegate, const. conv., 380.

Johnson, Jeremiah, representative, Marion Co. (1834), *220.

Johnson, John, lieutenant governor (1816), 159.

Johnson, John, representative, Gibson Co. (1816), *183; (1818), *185; Pike Co. (1821), *188; (1822), *190; (1823), *192; (1824), *193; (1825), *195; Dubois and Pike (1826), *196; (1827), *198.

Johnson, John B., representative, Montgomery Co. (1847), 317.

Johnson, John D., representative, Dearborn Co. (1840), 256n; (1846),

Johnson, John D. (Cont.)
*303; (1848), *325; delegate, const. conv., *381.
Johnson, Joseph, representative, Grant Co. (1848), 326.
Johnson, Joseph, representative, Marion Co. (1846), 306.
Johnson, Lewis, senator, Fayette and Union cos. (1822), *190.
Johnson, Lewis, representative, Wayne Co. (1818), *185.
Johnson, Nathan, senator, Wayne Co. (1847), 323.
Johnson, Richard M., vice-president (1836), 25-28; (1840), 33-36.
Johnson, Robert, representative, Carroll Co. etc. (1829), 204n.
Johnson, Samuel, representative, Wayne Co. (1841), 263n.
Johnson, T. ———, representative, Allen Co. (1842), 265.
Johnson, Thomas, representative, Marion Co. (1842), *266.
Johnson, W., delegate, const. conv., Spencer Co., 380.
Johnson, William R., delegate, const. conv., Orange Co., *383n.
Johnston, Archibald, representative, Putnam Co. (1848), *329; (1850), *351.
Johnston, General Washington, lieutenant governor (1825), 161-62n; contests election (1818), 186n; representative, Knox Co. (1821), *188. (1822), *190; (1826), *197; (1829), *203.
Johnston, George H., representative, Monroe Co. (1838), *242.
Johnston, John M., presidential elector (1844), *38-42; representative, Franklin Co. (1834), *219; (1835), *224.
Johnston, Samuel H., representative, Parke Co. (1849), *339.
Jolliff, E. H., 298n.
Jolly, Jacob, representative, Ripley Co. (1847), 318.
Jones, Andrew M., representative, Harrison Co. (1843), 273; (1850), 347.
Jones, Aquilla, representative, Bartholomew Co. (1842), *267.
Jones, C. V., senator, Fountain Co. (1843), *277.
Jones, Charles, representative, Bartholomew Co. (1847), *313; (1848), *323.
Jones, Charles T., representative, Ohio and Switzerland cos. (1847), *317.
Jones, David M., representative, Vigo Co. (1844), *285.
Jones, Edwin M., 97n.
Jones, James R., representative, Franklin Co. (1843), *275.
Jones, Jesse, representative, La Porte Co. (1844), 282, 286n.
Jones, John, representative, Floyd Co. (1844), 280; (1845), *291.
Jones, John, representative, Wayne Co. (1827), *199; (1829), *203; (1830), 205; (1831), *209; (1833), *216; (1835), 227; (1837), 238n; (1841), 260.
Jones, John, Jr., representative, Greene Co. (1846), *304.
Jones, John F., representative, Bartholomew Co. (1847), 313.
Jones, John P., representative, La Grange Co. (1850), *348.
Jones, John R., representative, Fountain Co. (1843), *275; (1844), *280.
Jones, Lewis, representative, Daviess and Martin cos. (1835), *226.
Jones, Newton C., representative, Bartholomew Co. (1828), *200; death, 201n.
Jones, Samuel, representative, Huntington and Whitley cos. (1848), *327.
Jones, Smith, delegate, const. conv., Bartholomew Co., *381.
Jones, Thomas, senator, Jefferson Co. (1844), 287.
Jones, William, representative, Jay and Blackford cos. (1846), *301; (1851), 355.
Jones, William, representative, Spencer Co. (1838), *244; Perry and Spencer cos. (1839), *247; (1840), *254.

Jones, William, representative, Wayne Co. (1823), *192.

Jones, William T. T., representative, Vanderburgh Co. (1836), *232; (1837), *238.

Jordan, John, representative, Wayne Co. (1822), *190.

Jordan, Peter, representative, Jefferson Co. (1844), 281.

Jordan, Russell, representative, Henry Co. (1850), *347.

Jordan, Thomas N., representative, Washington Co. (1850), 351.

Judah, Samuel, U. S. Senator (1831), 128; (1838), 132-33; representative, Knox Co. (1827), *199; (1828), *201; (1833), 215; (1837), *236; (1838), *241; (1839), *247; (1840), *253; (1841), 259; senator, Knox Co. etc. (1836), 233; speaker of the House, xx.

Julian, George W., presidential elector (1848), 63-67; representative, U. S. Congress (1849), *119; (1851), 123; representative, Wayne Co. (1845), *297.

Julian, Isaac, representative, Wayne Co. (1822), *190.

Julian, Jacob B., representative, Wayne Co. (1846), *309; (1848), *331.

Julien, John C., representative, Hendricks Co. (1832), 212.

Jumper, Alden H., representative, Dearborn Co. (1850), 346.

Justus, Aquilla, representative, Parke Co. (1846), 306.

Kahill, William, 298n.

Kearns (Kerns), William, representative, Benton Co. etc. (1849), 334.

Keath, Joseph, representative, Boone Co. (1850), 345; (1851), 355.

Keen, William C., representative, Switzerland Co. (1825), *195.

Keeney, Rufus D., representative, La Grange and Noble cos. (1849), *338.

Keep, Luther, 309n.

Keiser, Peter, representative, Allen Co. (1847), *312.

Kelley, Richard, representative, Ripley Co. (1848), *329.

Kelly, John, representative, Washington Co. (1843), *276; (1844), *285.

Kelly, Richard M., representative, Bartholomew Co. (1848), 323; (1849), 334.

Kelsay, John, representative, Madison Co. (1846), 306.

Kelso, Andrew F., representative, Dubois Co. (1844), 280.

Kelso, Daniel, representative, Switzerland Co. (1832), 212; (1833), *215; (1834), *220; (1836), 230; (1839), 247; (1848), *329; (1851), 359; senator (1837), 239; (1842), *271, 271n; (1843), 277; (1844), 288; (1846), 312; delegate, const. conv., *380; contests election, 278n.

Kemmer (Keimer), Peter, senator, Blackford Co. etc. (1843), *272.

Kendall, Harrison, delegate, const. conv., Miami and Wabash cos., *385.

Kendall, Robert C., senator, Benton Co. etc. (1851), *362; delegate, const. conv., *383.

Kennard, Thomas, representative, Clinton and Tipton cos. (1847), *314.

Kennedy, Andrew, presidential elector (1840), *33-36; representative, U. S. Congress (1841), *103; (1843), *109; (1845), *113; senator, Delaware and Randolph cos. (1836), *235; (1837), *239.

Kennedy, Archibald, senator, Rush Co. (1847), 323.

Kennedy, John Y., senator, Shelby Co. (1842), *271, 271n.

Kennedy, Robert, representative, Ripley Co. (1823), *192.

Kennedy, Thomas, senator, Franklin Co. (1847), 321.

Kent, Phineas M., representative, Floyd Co. (1851), *356; delegate, const. conv., *384.

Kenton, William M., representative, Jasper Co. etc. (1837), *237; (1838), *243.

Kenworthy, Jehu, representative, Montgomery Co. (1849), 339.
Kern, J. H., representative, Cass and Howard cos. (1847), 313.
Kerr, James, representative, Parke Co. (1840), *256; (1843), *275; (1844), *283; (1845), *295; (1846), *306.
Kersey, D., representative, Hendricks Co. (1849), 337.
Kersey, J. C., representative, Hendricks Co. (1849), 342n.
Kersey, James, representative, Hendricks Co. (1849), 337.
Kester, Joel, representative, Vigo Co. (1846), 308.
Ketcham, John, presidential elector (1832), *14-16; representative, Monroe Co. (1825), *195; (1826), *197; (1829), *203; (1837), 235; (1849), 335; senator, Monroe Co. etc. (1830), 207; Monroe Co. (1839), 250.
Key, William, representative, Orange Co. (1847), 317.
Kile, William, representative, Vermillion Co. (1841), 260.
Kilgore, ———, 132-33.
Kilgore, David, presidential elector (1848), 58-62; representative, U. S. Congress (1849), 121-22; representative, Delaware Co. etc. (1833), *216; (1834), *221; (1835), *226; (1838), *241; delegate, const. conv., *381.
Kilgore, George, representative, Delaware Co. (1851), 356.
Kimball, Nathan, senator, Washington Co. (1847), 323.
Kimberlin, Robert P., representative, Hamilton and Tipton cos. (1845), *292.
Kimberly, Zenas, representative, Jennings Co. (1821), *188.
King, Francis, representative, Wayne Co. (1846), 309.
King, James H., representative, Monroe Co. (1838), 242.
King, John L., representative, Jefferson Co. (1851), *357.
Kingsbury, John, representative, Washington Co. (1829), *203.
Kinison, Lawrence, representative, Warren Co. (1846), 308.
Kinley, Isaac, delegate, const. conv., Henry Co., *387.
Kinnard, George L., 82n; representative, U. S. Congress (1833), *89; (1835), *92; representative, Marion Co. (1827), *199; (1828), *201; (1829), *203; senator, Marion and Hamilton cos. (1831), 210; death, 93n.
Kinnard, Thomas, senator, Carroll and Clinton cos. (1849), *342.
Kinnear, C., representative, Jefferson Co. (1830), 204.
Kinnear, Robert, representative, Jefferson Co. (1834), 219.
Kinney, Amory, representative, Vigo Co. (1830), *205; (1838), *244; (1847), *319; delegate, const. conv., 383n.
Kintner, Jacob L., representative, Harrison Co. (1846), 304.
Kinzer, Henry, senator, Harrison Co. (1839), *250.
Kirkpatrick, Absalom, representative, Montgomery Co. (1847), 317.
Kirkpatrick, Moses, representative, Floyd Co. (1821), *188.
Kiser, William P., representative, Bartholomew Co. (1833), *216.
Kizer, Elias, senator, Jay and Randolph cos. (1851), 363.
Knapp, Squire H., 67n; representative, Ripley Co. (1851), 360.
Knight, Job L., delegate, const. conv., Miami and Wabash cos., 385.
Knight, L. M., senator, Putnam Co. (1833), 218.
Knott, John, 97n.
Knowland, Obadiah, representative, Clark Co. (1844), 279; (1847), 313.
Knowlton, Hiram, representative, Ripley Co. (1849), *340; senator (1850), *354.
Knox, Turner A., representative, Benton Co. etc. (1848), 324.

Krutz, Charles F., representative, Switzerland Co. (1830), 205; (1833), 215.

Kuykendall, Jacob, presidential elector (1832), 17-20.

Kyle, William, representative, Vermillion Co. (1840), *254.

Kyler, Sapington B., representative, Elkhart Co. (1844), 280.

Lacy, John, representative, Wayne Co. (1845), 297.

Lafferty, James, representative, Posey Co. (1849), 340.

Lagow, Wilson, senator, Knox Co. etc. (1830), 207.

Laird, David T., senator, Perry Co. etc. (1851), 364.

Lancaster, Morris, representative, Wayne Co. (1839), *249; (1840), *256.

Landers, Jeremiah, representative, Boone Co. (1851), 355.

Landers, W., representative, Morgan Co. (1838), 242.

Landiss, John, representative, Crawford Co. (1849), *335.

Lane, Amos, representative, U. S. Congress (1833), *88; (1835), *91; (1837), 95; lieutenant governor (1816), 159; (1831), 165n; representative, Dearborn Co. (1816), *183; (1817), *184; (1821), *188; (1839), *246.

Lane, Daniel C., senator, Harrison Co. (1827), *200.

Lane, George W., representative, Dearborn Co. (1847), *314.

Lane, Henry S., 118n; presidential elector (1844), 43-47; representative, U. S. Congress (1840, special), *101; (1841), *104-5; (1849), 120-21; representative, Montgomery Co. (1837), *237.

Lane, Higgins, representative, Putnam Co. (1849), *340.

Lane, James H., lieutenant governor (1849), *178-80n; representative, Dearborn and Ohio cos. (1845), 290, 298n.

Lane, Joseph, representative, Vanderburgh and Warrick cos. (1822), *190; (1830), *206n; (1831), *209; (1832), *213; (1838), *244; senator (1839), *251; (1844), *288.

Langton, Daniel, representative, Knox Co. (1824), *193.

Langton, Samuel, representative, Knox Co. (1839), 247.

Lanius, William, representative, Dearborn Co. (1839), *246; (1844), *280; (1845), *290, 298n.

Lank, Elza, representative, Randolph Co. (1849), *340; (1850), *350.

Latshaw, Joseph, representative, Sullivan Co. (1834), *221.

Latta, James, representative, Noble and La Grange cos. (1841), 259.

Laughlin, William B., senator, Franklin Co. (1821), *189.

Laughlin, William M., representative, Wayne Co. (1849), 341.

Laughmiller, Joseph, representative, Washington Co. (1850), 351.

Laverty, John, representative, Morgan Co. (1851), *359; delegate, const. conv., 386.

Law, John, representative, U. S. Congress (1831), 84-85, 87n; (1833), 87-88; (1837), 94; U. S. Senator (1830), xx, 128; (1832), 129; (1848), 134; representative, Knox Co. (1823), *191.

Lawlis (or Lawlyes), William A., representative, Vermillion Co. (1846), 308; (1847), 319.

Lawrence, Archibald, representative, Jefferson Co. (1841), *259; (1842), 266; (1843), 273; (1845), 298n; senator (1844), 287.

Lawrence, Edmund, representative, Wayne Co. (1850), *351; (1851), *361.

Lawrence, John, representative, Dearborn Co. (1838), 244n.

Layne, Elisha G., representative, Tippecanoe Co. (1842), 267.

Leavenworth, *see* Levenworth.

Ledbetter, William F., representative, Vanderburgh Co. (1850), 350.

Ledgerwood, Samuel, representative, Sullivan Co. (1841), 260.

Lee, Abraham, representative, Franklin Co. (1845), 291.

Lee, Azra, representative, Posey Co. (1841), *262; (1842), *269; (1843), *273; (1844), 284; (1845), 295.

Lee, Henry, representative, Clinton and Montgomery cos. (1835), *224; (1836), *230; (1839), *248.

Lee, James H., representative, Franklin Co. (1845), 291.

Lee, Stephen, representative, Jefferson Co. (1843), *273.

Lee, Thomas G., representative, Bartholomew Co. (1835), *226; (1836), *231; (1837), *237; (1838), *242.

Leech, George, representative, Knox Co. (1842), 266.

Leedom, Thomas, senator, Blackford Co. etc. (1849), 342.

Leeds, Warner M., representative, Wayne Co. (1838), 244n.

Leeland, Moses N., representative, Fulton and Marshall cos. (1848), 326.

Leeper, Joseph H., 67n; representative, Elkhart Co. (1848), 326.

Legg, Walter, representative, Wayne Co. (1844), *285; (1845), *297.

Lemon, John, representative, Clark Co. (1825), *194; (1826), *196; (1827), *198; (1828), *200.

Lemon, John M., presidential elector (1840), 33-36; senator, Clark and Floyd cos. (1829), *203; (1832), *214; resignation (1833), 219n; senator, La Porte Co. etc. (1846), 311.

Lemonds (Lemmons), George W., representative, Dubois Co. (1845), *291; (1846), *303; (1847), 314.

Leslie, ——, senator, Clark and Floyd cos. (1835), 228.

Leslie, Frederick, representative, Harrison Co. (1833), *215; (1834), *219; (1839), 246; (1840), *253 (1841), *259; (1842), *266; (1844), *285; delegate, const. conv., 379.

Levenworth, Seth M., representative, U. S. Congress (1833), 87; U. S. Senator (1838), 132-33; representative, Crawford Co. (1826), *196; (1827), *198; (1828), *200; (1829), *202.

Levenworth, Zebulon, representative, Crawford Co. (1830), *206; (1832), *212; (1833), *216.

Leviston, James, representative, Union Co. (1828), *201; (1829), *203; (1837), 238; (1849), *341; (1851), *361; senator, Fayette and Union cos. (1831), *211; (1843), *277.

Lewis, ———, representative, Warrick Co. (1844), 285.

Lewis, Allen W., representative, Wayne Co. (1845), 297; (1846), 309n; (1847), 320n; (1848), 331; (1850), 351.

Lewis, Caleb, representative, Wayne Co. (1825), *195; (1826), *197; (1832), *213; (1837), 238n; (1838), *242; (1841), 260; (1843), 274; senator (1847), 323.

Lewis, David S., representative, Lawrence Co. (1845), 294.

Lewis, Eli, representative, Warrick Co. (1850), *351; (1851), *361.

Lewis, James, representative, Grant Co. (1849), 336.

Lewis, John, representative, Clay Co. (1846), *302; (1847), 313.

Lewis, John, representative, Dearborn Co. (1842), *268; (1844), *280.

Lewis, Joseph, representative, Wayne Co. (1830), 206n; (1844), *285; (1845), *297.

Lewis, Madison, representative, Parke Co. (1851), 359.

Lewis, Nathan, delegate, const. conv., Shelby Co., 380.

Lewis, Samuel, representative, Franklin Co. (1825), *196n; (1826), *196.

Lewis, William, representative, Union Co. (1827), *200n.

Lewis, William B., representative, Decatur Co. (1845), 291.

Leyman, William L., representative, Tippecanoe Co. (1842), *267; (1845), *296.

Liberty party, in presidential election (1840), xxiii, 37; (1844), xxiv, 48-52; in gubernatorial elections (1843, 1846), xxiv, 150-55.

Lichtenberger, Adam, representative, Posey Co. (1846), 307; (1847), *318.

Lieutenant governor, term of office, ix; acting governor, ix.

Lightner, Daniel D., representative, Clinton and Tipton cos. (1846), 302.

Lillard, John P., representative, Switzerland Co. (1833), 215.

Lilleston, Elijah, representative, Posey Co. (1850), 349.

Lilleston, John W., representative, Vanderburgh Co. (1842), 267; (1843), 274, 276n; senator, Posey and Vanderburgh cos. (1844), 288.

Lilly, John, senator, Tippecanoe Co. (1849), 344.

Lincoln, Moses J., 286n.

Lindley, Jonathan, representative, Orange Co. (1816), *183.

Lindley, Samuel, representative, Washington Co. (1819), *186.

Lindsay, Nathaniel R., representative, Howard and Tipton cos. (1851), *357.

Lindsey, John, representative, Bartholomew Co. (1821), *187.

Lindsey, John V., representative, Fayette Co. (1850), *346; (1851), *356.

Line, Aaron B., representative, Franklin Co. (1847), *315; (1848), *326.

Lingle, Henry, representative, Orange Co. (1841), *262; (1842), *268.

Linton, William C., representative, U. S. Congress (1833), 87-88; U. S. Senator (1832), 129-30; senator, Vigo Co. etc. (1828), *201; representative, Vigo Co. (1831), 208.

Liston, Jonathan A., representative, La Porte and St. Joseph cos. (1834), *220; (1835), *225; senator, Kosciusko Co. etc. (1836), *234, 235n.

Litchfield, David B., representative, Whitley Co. (1851), *361.

Litle (Little), Aaron, representative, Lake and Porter cos. (1845), 294; delegate, const. conv., 385.

Littell, William D., representative, Harrison Co. (1817), *184.

Little, Alexander, representative, Hendricks Co. (1832), 212; senator (1836), *234.

Little, Alexander, representative, Washington Co. (1816), *183; (1817), *184; (1826), *197; (1827), *199; (1829), *203; senator (1819), *186, 186n.

Little, John, representative, Tippecanoe Co. (1851), 360.

Little, Nathaniel, presidential elector (1848), 63-67.

Little, Samuel, representative, Fayette Co. (1844), *280; (1847), *314; (1850), 352n.

Littlefield, John, representative, Ohio and Switzerland cos. (1849), 339.

Livingston, Hugh L., representative, U. S. Congress (1833), 87-88; representative, Lawrence Co. (1831), *209 (1832), *213.

Locke, William, representative, Wayne Co. (1838), 244n.

Lockhart, James, representative, U. S. Congress (1841), 101-2; (1851), *122; delegate, const. conv., Posey and Vanderburgh cos., *386.

Lockhart, Levi, representative, Pike Co. (1851), 359.

Lockhart, Levi P., representative, Washington Co. (1834), *222; (1835), 226.

Lockridge, Robert, representative, Sullivan Co. (1851), 360.

Lockwood, Rufus, representative, Tippecanoe Co. (1847), 319.

Lockwood, Stephen H., representative, Greene Co. (1847), *315.

Logan, Benjamin S., representative, Harrison Co. (1842), 266.

Logan, Ezekiel D., representative, Washington Co. (1829), *204n; (1830), *205; (1831), *209; (1842), *269; (1843), *276; senator (1832), *214; resignation (1834), 223n; senator (1844), *288; delegate, const. conv., *381.

Logan, Reuben D., representative, Rush Co. (1845), 295; senator (1850), *354.

Logan, Robert, representative, Pike Co. (1843), *275; (1845), *295; (1846), *307.

Lomax, Abel, presidential elector (1832), 17-20; representative, (1823), *192; (1824), *194; (1825), *195; (1826), *197; (1827), *199; (1828), *201; (1833), 216; senator (1829), 204.

Lomax, William, representative, Grant Co. (1847), 315.

Long, Elisha, presidential elector (1828), *25-28; representative, Henry Co. etc. (1826), *197; (1827), *199; (1828), *200; (1829), *202; (1830), *206; Franklin Co. (1839), *246; senator (1831), *211, 211n; (1832), *214.

Long, Joel, representative, Kosciusko Co. etc. (1836), *230.

Long, William, representative, Putnam Co. (1848), 329.

Longley, Abner H., representative, Boone Co. (1836), *231.

Longshore, Thomas M. D., senator, Jay and Randolph cos. (1851), *363.

Lonsberry, Elihu, representative, Franklin Co. (1845), 291.

Loudermilk, ——, senator, Knox Co. (1843), 277.

Love, Abraham, representative, Jackson Co. (1846), 304.

Lovejoy, John K., presidential elector (1844), 48-52; senator, Benton Co. etc. (1845), 298; representative (1846), 301.

Lowe, Enos, representative, Parke Co. (1834), *220; senator (1835), 228.

Lowe, Frederick, representative, Boone Co. (1844), 279.

Lowe, Jacob, 13n.

Lowe, Jacob B., representative, U. S. Congress (1835), 92; representative, Brown and Monroe cos. (1845), *289; (1847), *313.

Lowe, John, representative, Carroll and Howard cos. (1844), 279.

Lowe, Joseph, representative, Rush Co. (1832), *213; (1842), *267; senator (1835), 228; (1838), *245.

Lowe, William, presidential elector (1828), *10-11.

Lowry, Alexander, representative, Scott Co. (1830), *206.

Lozier, George M., representative, Dearborn Co. (1848), *325.

Lucas, Ebenezer F., senator, Warren Co. etc. (1845), 298; representative, Warren Co. (1851), 361.

Lucas, Joshua B., representative, Shelby Co. (1840), *256.

Lucas, Joshua H., representative, Monroe Co. (1822), *190.

Lucas, Simeon H., representative, Randolph Co. (1846), 307.

Luce, Cyrus G., representative, De Kalb and Steuben cos. (1848), 325.

Ludlow, Stephen, presidential elector (1832), 17-20.

Lusk, James, representative, Johnson Co. (1836), *232.

Lutz, Jesse, representative, Hamilton Co. (1846), *304.

Lutz, Jesse B., representative, Tippecanoe Co. (1848), 330.

Lynd, James, representative, Orange Co. (1828), *201; (1830), *206; (1831), *209; (1832), *213.

Lynn, Dan, representative, Posey Co. (1816), *183; (1817), *184; (1819), *186.

Lynn, Joel, representative, Dearborn Co. (1839), 249n.

Lynn, John, representative, Warrick Co. (1845), 297.

Lyon, Jonathan, representative, Washington Co. (1818), *185.

Lyon, Robert W., senator, Fountain Co. (1849), *343; death, 354n.

McAllister, Thomas, representative, Madison Co. (1841), *262; (1843), *275; (1844), *282; (1851), *358.

McBean, Gillis, representative, Carroll and Cass cos. (1833), *215 (1835), *224.

McBride, Allen, representative, Sullivan Co. (1845), 296.
McBride, Henry, 298n.
McBride, William C., representative, Sullivan Co. (1849), 341.
McCall, James B., representative, Knox Co. (1823), *191.
McCalley, Eli, representative, Clark Co. (1834), *221.
McCampbell, James, representative, Parke Co. (1845), 295.
McCarty, Abner, representative, Franklin Co. (1838), *243.
McCarty, Benjamin, representative, La Porte and St. Joseph cos. (1834), 220; Porter and Newton cos. (1836), *230.
McCarty, Elijah, representative, Putnam Co. (1849), 340; (1850), *351.
McCarty, Enoch, presidential elector (1836), *21-24; representative, U. S. Congress (1833), 88; senator, Franklin Co. (1831), *211; representative (1835), *224; (1836), *229.
McCarty, Green B., representative, Shelby Co. (1850), 350.
McCarty, Jonathan, presidential elector (1824), *4-5; (1840), *29-32; representative, U. S. Congress (1828), 84; (1831), *86; (1833), *88-89; (1835), *91-92; (1837), 95-96; (1839), 99, 100n; (1841), 103, 105n; U. S. Senator (1832), 129; (1843), 134; representative, Franklin Co. (1818), *185.
McCarty, Nicholas, representative, U. S. Congress (1847), 115; senator, Marion Co. (1849), *344.
McCarty, William M., presidential elector (1848), *53-57; senator, Franklin Co. (1847), *321.
McCleery, William, representative, Franklin Co. (1822), *189.
McClelland, Beattie, delegate, const. conv., Randolph Co. *382.
McClelland, David D., representative, Jefferson Co. (1849), 337.
McClelland, James S., representative, Clinton and Tipton cos. (1850), *345.
McClure, Charles, representative, La Porte Co. (1837), *237; (1838), *241.
McClure, Daniel G., representative, Knox Co. (1844), *282.
McClure, David, representative, Scott Co. (1843), *275; (1844), *285; (1846), 307.
McClure, John, representative, Knox Co. (1817), *184.
McClure, Nathaniel, representative, Fayette Co. (1845), 291.
McClure, Thomas, representative, Knox Co. (1827), *199.
McClure, William, 298n.
McConnell, David, representative, Benton Co. etc. (1843), *272; (1847), *313.
McConnell, George W., representative, De Kalb and Steuben cos. (1851), *356.
McCord, Samuel H., senator, Parke Co. (1840), *258.
McCorkle, John, representative, Johnson Co. (1849), 338.
McCorkle, S. M., representative, Parke Co. (1834), 220.
McCorkle, T. J., representative, Boone Co. (1847), 313.
McCormack, Joseph, representative, Fountain Co. (1838), *243; (1839), *248; (1842), *268.
McCormick, Philip, representative, Tippecanoe Co. (1846), *308; (1847), *319; (1848), 330.
McCormick, Samuel, representative, Tippecanoe Co. (1844), 284; (1845), *296.
McCoy, Angus C., representative, U. S. Congress (1845), 110-11.
McCoy, John, representative, Jefferson Co. (1836), 229; (1841), 259; (1850), 348.
McCoy, William W., representative, Shelby Co. (1839), *249; (1840), *256.
McCoy, William W., senator, Lake Co. etc. (1849), 344.

McCracken, Mark, senator, Dearborn, Co. (1837), 239; representative, (1840), 252.

McCreery, John, representative, Vanderburgh and Warrick cos. (1824), *194.

McCrilles, Aaron B., representative, Crawford and Dubois cos. (1837), *237; Dubois and Pike (1840), *252.

McCulley, James, representative, Carroll Co. (1840), *255.

McCullough, Harvey W., representative, Ripley Co. (1850), 350.

McCullough, William B., senator, Dearborn Co. (1846), 310.

McCune, George C., representative, Henry Co. (1845), 293.

McDonald, Alexander, representative, Lake and Porter cos. (1843), *275; (1845), *294; (1847), *316; Lake Co. (1851), *358.

McDonald, David, 126n; representative, Daviess and Martin cos. (1833), *216.

McDonald, David, representative, Adams and Wells cos. (1847), *312.

McDonald, James, representative, Daviess Co. (1841), 259.

McDonald, John, representative, Knox Co. (1820), *187.

McDonald, Joseph E., representative, U. S. Congress (1849), *120-21.

McDougal, Levi, representative, Washington Co. (1845), 297; (1846), 308; (1848), 331.

McDougle (McDougall), Levi, 122n; representative, Floyd Co. (1834), *221; (1835), 224; delegate, const. conv., 384.

McDowell, George, representative, Huntington and Wells cos. (1851), *357.

McDowell, William, representative, Blackford and Jay cos. (1846), 301.

McDuffie, Gabriel C., senator, Rush Co. (1844), 288.

Mace, Daniel, presidential elector (1848), *53-57; representative, U. S. Congress (1851), *125; representative, Warren and Jasper cos. (1836), *231.

Macey, John W., representative, Rush Co. (1850), 350. *See also* Macy.

McFadin, Samuel L., representative, Cass and Howard cos. (1850), 345.

McFarland, Demas L., representative, Marion Co. (1844), 283.

McFarland, Joel B., delegate, const. conv., Tippecanoe Co., *386.

McGaughey, Edward, presidential elector (1848), 58-62; representative, U. S. Congress (1843), 107-8, 109n; (1845), *112; (1849), *120; (1851), 124-25; representative, Putnam Co. (1839), *248; senator (1842), *270; resignation (1843), 278n.

McGaughey, James P., representative, Daviess Co. (1844), *279.

McGrew, Burr, representative, Sullivan Co. (1841), 260.

McHenry, ——, representative, Switzerland Co. (1830), 206n.

McIntyre, Robert, representative, Fountain Co. (1834), *219; (1836), *233n.

McIntyre, Robert, representative, Washington Co. (1824), *194; (1828), *201.

McJunkin, Erasmus, representative, Daviess and Martin cos. (1832), *212.

McKay, William, representative, Spencer Co. (1843), 273.

McKee, Archibald, representative, Knox Co. (1837), 236.

McKee, David, representative, Rush Co. (1847), 318.

McKeehan, Samuel B., representative, Bartholomew Co. (1845), 289.

McKenn, George W., representative, Montgomery Co. (1849), 339.

McKenzie, William A., representative, Putnam Co. (1847), *318.

McKim, John, representative, Perry Co. (1850), *349.

McKinley, George G., representative, Clay Co. (1848), 324.

McKinney, Callin, representative, Bartholomew Co. (1850), *351; death, 352n.

McKinney, J., representative, Parke Co. (1834), 220.

McKinney, John, representative, Bartholomew and Brown cos. (1836), *231.

McKinney, John T., representative, Franklin Co. (1826), *196; (1827), *198; senator (1828), *201.

McKinney, John W., representative, Fountain Co. (1850), 347.

McKinney, Presley L., representative, Fountain Co. (1846), 303.

McKnight, James, 160n.

McLain, Nelson, representative, Allen Co. (1846), 301.

McLane, Lewis, representative, Wayne Co. (1834), 222n.

McLean, William, delegate, const. conv., Boone Co., *381.

McMahan, ——, representative, Washington Co. (1840), 255.

McMakin, Robert W., representative, Montgomery Co. (1850), *349.

McMillan, John, representative, Rush Co. (1846), 307.

McNamee, Elias, presidential elector (1824), *4-5; U. S. Senator (1816), 127.

McNary, John, representative, Clay and Putnam cos. (1829), *202; (1830), *205; Putnam Co. (1832), *213; (1835), 225; (1838), *243.

McNeal, Daniel W., representative, Blackford and Jay cos. (1848), 324.

McPheeters, Hugh, representative, Washington Co. (1827), *199; (1828), *201; (1830), *205.

McPheeters, Joseph G., representative, Monroe Co. (1851), 359.

McQueen, William, representative, Randolph Co. (1851), 360.

McRae, Daniel A., representative, Crawford Co. (1845), *290.

McRae, Franklin, representative, Harrison Co. (1843), *273; (1845), 292; (1847), 315.

McWhinney, Johnson, representative, Vigo Co. (1839), 247.

Macy, David, representative, Dearborn Co. (1843), *274.

Macy, David, representative, Henry Co. (1835), *226; (1836), *232; (1837), *237.

Madden, William, 122n.

Maddox, Finley L., representative, Fountain Co. (1845), 291; (1848), *326; senator (1846), 311.

Maddox, John W., representative, Gibson Co. (1819), *186.

Magill, William, representative, Johnson Co. (1846), 305.

Maguire, Douglass, representative, Marion Co. (1837), 236; (1838), 242; delegate, const. conv., *380.

Mahan, Isaac, representative, Putnam Co. (1836), *232.

Major, Andrew, representative, Clinton Co. (1837), *237; (1838), *242; (1842), *268; senator, Clinton and Carroll cos. (1843), *276.

Major, William, representative, Shelby Co. (1845), *319; (1851), *360.

Mallory, William H., representative, Fountain Co. (1846), 303; delegate, const. conv., 384.

Malott, Michael A., senator, Lawrence Co. (1847), *322.

Manker, William J., representative, Morgan Co. (1848), 329.

Mann, Josiah, representative, Sullivan Co. (1824), *193.

Manson, Mahlon D., representative, Montgomery Co. (1849), 339; (1851), *359.

Manville, Silvanus, representative, Brown Co. (1844), *279; (1851), 355.

March, Walter, delegate, const. conv., Delaware and Grant cos., *387.

Markle, Abraham, 160n.

Marks, John, representative, Sullivan Co. (1846), 308; (1849), 341; (1851), 360.

Marks, Thomas, representative, Sullivan Co. (1845), 296; (1848), 332n.

Marks, William, representative, Fayette Co. (1844), 280.

Markwell, ———, representative, Washington Co. (1840), 256n.

Marlin, Hugh, representative, Monroe Co. (1851), 359.

Marquess, William K., representative, Fountain Co. (1850), *347.

Marquis, James, 118n; representative, Blackford and Jay cos. (1848), 324.

Marrs, Urbin, representative, Posey Co. (1851), *360.

Marsh, John J., representative, Ohio and Switzerland cos. (1848), 329.

Marsh, Madison, representative, De Kalb Co. etc. (1840), 252; (1841), *259; (1842), 265; senator (1846), *311.

Marshall, ——, U. S. Senator (1832), 129-30.

Marshall, Joseph G., presidential elector (1840), *29-32; (1844), 43-47; (1848), 58-62; U. S. Senator (1843, 1845, 1848), 134; governor (1846), 153-55; representative, Jefferson Co. (1834), *219; (1835), 225; (1836), *229; (1837), *237; (1838), *241; (1841), *259; senator (1850), *353.

Marshall, Miles, representative, Wayne Co. (1850), *351.

Marshall, William, representative, Jackson Co. (1822), *190; (1823), *191; (1825), *195; (1826), *197; (1827), *199; (1828), *200; (1836), *232.

Marshel, Blaine, representative, Floyd Co. (1848), 326.

Marsters, Stephen, representative, Kosciusko Co. etc. (1836), 230.

Martin, Abner, representative, Washington Co. (1826), *197.

Martin, Archibald F., representative, Fayette Co. (1851), 356.

Martin, Delavan, representative, La Grange Co. (1846), 305; senator, La Grange and Elkhart (1847), *321, 323n.

Martin, Isaac, representative, Fountain Co. (1834), 219.

Martin, J., representative, Wayne Co. (1833), 217n.

Martin, James W., delegate, const. conv., Washington Co., 381.

Martin, Josephus, representative, Adams and Jay cos. (1841), 258; (1842), 265.

Martin, Roger, representative, U. S. Congress (1845), 110; (1851), 123.

Martindale, John, representative, Wayne Co. (1846), 309.

Martle, David T., representative, Posey Co. (1851), 360.

Marvin, Henry H., representative, Hendricks Co. (1834), 219; (1842), *266; (1845), 293; (1851), 357.

Marvin, Henry M., representative, Boone Co. (1850), *345.

Marvin, W. H., 67n.

Mason, Charles H., 126n.

Mason, Horatio, representative, Fayette Co. (1850), 346.

Mason, Martin B., representative, Spencer Co. (1851), 360.

Mason, Philip, representative, Fayette Co. (1835), *226; (1838), *242; (1840), *255.

Mason, William, representative, Fulton Co. etc. (1847), 315.

Mason, William M., representative, Brown Co. (1846), *301.

Massey, John H., representative, Knox Co. (1849), 338; (1850), 348.

Mastin, Lewis, representative, Hendricks and Morgan cos. (1830), 204; Hendricks Co. (1831), *208; (1832), *212; senator, Hendricks Co. etc. (1833), *218; Hendricks Co. (1836), 234.

Matchett, Dr. ———, senator, Elkhart Co. etc. (1845), 299.

Matheny, Francis A., representative, Morgan Co. (1841), *262; (1842), *268; (1843), *275.

Mather, Joseph H., delegate, const. conv., Elkhart and La Grange cos., *384.

Mathers, Joseph, representative, Hancock Co. (1842), *268.

Mathes, ———, representative, Clark Co. (1847), 313.

Mathis, Frederick W., representative, Harrison Co. (1849), 337.

Mathis, John, delegate, const. conv., Harrison Co., *379.

Matkins, Isaac, representative, Putnam Co. (1843), 273.

Matlock, Thomas J., representative, Hendricks Co. etc. (1826), *197; (1827), *199; (1828), *200.

Matlock, William T., representative, Hendricks Co. (1836), 229; (1837), *236; (1844), *281.

Matson, John A., presidential elector (1844), 43-47; representative, U. S. Congress (1843), 106; governor (1849), 155-58; representative, Franklin Co. (1838), *243; (1840), *252; resignation, 256n.

Matthews, Hiram, representative, Morgan Co. (1836), *232.

Mattingly, Ignatius, representative, Harrison Co. (1838), 241.

Mauck, Peter, representative, Harrison Co. (1822), *190.

Mavity, Michael, representative, Orange Co. (1847), 317.

Maxson, Leo H. T., representative, La Porte Co. (1836), *232.

Maxwell, ———, representative, Union Co. (1844), 285.

Maxwell, David H., 77n; lieutenant governor (1822), 160-61n; representative, Monroe Co. (1821), *188; (1823), *191; (1824), *193; senator, Monroe Co. etc. (1826), *198, 198n; (1827), *200.

Maxwell, Edward R., representative, Jefferson Co. (1831), *208; (1832), 212; (1833), 215.

Maxwell, S. F., representative, Parke Co. (1851), 359.

Maxwell, Samuel D., representative, Clinton Co. (1844), 279; (1848), 325; (1849), 335.

Maxwell, Thomas, representative, Union Co. (1845), 296.

May, Edward R., representative, De Kalb and Steuben cos. (1849), *336; (1850), 352n; delegate, const. conv., *379.

May, George, representative, Washington Co. (1841), *260; (1847), *320.

May, George, representative, Fountain Co. (1846), *303; senator (1850), 353.

Mayfield, Francis F., representative, Jefferson Co. (1851), *357.

Meacham, ———, representative, Orange Co. (1838), 242.

Meacham, John, representative, Parke Co. (1848), *329.

Means, Thomas, representative, Wayne Co. (1848), 331.

Means, William P., representative, De Kalb and Steuben cos. (1846), 303, 309n.

Meek, Jesse, representative, Wayne Co. (1843), 274.

Meeker, Miner, representative, Fayette Co. (1841), *261; (1842), *268; (1845), *291.

Mehaffey, Robert, delegate, const. conv., Cass Co. etc., 384.

Menaugh, John L., representative, Washington Co. (1849), *341.

Mendenhall, Absalom, senator, Fountain Co. (1840), *258; resignation (1841), 265n.

Mendenhall, James R., representative, Union Co. (1834), *221.

Mercer, Milton, representative, Elkhart Co. (1850), *346; (1851), 356.

Meredith, Andrew, representative, Wayne Co. (1843), 276n.

Meredith, Solomon, representative, Wayne Co. (1846), *309; (1847), *320; (1848), *331.

Merrifield, George C., representative, St. Joseph Co. (1842), 267; (1844), 284.

Merrill, J. F., representative, Adams Co. etc. (1838), 240.

Merrill, Samuel, representative, Switzerland Co. (1819), *186; (1820), *187; (1821), *188; Marion Co. (1849), 338.

Mickle, Samuel S., representative, Adams and Jay cos. (1843), *272; (1845), *289; Adams and Wells cos. (1849), *334; senator, Adams, Allen, Wells (1850), *352.

Mieure, William, representative, Knox Co. (1837), 236.

Milam, Elijah, representative, Sullivan Co. (1851), 360.

Milburn, John, representative, Gibson Co. (1823), *191.

Miller, Benjamin, representative, Union Co. (1847), 319.

Miller, Cornelius J., delegate, const. conv., Clinton and Tipton cos., *378.

Miller, Daniel, representative, Vanderburgh Co. (1843), *274.

Miller, Daniel B., representative, Randolph Co. (1847), 318.

Miller, Hugh, representative, Fulton Co. etc. (1849), *336; (1851), *362; delegate, const. conv., *385.

Miller, Huston, representative, Crawford Co. (1843), *274; senator, Crawford and Orange cos. (1844), *286; (1850), *352.

Miller, Jacob, representative, Floyd Co. (1840), *255.

Miller, James F., representative, Owen Co. (1849), *339.

Miller, John, representative, Clark Co. (1821), *187.

Miller, Noah, senator, Franklin Co. (1849), 343.

Miller, Samuel, representative, Fayette Co. (1847), 314.

Miller, Samuel, representative, La Porte and St. Joseph cos. (1834), 220; La Porte Co. (1835), 225.

Miller, Smith, representative, Gibson Co. (1835), *226; (1836), *232; (1837), *237; (1839), *248; (1845), 292; (1846), *304; senator, Gibson Co. etc. (1841), *264; (1847), *321; delegate, const. conv., *384.

Miller, William, representative, St. Joseph Co. (1844), *284; (1847), *318; (1848), *330; senator, St. Joseph Co. etc. (1849), 344.

Milligan, Dixon, senator, Blackford Co. etc. (1846), *310; delegate, const. conv., *378.

Milligan, Lampden P., senator, Huntington Co. etc. (1848), 333; representative (1850), 348.

Milligan, Lewis, 309n.

Milligan, William, 312n.

Millikan, James P., 126n; representative, Dearborn Co. (1835), 224; (1841), *259; (1842), *268; senator (1846), *310; (1849), *343.

Millikan (Millikin), William, representative, La Porte Co. (1849), *338; (1850), *348.

Mills, Felix, representative, Posey Co. (1847), *318; (1848), *329; (1850), 349; (1851), 360.

Mills, Henry I., representative, Knox Co. (1816), *183.

Milroy, Henry B., representative, Carroll Co. (1839), *246.

Milroy, John, representative, Lawrence Co. (1821), *188; senator, Lawrence and Orange cos. (1826), *198.

Milroy, Robert H., delegate, const. conv., Carroll Co., *378.

Milroy, Samuel, 109n, 163n; presidential elector (1824), *4-5; lieutenant governor (1825), 161-62n; representative, Washington Co. (1816), *183; (1817), *184; (1818), *185; (1819), *186; (1820), *187; (1821), *188; representative, Carroll Co. etc. (1829), *202; resignation, 204n; (1837), *237; (1838), *242; senator, Washington Co. (1823), *192; succeeded, 196n; senator, Carroll Co. etc. (1834), 222, 223n; (1836), *234, 235n.

Miner, Noah W., representative, Wayne Co. (1850), 351.

Misner, Charles, 298n.

Misner, John T., senator, Franklin Co. (1849), 343.

Mitchell, David G., anti-Mason, xx-xxi, 20n; representative, U. S. Congress (1833), 87; U. S. Senator (1838), 132-33; representative, Harrison Co. (1821), *189n; (1832), *213; senator (1836), *233.

Mitchell, Giles B., senator, Morgan Co. (1850), 353.

Mitchell, Pleasant L. D., senator, Brown and Monroe cos. (1851), 363.

Mitchell, Samuel C., representative, Hendricks Co. (1844), 281; (1846), 304.

Mitchell, Samuel G., representative, Marion Co. (1831), 208; (1832), 212.

Mitchell, William, representative, Noble and La Grange cos. (1842), *266; senator, De Kalb Co. etc. (1843), 276; delegate, const. conv., 384.

Mitchell, William B., representative, Elkhart Co. (1841), *261; senator, Elkhart Co. etc. (1842), *270.

Moffatt, James T., 109n; representative, Knox Co. (1825), *195; Vigo Co. (1831), 209n; senator, Vigo Co. etc. (1837), *239; (1840), *255; (1846), 310.

Moffitt, William, representative, Rush Co. (1844), 284.

Monk, Simon S., representative, Crawford and Orange cos. (1846), *302.

Monroe, Henry C., representative, Washington Co. (1833), *217; (1837), *238; (1838), *244; (1839), *249; (1841), *260; (1845), *297; (1847), 320.

Monroe, James, elected president, xii, 3.

Montague, David, representative, Decatur Co. (1842), *268; (1843), *274.

Montgomery, Isaac, presidential elector (1828), *12-13; senator, Gibson and Pike cos. (1817), *185; (1823), *192; (1826), *197; representative, Gibson Co. (1840), *255.

Montgomery, Matthew P., representative, Allen Co. (1847), 312.

Montgomery, Thomas J., representative, Gibson Co. (1844), 281.

Montgomery, William, representative, Gibson Co. (1843), *275; (1844), *281.

Montgomery, William G., representative, Warren Co. (1839), *249; (1840), *256; (1841), *262; (1845), 298n; senator, Warren Co. etc. (1845), *298; (1848), *332.

Moodey, James C., representative, Floyd Co. (1850), 347.

Moody, John M., representative, Ohio Co. (1851), 362n.

Moon, Henry, 286n.

Mooney, Samuel P., representative, Jackson Co. (1843 special), *269n; (1843), *275; (1844), *281; (1845), *293; delegate, const. conv., *382.

Moore, A. G., representative, Carroll Co. (1849), 335.

Moore, Daniel, representative, Marion Co. (1846), 306.

Moore, Frederick, senator, Montgomery Co. (1843), *278.

Moore, George W., presidential elector (1836), 25-28; representative, Owen Co. (1833), *216; (1834), *221; (1835), *227; (1839), *248; (1842), *268; (1843), *275; (1845), *295; delegate, const. conv., *382.

Moore, Harbin H., representative, U. S. Congress (1833), 88; U. S. Senator (1832), 129; governor (1828), xix, 140-41; representative, Harrison Co. (1818), *185; (1826), *197; (1827), *199; (1831), *209, (1832), *213.

Moore, John, delegate, const. conv., Elkhart and La Grange cos., 384.

Moore, Joseph, representative, Vermillion Co. (1839), *249; (1840), 254.

Moore, Nathaniel, representative, Floyd Co. (1842), *268.

Moore, Samuel A., representative, Bartholomew Co. (1850), *351; (1851), 354.

Moore, Thomas C., senator, Daviess Co. etc. (1836), *233.

Moore, Widdows, P., 298n.

Moore, William, representative, Marion Co. (1839), 247; delegate, const. conv., 380.

Moore, William J., representative, Marion Co. (1846), *306.

Moore, William J., representative, Delaware Co. (1850), 346.

Morehead, A., representative, Vermillion Co. (1835), 226.

Morehouse, Jay, representative, Vanderburgh and Warrick cos. (1830), *206; death, 206n.

Morgan, A., representative, Fayette Co. (1830), 204.

Morgan, Amaziah, presidential elector (1828), 12-13; senator, Rush Co. etc. (1826), *197, 198n; (1829), *204; Rush Co. (1832), *214; (1835), *228.

Morgan, Benjamin, representative, Marion Co. (1850), *349.

Morgan, Henry, senator, Hendricks Co. (1845), 299.

Morgan, Isaac, representative, Dearborn Co. (1819), *186.

Morgan, James, senator, Decatur Co. (1837), *239; (1840), *258; (1843), *277; (1849), *343; representative (1848), *331.

Morgan, James S., representative, Daviess and Martin cos. (1848), 325; (1849), 335.

Morgan, Jesse, representative, Daviess Co. (1844), 279; (1845), 290; (1850), 346.

Morgan, Jesse, representative, Rush Co. (1838), *243; (1839), *249; (1840), *254; (1843), *275; senator (1841), 263; (1844), *288; delegate, const. conv., *387.

Morgan, John, 20n.

Morgan, Lewis, representative, Johnson and Shelby cos. (1826), *197.

Morgan, Oliver, representative, Spencer Co. (1844), 284.

Morgan, Thomas, representative, Washington Co. (1847), 320.

Morley, Israel D., representative, De Kalb and Steuben cos. (1851), 356.

Morris, Austin W., presidential elector (1836), *21-24; senator, Marion and Hamilton cos. (1833), 217; Marion Co. (1837), 239; representative (1835), *225; (1836), *230; (1841), 260.

Morris, Bethuel F., U. S. Senator (1832), 129.

Morris, Daniel M., representative, Parke Co. (1844), 283.

Morris, Isaac H., representative, Henry Co. (1851), *357.

Morris, Morris, representative, Marion Co. (1826), *197.

Morris, Sylvan B., representative, Johnson and Shelby cos. (1828), *201; Shelby Co. (1831), *209.

Morris, Thomas, vice-president (1844), 48-52.

Morrison, Alexander F., representative, Clark Co. (1829), *202; Marion Co. (1836), 230; (1837), *236; (1840), 253; senator, Marion and Hamilton cos. (1833), *217, 218n; Marion Co. (1843), 277; delegate, const. conv., *385.

Morrison, Alonzo A., representative, Scott Co. (1847), *319; (1849), *340.

Morrison, John I., representative, Washington Co. (1839), *249; senator (1847), *323; delegate, const. conv., *386.

Morrow, Joseph, presidential elector (1848), 67n; representative, Wayne Co. (1837), 238n; (1838), *242.

Morrow, Joseph, representative, Grant Co. (1844), 281; (1845), *292; (1850), *347.

Morse, Hugh, 20n.

Morton, Oliver P., 122n.

Mosier, John, representative, Martin Co. (1847), 317.

Moulder, Jacob, representative, Orange Co. (1822), *190.

Mount, David, representative, Franklin Co. (1816), *183; senator (1837), *239; (1840), *257.

Mowrer, Daniel, delegate, const. conv., Henry Co., *382.

Moyer, John B., representative, Orange Co. (1828), *201; (1829), *203; (1831), *209.
Mudget, Gilman C., representative, De Kalb and Steuben cos. (1850), 352n; (1851), *356.
Muhler, Charles M., representative, Allen Co. (1849), 334.
Murdock, George L., representative, Franklin Co. (1816), *184n; (1821), *188; (1823), *191.
Murphey, Eli, senator, Henry Co. (1845), *300.
Murphy, Miles, representative, Henry Co. (1837), *237; (1844), 281.
Murray, Charles D., representative, Cass and Howard cos. (1846), 302; (1849), *335.
Murray, Elias, representative, Delaware Co. etc. (1831), *209; Huntington Co. etc. (1841), *261; senator (1847), *322; delegate, const. conv., *385.
Murray, James, representative, Dearborn Co. (1831), 209n; (1838), 244n.
Murray, John, representative, Orange Co. (1835), *227.
Murray, Seth W., representative, De Kalb and Steuben cos. (1841), 259.
Myer, Philip P., representative, Fountain Co. (1849), 336.
Myers, John, presidential elector (1836), 25-28; representative, Knox Co. (1835), *225; (1836), *230; (1839), 247; (1841), *259; (1842), *266; senator (1843), 277.

Nave, Christian C., representative, Hendricks Co. (1833), 215; (1834), *219; (1835), *224; (1837), 236; (1849), 342n; senator (1839), *251; (1845), 299; (1851), 363; delegate, const. conv., *379.
Naylor, Charles B., representative, Washington Co. (1829), *203; election contested, 204n; (1830), 205.
Naylor, Isaac, representative, Montgomery Co. (1836), 230.
Naylor, William, representative, Hendricks Co. (1834), 219.
Naylor, William, representative, Vigo Co. (1847), 320n; delegate, const. conv., 383n.
Neal, John, representative, Dearborn Co. (1837), 238n.
Neal, Stephen, representative, Boone Co. (1846), *301; (1847), *313.
Neely, John I., presidential elector (1832), 17-20.
Nees, John B., representative, Clay Co. (1842), *268; (1843), *274.
Neff, Elias, representative, Putnam Co. (1842), 267.
Neff, Henry H., representative, Randolph Co. (1847), *318.
Neff, Orange H., representative, Rush Co. (1842), 267.
Nelson, Daniel, representative, Jefferson Co. (1845), 298n; (1847), 316; (1851), 357.
Nelson, Isaac D. G., representative, Allen Co. (1851), *354.
Nelson, John, representative, Clinton and Montgomery cos. (1831), *208; (1832), 211; (1836), 230; (1839), *248; (1841), *262; (1842), *268; (1845), *294; senator (1846), 311.
Nelson, John H., representative, Boone Co. (1838), *242; (1839), *247; (1850), *345.
Nelson, Reuben W., representative, U. S. Congress (1818), xix, 72-73; (1820), xix, 73-74; representative, Clark Co. (1823), *191; (1824), *192.
Newell, Curtis, representative, Fountain Co. (1844), 280; (1845), 291.
Newell (Newel), Davis, representative, Fountain Co. (1840), *255; (1847), 315, 320n.
Newell (Newel), Robert, representative, Jasper Co. etc. (1836), *232; (1840), *253.
Newell, William, representative, Rush Co. (1827), *199.
Newland, Elijah, presidential elector (1844), *38-42.
Newland, John H., representative, Marion Co. (1837), 236.

Newman, John S., representative, Wayne Co. (1834), *220; delegate, const. conv., *386.

Niblack, William E., representative, Martin Co. (1849), *338; senator, Daviess and Martin (1850), *352.

Nichols, Drusus, representative, De Kalb Co. etc. (1838), 241.

Nichols, Thomas, representative, Hendricks Co. (1833), *215; (1834), 219; (1836), *229; senator (1848), 333.

Nicholson, David D., representative, Montgomery Co. (1848), *328.

Nickoll, Joseph B., representative, Shelby Co. (1837), *239n; senator (1839), *251.

Niles, John B., delegate, const. conv., La Porte Co., *379.

Nimmon, William H., representative, Noble Co. etc. (1844), *282; (1847), *316; (1849), 349; senator (1846), 311.

Nixon, Jeremy, representative, Lake and Porter cos. (1850), 348.

Noble, Benjamin S., presidential elector (1844), 48-52; representative, Franklin Co. (1829), *202; (1831), *209; (1833), *216; (1834), 219; Johnson Co. (1837), *237.

Noble, James, U. S. Senator (1816), *xii, xvii, 127; (1820), *127; (1826), *127; representative, Franklin Co. (1816), *183; resignation, 184n; death, xx.

Noble, Noah, U. S. Senator (1832), 129; (1836), xxii, 131; (1838), xxii-xxiii, 132-33; governor (1831), *xvi, xx, 141-43; (1834), *xxii, 143-45; term of service, 395; representative, Franklin Co. (1824), *193; (1825), *194; resignation, 196n.

Noel, Samuel V. B., representative, Marion Co. (1846), *306; (1848), 328.

Noel, William T., senator, Parke Co. (1835), 228; representative (1837), *238; (1838), *243.

Nofsinger, William R., representative, Parke Co. (1845), *295; (1846), *306; delegate, const. conv., *382.

Norris, Isaiah M., representative, Johnson Co. (1847), *316.

North, Abijah, representative, Dearborn Co. (1840), *252.

North, Royal F., representative, Switzerland Co. (1837), 236.

Norton, Asa, representative, Elkhart Co. (1846), *303.

Norvell, Ralph G., representative, Lawrence Co. (1841), *262; (1842), *268; (1843), *275.

Nowland, Matthias T., representative, Marion Co. (1833), 215; (1834), 220.

Nutter, Charles, representative, Union Co. (1843), *275; (1844), *285.

Nuzum, Richard R., representative, Fayette Co. (1847), 314.

Odell, James, representative, Carroll Co. (1848), *324.

Odell, John W., representative, Tippecanoe Co. (1836), *230; (1844), *284; senator (1842), *271; (1849), *344.

Ogden, Daniel, representative, Union Co. (1841), *262.

Ogdon, William B., 67n.

O'Haver, James K., representative, Sullivan Co. (1849), *341.

Oiler, Dr. ———, 126n.

Oliver, David, representative, Franklin Co. (1823), *191; (1824), *193; senator (1825), *196.

Olmstead, John S., representative, Ohio and Switzerland cos. (1850), 349.

Olmstead, William, representative, Vanderburgh Co. (1844), 285.

O'Neal, Hugh, presidential elector (1844), 43-47.

O'Neal, John F., representative, Greene Co. (1841), *261; (1842), *268; (1843), *275; senator, Greene and Owen (1844), 287; (1847), 322.

O'Neal, Thomas H., representative, Tippecanoe Co. (1849), *341; (1850), *350.

O'Neall, Abijah, representative, Montgomery Co. (1839), *248; senator (1849), 344.

Orr, Joseph, presidential elector (1828), 12-13; representative, Clay and Putnam cos. (1828), *200; senator, Carroll Co. etc. (1829), *203; (1830), *207.

Orr, Samuel, representative, Delaware Co. (1847), *314; (1848), 325; (1849), *336.

Orth, Godlove S., 178n; presidential elector (1848), 58-62; senator, Tippecanoe Co. (1843), *278; (1846), *312.

Orton, Harlow S., representative, Lake and Porter cos. (1847), 316.

Orton, Myron H., representative, La Porte Co. (1847), *316.

Osbon, James, representative, Union Co. (1845), 296.

Osborn, Andrew L., representative, La Porte Co. (1838), 241; (1844), *282, 286n; (1845), *297; senator, La Porte Co. etc. (1846), *311.

Osborn, Isaiah, representative, Wayne Co. (1842), 269n; (1844), 285.

Osborn, James, representative, Union Co. (1836), 230; (1839), *249; (1842), *269.

Osborn, James, representative, Vermillion Co. (1832), *213.

Osborn, Job, representative, Hendricks Co. (1835), 224.

Osborn, John, representative, Clay Co. (1839), *248.

Osborn, Redin, representative, Franklin Co. (1837), *237; (1839), *246.

Osborn, Silas, representative, Sullivan Co. (1845), *296; (1846), *308; (1847), 319; (1848), *330.

Ounghst, H., representative, Warren Co. etc. (1836), 231.

Overman, Ephraim, representative, Wayne Co. (1816), *183.

Owen (or Owens), John, representative, Monroe Co. (1830), *205.

Owen, Robert Dale, presidential elector (1840), 33-36, 37n; (1848), *53-57; representative, U. S. Congress (1839), 97; (1843), *105-6, 109n; (1845), *110; (1847), 114; representative, Posey Co. (1836), *232; (1837), *238; (1838), *243; (1851), *360; delegate, const. conv., *382.

Pabody, Ezra F., representative, Jennings Co. (1827), *199; (1828), *201; (1829), *203; (1836), *232; (1837), *237.

Paddacks, Joseph, representative, Harrison Co. (1825), *195; (1830), *206; (1831), *209.

Paine, Frederick C., senator, Fountain Co. (1833), *218, 219n; (1834), 223.

Painter, Henry, representative, Washington Co. (1850), *351.

Palmer, Henry D., representative, Sullivan Co. (1822), *190; (1823), *192.

Palmer, Hiram, representative, Daviess and Martin cos. (1846), 302.

Palmer, Joel, representative, Franklin Co. (1843), *275; (1844), *280.

Palmer, Nathan B., presidential elector (1832), *14-16; representative, U. S. Congress (1841), 104; representative, Jefferson Co. (1824), *192; (1825), *195; (1828), *201; (1832), *212; (1833), *215.

Palmer, William S., representative, Cass Co. (1844), 279; (1846), *302.

Pancake, Abraham, representative, Noble Co. (1850), *349.

Parcels, James, representative, Miami Co. (1851), 358.

Park, Moody, delegate, const. conv., Jefferson Co., 379.

Park, Wesley, representative, De Kalb and Steuben cos. (1847), 314; (1851), 356; delegate, const. conv., 379.

Parker, Christian, representative, Allen Co. (1845), *289; (1846), *301; (1847), *312; (1848), *323.

Parker, Hiram, 170n.

Parker, Isaac, representative, Henry Co. (1842), *268; (1844), *281.

Parker, J., delegate, const. conv., Spencer Co., 380.

Parker, John C., representative, Clark Co. (1832), *212.

Parker, Patterson C., representative, Brown Co. (1848), *324.

Parker, Samuel W., presidential elector (1844), 43-47; representative, U. S. Congress (1849), 119; (1851), *123; representative, Fayette Co. (1839), *248; (1843), *274; senator, Fayette and Union cos. (1840), *258.

Parker, Woodbridge, representative, Washington Co. (1830), 205; (1833), *217; (1838), *244.

Parks, James, representative, Hendricks Co. (1848), 327.

Parks, James, representative, Monroe Co. (1832), *213.

Parks, James O., representative, Fulton and Marshall cos. (1846), *303.

Parks, Parmenter M., senator, Morgan Co. (1841), *264; (1844), *288; representative (1849), 339.

Parks, Pleasant, representative, Lawrence Co. (1829), *203; (1830), *206; (1831), *209; (1834), *221; senator (1850), 353.

Parmelee, William H., representative, Adams and Wells cos. (1846), 301.

Parret, Elisha E., representative, Adams and Jay cos. (1842), 265.

Parton, H. E., representative, Jefferson Co. (1841), 262n.

Pate, C. Bird, representative, Dearborn and Ohio cos. (1845), 298n.

Patrick, John M., 67n.

Patrick, Septer, representative, Vigo Co. (1842), *269.

Patterson, Alexander L., representative, Tippecanoe Co. (1849), *341; (1850), *350.

Patterson, Arthur, presidential elector (1832), *14-16; U. S. Senator (1832), 129; senator, Parke Co. (1831), 210.

Patterson, Peter H., representative, Fountain Co. (1836), 233n.

Patterson, Thomas, representative, Harrison Co. (1851), 357.

Patterson, William, representative, Knox Co. (1837), 236; (1840), 253.

Patterson, William M., representative, Fulton Co. etc. (1850), *347.

Paul, John, senator, Jefferson and Switzerland cos. (1816), *183, 184n.

Paul, William, 52n.

Pavy, John, representative, Switzerland Co. (1834), 220.

Paxton, James, representative, Marion Co. etc. (1823), *191; (1825), *194.

Paxton, James, representative, Rush Co. (1845), 295.

Payne, H. B., representative, Wayne Co. (1842), 269n; (1847), 320n.

Payne, John W., presidential elector (1840), *29-32; representative, U. S. Congress (1843), 105-6, 109n; senator, Harrison Co. (1830), 207; (1833), *218; representative (1832), *213.

Pearcy, George, Jr., representative, Putnam Co. (1841), *262. *See also* Piercy.

Pearson, Isaac, representative, Vermillion Co. (1833), *217; (1835), 226.

Pearson, John, representative, Hendricks Co. (1849), 342n.

Peaslee, William J., presidential elector (1840), 33-36; representative, Shelby Co. (1837), *238; (1838), *243.

Peck, Joseph, representative, Rush Co. (1840), *254.

Peck, Willys, representative, La Porte Co. (1844), 282, 286n.

Peckenpaugh, Nicholas, representative, Crawford Co. (1850), *346.

Peek (Peak), Cager, representative, Martin Co. (1841), *262; (1842), *268; (1844), *283; (1846), 310.

Pelham, William C., senator, Posey and Vanderburgh cos. (1844), 288.

Pendleton, Z. W., representative, Wayne Co. (1833), 217n.

Pennington, Dennis, presidential elector (1832), 17-20; representative,

U. S. Congress (1833), 87; lieutenant governor, 160n; (1825), 161-62n; senator, Harrison Co. (1816), *183, 184n; Crawford and Harrison (1818), *185; resignation (1820), 187n; representative, Harrison Co. (1822), *190; (1823), *191; (1828), *200; (1829), *203; (1845), *292; senator (1824), *194; (1830), *207; (1839), 250; (1842), *270.

Pennington, Robert B., representative, Harrison Co. (1846), 304.

Pepper, Abel C., 148n; U. S. Senator (1832), 129-30; lieutenant governor (1828), 161-62; (1837), 170n; representative, Dearborn Co. (1824), *192; (1825), *194; (1836), *229; senator (1840), 257; delegate, const. conv., Ohio and Switzerland cos., *386.

Pepper, Samuel, representative, Crawford Co. (1851), 355; delegate, const. conv., *381.

Perine, Aaron M., representative, Kosciusko Co. etc. (1837), *237; (1838), *243.

Perkins, Samuel E., presidential elector (1844), *38-42.

Perrin, John Q. A., representative, Clinton and Tipton cos. (1848), 325.

Perry, Lewis F., representative, Crawford and Orange cos. (1848), 325.

Perry, William, representative, Dearborn Co. (1839), *246.

Perssuant, W. W., *see* Purviance, Lewis W.

Pettit, John, representative, U. S. Congress (1843), *108; (1845), *112; (1847), 116, 118n; representative, Tippecanoe Co. (1835), 225; (1838), *244; (1841), 260; delegate, const. conv., *380.

Pettit, John U., 122n; representative, Miami and Wabash cos. (1844), *283; (1847), 322.

Peugh, Isaiah, senator, Washington Co. (1844), 288.

Peyton, Jared, representative, Clay Co. (1831), *208; (1832), *212.

Pfaff, Israel S., senator, Hamilton Co. etc. (1848), 332.

Pfaff, Jacob L., representative, Hamilton Co. etc. (1844), 281; (1847), 315; senator (1845), 299; (1848), 332.

Phelps, Joseph N., representative, Crawford Co. (1834), *220; (1835), *226.

Phillips, Brannack, representative, Jennings Co. (1850), *348.

Piatt, John B., representative, Dearborn Co. (1841), 259.

Piatt, William, senator, Fountain Co. (1846), 311; representative (1851), 356.

Pickens, Samuel, representative, Owen Co. (1848), 329.

Picket (Pickett), Elihu, representative, Hamilton and Tipton cos. (1845), 292; (1846), 304.

Pierce, Lavinius, representative, Elkhart Co. (1848), *326.

Pierce, Oliver P., representative, Martin Co. (1849), 338.

Pierce, S., representative, Wayne Co. (1833), 217n.

Piercy (Pearcy), George, representative, Clay and Putnam cos. (1826), *196; (1827), *198; Putnam Co. (1833), *215; (1835), 227n; (1840), 254.

Pile, Burdet C., senator, Clark Co. (1850), 352.

Pitcher, John, presidential elector (1818), 67n; representative, U. S. Congress (1837), 94; representative, Perry and Spencer cos. (1830), *206; senator, Posey and Vanderburgh cos. (1841), *264, 265n, 271n; delegate, const. conv., 386.

Pitman, Anthony, representative, Adams and Jay cos. (1845), 289.

Place, Willard A., representative, La Porte Co. (1839), 247; (1840), 253; (1848), *328; (1849), 338.

Plummer, Benjamin, representative, Dearborn and Ohio cos. (1844), 280.

Plummer, Daniel, senator, Dearborn Co. (1834), *222.

Pogue, Jacob L., representative, Monroe Co. (1850), 349.

Politics, beginning of party machinery, xviii-ix; personal, xxviii-xix; part played in Indiana elections, xx-xxiv.

Polk, James K., president (1844), *38-42.

Polke, Richard, representative, Perry and Spencer cos. (1829), *203; (1831), *209.

Polke, William, lieutenant governor (1822), 160-61n; senator, Knox Co. (1816), *183, 184n; Knox Co. etc. (1818), *185.

Pollard, Philip, representative, Carroll and Cass cos. (1833), 215.

Pollock, James T., representative, Dearborn Co. (1827), *198; (1828), *200; (1829), *202; (1830), *204; senator (1831), *210; resignation (1833), 218n.

Pomeroy, Ralph M., representative, Randolph Co. (1848), 329.

Pomeroy, William G., representative, Fulton and Marshall cos. (1844), *281; (1850), 347; senator, Fulton Co. etc. (1845), *299; (1846), 311.

Poor, ———, representative, Washington Co. (1840), 255; senator (1841), 263.

Porter, John, representative, Vermillion Co. (1837), *238.

Porter, Samuel, representative, Ohio and Switzerland cos. (1851), *359.

Porter, William A., representative, Harrison Co. (1836), *229; (1838), 241; (1841), 259; (1845), *292; (1846), *304; (1847), *315; senator (1848), *333; delegate, const. conv., 385.

Porter, William M., representative, Tippecanoe Co. (1839), *249.

Posey, Alfred, representative, Rush Co. (1835), *225; (1836), *232.

Posey, Thomas, representative, U. S. Congress (1817), xix, 71-72; governor (1816), xvi, 137.

Posey, Thomas, representative, Harrison Co. (1824), *193; (1825), *195.

Potter, William, representative, Carroll Co. (1848), 324.

Potter, William, representative, Tippecanoe Co. (1845), 296.

Pottinger, Dennis G., representative, Montgomery Co. (1849), 339.

Poulson, John, representative, Dubois Co. (1841), *261.

Powell, Erasmus, lieutenant governor (1822), 160-61n; representative, Dearborn Co. (1816), *183; (1817), *185n; (1818), *185; (1820), *187; (1821), *188; (1836), *232; (1838), *243.

Powell, John, representative, Henry Co. (1846), *309.

Powell, William, representative, Jefferson Co. (1830), 204; (1836), 229.

Powers, Clark, representative, De Kalb and Steuben cos. (1845), *291.

Prather, Hiram, representative, Jennings Co. (1847), *320; (1849), *337; delegate, const. conv., Bartholomew and Jennings cos., *387.

Prather, Thomas W., representative, Clark Co. (1845), 290.

Pratt, Daniel D., presidential elector (1848), 58-62; representative, U. S. Congress (1847), 116-17, 118n; representative, Cass and Howard cos. (1850), *345.

Pratt, Joseph H., representative, Huntington and Whitley cos. (1847), 316.

Presidential electors, method of choosing, xii, xvii-xviii; elected by General Assembly (1816, 1820), 3; vote for (1824), 4-10; (1828), 10-13; (1832), 14-20; (1836), 21-28; (1840), 29-37; (1844), 38-52; (1848), 53-67.

Price, Andrew B., representative, Lake and Porter cos. (1848), 328.

Price, William, representative, Sullivan Co. (1845), 296.

Prickett, Benjamin, representative, Randolph Co. (1847), 318.

Prilliman, William, representative, Blackford Co. etc. (1842), *267.

Primley, J., 67n.

Prince, William, representative, U. S. Congress (1822), *76; senator, Gibson Co. (1816), *183, 184n; representative (1821), *188; death, 80n.

Proctor, James, representative, Spencer Co. (1846), 307.

Proctor, John, representative, Spencer Co. (1841), *262; (1842), *269.

Proctor, William, 67n.

Proffit, George H., representative, U. S. Congress (1839), *97; (1841), *101-2; representative, Dubois and Pike cos. (1831), *209; (1832), *212; (1836), *231; (1837), *238; (1838), *242.

Pruitt, Richard, representative, Parke Co. (1832), *213.

Puckett, Zachariah, representative, Randolph Co. (1834), *221; (1836), *232; (1837), *238; senator, Randolph Co. etc. (1849), 342.

Puett, Austin M., presidential elector (1844), *38-42; senator, Parke Co. (1835), *228; representative (1838), *243.

Pulse, John D., representative, Blackford Co. etc. (1845), 289.

Purcel (Pursel), Thomas, senator, Franklin Co. (1840), 257; (1845), 298n.

Pursell (Purcel?), Aaron, representative, Dearborn and Ohio cos. (1844), 286n.

Purviance, Lewis W. (Purssuant, W. W.), representative, Adams Co. etc. (1839), *245.

Quick, Tunis, representative, Bartholomew and Brown cos. (1840), *255; (1841), *261.

Quigg, Joseph, representative, Wayne Co. (1845), 298n; (1846), 309n.

Quinn, John, representative, Jefferson Co. (1849), 342n.

Rabb, David G., representative, Dearborn and Ohio cos. (1845), 298n.

Rader, Jesse, representative, Monroe Co. (1838), 242.

Railsback, Edward, representative, Hendricks Co. (1836), 229.

Rambo, Smith, representative, Huntington and Whitley cos. (1847), 316.

Rand, James, representative, Dearborn Co. (1841), *259.

Randall, Franklin P., representative, Allen Co. (1845), 289; senator, Allen Co. etc. (1847), *321.

Randall, Joshua R., representative, Adams and Wells cos. (1849), 334.

Rannells, William, representative, Fulton and Marshall cos. (1841), *261.

Raper, William, representative, Knox Co. (1833), 215.

Rariden, James, 105n; presidential elector (1824), 6-7; representative, U. S. Congress (1835), 91-92; (1837), *95-96, 97n; (1839), *99, 100n; U. S. Senator (1831), 128; (1832), 129; senator, Randolph and Wayne cos. (1823), *192; Wayne Co. (1826), *198; representative, (1829), *203; (1832), *213; delegate, const. conv., *381.

Ratliff, Cornelius, representative, Wayne Co. (1836), 231.

Rawlings, Aaron, representative, Scott Co. (1840), *256; (1841), *262.

Ray, James Brown, representative, U. S. Congress (1824), 79; (1831), 85-86; (1833), 89; (1837), 96-97n; U. S. Senator (1832), 129-30; governor (1825), *xix, 138-39n; (1828), *xix, 140-41; lieutenant governor (1831), 165n; acting governor, ixn, xix, 395; representative Franklin Co. (1821), *188; senator (1822), *190.

Ray, Joel, representative, Crawford Co. (1851), *355.

Ray, Martin M., representative, Fayette Co. (1826), *196; Wayne Co. (1834), *220; (1835), *226; senator, Shelby Co. (1848), 334.

Ray, William, representative, Vigo Co. (1840), 255; delegate, const. conv., 383n.

Raymond, Felix L., representative, Lawrence Co. (1849), 338.

Raymond, Nathan H., representative, Wayne Co. (1851), 361.

Read, Daniel, delegate, const. conv., Brown and Monroe cos., *383.

Read, James G., presidential elector (1844), *38-42; U. S. Senator (1832), 129; governor (1831), xx, 141-43; (1834), xxii, 143-45; representative, Daviess and Martin cos. (1821), *188; (1823), *191; (1824), *192; (1826), *196; (1827), *198; (1828), *200; (1829), *202; (1830), *206; Clark Co. (1839), *248; (1840), *255; senator (1841), *264; (1844), *286; (1847), *321; delegate, const. conv., *387.

Read, Joshua W., representative, Scott Co. (1847), 319.

Reagin, Wilks, representative, Vanderburgh Co. (1846), 308.

Rector, W., representative, Marion Co. (1836), 230.

Reding, John W., senator, Marion Co. (1834), 223.

Redlon, Ebenezer, *see* Ridlin.

Reed, Archibald C., representative, Marion Co. (1834), 220; (1835), 225.

Reed, Armer, representative, Warrick Co. (1849), *341; (1850), 351.

Reed, David W., representative, Wayne Co. (1851), 361.

Reed, Ezra, 126n.

Reed, Isaac C., 105n.

Reed, Joel, representative, Henry Co. (1841), *261; (1843), *275; (1850), 347.

Reel, John, representative, Putnam Co. (1842), *267.

Reeve, Benjamin F., representative, Rush Co. (1836), *232; (1837), *238; senator (1841), *263; (1850), 354.

Referendums, on method of voting, xin; on revision of the Constitution, xxiv-xxv, 367-77.

Reid, John, representative, Franklin Co. (1825), *194; (1827), *198; (1830), *206; (1831), *209; (1832), *213; (1833), *216; senator (1834), *223; (1835), *228; death, 228n.

Reid, John S., representative, Union Co. (1846), 308; senator, Fayette and Union cos. (1849), *343.

Reiley, John, representative, Martin Co. (1836), *232; (1838), *243.

Reily, John C., representative, Knox Co. (1828), *201; (1829), *203; (1830), *205.

Reyburn, William M., representative, Fulton and Miami cos. (1839), 246; (1840), *252; senator, Miami Co. etc. (1843), *277; delegate, const. conv., 380.

Reynearson, John representative, Hendricks Co. (1849), 337; delegate, const. conv., 379.

Reynolds, Berrian, representative, Johnson Co. (1838), *243.

Reynolds, Eli, representative, Vermillion Co. (1831), *209.

Reynolds, John, representative, St. Joseph Co. (1850), *350.

Reynolds, Zimri, representative, Grant Co. (1851), *362.

Rhorer (Rorer), John, representative, Elkhart Co. (1847), 314.

Rhorer, Samuel, representative, Marion Co. (1846), 309n.

Ribble, David, representative, Delaware Co. etc. (1832), *212.

Rice, James, representative, Montgomery Co. (1851), 359.

Rice, John W., representative, Crawford Co. (1847), 314; (1848), *325; (1850), *349.

Rich, DeWitt C., representative, Jennings Co. (1842), *268; (1843), *275; (1844), *282; senator, Bartholomew and Jennings cos. (1845), *298.

Richards, Harlin, representative, Owen Co. (1844), 283.

Richardson, Augustine P., representative, St. Joseph Co. (1845), 296; (1846), 307.

Richardson, James H., representative, Posey Co. (1824), *193; (1825), *195; (1826), *197.

Richardson, William B., representative, Spencer Co. (1848), 330; (1849), *340, 342n.
Richey, John, representative, Boone Co. (1844), 279.
Richey, John, representative, Ripley Co. (1824), *193.
Richey (Richie), John, representative, Delaware Co. (1837), *238; (1838), 241.
Richey, Samuel W., representative, U. S. Congress (1847), 116; senator, Fountain Co. (1846), 311.
Richmond, Corydon, representative, Cass and Howard cos. (1847), *313.
Ridgway, David, representative, Huntington and Whitley cos. (1849), 337.
Ridlin (Redlon), Ebenezer, 113n; representative, Ripley Co. (1845), 295; (1849), 340.
Rifner, William A., representative, Henry Co. (1848), *327; senator (1851), 363.
Riley, David, representative, Orange Co. (1844), 283.
Riley, Davis, representative, Rush Co. (1850), *350.
Riley, Ezekiel S., representative, Orange Co. (1823), *192; (1825), *195; senator (1838), *245.
Riley, Reuben A., representative, Hancock Co. (1845), *292; (1848), *327; delegate, const. conv., Hancock and Madison cos., 385.
Rinehart, Enoch, representative, Carroll Co. (1848), 324.
Rippey, David, representative, Kosciusko Co. etc. (1845), *293; senator (1847), 322.
Rippey, Matthew, representative, Elkhart Co. (1839), *248; (1840), *255; (1848), *326; senator, Elkhart Co. etc. (1844), *287.
Ristine, Henry, representative, Montgomery Co. etc. (1826), *196; (1835), *224; (1837), *237.
Ristine, Joseph, delegate, const. conv., Fountain Co. *379.
Ritchey, James, presidential elector (1848), *53-57; representative, Johnson Co. (1840), *255; (1841), *261; (1846), 305; senator (1842), *271; delegate, const. conv., *387.
Ritchey, John, senator, Johnson Co. (1845), 300.
Ritchey, John, representative, Cass Co. (1841), 258.
Ritchie, James, representative, Dubois and Pike cos. (1828), *200.
Roache, Addison L., representative, Parke Co. (1847), *318; senator, Parke and Vermillion cos. (1848), 333.
Robb, David, presidential elector (1824), *4-5; (1828), 13n; U. S. Senator (1832), 129; representative, Gibson Co. (1820), *187; (1822), *189; (1824), *193; (1828), *200; senator, Gibson Co. etc. (1829), *203; (1832), *214; resignation (1833), 219n.
Robbins, Isaac, representative, Parke Co. (1850), *351.
Robbins, Jacob, representative, Hamilton Co. (1837), *237; (1840), *255.
Robbins, James H., 298n, 309n.
Robbins, Joseph, representative, Fulton and Marshall cos. (1843), *275; (1845), 292.
Robe, Andrew, representative, Marion Co. (1834), 220.
Roberts, Daniel, representative, Dearborn Co. (1836), 233.
Roberts, Ferdinand, representative, La Porte Co. (1843), *273.
Roberts, Gaines H., senator, Posey Co. etc. (1840), *258; shifted to new district, 265n.
Roberts, John H., representative, Putnam Co. (1842), *267; (1843), *273; (1844), 284; senator (1845), 300.
Roberts, John S., representative, Ohio Co. (1851), 362n.
Roberts, Lewis, representative, Lawrence Co. (1826), *197; (1827), *199.

Roberts, Peter H., senator, Greene and Owen cos. (1850), 353.

Roberts, William S., representative, Brown Co. (1848), 324.

Robertson, Amos, representative, Montgomery Co. etc. (1823), *191; (1824), *193; (1825), *195; senator (1826), *197, 198n.

Robertson, Andrew, representative, Jackson Co. (1847), 316.

Robertson, Henry, representative, Benton Co. etc. (1844), 278; (1851), 355.

Robertson, James, representative, Clark Co. (1844), 279; (1845), 290.

Robertson, William, representative, Jackson Co. (1848), 327.

Robinson, Alexander H., representative, La Porte Co. (1848), 328; (1849), *338; (1850), 348.

Robinson, Andrew L., 126n; delegate, const. conv., Posey and Vanderburgh cos., 386.

Robinson, Andrew L., representative, Carroll Co. (1841), *258, 262n; (1842), *265; (1843), *272; Carroll and Howard cos. (1844), *279.

Robinson, George, representative, Jefferson Co. (1839), *248; (1840), *253.

Robinson, H., representative, Benton Co. etc. (1843), 272.

Robinson, Isaiah, presidential elector (1848), 67n; senator, Ripley Co. (1847), 323; representative, Switzerland Co. (1837), 236; (1839), 247.

Robinson, John L., presidential elector (1840), 33-36; representative, U. S. Congress (1847), *114-15; (1849), *119; (1851), *123.

Robinson, Joseph, representative, U. S. Congress (1849), 119; representative, Ripley Co. (1831), *209; (1839), *249; Decatur Co. (1844), *280; senator (1846), *312; delegate, const. conv., *381.

Robinson, Osmyn, representative, Rush Co. (1839), *249; (1840), 254.

Robinson, William C., representative, Rush Co. (1841), *260; (1842), 267; (1847), *318.

Robinson, William J., representative, Decatur Co. (1845), *291 (1849), *335.

Robinson, William W., representative, Tippecanoe Co. (1845), 296.

Robson, William, representative, Marion Co. (1849), *338.

Rockhill, William, presidential elector (1836), 25-28; representative, U. S. Congress (1847), *117; representative, Allen Co. etc. (1834), *220; (1836), *231; senator (1844), *286.

Roe, Jeremiah, 147n.

Roe, John E., representative, Clark Co. (1830), *205; Scott Co. (1837), *238.

Rogers, George B., senator, Henry Co. (1845), 300.

Rogers, John, representative, Kosciusko Co. (1850), 348.

Rogers, Jonathan, representative, Vigo Co. (1846), 308.

Rollin, M. H., representative, Elkhart Co. (1845), 291.

Romine, Benjamin, representative, Spencer Co. (1850), 350.

Rooker, William D., representative, Hamilton Co. (1841), *261.

Roop, John, representative, Franklin Co. (1832), *213.

Rose, Allen T., representative, Clay Co. (1844), *279.

Rose, Erasmus, representative, Union Co. (1838), *244.

Rose, John B., representative, Union Co. (1825), *195; (1831), *209; (1840), *256.

Rose, Jonathan H., representative, Boone Co. (1842), *268.

Roseman, Joseph, representative, Knox Co. (1830), 205.

Ross, ——, representative, Clinton and Montgomery cos. (1834), 224.

Ross, Andrew J., representative, Franklin Co. (1849), *336; (1850), *347; (1851), 356.

Ross, James M., representative, Rush Co. (1840), *254.

Ross, John F., representative, Clark Co. (1819), *186; (1820), *187.

Ross, Nathan O., representative, Miami Co. (1848), *328.

Ross, William T., representative, Wabash Co. (1848), *331.

Roszell, Elliott, representative, Ripley Co. (1846), 307.

Rousseau, Lovel (Lovell) H., presidential elector (1848), 58-62; representative, Greene Co. (1844), *281; (1845), *292; senator, Greene and Owen cos. (1847), *322.

Rousseau, Richard H., representative, Greene Co. (1848), *332n; (1851), 356.

Routt, William H., representative, Daviess and Martin cos. (1822), *189.

Rowland, Daniel A., representative, Dearborn Co. (1848), 331n.

Rowley, Nathan, representative, Vanderburgh Co. (1848), 330.

Royston, Barney, representative, Vanderburgh Co. (1845), 296.

Ruby, Ambrose S., representative, Union Co. (1845), *296.

Ruddick, Jesse, representative, Bartholomew Co. (1831), *208; (1832), *212.

Rudisill, Ephraim, senator, Montgomery Co. (1849), 344.

Rulon, Morrison, representative, Adams Co. etc. (1840), *251; Adams and Jay cos. (1841), 258; Jay and Blackford cos. (1847), *320n.

Runyan, Peter L., representative, Kosciusko Co. etc. (1840), *255; (1841), *261.

Rush, Greenberry, representative, Rush Co. (1849), *340; (1850), 350.

Rush, John, representative, Miami Co. (1850), 349.

Rush, Leonard, representative, St. Joseph Co. (1839), *249.

Rush, Richard, vice-president (1828), 12-13.

Rush, William P., representative, U. S. Congress (1851), 124; representative, Rush Co. (1835), 225; (1836), *232; (1838), *243; (1841), 260.

Rushton, Solomon, representative, Hendricks Co. (1847), 315.

Russell, Alexander W., representative, Marion Co. (1830), *205.

Russell, John, representative, Vermillion Co. (1840), *254.

Russell, Samuel A., representative, (1849), *337; (1850), 347.

Rust, John B., senator, Jackson and Scott cos. (1845), 300.

Ryan, Townsend, representative, Madison Co. (1848), *328.

Ryman, John, representative, Dearborn Co. (1848), 325.

Sabin, Stephen, representative, De Kalb and Steuben cos. (1846), 303.

Sacket, Erastus, representative, Perry Co. (1847), *318.

Saffer, William M., representative, Harrison Co. (1839), 246; (1841), *259; (1842), 266; (1843), *273; (1845), 292; senator (1851), *363; delegate, const. conv., 385.

Sailor, Conrad, representative, Franklin Co. (1819), *186.

St. Clair, Arthur, representative, Dearborn Co. (1828), *200.

St. John, Daniel, representative, Franklin Co. (1828), *200.

St. John, J. O. (?), 298n.

St. John, Seth, representative, Warren Co. (1849), 341.

Sale, T. C. W., delegate, const. conv., Vermillion Co., 381

Salter, William H., senator, Benton Co. etc. (1848), 332; representative. (1849), *334; (1851), 357.

Sample, Samuel C., presidential elector (1840), *29-32; representative, U. S. Congress (1843), *108; (1845), 112-13; representative, Fayette Co. (1828), *200.

Samsel, Isaac, senator, Brown and Monroe cos. (1845), 299.

Sandbach, ——, representative, Harrison Co. (1840), 253.

Sanders, William, representative, Marion Co. (1833), 215.

Sands, Isaac, representative, Crawford Co. (1836), *231; (1840), 252; senator, Crawford and Orange cos. (1841), *264; (1844), 286.

Sands, Lewis H., representative, Putnam Co. (1832), *213.

Sands, Samuel, representative, Crawford Co. (1838), *240; (1839), *246; (1840), 252.

Sandusky, Isaac B., representative, Marion Co. (1851), 358.

Sanford, Nathan, vice-president (1824), 6-7.

Sargeant, Absalom, representative, Washington Co. (1826), *197.

Saunders, James, representative, Decatur Co. (1841), *261; (1850), 346.

Sawin, George, representative, La Porte Co. (1846), 305.

Saylor, Martin Z., representative, Clinton Co. (1840), *255; (1841), *261.

Schnee, John, representative, Posey Co. (1823), *192.

Schooling, Joseph, representative, Vermillion Co. (1834), *221; (1835), 226.

Schooly, Isaac, senator, Delaware and Grant cos. (1845), 299.

Schoonover, Rudolphus, representative, Washington Co. (1830), *205; (1832), *213; (1835), 226; (1840), *255; (1851), *361; delegate, const. conv., *381.

Schwartz, George, representative, Clark Co. (1850), *345.

Scoby, T. B., 298n.

Scott, ———, representative, Switzerland Co. (1830), 205.

Scott, Andrew F., representative, Wayne Co. (1841), 260.

Scott, David, representative, Putnam Co. (1846), *307.

Scott, Hugh S., representative, Fountain Co. (1845), *291; (1847), 315.

Scott, James, 75n; presidential elector (1824), 8-9; representative, U. S. Congress (1822), 76-77; U. S. Senator (1816, 1818), 127; (1832), 129; governor (1834), 143n.

Scott, James H., senator, Switzerland Co. (1837), 239.

Scott, John, representative, Wayne Co. (1816), *183; (1817), *184.

Scott, John H., 82n.

Scott, Lucius H., representative, Parke and Vigo cos. (1822), *190.

Scott, Thomas J., representative, Montgomery Co. (1851), 359.

Scott, W. H. H., senator, Jasper Co. etc. (1836), 234.

Scott, Warner L., representative, Pike Co. (1846), 307.

Scott, William, representative, Switzerland Co. (1835), 225.

Scoville, Linus, representative, Switzerland Co. (1822), *190.

Scruggs, William, representative, Rush Co. (1844), 284; (1845), 295.

Scudder, John, representative, Daviess Co. (1851), *355.

Seamans, David, representative, Delaware and Randolph cos. (1830), *206.

Searce, William, representative, Wayne Co. (1830), 206.

Seawright, Wilson, representative, Clinton Co. (1845), *290; Clinton and Tipton cos. (1846), 302.

Sebastian, Alexander, senator, Ripley and Switzerland cos. (1834), 223; representative, Switzerland Co. (1835), 225; (1844), 284.

Secrest, Henry, presidential elector (1840), 33-36; (1848), 67n; representative, Putnam Co. (1845), *295; (1846), *307; senator (1851), *364.

Secrest, James, representative, Putnam Co. (1831), *209; (1833), 215.

Seller, James, representative, Montgomery Co. (1843), *275.

Semans, David, representative, Putnam Co. (1845), 295. *See also* Simmons.

Senate, classification of members (1816), 184n; (1821), 189n; (1826), 198n; (1831), 211n; (1836), 235n; (1841), 264n-65n; number of members, ix. *See also* General Assembly.

Sergeant, John, vice-president (1832), 18-20.

Sering, John, senator, Jefferson and Jennings cos. (1828), *201; (1829), *203.

Serring, E., 298n.

Servis, Aaron, 286n.

Settle, William B., representative, Jefferson Co. (1841), 262n.

Seward, A. D., representative, Miami and Wabash cos. (1845), 294; Wabash Co. (1846), 308.

Seward, Austin, representative, Monroe Co. (1844), 283.

Shank, Jacob, representative, Shelby Co. (1834), *221.

Shanklin, Andrew, representative, Madison Co. (1851), *358.

Shanks (Shank), William, representative, Washington Co. (1830), 205; (1840), *255; (1844), *285; (1845), *297; (1846), 308; senator (1841), 263.

Shannon, David A., representative, Montgomery Co. (1846), 306; delegate, const. conv., *382.

Shaw, Griffin M., representative, Hamilton Co. (1848), *326.

Shaw, Henry M., senator, Knox Co. etc. (1833), 217; (1835), *228; representative, Knox Co. (1834), *219.

Shaw, Jonathan, representative, Wayne Co. (1834), 222n.

Shawhan, David C., representative, Henry Co. (1840), *255.

Sheets, Zebulon, senator, Benton Co. etc. (1841), *264, 264n.

Shelby, Isaac, representative, Tippecanoe Co. (1842), *267; (1843), *275; (1844), *284; (1847), 319; (1849), *341; delegate, const. conv., 380.

Shelby, Joseph, representative, Parke and Vigo cos. (1821), *188.

Sheldon, Benjamin D., 67n.

Sheldon, George W., representative, La Grange and Noble cos. (1847), 316.

Shell, ———, representative, Morgan Co. (1835), 225.

Shepard (Shepherd), Horace B., representative, Knox Co. (1846), 305; (1849), *338.

Shepherd, Thomas S., representative, Cass and Howard cos. (1849), 335.

Sherrod, William F., representative, Orange Co. (1849), *339; delegate, const. conv., Orange and Crawford cos., *384.

Shields, Meedy W., representative, Jackson Co. (1846), *304.

Shields, Pleasant S., senator, Floyd Co. (1849), 343.

Shields, William, representative, Jackson Co. (1839), *248.

Shimer, Ellis N., representative, Marion Co. (1844), 283.

Shirk, Samuel, representative, Franklin Co. (1845), 291.

Shively, James S., representative, Grant and Wabash cos. (1839), *248; (1840), 252; Grant Co. (1841), *261; (1844), *281.

Shoemaker, Daniel, representative, Kosciusko Co. (1848), 327.

Shoemaker, Leonard, representative, Howard and Tipton cos. (1851), 357.

Shook, Hezekiah, representative, Ripley Co. (1834), 220; (1836), *232; (1837), *238.

Shook, Luther, representative, Ripley Co. (1850), *350.

Short, Milton, presidential elector (1848), 63-67.

Short, Samuel W., representative, Lawrence Co. (1847), *317.

Shortridge, Lemuel, Benton Co. etc. (1846), 301.

Shortridge, Morgan, representative, Tippecanoe Co. (1832), *213; (1840), *254.

Shoults, Frederick, senator, Daviess Co. etc. (1821), *189.

Shoup, George G., representative, Franklin Co. (1840), 252; (1840, special), *256n; (1841), *261; (1842), *268; senator (1849), 343; delegate, const. conv., *382.

Shryer, Marcus H., representative, Greene Co. (1849), 337.
Shryock, John J., representative, Fulton Co. etc. (1847), *315.
Shuck, William, representative, Clinton Co. (1845), 290.
Shuler, Lawrence S., representative, U. S. Congress (1826), 80-81.
Shull, William T., representative, Blackford and Jay cos. (1846), 301; (1850), *345.
Sigler, Daniel, senator, Putnam Co. (1833), *218; (1836), *235.
Simler, John, representative, Harrison Co. (1850), *347; (1851), 357.
Simmons (Semans), David, senator, Blackford Co. etc. (1846), 310.
Simmons, George W., representative, Dubois Co. (1851), 356.
Simmons, J. M., 37n.
Simonson, John S., representative, U. S. Congress (1837), 94-95; senator, Clark and Floyd cos. (1826), *197; representative, Clark Co. (1838), 240; (1841), *261; (1842), *268; (1843), *274; (1844), *279; (1845), *290.
Simpson, Henry, representative, Fayette Co. (1843), *274; senator, Fayette and Union cos. (1846), *311.
Sims, John, representative, Morgan Co. etc. (1825), *194; Morgan Co. (1837), *238.
Sims, Stephen, senator, Clinton and Carroll cos. (1843), 276; delegate, const. conv., Clinton and Tipton cos., *378.
Sims, William, representative, Tippecanoe Co. (1842), 267.
Sinclair, ———, representative, Putnam Co. (1835), 225.
Sinclair, Joseph, representative, Allen Co. (1840), 251; senator, Allen Co. etc. (1841), *263.
Sinks, Daniel, representative, Wayne Co. (1841), *260.
Skeen, William, representative, Ripley Co. (1830), *206; (1832), *213.
Skinner, Albert G., representative, Greene Co. (1845), 292.
Skinner, John N., representative, Porter Co. (1851), 359.
Slack, James R., senator, Huntington and Wells cos. (1851), *363.
Slater, Francis, representative, Pike Co. (1851), 359.
Slater, Isaac, representative, Blackford Co. (1851), 355.
Slater, John, representative, Johnson Co. (1844), 282; (1845), 293.
Slater, John R., representative, Johnson Co. (1844), 282.
Slater, Richard D., representative, Dearborn and Ohio cos. (1845), *290; Dearborn Co. (1847), *314; senator (1849), 343.
Slaughter, James B., representative, Harrison Co. (1817), *184; (1818), *185; (1826), *197; (1827), *199; (1828), *200; (1829), *203; (1831), *209; senator, Harrison Co. etc. (1820), *187, 187n; (1821), *189.
Slaughter, William B., representative, Lawrence Co. (1832), *213.
Sleeth, James M., representative, Shelby Co. (1845), *296; (1846), *307; senator (1848), *334; (1851), *364.
Sleight, Jacob G., representative, La Porte Co. (1846), 305; (1847), 316.
Slinkard, Frederick, representative, Greene Co. (1844), 281.
Sloan, James G., representative, Crawford Co. (1840), *252; (1844), 279.
Sluss, John M., representative, Brown and Monroe cos. (1842), *268.
Small, Abner B., representative, Vermillion Co. (1844), 285.
Smiley, John, representative, Johnson and Shelby cos. (1827), *199; (1830), *204; Johnson Co. (1831), *209; senator (1845), 300.
Smiley, Ross, presidential elector (1828), *10-11; lieutenant governor (1831), 164-65; (1834), 167n; senator, Fayette and Union cos. (1825), *196; (1834), 222; (1846), 311; representative, Union Co. (1829), *203; delegate, const. conv., Fayette Co., *382; speaker of the House, xx.

Smiley, Thomas, senator, Tippecanoe Co. (1839), *251; representative (1846), *308; (1847), *319.
Smith, ——, representative, Perry and Spencer cos. (1839), 247.
Smith, Anthony F., representative, Fulton and Marshall cos. (1845), *292.
Smith, Caleb B., presidential elector (1840), *29-32; representative, U. S. Congress (1841), 103; (1843), *106; (1845), *111; (1847), *115; U. S. Senator (1848), 134; representative, Fayette Co. (1833), *216; (1834), *219; (1835), *226; (1836), *232; (1840), *255.
Smith, Hezekiah S., representative, Scott Co. (1848), *330; delegate, const. conv., *382.
Smith, Isaac, representative, Marion Co. (1851), *358.
Smith, J., senator, Allen Co. etc. (1832), 214.
Smith, Jacob T., representative, Floyd Co. (1845), 291.
Smith, Jeremiah, representative, Randolph Co. (1844), 284; delegate, const. conv., Randolph Co. etc., 383.
Smith, John, 126n.
Smith, Nathan, representative, Wayne Co. (1836), *231; (1837), *236; senator (1838), *245.
Smith, Nathaniel, representative, Rush Co. (1832), *213.
Smith, Oliver H., representative, U. S. Congress (1826), *82; (1831), 86; (1833), 88-89; U. S. Senator (1832), 129; (1836), *xxii, 131; (1843), 134; representative, Fayette Co. (1822), *189.
Smith, Robert, representative, Clinton and Montgomery cos. (1832), 211.
Smith, Samuel, Jr., representative, Knox Co. (1833), *215.
Smith, Thomas, representative, Dearborn and Ohio cos. (1845), 298n.
Smith, Thomas, presidential elector (1848), 67n; representative, U. S. Congress (1839), *98; (1841), 103; (1843), *106; (1845), *110-11; representative, Ripley Co. (1829), *203; (1833), *216; (1834), *220; (1835), *227; senator (1836), *235, 235n; (1838), *245; succeeded (1839), 251; delegate, const. conv., *387.
Smith, Thomas M., representative, Spencer Co. (1843), *273; (1844), *284; (1845), 296; (1850), 350; (1851), *360.
Smith, Wesley, representative, Boone Co. (1847), 313.
Smith, Zachariah, representative, Adams and Jay cos. (1843), 272.
Smith, Zenas, representative, Vigo Co. (1850), 351.
Smock, Isaac, representative, Johnson Co. (1846), 305.
Smock, John, representative, Jefferson Co. (1834), 219; (1836), 229; (1838), 241; (1845), 293; (1846), 305.
Smock, John R., representative, Johnson Co. (1845), 293.
Smock, Simon, representative, Marion Co. (1845), 294.
Smydth, Samuel H., representative, Clay Co. (1837), *237; (1838), *242; Daviess Co. (1840), *255; senator, Daviess and Martin cos. (1842), *271; resignation, 271n.
Snapp, John F., representative, Knox Co. (1831), 208; (1833), *215; (1834), 219.
Snethen, Abraham, representative, Benton Co. etc. (1846), 301.
Snoddy, Martin, representative, Owen Co. (1841), *262.
Snook, Henry T., representative, Montgomery Co. (1841), *262; (1842), *268; (1844), *283; (1845), *294; (1848), *328; delegate, const. conv., *387.
Snowden, James, representative, Franklin Co. (1817), *184.
Soper, Henry L., representative, Jennings Co. (1830), *206.
Southard, Matthew R., representative, Posey Co. (1839), *248.
Southern, James, representative, Orange Co. (1849), 339.

Southwick, Emory, representative, Henry Co. (1845), 293; (1848), 327; (1850), 347.
Sowder, John, representative, Washington Co. (1846), 308.
Spann, John L., representative, Jefferson Co. (1826), *197; (1827), *199; Jennings Co. (1838), *243; (1839), *248; (1848), 327; senator, Bartholomew and Jennings cos. (1851), *362; delegate, const. conv., *382.
Spaulding, Thomas I., representative, La Grange and Noble cos. (1844), 282.
Spencer, Benjamin N., representative, Lake and Porter cos. (1848), *328.
Spencer, John A., 105n.
Spencer, John W., representative, Ohio and Switzerland cos. (1849), *339; (1851), *359.
Spicely, William L., representative, Orange Co. (1851), 359.
Spicknall, Richard N., representative, Dearborn Co. (1843), *274.
Squibb, Nathaniel L., representative, Dearborn Co. (1837), 238n.
Stafford, Grant, representative, Morgan Co. (1833), *216; (1834), *220; senator (1836), *235, 235n; (1838), *245.
Staley, John H., representative, Fulton Co. etc. (1847), 315.
Stanfield, Thomas S., lieutenant governor (1849), 178-80; representative, St. Joseph Co. (1845), *296; (1846), *307; (1851), *360.
Stanford, Thomas R., representative, Henry Co. etc. (1825), *194; Henry Co. (1831), *209; (1832), *213; (1833), *216; (1834), *221; (1840), *255; senator (1836), *235, 235n; (1842), *271.
Stanton, Stephen B., representative, Wayne Co. (1847), *320; (1848), *331.
Stapp, Milton, presidential elector (1836), *21-24; U. S. Senator (1838), 132-33; governor (1831), 141-43; lieutenant governor (1828), *162-63; representative, Jefferson Co. (1822), *190; (1827), *199; (1835), *225; (1836), *229; (1837), *237; (1844), *281; (1845), *293; senator, Jefferson and Jennings cos. (1823), *190.
Starbuck, George C., representative, Union Co. (1848), *330.
Start, Solomon C., senator, Carroll and Clinton cos. (1846), 310.
State bank, created, xxi-xxii.
Staton, William, representative, Boone Co. (1851), *355.
Stayner, John, representative, De Kalb and Steuben cos. (1850), *346.
Steele, George K., representative, Parke Co. (1835), *225; (1836), *232; (1842), *269; delegate, const. conv., Parke and Vermillion cos., 386.
Steele, William, 153n; delegate, const. conv., Wabash Co., *382.
Steele, William, representative, Wayne Co. (1827), *199; (1828), *201; (1830), 205; (1831), *209; (1832), *213; (1833), *216.
Steichelman, Michael, representative, Lake and Porter cos. (1846), 305.
Stephens, John F., representative, Decatur Co. (1851), *362.
Stephenson, Edward, representative, Dubois Co. (1851), 356.
Stephenson, J. C., 155n.
Stephenson, John, 286n.
Stevens, Stephen C., 122n; presidential elector (1844), 48-52; governor (1846), xxiv, 153-55; representative, Franklin Co. (1817), *184; Switzerland Co. (1823), *192; (1824), *193; (1826), *197; (1827), *199; senator, Ripley and Switzerland cos. (1828), *201.
Stevenson, Alexander C., lieutenant governor (1846), 175-78n; representative, Putnam Co. (1831), *209; (1844), *284; senator (1839), *251; delegate, const. conv., *387.
Stevenson, Joseph G., representative, Owen Co. (1851), 362n.
Stewart, David, representative, Crawford Co. (1825), *194.

Stewart, George W., representative, Sullivan Co. (1846), 308.
Stewart, Isaac, representative, Floyd Co. (1828), *200; (1838), *241; (1839), *248.
Stewart, John, representative, Fountain Co. (1842), *268.
Stewart, M., representative, Dearborn Co. (1831), 208.
Stewart, Robert, representative, U. S. Congress (1847), 116-17, 118n; (1851), 126n; senator, Lake Co. etc. (1846), 311.
Stewart, Robert, representative, De Kalb and Steuben cos. (1847), 314.
Stewart, Samuel, representative, La Porte Co. (1846), *305.
Stewart, Samuel J., representative, Clark Co. (1833), *216.
Stewart, Samuel W., representative, Henry Co. (1849), *342.
Stewart, Thomas C., presidential elector (1836), 25-28; representative, Dubois and Pike cos. (1829), *202; (1830), *206; (1839), 247; (1840), 252; senator, Dubois, Gibson, Pike cos. (1835), *228.
Stewart, Warren, representative, Delaware Co. (1847), 314.
Stewart, William, representative, Fayette Co. (1845), *291; (1846), *303.
Stewart, William, senator, Marion Co. (1846), *311.
Stinson, Jack, delegate, const. conv., Warren Co., 381.
Stirlin, Thomas, representative, Carroll Co. (1842), 265.
Stitt, John B., representative, Wayne Co. (1849), 341.
Stockton, Charles L., representative, Lake and Porter cos. (1845), 294.
Stockton, Lawrence B., representative, Tippecanoe Co. (1850), 350; (1851), 360.
Stockwell, William H., senator, Posey and Vanderburgh cos. (1846), *312.
Stokes, ———, representative, Vermillion Co. (1836), 231.
Stone, Asahel, representative, Randolph Co. (1847), *318.
Stone, Charles M., representative, Fayette Co. (1849), *336; (1850), *346.
Stone, Earl S., representative, Hamilton Co. (1847), 315.
Stoops, William, representative, Hamilton Co. (1845), 298n; (1846), 304; (1849), *337.
Stophlet, Samuel, representative, Allen Co. (1844), *278.
Storm, Joseph P., representative, Greene Co. (1834), *221; (1835), *226; (1836), *232.
Stott, James M., representative, Jennings Co. (1846), 305.
Stout, Levi, 109n.
Stover, Daniel C., representative, Montgomery Co. (1851), *359.
Strain, John, representative, Vigo Co. (1842), *269.
Strain, Robert, representative, Washington Co. (1834), *222; (1835), *226; (1836), *233.
Strain, William, representative, Washington Co. (1849), 341.
Strange, James, representative, Parke Co. (1834), 220.
Stratton, Daniel, representative, Wayne Co. (1840), *256; (1841), *260; (1842), *267.
Stratton, Jonathan D., representative, Howard and Tipton cos. (1851), 357.
Stretch, James A., representative, Grant Co. (1848), 326.
Strong, A. B., representative, Marion Co. (1836), 230.
Strong, Samuel S., representative, Boone Co. (1846), 301.
Struble, Joseph, representative, Bartholomew Co. (1851), *354.
Stryker, Peter J., representative, Parke Co. (1847), 318.
Stuart, William Z., representative, Cass Co. (1851), *355.
Stucker, David, representative, Harrison Co. (1842), 266.
Studabaker, John, representative, Huntington and Wells cos. (1851), 357.

Sturgeon, Hume, representative, Johnson Co. (1847), 316.
Sturgis, Charles E., delegate, const. conv., Allen Co., 378.
Sturgus, Robert, representative, Knox Co. (1820), *187.
Suffrage, qualification of voters, x.
Sugg, ———, representative, Washington Co. (1841), 260.
Suit, James F., presidential elector (1848), 58-62; representative, Clinton and Tipton cos. (1846), *302; Clinton Co. (1851), *355.
Sullivan, George R. C., representative, U. S. Congress (1816), 71; representative, Knox Co. (1817), *184; (1818), *185; (1820), *187.
Sullivan, Jeremiah, representative, U. S. Congress (1824), 78-79; (1826), 82n; representative, Jefferson Co. (1819), *186; (1820), *187.
Sullivan, John H., representative, Clark Co. (1817), *313.
Sullivan, Thomas L., representative, Jefferson Co. (1844), *281.
Sullivan, William C., representative, Jefferson Co. (1834), 219.
Summers, Jacob, Sr., delegate, const. conv., Floyd Co., 379.
Summers, Simon, representative, Henry Co. (1842), *268; (1846), *309; (1849), *342.
Sumner, Allen, representative, Hamilton Co. (1842), *268.
Sumner, Eli J., presidential elector (1844), 48-52; senator, Morgan Co. (1844), 288; (1847), 322; representative (1845), 295; (1846), 306.
Sumner, Thomas, representative, Marshall and Starke cos. (1851), *362.
Sunman, John, representative, Ripley Co. (1847), 318.
Sutherland, John, representative, Marion Co. (1843), *273.
Sutherland, John, representative, Wayne Co. (1818), *185; (1819), *186.
Suttenfield, William, representative, Allen Co. etc. (1833), 214.
Swain, Ira, representative, Randolph Co. (1844), 284; (1848), 329.
Swain, Thomas, representative, Wayne Co. (1820), *187.
Sweeney, Thomas W., senator, Adams Co. etc. (1838), 244.
Sweet, James, representative, Grant Co. (1846), 304.
Sweet, Jerome, representative, Noble Co. (1851), *359.
Sweetser, James, representative, Grant and Wabash cos. (1840), *252.
Sweetser, M., representative, Allen Co. (1843), 272.
Sweetser, Philip, representative, Bartholomew Co. (1825), *194; (1826), *196; (1828), *201n; Marion Co. (1839), *247; (1840), *253; senator, Bartholomew Co. etc. (1830), 207.
Swihart, Gabriel, representative, Miami and Wabash cos. (1842), *266; Wabash Co. (1846), 308; (1850), *351.
Swihart, Henry, representative, Huntington and Whitley cos. (1847), *316; (1848), 327; (1850), *348; senator, Kosciusko, Noble, Whitley cos. (1851), 363.
Swinney, Thomas W., senator, Adams, Allen, Wells cos. (1850), 352.

Tabbs, Moses, presidential elector (1824), 6-7.
Taber, Cyrus, senator, Cass Co. etc. (1837), 239; Cass Co. (1846), *310; representative (1845), *290.
Tackitt, Isaac W., representative, Morgan Co. (1846), *306; (1847), 317; delegate, const. conv., 380.
Tadlock, Elisha, representative, Crawford Co. (1823), *191; (1824), *192.
Taffee, Samuel A., 67n.
Taggart, James, Jr., representative, Brown Co. (1844), 279.
Taggart, William, representative, Brown Co. (1851), *355.
Tague, George, representative, Hancock Co. (1844), *281; delegate, const. conv., *379.

Tait, John, Jr., representative, Dearborn Co. (1838), 240; Dearborn and Ohio (1844), 280; Switzerland and Ohio (1846), *306; (1848), 329; (1849), 339.

Talbott, E. P., representative, Montgomery Co. (1850), 349.

Talbott, James M., representative, Decatur Co. (1844), 280.

Talbott, John S., representative, Putnam Co. (1836), *232.

Talbott, William K., representative, Lake and Porter cos. (1840), 253.

Talbut, Elihu, representative, Union Co. (1846), 308.

Tannehill, Zachariah, senator, Bartholomew and Jennings cos. (1833), *218, 218n; (1839), *250; (1842), *270; (1848), 332; delegate, const. conv., *381; representative, Bartholomew and Brown cos. (1837), *237.

Tate, George, representative, Adams Co. (1837), 235.

Tatman, John, representative, De Kalb and Steuben cos. (1849), 336.

Taylor, Daniel, representative, Dearborn Co. (1840), 256n.

Taylor, Edmund D., delegate, const. conv., La Porte Co., *379.

Taylor, Gamaliel, 148n; lieutenant governor (1837), 170n; representative, Jefferson Co. (1840), 253.

Taylor, Robert, representative, Fountain Co. etc. (1828), *200.

Taylor, Robert N., representative, Fayette Co. (1846), 303.

Taylor, Waller, 73n; U. S. Senator (1816, 1818), *xii, 127.

Taylor, William, representative, La Porte Co. (1847), 316.

Taylor, Zachary, president (1848), 58-62.

Tebbs, Alvin G., representative, Dearborn Co. (1846), *303.

Tebbs, Warren, representative, Dearborn Co. (1831), *208; (1833), 215; (1835), 224.

Tedford, Henry P., representative, Carroll and Howard cos. (1845), *290; Carroll Co. (1847), 313.

Teegarden, Abraham, senator, Lake Co. etc. (1849), *344.

Templeton, R., 298n.

Templeton, William, representative, Fountain Co. (1835), *224; (1836), *229; death, 233n.

Templin, John, senator, Hancock and Madison cos. (1847), 322.

Terrell, Williamson, representative, Bartholomew and Brown cos. (1838), *242; (1840), *255.

Terry, Elias S., senator, Daviess and Martin cos. (1841), 263; representative, Daviess Co. (1847), *314; delegate, const. conv., *387; resignation, 387n.

Test, Charles H., presidential elector (1848), *53-57; representative, U. S. Congress (1841), 105n; (1843), 106; (1847), 115; representative, Rush Co. (1826), *197; senator, Wayne Co. (1840), *258; (1841), 264.

Test, John, representative, U. S. Congress (1822), *77; (1824), *79; (1826), 82; (1828), *xx, 84; (1831), 86; (1833), 88; U. S. Senator (1832), 129-30.

Tevis, Benjamin, representative, Jefferson Co. (1843), *273; (1845), 293.

Tevis, Fletcher, representative, Shelby Co. (1842), *269.

Thackery, Samuel, representative, Ripley Co. (1851), 362n.

Thatcher, Jesse, 180n.

Thom, Alexander C., representative, Jefferson Co. (1849), *337.

Thom, Allan D., representative, U. S. Congress (1816), 71.

Thomas, David, representative, Clay Co. (1846), 302.

Thomas, George W., representative, Posey Co. (1849), *340.

Thomas, Harrison R., representative, U. S. Congress (1833), 89-90.

Thomas, W. G., delegate, const. conv., Spencer Co., 380.

Thomas, William, representative, Rush Co. (1846), *307.

Thomas, William W., delegate, const. conv., Fayette Co., *382.

Thomasson, William P., representative, Harrison Co. (1818), *185; (1819), *186.

Thompson, ———, representative, Rush Co. (1841), 260.

Thompson, Aaron, representative, La Grange Co. (1846), 305.

Thompson, Ebenezer, senator, Huntington and Wells cos. (1851), 363.

Thompson, George Burton, senator, Crawford Co. etc. (1833), *218; (1836), *234; (1839), *250; resignation (1841), 264n; representative, Perry Co. (1845), *295; (1846), *307.

Thompson, George W., representative, Gibson Co. (1847), *315.

Thompson, J. D., representative, Fayette Co. (1830), 204.

Thompson, John, representative, Noble and La Grange cos. (1841), *259; (1842), 266.

Thompson, John C., senator, Washington (1850), 354.

Thompson, John H., presidential elector (1820), 3; representative, U. S. Congress (1828), 83-84; (1831), 85-86; lieutenant governor (1825), *161-62n; U. S. Senator (1838), 132-33; representative, Clark Co. (1818), *185; (1819), *186; (1821), *187; (1833), *216; senator, Clark and Floyd cos. (1822), *190, 190n; (1823), *192; succeeded (1825), 196n.

Thompson, John S., representative, Johnson Co. (1835), *227; senator (1836), *235, 235n.

Thompson, Lewis G., presidential elector (1844), 43-47; representative, U. S. Congress (1843), 109; (1845), 113; representative, Allen and Huntington cos. (1835), *226; Allen Co. (1837), *237; (1838), *242; (1839), *247; (1842), *269n.

Thompson, Michael, representative, Delaware Co. (1850), *346; (1851), *356.

Thompson, Richard W., presidential elector (1840), *29-32; (1844), 43-47; representative, U. S. Congress (1841), *102, 105n; (1847), *116; (1851), 126n; U. S. Senator (1838), 132-33; representative, Lawrence Co. (1834), *221; (1835), *227; senator (1836), *235, 235n.

Thompson, Thomas, representative, Carroll Co. (1846), 301; (1847), *313; (1850), *345; (1851), 355.

Thompson, William, representative, U. S. Congress (1839), 99, 100n; representative, Washington Co. (1848), *331.

Thompson, William A., representative, Madison Co. (1851), 358.

Thompson, Wilson, representative, U. S. Congress (1843), 106; representative, Fayette Co. (1837), *237; (1841), *261; (1844), 280.

Thorn, James, representative, Knox Co. (1831), 208; (1850), *348.

Thornberry, Abel, representative, Wayne Co. (1833), *216; (1834), 220.

Thornton, Henry P., 75n; representative, Washington Co. (1831), *209; Floyd Co. (1836), *232; (1838), 241; delegate, const. conv., *379.

Tiffany, William S., representative, Jennings Co. (1849), 337.

Tift, Russell G., representative, Perry

Tillotson, Jeremiah, 148n.

Tillotson, Luther, representative, Warren and Jasper cos. (1836), 231.

Co. (1849), 339; (1850), 349.

Tinbrook, Andrew, representative, Parke Co. (1849), *339.

Tinbrook, William, representative, Parke Co. (1846), 306; (1847), *318; (1849), 339.

Tingley, George B., representative, Rush Co. (1842), *267; (1844), *284.

Tipton, John, U. S. Senator (1831), *xx, 128; (1832), *xxi, 129; (1838), 132-33; representative, Harrison Co. (1820), *187; (1821), *188.

Tipton, Spear S., representative, Cass Co. (1840), 251.

Tisdale, Robert D., representative, Adams and Jay cos. (1841), *258.

Todd, Henry G., representative, Hendricks Co. (1847), 320n; (1848), 327; delegate, const. conv., *385.

Todd, Levi S., delegate, const. conv., Marion Co., 380.

Todd, Samuel, representative, Decatur Co. (1849), 335.

Todd, Thomas J., representative, Marion Co. (1842), 266; senator (1843), *277.

Tomlinson, John, representative, Delaware Co. (1844), *280; (1845), *297.

Tomlinson, Samuel, representative, Knox Co. (1832), 212.

Tompkins, Daniel D., elected vice-president, xii, 3.

Torbet, Nelson H., representative, Dearborn Co. (1834), *219.

Torbet, Oliver B., representative, Dearborn Co. (1851), *355.

Torrey, Levi F., 67n.

Tower, Nehemiah, representative, Crawford Co. (1849), 335.

Townsend, James, representative, Putnam Co. (1838), *243.

Townsend, John C., representative, Washington Co. (1848), 331.

Townsend, William, representative, Hendricks Co. (1841), *261; senator (1842), 270; (1845), 299.

Trafton, William, representative, Vanderburgh and Warrick cos. (1828), *201.

Trask, Ezra S., senator, Grant Co. etc. (1836), *235, 235n.

Treat, Samuel, representative, La Porte Co. (1844), 282, 286n.

Trembly, Daniel, representative, Union Co. (1847), *319; (1848), 330; delegate, const. conv., Fayette and Union cos., *387.

Trimble, Henry H., representative, Shelby Co. (1849), 340.

Trimble, James, senator, Grant Co. etc. (1838), *245.

Trimble, John, representative, Delaware Co. (1846), *303.

Troutwine, H., representative, Jefferson Co. (1841), 259; (1842), 266.

Trowbridge, Charles, representative, Vermillion Co. (1848), 330.

Truelock, William, representative, Scott Co. (1838), *243.

Tucker, Cornelius W., representative, Brown Co. (1846), 301.

Tucker, Ebenezer, representative, Randolph Co. (1849), 340.

Tucker, William, representative, Dearborn Co. (1830), 206n.

Tufts, Servetus, representative, Dearborn Co. (1848), 325.

Tuley, Benjamin S., lieutenant governor (1840), 170-72n.

Tuley, Preston F., senator, Floyd Co. (1837), *239.

Turman, Simon, senator, Warren Co. etc. (1836), *234.

Turman, Solon, senator, Fountain Co. (1850), *353.

Turman, Thomas, representative, Sullivan Co. (1843), *275; (1844), *285.

Turner, Robert B., representative, Blackford Co. etc. (1845), *289.

Tutt, Francis R., delegate, const. conv., Fulton, Marshall, Starke cos., 385.

Tuttle, Enos S., representative, Fulton and Marshall cos. (1848), *326.

Tuttle, James, 298n.

Tyler, Charles, representative, Fountain Co. (1845), 291.

Tyler, John, vice-president (1840), *29-32.

Tyner, Thomas, representative, Wayne Co. (1837), 236.

Tyson, Samuel, senator, Hancock and Madison cos. (1847), 322.

Underhill, William, representative, Floyd Co. (1847), 314.

Underwood, Isaac, representative, Blackford and Jay cos. (1850), 345.

United States Congress, apportionment of representatives, 77n, 90n, 396-98; election of senators (1816-51), x, xxi, xxii, xxii-xxiii, 127-34; time

of holding elections changed, xix-xx, 87n.
Unthank, Jonathan, representative, Wayne Co. (1844), 285.
Usher, John P., 126n; representative, Vigo Co. (1850), *351.
Utter, William, senator, Vermillion Co. (1844), 288.

Vanbenthusen, James, delegate, const. conv., Shelby Co., *380; death, 383n.
Van Buren, Martin, vice-president (1832), *14-15; president (1836), 25-28; (1840), xxiii, 33-36; (1848), xxiv, 63-67.
Vance, Arthur S., representative, Marion Co. (1848), *328.
Vance, David, representative, Clinton and Montgomery cos. (1833), *216; senator (1834), 222.
Vance, Samuel C., representative, U. S. Congress (1822), 77.
Vance, William, representative, Adams Co. etc. (1836), 229; (1837), *235; (1838), *240; (1839), 245.
Vandeveer, Joel, representative Orange Co. (1833), *216; (1834), *221; (1835), *227; (1836), *232; (1837), *238; (1844), *283; (1845), *297; senator (1838), 245.
Vandeveer, Thomas, representative, Dubois Co. etc. (1821), *188.
Vanmetre, William, representative, Delaware Co. (1836), *231.
Van Ornum, Ara C., representative, La Grange and Noble cos. (1849), 338.
Vanosdol, James, representative, Ripley Co. (1849), 340.
Van Sandt, Elijah, representative, Union Co. (1844), 285.
Vanvactor, David, representative, Fulton and Marshall cos. (1846), 303.
Vaughn, Sterling, representative, Jackson Co. (1846), 309n.
Vawter, John, lieutenant governor (1816), 159; representative, Jennings Co. (1831), *209; (1832), *212; (1834), *221; (1835), *227; senator, Jennings Co. etc. (1833), 218; (1836), *234.
Vawter, Smith, representative, Jennings Co. (1848), *327; senator, Bartholomew and Jennings cos. (1851), 362.
Veach, Jeremiah, representative, Henry Co. (1848), 327.
Veatch, Isaac, representative, Perry and Spencer cos. (1827), *199.
Venneman, Theodore, representative, Vanderburgh Co. (1850), 350.
Verbrike, Samuel A., representative, Hendricks Co. (1838), 241; (1843), *275; senator (1845), *299.
Vice-presidents, vote for Indiana electors (1816-51), 3-67.
Vickers, Corson, representative, Marion Co. (1840), 253.
Vigus, Jordan, representative, Cass Co. (1838), 240.
Vineyard, Nicholas, representative, Switzerland and Ohio cos. (1846), 306.
Violette (Violett), John W., representative, Elkhart Co. (1843), 272; senator, Elkhart Co. etc. (1844), 287.
Voorees, H. M., representative, Hendricks Co. (1840), 253.

Wade, David, representative, Hendricks Co. (1848), *327.
Wade, E., representative, Fountain Co. (1836), 229.
Wade, Jethro, representative, Tippecanoe Co. (1848), 330.
Waer, R., delegate, const. conv., Spencer Co., 380.
Waggoner, James N., 117n.
Wakefield, Andrew, representative, Allen Co. (1847), 312.
Walden, Ariel, representative, De Kalb and Steuben cos. (1844), 280.
Walden, Benjamin, representative, Putnam Co. (1844), 284.
Waldo, Loring A., representative, Wayne Co. (1821), *188.
Walker, Charles E., representative, Clark Co. (1848), 324.

Walker, George, 67n.
Walker, George B., representative, Cass Co. (1848), 324; senator (1849), *343.
Walker, Henry, representative, Dearborn Co. (1835), *224.
Walker, James, representative, Dearborn Co. (1830), 204; (1834), *219; (1836), 229.
Walker, James T., representative, Vanderburgh Co. (1844), *285; (1846), 308.
Walker, John, representative, Jennings Co. (1824), *193; (1825), *195.
Walker, John, representative, Shelby Co. (1835), *227; senator (1836), *235, 235n.
Walker, Jonas, 67n.
Walker, Milton, representative, Perry Co. (1851), *359.
Walker, Zachariah, representative, Daviess and Martin cos. (1846), *302; (1847), 314.
Wallace, Alexander, representative, Orange Co. (1821), *188; (1824), *193; (1826), *197; (1827), *199.
Wallace, Benjamin F., senator, Fountain Co. (1831), *211, 211n; resignation (1833), 219n.
Wallace, Coleman C., representative, Daviess and Martin cos. (1848), 325.
Wallace, David, 155n; representative, U. S. Congress (1841), *104; (1843), 107; U. S. Senator (1832), 129; governor (1837), *xxii, *145-48, 395; lieutenant governor (1831), 164-65; (1834), *166-67n; representative, Franklin Co. (1828), *200; (1829), *202; (1830), *206; delegate, const. conv., Marion Co., *380.
Wallace, James H., representative, Jefferson Co. (1829), *203; (1830), *204; (1831), 208; (1833), *215; (1834), *219.
Wallace, William, representative, Daviess and Martin cos. (1825), *194; (1831), *208; (1832), *211; senator, Daviess Co. etc. (1833), *217; death (1835), 228n.
Walls, John, representative, Spencer Co. (1850), *350; (1851), 360.
Walpole, Thomas D., presidential elector (1848), 58-62; representative, Hancock Co. (1836), *232; (1837), *237; (1840), *255; senator, Hancock and Madison cos. (1841), *264; (1844), 287; (1847), *322; delegate, const. conv., *385.
Walters, Ephraim, representative, Noble Co. (1851), 359; delegate, const. conv., 384.
Wampler, Jefferson, representative, Owen Co. (1849), 339.
Ward, Ebenezer, 105n.
Ward, John, representative, Fountain Co. (1835), 224.
Ward, Oliver C., representative, De Kalb Co. etc. (1838), 241.
Ward, Samuel, representative, Cass Co. (1838), 240.
Warner, Joseph, 162n; representative, Knox and Sullivan cos. (1818), *185; election contested, 186n; representative, Knox Co. etc. (1819), *186; Daviess and Martin (1848), 325.
Warner, Peter, representative, Parke Co. (1848), 329.
Warriner, Lewis, representative, Lake and Porter cos. (1841), *261; (1845), 294; (1849), *338.
Washburn, Thomas, senator, Kosciusko Co. etc. (1851), *363.
Washer, Solomon, representative, Switzerland Co. (1833), 215.
Waters, Philip, representative, Carroll and Howard cos. (1845), 290; senator, Carroll and Clinton cos. (1846), *310; (1849), 342; delegate, const. conv., 378.
Watkins, Joseph F., representative, Dearborn Co. (1849), *335.
Watson, Ebenezer S., representative, Hendricks Co. (1851), *357.
Watson, Jonathan, representative, Brown Co. (1850), *351.
Watson, Thomas, representative, Tippecanoe Co. (1836), 230; (1837), *238.

Watt, William, representative, Union Co. (1832), *213; (1835), *227; (1836), *230; (1845), *296; (1850), *350; (1851), 361; senator, Fayette and Union cos. (1837), *239.

Watts, Arthur, representative, Scott Co. (1827), *199.

Watts, Howard, representative, Jefferson Co. (1850), *348; (1851), 357.

Watts, John, presidential elector (1828), 12-13; representative, Dearborn Co. (1818), *185; resignation, 185; senator (1825), *195; (1828), *201.

Watts, John S., representative, U. S. Congress (1849), 120; representative, Monroe Co. (1846), *309n.

Watts, Johnson, representative, U. S. Congress (1851), 123; representative, Dearborn Co. (1826), *196; senator (1833), 217; (1837), *239; (1840), *257; delegate, const. conv., *381.

Watts, Joseph, 13n.

Weatherly, Jesse, representative, Harrison Co. (1834), 219.

Weaver, Davis, representative, Dearborn Co. (1830), 206n.

Weaver, John, representative, Wayne Co. (1851), 361.

Weaver, Samuel, representative, Carroll Co. (1849), *335.

Webb, Daniel, representative, Johnson Co. (1845), *293.

Webb, Madison, representative, Marion Co. (1850), 349.

Webber, Nathaniel B., representative, Marion Co. (1845), *294.

Webster, Elijah A., representative, La Grange and Noble cos. (1848), *328.

Webster, Johnson, representative, Parke Co. (1845), 295.

Weir, James H., representative, Sullivan Co. (1849), *341.

Welborn, John Y., representative, Posey Co. (1828), *201.

Welch, Presley, representative, Jennings Co. (1840), *255.

Welch, Samuel, representative, Jefferson Co. (1833), 215; (1835), 225; (1841), 262n; senator (1838), 244.

Wells, Samuel T., representative, Jackson Co. (1849), *337; (1851), *357.

Welton, Ebenezer, representative, Knox Co. (1830), 205.

West, Nathaniel, senator, Marion Co. (1841), *263, 264n.

West, T. N., representative, La Porte Co. (1846), 305.

Westervelt, John L., representative, Fulton and Marshall cos. (1846), 303.

Wharry, Robert, representative, Vigo Co. (1849), 341.

Wheeler, Amzi L., representative, Marshall Co. etc. (1839), *248; (1842), *268; (1844), 281; senator (1843), 277; delegate, const. conv., *382.

Wheeler, David B., representative, De Kalb and Steuben cos. (1846), *303; death, 309n.

Wheeler, Samuel, representative, Vigo Co. (1841), 260.

Whetzel, Cyrus, representative, Morgan Co. (1846), 306.

Whig party, in state and presidential elections, xxii-xxiv.

Whight, Alvan T., representative, Pike Co. (1841), *262; (1842), *266; (1844), *284.

Whinery, Mark, representative, St. Joseph Co. (1849), *340.

Whitcomb, James, U. S. Senator (1848), *134; governor (1843), *150-53n; (1846), *153-55; term of service, 395; senator, Monroe Co. etc. (1830), *207; (1833), *218.

White, ———, representative, Carroll Co. etc. (1830), 204.

White, Albert S., presidential elector (1836), *21-24; representative, U. S. Congress (1833), 89-90; (1837), *96-97n; U. S. Senator (1838), xxiii, 132-33; representative, Tippecanoe Co. (1847), 319.

White, C. F., representative, Miami Co. (1842), 266.

White, George, representative, Hamilton Co. (1850), 347.
White, James, representative, Tippecanoe Co. (1839), *249.
White, Joab, representative, Warren Co. (1848), 331.
White, Joseph L., presidential elector (1840), *29-32; representative, U. S. Congress (1841), *102; (1843), 106.
White, Wesley, senator, Morgan Co. (1847), 322.
White, William, presidential elector (1836), 25-28.
Whitinger, Daniel, representative, Kosciusko Co. (1848), 327.
Whitlock, Abel A., representative, St. Joseph Co. (1847), 318; (1848), 330; (1850), 350.
Whitman, George W., representative, Wayne Co. (1841), 263n; (1849), 341.
Whitman, Shepherd, representative, Floyd Co. (1835), *224; (1837), *237.
Whitson, B. F., representative, Jefferson Co. (1850), 348.
Wick, William W., presidential elector (1824), 6-7; (1844), *38-42; representative, U. S. Congress (1831), 85-86; (1833), 89; (1837, special), 93; (1839), *99-100; (1845), 111; (1847), *115; U. S. Senator (1832), 129; (1838), 132-33.
Wicker, James P., senator, Elkhart and La Grange cos. (1847), 321.
Wickersham, M. R., delegate, const. conv., Cass and Howard cos., 378.
Widney, John P., representative, De Kalb and Steuben cos. (1847), *314.
Wilber, Shadrach, senator, Jefferson Co. (1841), 263; (1843), *277, 278n; representative (1845), 293; (1846), 305.
Wilcox, Alfred, representative, Kosciusko Co. (1851), 358.
Wildey, Morris, representative, Jennings Co. (1847), 337; (1851), 358.
Wiley, Moses, representative, Dearborn Co. (1817), *184; resignation, 185n.
Wiley, Spencer, representative, Franklin Co. (1836), 229; (1845), *291; (1846), *303; delegate, const. conv., *382.
Wilkinson, R., representative, Jefferson Co. (1850), 348.
Willard, Ashbel P., representative, Floyd Co. (1850), *347.
Willard, Orson, representative, Sullivan Co. (1848), 330.
Willer (?), James W., representative, Adams Co. (1837), 235.
Willett, Isaac, delegate, const. conv., Hancock Co., 379.
Willett, Marinus, presidential elector (1836), 25-28; representative, Rush Co. (1830), 205; (1831), *209; (1833), *216; (1834), *220; (1835), *225.
Willett, Marinus, representative, Wayne Co. (1830), 206n.
Willey, John, representative, Fayette Co. (1838), *242.
Willey, John F., representative, Clark Co. (1846), 302; (1847), 313; (1851), 355.
Williams, Achilles, presidential elector (1836), *21-24; representative, Wayne Co. (1837), *236; senator (1838), *245.
Williams, Alfred, representative, Lake and Porter cos. (1846), 305.
Williams, Andrew, 298n.
Williams, James D., representative, Knox Co. (1843), *273; (1845), 293; (1847), *316; (1851), *358; senator (1848), 333.
Williams, John M., representative, Daviess and Martin cos. (1848), 325.
Williams, Jonathan, presidential elector (1836), 25-28; representative, Morgan Co. (1838), *242.
Williams, Joseph, representative, Hendricks Co. (1846), 304.
Williams, Joseph, representative, Wayne Co. (1846), 309n; (1847), 320n; (1848), 331.
Williams, Merrill, senator, Fulton Co. etc. (1845), 299.

Williams, Robert N., representative, Madison Co. (1842), *268; (1846), 306; (1847), *320; (1848), 328; (1849), 338.

Williams, Samuel, 170n.

Williams, Urbane, representative, Posey Co. (1847), 318.

Williams, Vinson, representative, Lawrence Co. (1823), *191; (1825), *195; (1828), *201; (1836), *232; (1837), *237.

Williams, Ward W., representative, Rush Co. (1837), *238.

Williams, William, representative, Floyd Co. (1831), *209; (1833), *216; (1835), 224.

Williams, William W., representative, Henry Co. (1851), 357.

Williamson, Delana E., representative, Clay Co. (1847), 313; (1850), *351.

Williamson, Jeremiah S., representative, Union Co. (1841), *262.

Williamson, John W., representative, Wayne Co. (1843), *274.

Wills, David, representative, Putnam Co. (1842), 267; (1844), *284.

Willson, Samuel C., 118n; representative, Montgomery Co. (1844), 283.

Wilson, ———, senator, Clay Co. etc. (1840), 257.

Wilson, Alexander, representative, Fulton and Miami cos. (1838), *243; (1839), *246.

Wilson, Alexander, representative, Marion Co. (1838), 242; (1839), 247.

Wilson, Alphonso, representative, St. Joseph Co. (1850), 350.

Wilson, Creed Y., representative, Lawrence Co. (1848), 328.

Wilson, George P. R., representative, U. S. Congress (1845), 110; representative, Harrison Co. (1833), *215; (1834), *219; (1835), *224; (1837), *237; (1838), *241; (1841), 259; (1842), *266; (1844), *285; (1848), *327; (1849), *337; senator (1836), 233; (1839), 250; delegate, const. conv., 379.

Wilson, Gideon, representative, Hendricks Co. (1832), 212; (1833), 215.

Wilson, J. A., representative, Fayette Co. (1834), 219.

Wilson, James W., 109n; representative, Tippecanoe Co. (1841), 260; senator, Carroll and Clinton cos. (1846), 310.

Wilson, John, representative, Montgomery Co. (1840), *255; (1848), 328.

Wilson, John, representative, Randolph Co. (1851), *360.

Wilson, John B., representative, Jasper Co. etc. (1839), *248; (1840), 253.

Wilson, John H., representative, Sullivan Co. (1845), *296; (1850), *351.

Wilson, Lewis, representative, Gibson Co. (1846), 304.

Wilson, Paton, representative, Parke Co. (1834), *220; (1835), 225.

Wilson, Philip D., representative, Posey Co. (1848), 329; senator, Posey and Vanderburgh cos. (1850), 354.

Wilson, Ralph, representative, Vigo Co. (1831), 210n; (1834), 221.

Wilson, Robert, representative, Grant Co. (1847), 315.

Wilson, Robert, representative, Posey Co. (1843), 273.

Wilson, Theophilus, 309n; senator, Jay Co. etc. (1846), 310.

Wilson, Thomas H., representative, La Grange and Noble cos. (1845), *294; (1846), *306.

Wilson, Walter, presidential elector (1824), 6-7; (1832), 17-20; U. S. Senator (1816), 127; (1832), 129; representative, Knox Co. (1816), *183; Gibson Co. (1826), *196; (1827), *198; Carroll and Cass cos. (1831), *208; (1832), *212.

Wilson, William, representative, Madison Co. (1844), 282.

Wilson, Young E. R., representative, Marion Co. (1845), *294.

Wilstach, John A., representative, Tippecanoe Co. (1849), 341.

Wiltse, George, representative, Rush Co. (1849), 340; (1851), 360.

Winans, C. S., representative, Fountain Co. (1835), 224.

Winchell, R., representative, Franklin Co. (1836), 229.

Winchell, Richard, senator, Delaware and Grant cos. (1845), *299.

Winder, Daniel, representative, Wayne Co. (1841), 263.

Windsor, Abner, representative, De Kalb and Steuben cos. (1846), 309n.

Wines, Josiah L., representative, Grant and Wabash cos. (1836), *232; (1837), *237; (1838), *243.

Wines, Marshall S., representative, Allen Co. (1841), *261; (1842), *265; death, 269n.

Wines, William, representative, Vigo Co. (1836), *232; (1837), *238; (1841), *260.

Wingate, Smith, representative, Shelby Co. (1847), 319.

Winship, Edwin, representative, Clinton and Montgomery cos. (1835), 224; (1836), *231.

Winstandley, John B., representative, Floyd Co. (1847), *314; (1848), *326; senator (1849), *343.

Wirt, William, candidate for president, xx.

Wise, Thomas, representative, Jefferson Co. (1845), *293; (1846), *305.

Witherow, David, delegate, const. conv., Carroll and Clinton cos., 384.

Witherow, John, senator, Hendricks Co. (1851), *363.

Withers, Emanuel, representative, Franklin Co. (1850), *347; (1851), *356.

Withers, James R., representative, Pike Co. (1847), 318; (1848), *329; (1849), *340.

Wittenmyer, Benjamin, representative, Vermillion Co. (1849), 341; (1850), *350.

Wolf, Daniel, representative, Franklin Co. (1848), 326; (1849), 336.

Wolf, George J., representative, Floyd Co. (1843), *275; (1844), *280; (1849), 336.

Wolfe, Benjamin D., representative, Sullivan Co. (1846), *308; (1847), *319; (1848), *330; (1849), 341; delegate, const. conv., *382.

Wolfe, Simeon K., senator, Harrison Co. (1851), 363.

Wood, Isaac, representative, Vanderburgh Co. (1850), 350.

Wood, Isaac F., senator, Blackford Co. etc. (1843), *277; representative, Randolph Co. (1848), *329.

Wood, James, representative, Vanderburgh Co. (1849), 341; (1851), 361.

Woodard, Charles, representative, Jefferson Co. (1839), *248; (1840), *253; (1841), 259; (1843), 273.

Woodbridge, George A., representative, Lake and Porter cos. (1849), 338.

Wooden, Robert M., representative, Owen Co. (1831), *209; (1832), *213.

Woodruff, Harvey E., representative, Lake and Porter cos. (1846), *305.

Woodruff, Joab, representative, Johnson Co. (1832), *213; (1833), *216; (1834), *221.

Woods, James, representative, Warrick Co. (1845), 297.

Woods, John, senator, Ohio and Switzerland cos. (1849), *344.

Woods, Joseph, delegate, const. conv., Jefferson Co., 385.

Woods, William, representative, Ohio and Switzerland cos. (1851), 359.

Woodsmall, Jefferson H., representative, Owen Co. (1847), 318.

Woodward, Nathaniel A., representative, Allen Co. (1844), 278.

Woolman, Samuel L., representative, Grant Co. (1843), *275.

Work, Joseph, representative, Clark Co. (1826), *196; (1827), *198; (1828), *200; (1830), *205.

Work, Robert, delegate, const. conv., De Kalb Co. etc., *384.

Workman, James M., representative, Boone Co. (1849), 335.

Workman, Richard, 67n.

Worster, Thomas, representative, Rush Co. (1839), *249.

Worth, Alexander, representative, Hendricks and Morgan cos. (1830), *204.

Worth, Daniel, 105n, 118n; presidential elector (1844), 48-52; (1848), 63-67n; representative, U. S. Congress (1845), 113; representative, Allen and Randolph cos. (1824), *192; (1825), *194; (1828), *200; senator, Allen Co. etc. (1829), *203; Delaware and Grant (1845), 299.

Worthington, William, representative, Fountain Co. (1834), 219.

Wright, ———, senator, Washington Co. (1835), 228; representative (1840), 255.

Wright, Arvin, representative, Clark Co. (1848), 324; Washington Co. (1845), 297.

Wright, Eli, representative, Wayne Co. (1830), *205; (1844), *285.

Wright, Herman, 105n.

Wright, Isaiah, representative, Putnam Co. (1848), 329.

Wright, John, 122n; representative, Randolph Co. (1821), *188; (1822), *190; (1823), *192.

Wright, John W., lieutenant governor (1849), 178-80n.

Wright, John W., representative, Ohio and Switzerland cos. (1849), *339.

Wright, Joseph A., representative, U. S. Congress (1843), *107-8, 109n; (1845), 112; (1847), 116; governor (1849), *155-58, 395; representative, Parke Co. (1833), *216; (1836), *232; senator, Parke Co. (1839), *251.

Wright, Noah, representative, Washington Co. (1821), *188; (1822), *190.

Wright, Thomas T., representative, Switzerland Co. (1843), *274; (1844), *284.

Wright, William, representative, La Porte Co. (1846), 305.

Wright, William M., representative, Dubois and Pike cos. (1833), *216; (1834), *221.

Wright, Williamson, representative, U. S. Congress (1849), 121; senator, Cass Co. etc. (1840), *257.

Wunderlich, Jacob, delegate, const. conv., Huntington and Whitley cos., *382.

Wyland, Jonathan, senator, Elkhart and La Grange cos. (1850), 353.

Wyman, Henry, representative, Madison Co. (1837), *237; (1838), *243; (1840), 253.

Wymond, James, representative, Dearborn and Ohio cos. (1845), 298n; Ohio Co. (1847), 320n.

Wynn, John, representative, Franklin Co. (1850), 352n.

Yandes, Simon, representative, Wayne Co. (1820), *187.

Yarnall, John, representative, Greene Co. (1847), 315; (1848), *326; succeeded, 332n.

Yaryan, James, representative, Union Co. (1846), *308.

Yaryan, John, senator, Fayette and Union cos. (1849), 343.

Yater, James L., 67n.

Yocom (Yocum), Francis B., representative, Clay Co. (1841), *261; (1845), *297; (1849), *335; delegate, const. conv., *381.

Yocom (Yocum), William, representative, Clay Co. (1833), *216.

Young, Alexander M., representative, Clinton and Tipton cos. (1848), *325.

Young, John, delegate, const. conv., Clinton and Tipton cos., 378.

Young, John M., representative, Greene and Owen cos. (1828), *200.

Young, William, representative, Madison Co. (1846), *306.

Zabriskie, George L., 286n.

Zeliff, David P., representative, Daviess Co. (1847), 314.

Zenor, Jacob, representative, Harrison Co. (1816), *183; (1817), *184; (1819), *186; (1820), *187.

Zenor, John, representative, Harrison Co. (1823), *191; (1830), *206; (1833), 215; (1835), *224; (1836), *229; (1837), *237; (1838), 241; (1839), *246; (1840), *253; senator (1845), *299; delegate, const. conv., *385.

Zenor, Philip, representative, Harrison Co. (1848), 327.

Zook, David, representative, Elkhart Co. (1848), 326.